Teaching Elementary Social Studies

A New Perspective

Teaching Elementary Social Studies

A New Perspective

Gene Edward Rooze
Leona Mitchell Foerster
Texas Technological University

CHARLES E. MERRILL PUBLISHING COMPANY
A Bell & Howell Company
Columbus, Ohio

International Standard Book Number: 0-675-09146-2

Library of Congress Catalog Card Number: 70-188177

1 2 3 4 5 6 7 8 9 10—76 75 74 73 72

Printed in the United States of America

TO

my creative wife, Wally, and children, Mark and Vernon, who have given of themselves so that I could create.

G.E.R.

TO

my deceased mother, Helen Linzer Mitchell, whose inspiration continues to live on in all my creative efforts.

L.M.F.

Preface

Although there have been many changes in the social studies in the 1960s, these were seemingly a preface to what is occurring in this decade. The revisions in curricula and materials have made their impact. The decade of the seventies is witnessing even greater changes in social studies. New materials to which we shall only allude in this text are now filtering into the schools. Changes which had been discussed only in national meetings, research centers, and universities are now classroom realities. Materials, however, are not the only innovations we are confronting. The role of the teacher has been radically redefined. No longer the mere purveyor of knowledge to students, the teacher is a designer of instruction, a guide to learning. The role of the student is shifting to that of the active inquirer who is guided in the development of thought processes through which he interprets his world and makes decisions. These roles and materials require us to look at social studies instruction through a new perspective.

Interwoven into the text of the book are behavioral objectives to guide the reader's interaction with what we have presented. General objectives have been developed to allow the instructor using the text to establish the criteria and set conditions for success. This approach seems imperative because of the differences of teaching styles and composition of classes. Also, you will find that these behavioral objectives are classified according to Bloom's Taxonomy which is explained in Chapter 5. Although this classification may be disturbing at first, after Chapter 5 you will begin to appreciate the specificity this allows in our communication. Thus, we would suggest that you bear the confusion that the insertion of this classification causes at the outset.

In the first two chapters of this book, we define social studies and provide the background the teacher needs to establish the purposes of social studies. In addition, we offer a model from which skills, knowledge, and values may be abstracted. The means of selecting content is discussed in Chapter 2.

Chapter 3 presents an analysis of the foundational disciplines of social studies content and provides a process model through which the teacher can develop an instructional plan.

Since concepts, generalizations, and constructs provide building blocks of the new social studies, Chapter 4 analyzes these frequently confusing terms and provides examples through which they can be developed.

Chapters 5, 6, 7, 8, and 9 analyze teaching and learning and present an interactive process through which you can systematically design and evaluate instruction.

Because of the emphasis on processes in the new social studies, the importance of communication skills has increased. Taking note of this trend, we have included a thorough discussion of appropriate techniques for enabling children to examine concepts, generalizations, and values. Chapter 11 focuses upon value development and offers means of helping students explore values and resolve conflicts.

Information processing skills are delineated in Chapter 12. This important area frequently has been discussed only in general terms, yet these skills provide the foundations for student operations in the new social studies. In addition to the more familiar skills, we have included ways in which elementary school students may utilize in social studies the statistical procedures presented in current mathematics programs.

To assist you in individualizing social studies, a generalized discussion of exceptional students is found in Chapter 13. One of the major themes of this book is that we must design instruction to fit children rather than attempt to force children into predesigned molds. But since students operate in a social milieu, group processes are extremely important. A learning sequence for these processes can be found in Chapter 14.

We would like to acknowledge Dr. Billie Everton of Texas Tech University, who was one of the initial readers of a portion of this manuscript, for her encouragement; Dr. Katherine Evans, Area Coordinator of Curriculum and Instruction of Texas Tech, for her untiring interest in the achievements of her staff; Mr. Robert Carter of the Midland Public Schools, an exemplary social studies educator, for the use of his photographs; Wally Rooze for many hours of arduous typing and constructive comments; Eugene Foerster for his continued support and understanding; and Charles Mitchell for his interest and encouragement.

In addition, we are indebted to Mr. Steve Branch, Mr. Monroe Prellop, and Ms. Corinne Smith of the Charles E. Merrill Publishing Company for making this text a reality.

G.E.R.

L.M.F.

Contents

Teaching Elementary Social Studies

I

What are the Social Studies

Chapter Outline

What are the Social Studies?

An anxious fifth-grader rushed up and said, "Mr. Rooze, this just won't work! Robert's production line can't keep up. We've got to shift some labor into the Top Assembly Division." This is exactly what the Model MR-24 Automobile Company decided to do at its next production meeting.

It all began as an activity in the study of the topic "The Manufacturer—Automation and Trade." The teacher was developing the concepts of *management, division of labor, standardization, techniques, production,* and *cost.* This activity was designed to aid the children in the following generalizations:

1. Division of labor allows man to produce more of the things he wants and needs.
2. Standardization of parts requires accurate systems of measure.
3. Man can vary the factors of production—resources, labor, capital, and management—according to his needs.
4. The goal of the manufacturer is to produce the most at the least possible cost.

This activity was initiated by having each child construct a paper model of an automobile. This took a great amount of time. By the end of the forty-five-minute period, twenty-two children had produced only eighteen cars. In a class discussion, the children concluded that if they were to attempt to sell these cars, some would not be marketable. Many of the styles created were too "far out" for general appeal.

The teacher asked the class, "How can we do a better and faster job?"

They came up with these answers:

"Nancy can do a better job of designing the car."

"Susan and Michael are good tracers. They can draw around the patterns that Nancy makes."

"Donald and Carol can cut better than Weldon and George."

Since Larry and Andrea didn't want to do any of these jobs, it was decided that they would help the group by carrying parts from place to place. This would furnish the transportation between the different work areas.

When the children were asked what had been accomplished, they responded quickly. "We've divided up the work." It was a simple step then to the concept of *division of labor.*

Since the children had already seen the Encyclopedia Britannica film *Eli Whitney*, the concept of *standardization* was not new to them, but it needed development. The automobile patterns, modeled after the Ford GT, permitted the students to make standardized parts of the same size and shape.

The remaining problem was one of planning. How could a class of twenty-two children be organized to do the best and most efficient job? The layout needed to be planned so that the procedure would run smoothly. Each job was to be as simple as possible. The children recognized that they were planning *techniques of production*.

The class decided that it was necessary to have six separate factories: the Top Assembly Division, the Front Body Division, the Rear Body Division, the Wheel Division, the Trim Division, and the Final Assembly Division. A separate division for transportation also had to be established.

Labor and capital were allocated (see Tables 1–1, 2, 3). The sub-assembly divisions consisted of a total of five tracers and nine cutters. The capital equipment required was nine scissors, five pencils, and five patterns.

The Final Assembly Division needed to be organized with one tracer and four assemblers. Four paste pads, one pencil, and a pair of scissors were needed as equipment. Groups were arranged in production line fashion, and production began.

Problems soon arose. The Top Assembly Division could not keep up. Their product was unsatisfactory, and they had to slow production. This

Table 1–1

Sub-Assembly Divisions

	Labor		Capital		
Divisions	Tracers	Cutters	Scissors	Pencils	Pattern
Top Assembly	1	1	1	1	1
Front Body	1	2	2	1	1
Rear Body	1	2	2	1	1
Wheel Assembly	1	2	2	1	1
Trim	1		2	1	1
TOTALS	5	9	9	5	5

prevented them from meeting the schedule. The body divisions had the most problems. At first, production along the individual lines went very well. Soon, it was discovered that the separate parts did not fit together at the Final Assembly Division. This stopped production in three factories. Production was stopped because the *system of measure* was not precise enough. The tracers were not following the patterns that had been planned.

Table 1–2

Transportation Division

	Type of Labor	Capital
Division	Carriers	Boxes
Transportation	2	2

Table 1–3

Final Assembly Division

	Type of Labor			Capital		
Station	Tracer	Assembler	Special	Scissors	Pencils	Paste
Brace			1	1		
Body		1				1
Top	1	1			1	1
Wheel		1				1
Trim		1				1
TOTALS	1	4	1	1	1	4

After these problems were corrected, production continued for the assigned thirty minutes. Eighteen cars had been produced. At this point, the company had a division meeting to plan the second day of production.

The teacher encouraged the children to discuss the problems they had encountered in their separate groups. They were to look for solutions to the problems and consider new methods of production. Solutions and recommendations were to be included in their report. These reports were to be presented to a meeting of all division managers. The recommendations from that meeting were as follows:

1. Increase labor in the Top Assembly Division.
2. Decrease labor in the Wheel and Trim Divisions.

3. Introduce an innovation—the auto bodies would be unitized instead of constructed in two halves.

Meeting of Division Managers

Labor problems were avoided by transferring the displaced workers to other positions. One tracer and one cutter were added to the Top Assembly Division. The operations in two of the factories were revised so that they produced the same product. It was decided to decrease the amount of labor in the Wheel and Trim Divisions. Therefore, production was stopped at those factories for ten minutes until their products were depleted.

Production ran very smoothly the second day. Thirty-four cars were produced in a thirty-minute period. When the class had evaluated their production, they turned to a discussion of cost. They counted only their labor, but they were quick to point out that a real manufacturer would have included many things that they could not include. Raw materials and profit were discussed as possible examples of these things. Finding a way to compute a simple *cost* was difficult, but with the teacher's help, the group developed these formulas:

Number of workers X minutes worked = man-minutes worked

Man-minutes worked ÷ cars produced = cost per car

Since the children had studied both multiplication and division, many of them were able to make these computations. As Table 1–4 indicates, the cost of the cars decreased drastically during the second day of mass production.

Table 1–4

Production Results

Production Method	Minutes Worked	Number of People	Units Produced	Cost per Car
Individual Production	40	22	18	*49 units
Mass Production				
Day #1**	30	22	16	41 units
Day #2	30	22	34	18 units

* Figures rounded to nearest whole number

** It will be noticed that the cost of production does not include the cost of preparing for production (tooling). This was done intentionally by the teacher.

The goal had been to produce the greatest number of cars at the least *cost.* The class accomplished this under their own *management* by using the *techniques of standardization* and the *division of labor.* By dividing the labor and using those most skilled in their jobs, the class was able to increase the *production* (Rooze).[1]

As you read through the foregoing example of a class engaged in a social studies learning game, perhaps you were taken by the differences between their activity and your own experience in elementary school social studies. What are some of these differences? Let's list them.

Children seem to be motivated.
Children were having fun.
Children were doing the work.
Children were giving their ideas.
Teacher did not seem to lecture.

Teacher was not the center of attention.
Teacher didn't do much "telling."
Children analyzed the situation.
Children arrived at conclusions.
There was no textbook.
Children had used a film.
Teacher did not seem to be looking for *a* correct answer.
Children were engaged in group work.

Perhaps you have a few items that you could add to this list.

What are some of the similarities you discovered?

Topic is familiar.
Children were working within a time period.
All children were working on the same theme.
One teacher was in charge of the entire class.
Arithmetic was mentioned.

We hope that you can add many more to this list.

We shall turn our attention now to some of the concerns in social studies education which have helped to bring about many of the changes in recent programs.

The social studies in this decade have the promise of creating in the minds of children some understanding of themselves, their environment, that environment's relationship to man, and man's relationship to other men. Although in the past, surveys have shown that students have despised the social studies because of their nebulous nature and the emphasis placed on the memorization of names, dates, and facts, present content can be a vehicle for the enrichment of the child's life now and in the future. This will enable the student to analyze his world and find his place within it.

Objectives

The reader will be able to:

Explain (1.0) the relationship between the social studies and the social sciences.

Justify (6.0) the inclusion of a given discipline on the basis of the reader's past experience with that discipline when given the three common factors on which the selected social sciences are based.

A Definition of the Social Studies

The social studies are those portions of the social science disciplines of anthropology, sociology, economics, psychology, political science, history, and geography, which have been selected for teaching purposes. (Wesley, 12–14) The rationale for the selection of these disciplines is that they are the social sciences which study the behavior of man. Although this generalization seems to exclude geography, it is held that elements of physical and cultural geography must be included because of their environmental effect upon man and man's manipulation of his environment. These disciplines are grouped together because of three common factors: *first,* the type of data they collect is descriptive of man's overt behavior; *second,* their experiments attempt to gain insight into the overt behavior of man; and *finally,* they extrapolate the meanings of their experiments to predict the behavior of man.

The relationship between the social studies and the social sciences is pointed out by Engle, the 1970 president of the National Council for the Social Studies. He states that social studies is the broader field ". . . which attempts to fuse scientific knowledge with ethical, philosophical, religious, and social considerations which arise in the process of decision-making. . . ." (Engle, 282)

Objectives

The reader will be able to:

Discuss (2.0) the five issues facing social studies curricula in the 1950s and 1960s and identify (1.0) questions which arise in facing these issues.

Explain (2.0) why "citizenship" is an unattainable goal in social studies education.

Explain (2.0) how the role of the school becomes an issue in dealing with social reality.

Contrast (2.0) the implications of the two views of content selection.

Differentiate (4.0) among the foci of the subject-centered, child-centered, and progressive views of education.

Evaluate (6.0) the validity of Tyler's criticisms of social

studies programs through an analysis (4.0) of their own experiences in social studies education.

Issues in the Social Studies

The ferment in social studies curricula of the 1950s and 1960s was caused by a total dissatisfaction with its content and methods. The reasons for discontent can be illustrated by reference to a leader in elementary school curricula, Sowards' (9–16) introduction to the report of the 1963 Stanford University Cubberly Conference called to discuss the future of the social studies.

Clarification of Objectives.

Sowards (10) identified the first issue in social studies education as the clarification of objectives. Are the social studies to teach citizenship? Classically, educators have listed this as the major objective of the social studies. This position assumes a great deal of any curricular area unless a concise definition is placed on the term "citizenship" and overt behaviors can be identified. Are the social studies alone responsible for such learnings? Is the school the only institution involved in this activity? These are related questions which we shall attempt to answer in the chapters that follow.

Dealing with social reality.

The second issue discussed was how far the social studies should go in dealing with social reality. If we are to teach citizenship, it can be argued, we must educate the student to meet the problems of society. It would seem to follow that social problems should be examined in a free and open climate. Assuming this is true, if students offer solutions to social problems which differ from those presently accepted by society, are they free to act according to the dictates of their consciences? Can youth be allowed to examine and attempt to change the values of established society? In other words, is the school to become an agent of social change?

Sources of social studies content.

Sources of social studies content was the third issue considered. Let's look at two major approaches to subject content. Is it the role of social studies to instill in the minds of students the glories of American political history and geography with little regard for distortions of facts, invalid generalizations, stereotypes, and nationalistic propaganda? Or are the social studies to draw their content from the social sciences which scrutinize the societies of man and study his behavior? The latter approach would result in the selection of concepts directly from the social sciences. It would also mean that the methods of social scientists would be used to create informed and active citizens able to evaluate, draw conclusions, and formulate their own values. If one were to choose this alternative, what criteria should be employed to select the concepts and methods which would be taught? Is this the responsibility of educators, or should scholars, who are closer to the disciplines, choose the important elements?

Focus of the curriculum.

These three problems are the product of a much broader unresolved conflict between the advocates of a subject-centered curriculum and the proponents of the child-centered curriculum, both of whom are attempting to dominate educational practice. The subject-centered curriculum is a relic of the past, having been transplanted from the Old World and well established in this country before the birth of our nation in the late eighteenth century. As Crosby (10) states in her book on elementary school curriculum:

> The subject-centered curriculum is founded upon the belief that the curriculum is composed of separate and distinct subjects, each of which embraces a body of content and skills which enable the learner to acquire knowledge of himself and his world.

The child-centered curriculum, on the other hand, is a product of the early twentieth century and is based upon the premise that instead of subjects, ". . . the child is the center of the educational process and the curriculum should be built upon his interest, needs, abilities, and purposes." (Crosby, 12)

There is an alternative, but few see it. Can the true tenets of progressive education be implemented? Proponents of this philosophy of curriculum maintain that although the institution of education cannot determine the direction of social change, it can develop the mental capacity for children to react intelligently to change.

Teachers and materials.

Central to the re-examination of the social studies is the competency of teachers in the classroom and the educational validity of the materials used. Tyler (119–32), a renowned leader in education, presents an excellent assessment of the state of social studies during the late 1950s and middle 1960s. Although there were exceptions, the social studies curriculum was the least effective of any of the areas taught. Pupils were not interested in the subject. It was dull, spiritless, and lacked clearly defined content and methods. The reasons for this, Tyler felt, were (1) the confusion over the purposes, (2) the lack of intellectual resources in the schools to aid teachers, (3) a poorly planned curriculum as a result of the confusion over purposes and the lack of intellectual resources, and (4) the assignment of this course to teachers who had neither the interest nor the training to teach the subject.

Objectives

The reader will be able to:

Relate (3.0) the problem-solving model to the solution of personal and social problems.

Explain (2.0) the relationship between society and its values.

Purposes of the Social Studies

Tyler (125) reminds us that the role of a subject area in education is not the furtherance of the subject. It should provide resources which can be used to equip students with ways of thinking, feeling, and acting. In turn, these skills will help them to live more effectively, with greater dignity and satisfaction.

Teaching of skills.

For years social studies educators have listed an objective similar to Tyler's. In 1962, a committee of the National Council for the Social Studies, a division of the National Education Association, indicated that the ultimate goal of education in social studies is the development of desirable socio-civic and personal behavior. "Man's behavior," they continued, "tends to reflect the values, ideals, beliefs, and attitudes which he accepts. . . . In a free society, behavior must rest upon reasoned convictions as well as emotional acceptance." (315) Knowledge and the ability to think should provide the basis upon which Americans can build the beliefs and behavior of free citizens.

The question then arises, how does one teach an individual to think? Long lists of social studies skill objectives have been identified by groups and national committees. When such specific objectives are analyzed, they can be subsumed under the following general objectives:

1. To teach the individual sources of information from which he can glean facts.
2. To teach the individual to evaluate the facts he has gathered in relationship to other facts on the same or different subjects.
3. To teach the individual several meaningful ways to organize data so that he may draw conclusions from it.
4. To teach the individual to draw conclusions and evaluate such conclusions according to other things known about the topic, and to relate such conclusions to his other knowledge.
5. To teach the individual channels for implementing action upon his conclusions.
6. To teach the individual ways of obtaining cooperation for action upon his conclusions.

These objectives of the social studies become a problem-solving model which the individual can use in the solution of personal and social problems. Each step has within it behaviors which can be developed and evaluated in the social studies classroom.

Teaching of knowledge.

Knowledge furnishes the student a frame through which he can view his world. The purpose of content is to provide the child with concepts and methods which he can use as tools of analysis. For many years, it has been argued by some that knowledge is an end in itself. This argument is valid only if such knowledge permits the individual greater understanding of his life space. Knowledge in the social studies is derived from the foundational disciplines of the social sciences. These disciplines are discussed in Chapter III.

Teaching of Values.

Generally, after the listing of knowledge and skills, educators continue by identifying the values of a people in a free society. This is the logical fallacy in which most social studies educators have been caught. They assume that all citizens of a free society will evolve the same set of values, regardless of their diverse social backgrounds and differing economic status. In the past, the problem encountered in the social studies has been that broad, general objectives have been stated which could not be developed in the microcosm of the classroom. These values had been highly idealized and stated as fixed values which describe a static rather than a dynamic society.

The current trend is to see pluralistic values which are developed in the process of obtaining wants and needs. Currently, values are viewed as being fluid, differing among social classes and institutions. Values, indeed, determine behavior. Values and attitudes are a result of man's knowledge and experience, interpreted in terms of successful acquisition of wants and needs.

Objectives

The reader will be able to:

Define (1.0) the term "institution" and identify (1.0) the institutions of American society.

Cite (1.0) an example showing the interrelationship of societal institutions

Identify (1.0) the role of education in relation to the other institutions of our society.

Relate (1.0) status in institutions to success in our society.

Describe (1.0) the characteristics of a pluralistic society.

Describe (1.0) the role of social studies education in American Society.

A Social Model.

The model illustrated in Figure 1 shows the relationship of individuals to our society. Individuals have wants and needs which society can fulfill. Society is not one element, but it is composed of many elements called institutions. Institutions can be defined as organized ways of fulfilling wants and needs. (Berelson, 383–84) They are formally recognized by the individuals in society and have established values and rules for pursuing wants and needs. These rules and values appear relatively stable because changes in them occur slowly over a period of time.

The types and numbers of institutions vary among societies because they are the products of the societies' attempts to satisfy the wants and needs of its members. The dominant institutions in a highly industrialized society, such as ours, can be identified as social, economic, political, religious, and educational. Although these institutions are depicted as separate in Figure 1, actually they are interrelated.

The population explosion is an issue that can be used to show this interrelationship. Although it might appear that this is purely a social and economic issue, the values held by the religious institution of our society, often upheld through legislation, inhibit the use of such controls as abortion, sterilization, euthanasia, and even methods of birth control. Since legislation is enacted through the political institution, the effect of the interaction between the religious and political institutions is readily apparent.

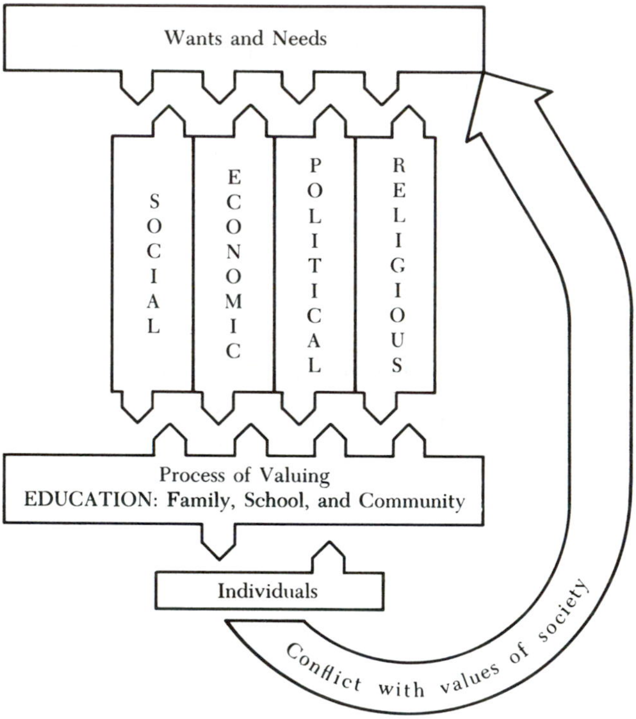

Figure 1. *Model of a Pluralistic Society*

Another example of this conflict comes from our nation's enactment of the prohibition laws of the 1920s. Following the lead of the religious institution, the political institution developed laws against the manufacture, transportation, and sale of alcoholic beverages in the United States. Neither the economic nor the social institution supported this legislation. Bootlegging became big business and speakeasies were popular gathering places. It took thirteen years for the political institution to reject forces in the religious institution and succumb to the pressures of the social and economic institutions which were working for repeal.

Returning to Figure 1, the reader will note that the institution of education is at the base of the other four institutions. It is the point of entrance into the others in industrialized societies. Education, which must be interpreted to include the influence of the family and community as well as the school, provides the means by which individuals gain the values, knowledge, and skills they need to operate successfully in other institutions.

Education has a reciprocal relationship with the other institutions because it interprets the values derived from them. It, in turn, has an effect on the values of the other institutions. Education, then, transmits values from the institutions to the individual, aiding him to become a successful participant in society.

Every individual within the society operates at a differing degree of success in specific institutions. The more successful an individual is in obtaining his wants and needs in any institution, the greater his success—measured in terms of status—in our society. Failure in one or more of the institutions, especially the social or economic, decreases the likelihood of success in the others. When the frustration of failure within the societal institutions becomes too great for the individual, it causes him to drop out of organized society. Since he drops out of society, he must turn to crime, rioting, or other means to achieve his wants and needs. These actions conflict with the values of established society.

Philosophical base for the social model.

Although this model is not new, the reasoning upon which it is based has been slow to receive acceptance. In a chapter of a recent book on the sociology of education, Beck et. al. (155–73) summarize the philosophical base for the argument the authors are presenting. Our society is pluralistic and, therefore, has many goals and sets of values.

Although the social, economic, political, and religious institutions are illustrated as entities in Figure 1, they are made up of many diverse groups. Each of these groups has its individual rules and values. Those of the economic system must take into account those of labor, management, capital, and government, yet many people continue to see society as having one set of values. The conflict between the values of labor and management is well documented and is adequate evidence of the pluralistic theory.

Characteristics of a pluralistic society.

At this point it would be helpful to examine the characteristics of a pluralistic society such as our own. First, a pluralistic society is flexible. It is deliberately organized and reorganized to accomplish changing social purposes, rather than to direct the total society toward predetermined goals. As a technological society changes, the wants and needs of its citizens change. This means that the values within institutions must change.

A second characteristic is that values ". . . are human constructs built up through social experience by men for the purposes of insuring the survival of society and enhancing human existence." (Beck, et. al, 158) The pluralistic society looks at tradition as an established way of satisfying wants and needs, but it realizes that established means will not fit a changing society. The pluralistic society is held together, not by a single set of fixed values and purposes or an inflexible code, but by several means within multiple institutions.

The third characteristic is that the role of education as an institution is active rather than passive. The educational institution of a pluralistic society provides access to all other institutions. It joins with these institutions in remaking itself and society. The schools of our pluralistic society transmit processes of inquiry and methods of dealing with facts, rather than fixed bodies of knowledge which must remain pure. Through these processes and methods, the individual becomes aware of existing institutional values. This awareness helps the individual to prepare himself for roles in these institutions.

The model of a pluralistic society is intended to provide the reader with some understanding of the transmission of values, as well as the relationship of values to institutions. Since the child is not a full participant in several institutions of society, the task falls to education and particularly social studies education to help the child develop and interpret societal values.

The role of social studies education is to supply the knowledge, skills, and values which will allow the individual to function more effectively in the institutions of society. Knowledge, skills, and values are developed from the child's testing of behaviors. The level of success he obtains determines the habits and values the child incorporates into his value complex. The consistency of success he meets in problem solving delimits the knowledge and skills he retains.

Objectives

The reader will be able to:

Cite (5.0) examples from his own classroom experiences to illustrate one of the value objectives listed in the text.

Explain (2.0) why processes are given an equal emphasis with content in the new social studies.

Values Derived from a Pluralistic Analysis

What are the values which can be influenced through social studies education; how may these values be developed? Through an analysis of the previous discussion concerning the characteristics of a pluralistic society, certain values can be identified. These values can be used to guide the selection of objectives for classroom instruction.

1. A free society implies that all men have inherent worth.
   In the classroom, children can be taught to *value* the *presence and contributions of all* individuals in the class.

2. Free men have rights to think, feel, act, and speak according to their beliefs.
   In our classrooms, children can be encouraged to *think and speak* according to their beliefs and *learn to accept* the ideas and beliefs of *others* in the class.

3. There are rules within society which men must follow if they are to be considered members of that society.
   Students can be assisted in *establishing, following, evaluating,* and *revising* classroom and school *rules.*

4. Our society allows the individual the choice of a specialized job. Advancement within this job is the reward of the individual's success within the economic institution. Social as well as economic status within society is the result.
   In our classrooms, children can be helped to *identify* the *successful behaviors* in tasks in which they succeed. They can be helped to *deal with failures* by evaluating them to determine their unsuccessful behaviors. Restructuring these experiences, they may *explore new behaviors* which might prove successful. Through their successes, pupils will gain status; through their failures, evaluations, and new attempts, they can *develop* some *tolerance for frustration.*

5. Specialized jobs require cooperation among individuals within a society. People are able to obtain more of their wants and needs through such cooperation.
   Situations can be arranged in our classrooms which permit the child to *experience* both *success and failure* in group work. If he succeeds, he will be rewarded. If he fails, he can learn to *evaluate group roles* and *behavior* and develop successful group strategies.

6. All men have the right to attempt to fulfill their wants and needs; as a result, they often come into conflict with the wants and needs of others. These conflicts can be resolved within our institutions.
   In our classrooms many conflicts develop. Teachers have abundant opportunities to *present alternative means* of resolving conflicts within the rules of the school.

7. A free society is open to new ideas and change. This change will create conflicts which can be resolved rationally.
   Situations and values change in the classroom, too. Again, some *means* of *resolution* can be *attempted* and *evaluated.*

8. Since wants and needs of individuals change, the values within institutions change. Each individual has a right to attempt to influence the values held by such institutions.
   To develop this value in the classroom, *respect for the rights* and *dignity* of the *individual* must become dominant.

These are the value objectives toward which teaching in the social studies can be directed. It is obvious that the fulfillment of these general objectives will require both the student and teacher to assume new roles. In the past, content received the major emphasis in the social studies, and it was assumed that values would develop through content learning. In other words, the fallacious assumption was made that transfer from knowledge to attitudes and behavior was automatic.

In the new social studies, processes are given an equal emphasis with content. The product is the value component which was merely verbalized in the past. Growth in the cognitive domain (knowledge) is accomplished through the content; growth in the affective domain (feelings, attitudes, and values) is assured through processes.

Objective

The reader will be able to:

Restate (2.0), in his own words, the criterion for the selection of content in the social studies.

A Social Studies Criterion

As stated previously, the overriding goal of the social studies is to equip the student with ways of thinking, feeling, and acting which will help him live more effectively, with greater dignity and satisfaction. Social studies educators can accomplish this by helping the student acquire those concepts and processes which will enable him to analyze his society, make judgments, and develop relevant values.

This is the focus that new curriculum projects have taken. The problem which still exists is that of attempting to find content which will accomplish this goal.

Jerome Bruner, considered by many the leader of current curriculum reform, points the way to developing a criterion when he states: ". . . whether, when fully developed, it is worth an adult's knowing and whether having known it as a child makes a person a better adult." (52) The importance of this statement is not realized until one focuses upon our changing world. Facts and even concepts change as man increases his depth and range of knowledge. If a man's knowledge allows him to understand himself, his environment, that environment's relation to man, and man's relationship to man, then that knowledge is indeed worth knowing. This is the criterion for the selection of content in the social studies.

References

Beck, Carlton E., et al. *Educating for Relevance.* New York: Houghton Mifflin Company 1968.

Berelson, Bernard, and Steiner, Gary. *Human Behavior: An Inventory of Scientific Findings.* New York: Harcourt, Brace and World, Inc., 1964.

Bruner, Jerome S. *The Process of Education.* New York: Random House, Inc., Vintage Book Edition, 1960.

Crosby, Muriel. *Curriculum Development for Elementary Schools in a Changing Society.* Boston: D. C. Heath and Company, 1964.

Engle, Shirley H. "Exploring the Meaning of Social Studies." *Social Education* 35 (March 1971): 280–288.

National Council for the Social Studies. "The Role of the Social Studies." *Social Education 26 (October 1962): 315.*

Rooze, Gene E. "Turning Out Make-Believe Cars Teaches Real Economics." Grade Teacher 84 (March 1967): 92–93, 167–168.

Sowards, G. Wesley, ed. *The Social Studies: Curriculum Proposals for the Future.* Chicago: Scott, Foresman, and Company, 1963.

Tyler, Ralph W. "An Assessment: The Edge of the Future." *The Social Studies: Curriculum Proposals for the Future.* Edited by G. Wesley

Sowards. Chicago: Scott, Foresman and Company, 1963.

Wesley, Edgar Bruce. "Teaching Social Studies." *Encyclopedia of Educational Research.* Edited by W. S. Monroe. New York: The Macmillan Company, 1950.

II

How Should Content Be Selected

Chapter Outline

How Should Content Be Selected?

Surveys of social studies materials during the early sixties indicated that the disciplines of history and geography received the greatest emphasis. Little attention was given to the other social sciences. Further, much of the material was grossly outdated. Social studies texts, and therefore the curriculum, did not provide a valid representation of current social studies knowledge. In order for you to gain some perspective of this educational problem, it will be helpful to examine traditional curriculum development. We shall look at the traditional model which is used in curriculum development and examine an alternative model which appears to be emerging.

Objectives

The reader will be able to:

Explain (2.0) the steps in the Traditional Model, as given in Figure 2–1.

Identify (1.0) the weaknesses of the Traditional Model.

Curriculum Development: A Traditional Model

Traditionally, the development of curriculum has been viewed as a responsibility of the school and the teacher (King, 493). In theory, the process of curriculum development (see Figure 2–1) is as follows: From the knowledge which has been identified by educators, educational purposes are derived which are translated into general objectives. Supposedly, these objectives reflect the assessed needs of students and society, as well as the nature or characteristics of the area of knowledge under study. Content is selected, organized, and sequenced. The curriculum is then implemented by means of activities which have been developed to fulfill the general objectives within the stated purposes. Evaluation is accomplished to insure that the objectives have been achieved.

Problems arise in the application of this model. First, educators are not sufficiently versed in many of the foundational disciplines which compose the elementary school curriculum. They are too far removed from the represented fields of knowledge to be aware of new developments and discoveries. Using this traditional model, there is a ten to twenty

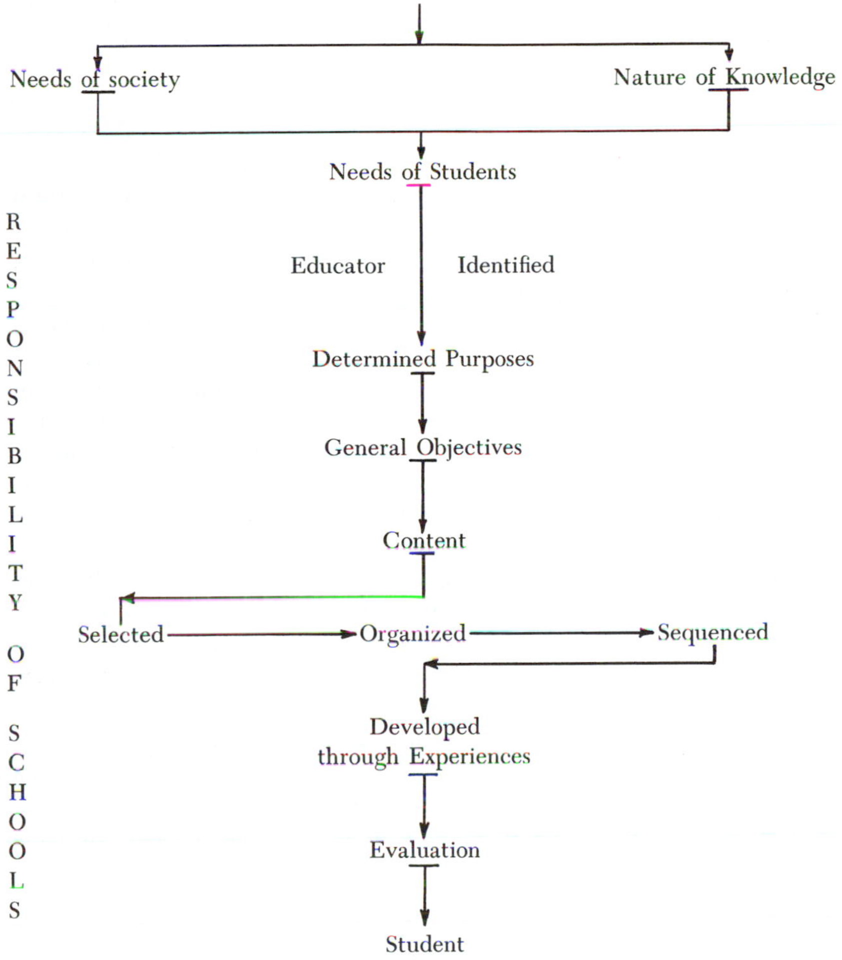

Figure 2–1. *Traditional Curriculum Model*

year lag between the discovery of knowledge and its implementation in textbooks or other materials.

Next, lip service has been given to the diagnosis of student needs. Curricula developed under this model tended to be prescriptive, in the sense that educators "knew" what was "good" and "necessary" for children. Frequently, objectives were based upon invalid assumptions about children's needs.

Additionally, the needs of society were assessed as static rather than dynamic. In recent educational history, such an interpretation was reasonably valid because the pace of change had not reached the momentum of present times. Harold Benjamin, in his satirical book entitled *The Saber Toothed Curriculum,* indicated the fallacy of retaining outdated content and skills in the curriculum on the basis of tradition. The fictitious society he described, even though primitive, had experienced changes in its technology and needs. Benjamin sardonically pointed to the fact that this society taught its youth the saber-tooth-tiger-scaring-with-fire technique with the zeal of an earlier day, although the chances of meeting such creatures had been considerably reduced. Yet, if you were to open the doors of a few classrooms today, you might find saber-tooth-tiger-fire-brandishing at the top of the study guide.

Third, objectives were stated in general, rather than specific terms. Statements, such as "the student will enjoy saber-tooth-tiger scaring," were open to varied interpretations. What does it mean to enjoy "saber-tooth-tiger-scaring," and how is such an objective to be evaluated? Would the student perform a ceremonial dance, jump from a high cliff, or brandish his torch with glee to show his pleasure in this activity? Such general objectives can be interpreted in many ways. They make planning for instruction difficult, give little help in the selection of appropriate activities, and evade effective evaluation. This method of curriculum development utilizes committees composed of teachers, principals, supervisors, and other educational specialists in charge of the program development process. The resulting products are curriculum packages, custom-made for the school system.

The fourth problem concerns the implementation of this model. Realistically, small school systems have little opportunity to develop curricula in this manner. They lack the financial resources and the specialized personnel needed to get the job done. In practice, the publishers of media control the curriculum in most schools. (King, 495) Principals, teachers, and supervisors, individually or as a team, make decisions regarding choice of textbooks. Little attempt is made to evaluate the effectiveness of such programs. The curriculum becomes what the teacher selects from what the textbook gives.

Textbooks have to be written by someone. Traditionally, the authors are professional educators. The major criticism has been that such persons are too far removed from the fields of knowledge to know current findings and relevant concepts from which they can prepare the required material.

Another interesting facet of the problem is that, until recently, there have been few scholars from the disciplines available to aid educators and publishers in the preparation of curricula or materials for the schools. For the scholars, such endeavors have not been valued by fellow social scientists as they are not in the high status research realm.

In conclusion, the problems encountered by school personnel in using the Traditional Model are twofold. In the first place, the model is not descriptive of practice. Educators are not prepared to deal with the myriad of new knowledge in the social sciences. The model is descriptive of curriculum development for which schools have neither the intellectual resources—they do not have access to scholars—nor the economic resources to develop new curriculum packages. Second, there have been practices developing which are unsound. Curricula have been designed which made conjectures about the needs of students, rather than assessing the students' actual needs. Such programs have not kept pace with changes in society. The objectives developed for skills, knowledge, and values have been vague and unrealistic in terms of what can be accomplished in the classroom.

Objectives

The reader will be able to:

Explain (2.0) the steps in the Alternative Model, given in Figure 3.

Contrast (2.0) the selection of content according to the Traditional and Alternative Models.

Explain (2.0) how the knowledge of the intellectual development of children is used in preparing material in the Alternative Model.

Defend (2.0) the utility of the Taxonomy of Educational Objectives.

Contrast (2.0) the type of thinking skills required in the older materials with those of newer programs.

Contrast (2.0) the expanding environment principle with spiral curriculum development.

Differentiate (2.0) between inductive and deductive teaching.

Suggest (3.0) both inductive and deductive teaching procedures, given a specific concept.

Contrast (2.0) the role of the teacher in the traditional and newer orientations.

Curriculum Development: An Alternative Model

Much research in school curricula was initiated in the late fifties and early sixties by various scholarly societies and the federal government.

The stated purposes of these projects included the upgrading of content and teaching methods of specific subject areas. Research and implementation continued in several of these studies into the seventies. Basically, the change achieved by the national curriculum projects has been one of placing intellectual resources within the financial reach of the public schools. Many individuals have seen this move as one of depositing direct control of the curriculum in the hands of scholars. This was nearly the case in some science projects, but most of the newer programs have been directed by university professors of education or nonprofit corporations with the cooperation of competent scholars of various fields. The process of curriculum development follows a Brunerian Model as illustrated in Figure 2–2, so named by the authors of this book because the ideas in the construct were adapted from Bruner.

DEVELOPED BY NATIONAL TEAMS

Knowledge—scholar identified
↓
Materials prepared by educators
↓
intellectual development of children considered
↓
acts of learning taken into account
↓
learning sequenced
↓
motives for teaching considered
↓
Developed through vicarious experiences
└both inductive
deductive
↓
Student

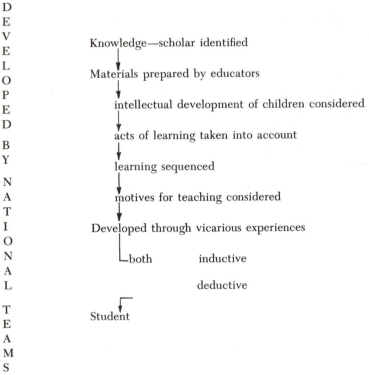

Figure 2–2. *Alternative Curriculum Model*

This model takes the structure of knowledge, defined by the scholars, as its content base. It differs from the Traditional Model because scholars from the foundational disciplines, rather than professional educators select the content initially. The advantage is that these scholars, closer to the specialized areas of knowledge, are more aware of the current developments in their disciplines and can place priorities as to what they assume is most relevant for the learner. Theoretically the use of this model prevents the selection of outdated concepts and methods, which was one of the major criticisms leveled at previous curriculum materials.

Intellectual development.

The substantive structure is then translated by professional educators into materials for children, taking into account the intellectual development of the student. Although Bruner makes reference to Piaget's stages of development, few projects have been bold enough to incorporate these ideas.

Jean Piaget, the famous Swiss developmental psychologist, has theorized that children pass through four distinct periods of intellectual development: sensory motor (birth to two years); pre-operational (two to seven years); concrete operational (seven to eleven years); and formal operational (above eleven years). These four levels determine the type of learning for which the child is ready. If learning is to be effective, the characteristics of the various stages must be considered.

Bruner's major concern is for readiness in terms of the child's way of viewing and explaining his world. If a subject can be organized with this in mind, Bruner contends, any subject can be learned by the child at any age.

For example, the complex economic concept of *division of labor* can be introduced to kindergarten children utilizing everyday experiences. A common activity is the sharing of responsibilities for room maintenance, such as dusting shelves, watering plants, and straightening books. Many variations of "helpers" charts indicating tasks and assignments for the day or week adorn schoolroom walls.

One teacher illustrated the importance of such sharing by assigning all of the maintenance tasks to two children who had volunteered and felt they could handle the responsibilities. It was soon evident to all that the helpers were not getting the job done in the allotted time. When questioned, the class concluded that more than two helpers were needed. The teacher helped the children to identify the tasks and then made daily assignments to each job. Soon the children decided that by dividing the work, they were able to complete all tasks quickly and had more time for other activities. The teacher supplied the label—*division of labor.*

This concept was once considered too advanced for elementary school children. But as Bruner points out, a concept becomes meaningful to the learner when it is placed in the proper learning context.

Acts of learning.

Translation of the content into materials for teaching must take into account acts of learning. Acts of learning refer to what a student must do in the learning process. According to Bruner, the child must first acquire new information; then, he must manipulate this information to fit the defined task. Bruner's third task is the evaluation of the adequateness of the fit. Again, few of the national projects have used this specific analysis. They have, however, analyzed and used levels of thinking. That is, developers of programs have designed the materials they produced in such a way as to call for different thinking skills than merely the lowest—memory—another criticism of the older material and methods of teaching in general.

The *Taxonomy of Educational Objectives, Handbook I* has served as a tool for several of the projects. This taxonomy is a means of classifying instructional objectives according to levels of complexity. It was developed by a committee of evaluation specialists from major colleges and universities. The Cognitive Taxonomy was edited by Benjamin S. Bloom, a recognized authority in testing and measurement. The major purpose of this taxonomy is to facilitate the communication of educational outcomes among educators and laymen by identifying six major categories of intellectual activity. They are listed as follows:

1.0 *Knowledge*, the lowest level, is the ability to recall facts, procedures, concepts, and generalizations.

2.0 *Comprehension* involves the manipulation of knowledge in the same or similar context in which it was taught.

3.0 *Application* involves the use of knowledge in new situations.

4.0 *Analysis* requires the individual to break phenomena into their component parts.

5.0 *Synthesis* is the combining of component parts in a new arrangement.

6.0 *Evaluation* is the judging of material according to some criteria.

As we have indicated, the identification of student behaviors, meaning the intended outcomes or objectives of the educational process, has been a major problem in school curriculum planning.

Guilford's (469–79) model of the intellect has also served as a tool for the identification of levels of thinking. J. P. Guilford, a noted psychologist in the area of learning and intelligence, has isolated five types of intellectual abilities. The operational areas, although developed for research purposes, have been utilized by teachers and program developers to insure the use of several types of questions in materials for children. Both the Taxonomy and Guilford's model facilitate the planning of many different levels of learning activities. Through their use, educators can communicate accurately specific behaviors to be elicited at each level.

Sequence of learning.

The third major area which must be considered, according to the Brunerian Model, is that of the sequence of learning. The structure of a subject must be presented in such a way that children meet major concepts at increasing levels of difficulty as they progress through the curriculum. This is known as *spiral curriculum* development. Consider the concept of *specialization.* Suppose we were to introduce this concept as it relates to the family in the primary grades; as it applies to industry in the intermediate grades; and as it pertains to the specialization of organisms in junior high school. This concept would be broadened and made more complex in meaning as the child progressed through the grades. Thus, the concept would become more meaningful and useful to the learner as he matures.

The traditional pattern of sequencing instruction in social studies has used the expanding environment principle. This was based upon the premise that children could comprehend only that environment nearest in time and space to their experiences. The child studied the home, school, neighborhood, community, state, region, and then the nation, in that order. Such a pattern ignored the impact of mass media to which children are exposed and which vastly increased their experiential base. In the spiral curriculum, advocated by Bruner, concern for the expanding environment of the child is negated in favor of the development of concepts and values that will aid him in becoming a functioning participant of society.

In communicating the structure of a subject to students, the educator, with the guidance of scholars, is concerned with providing experiences for children, most of which must be vicarious. It would be more effective to provide real experiences. Since this is impractical in many cases, we must depend upon vicarious ones. The study of a state could be accomplished through travel, but this is rather expensive and time consuming. Therefore, we settle for vicarious experiences, such as films, filmstrips, pictures, dramatic activities, and the like, to accomplish our objectives.

Learning is assumed to be more effective when inductive strategies are employed. These strategies allow the learner to experience a myriad of examples from which he infers a concept or generalization. But this process is often inefficient because of its trial and error nature and resulting expenditure of time. Deductive teaching, on the other hand, is used in many instances. This strategy presents a concept or generalization first, and then allows the student to test or experience examples. Although research on these strategies is inconclusive, educators contend that the inductive approach has greater payoff in terms of retention of what is learned.

Role of the teacher.

The role of the teacher must be examined to obtain the full impact of the newer curriculum projects. These projects place the teacher in a different posture than the traditional orientation. As illustrated below, traditionally we have seen the teacher as the mediator and purveyor of knowledge.

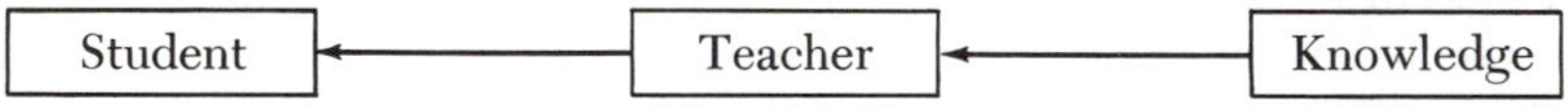

We fail to see the paradigm illustrated in Figure 2–3. This diagram places knowledge on one side and the student on the other. In between, there are many ways of conveying knowledge to the student. There are dramatizations, role playing, models, programmed materials, films, filmstrips, automated devices, texts, and other written materials. Note that the teacher can be considered one of the mediating devices, and he may be the manager of them all.

Content in the new curricula.

Recall now the concern of this chapter, how is content selected? In present programs, the content is selected by scholars of the disciplines and translated into learning experiences by professional educators. However, there remain vestiges of the past. Some school districts still attempt to develop their own curriculum packages with their limited intellectual and economic resources. Few of these districts rely on scholars to aid in the selection of content. Other districts still lack a cohesive social studies program because they rely on the selection of content from a limited number of textbooks.

Objectives

The reader will be able to:

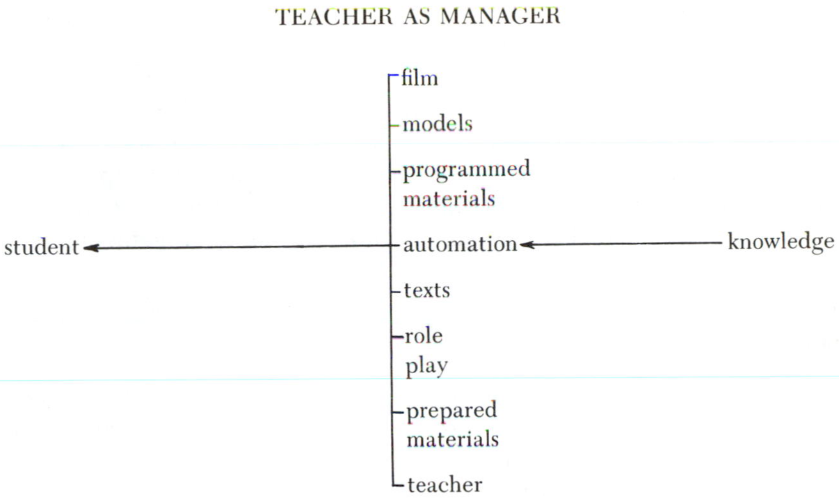

Figure 2–3. *The Teacher as Manager*

Identify (1.0) the three major components of the structure of a discipline.

Suggest (3.0) examples from personal experience which show the importance of the influence of a national association on one of its members.

Suggest (3.0) conceptions which are viewed differently by several scientists or social scientists in the same discipline.

Describe (1.0) the three different processes used in investigation.

State (1.0) the reason given for teaching children that knowledge can be revised.

The Structure of the Disciplines

We stated earlier that the social studies are those portions of the disciplines of anthropology, sociology, economics, psychology, political science, history, and geography which have been selected for teaching purposes. These are the foundational disciplines of the social studies. But this delineation is helpful only to the extent that it defines the disciplines we are going to use. This listing does not clarify "structure," and therefore, at this point, identification of content remains difficult.

Schwab, a leading theorist in education, elucidates the term "structure," in his discussion of the nature of knowledge. He identifies three major factors we must consider when describing the nature of a discipline. As shown in Figure 2–4, we must consider the people in the discipline and the organization that represents that discipline, the concepts (conceptions) its members use, and the methods or syntax employed in gathering and interpreting their data.

Membership and organization.

The first component, membership and organization, determines the subject matter studied, the academic expectations placed upon its individual members, the methods used in the research field, and the interpretations placed upon the literature of the specialized field. An interesting argument on membership of the social sciences surrounds history. The controversy still rages as to the validity of history as a social science because of the methods used by historians and the interpretations placed on their findings. A social science, the antagonists insist, must be predictive of human behavior rather than descriptive. Protagonists contend that history has a place because it furnishes a background for the younger disciplines.

Let's consider subject matter as an element of membership and organization. Is there a difference between the subject matter of physical and cultural geography? If so, this will make a difference in the portions of the discipline we select if we are interested in studying human behavior. The environmental factors which influence man's behavior must be analyzed if an adequate understanding of social behavior is to be developed. It is essential, then, for us to consider selected concepts drawn from physical geography to permit the student to investigate the relationship between man and his environment.

There are factors other than subject matter, that must be analyzed relating to membership. We must also consider the expectations placed upon the members of a discipline. What must each individual do to become a member? Are there specific methods he must use? What outcomes is one expected to derive from his study of data?

An excellent example comes to mind of the expectations placed on aspiring members of disciplines. A brilliant anthropology student spent eight years obtaining his PhD—eight years—he must have been a clod! Hardly. Specific procedures had been established by past research in his field. The methods he must use to obtain and interpret data on the language of an Indian tribe he was studying were rigorous. The expectation of his field was that he produce a significant contribution to the linguistic

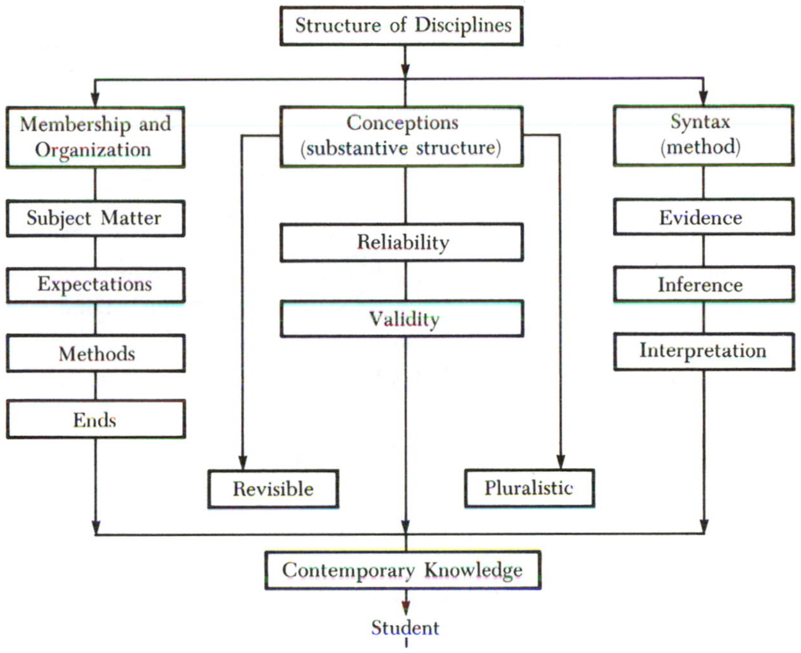

Figure 2–4. *The Structure of the Disciplines*

understanding of an unwritten language. The demands placed upon scholars in this discipline include diligent study and tenaciousness in the pursuit of knowledge. Considering such requirements, eight years in the pursuit of a PhD appears reasonable.

We have mentioned two elements of membership briefly in our previous examples. In the discussion of the controversy concerning history as a member of the social science disciplines, we pointed out that history uses methods which are open to question as scientific inquiry. Historians use diaries, letters, original sources, and secondary accounts in describing past events. Using such sources, they make assumptions and draw conclusions concerning these events. Social scientists claim that the assumptions made are too much the product of the particular historian's frame of reference. Therefore, the conclusions drawn cannot withstand objective evaluation through experimentation. Thus, because of the methods they use, historians are denied entrance to the social sciences by some scholars.

Ends, the fourth element of membership and organization, can be explained by using history as an example once more. The ends of a social science are to predict the behavior of man. Since history is descriptive of man's behavior rather than predictive, once more it may be denied membership in the social sciences. The example which described the young anthropologist can also be used to clarify ends. The aspirant was attempting to develop a description of an unwritten language which would allow the prediction of oral language behavior. Therefore, it is clearly seen that the ends of this study meet the requirements of a social science.

Conceptions.

Continuing the description of structure, conceptions of a discipline derived by the inquirers in the field comprise the second component. These conceptions allow fellow inquirers to communicate and evaluate their findings. An example may aid us in clarifying this confusing but necessary term, conceptions.

Since most of the readers will be familiar with the concept of IQ, it will serve as an illustration. Persons involved in the field of education know that the IQ score is relatively useful in predicting the success of an individual in the academic environment. IQ tests are reliable because similar results are obtained by individuals and groups when the same individuals and groups are retested. These tests are valid when used to predict school success. In other words, they appear to assess the factors that are needed for success in the school environment.

However, the IQ score is not as highly regarded as it once was. We have revised our interpretation of it. Previously, it was thought to measure only innate abilities. Research shows that this assumption is fallacious. It has been determined that intelligence tests measure a limited number of factors which make up the intellect. These factors depend upon the quantity and quality of experiences the individual has undergone. However, some unidentified factors exist. We now know that the IQ score can be raised by providing specific experiences in those areas measured by IQ tests. We can see from this discussion that the concept of IQ has been revised by educational psychologists. However, it remains a useful concept. Educationists disagree on some of the basic assumptions made by test and measurement specialists. But the need for the concept is generally accepted. It remains a useful concept even though we have pluralistic interpretations of IQ.

The conception of IQ is as much a part of the substantive structures of education as other concepts are of the substantive structures of the disciplines. As indicated in Figure 2–4, substantive structures of the disciplines must be reliable and valid. They are continually subjected to revision and assessment. Such structures are also pluralistic since the same concepts are not accepted by all of the scholars within an individual discipline.

Syntax.

The third element we must consider is the syntax or method of the disciplines. Syntax describes three different processes involved in investigation. First, a science has rules about what it will admit as data or evidence of an occurrence. In educational research, we have become more precise in measuring the success of curricula. Research specialists are not prone to accept subjective data, such as teacher opinion, for objective evidence of the effectiveness of a curriculum program. The criterion of student performance is considered more valid evidence of a program's success. Inferring is important to the syntax also. Inference implies the use of data. It also implies certain assumptions which are employed in the interpretation of data.

For example, a statistical technique is used frequently in educational research to indicate the relationship between two sets of variable measures. This idea is presented in the following example: Since the perimeter of each square is always four times the length of its side ($P = 4S$), it obviously follows that in any collection of squares, the one with the largest side will have the largest perimeter; the one with the second largest side will have the second largest perimeter, and so on. (Blommers, 361) However, educational statisticians would frown upon inferences from a study which indicated a high correlation between the size of the cranium of eight year old males and IQ scores. Such a study would be based on an assumption which educators feel is fallacious. Although a researcher might continue to obtain similar correlations, until his assumptions gained approval, his research would not receive acceptance.

The syntax of a science, as indicated above, limits the investigator to certain interpretations. As Schwab states:

> The significance of this variety of modes of inquiry, of patterns of discovery and verification, lies in this: most statements of most disciplines are like single words of a sentence. They take their most telling meanings, not from their dictionary sense, not from their sense in isolation, but from their context, their place in the syntax. The meaning of $F = MA$ or of free fall, of electron or neutrino, is understood properly only in the context of the inquiry that produced them. (24)

These, then, are the elements of the structure of knowledge which must be considered in selecting content for children. Using the disciplines from which we draw knowledge, scholars select the important conceptions and methods which are to be taught. One additional statement made by Schwab must be considered.

> If we dogmatically select one of the several bodies of theory in a given field and dogmatically teach this as the truth about its subject

> matter, we shall create division and failure of communication among our citizens. (29–30)

When the structure of a discipline is selected, we must caution students that all scientific knowledge is founded upon assumptions. Because of these assumptions the scientific findings are as limited as any other form of knowledge.

Since knowledge by its nature is open to constant revision, curriculum changes of great magnitude can be expected in the future. The minds of students must be prepared for such changes. We must help children understand that knowledge is based on presently known concepts and methods. It can be revised without destruction of their world. When the conceptions of a field change, knowledge changes. When methods of analyzing our world change, we gain new insights.

This is where the newer philosophy of curriculum differs from the traditional. The latter viewed knowledge as immutable. Any change in the body of knowledge meant a total destruction of a cognitive framework which had little tolerance for change. A chink in the framework caused the individual to distrust the total body of knowledge. Although the alternative model of curriculum development calls for reliance upon authorities in the fields of knowledge, it nevertheless leaves room for modification of the existing cognitive frame. New knowledge may be subsumed within the existing framework without creating the chaos of distrust. It also allows the child the opportunity to question knowledge.

Objectives

The reader will be able to:

Identify (1.0) the sources of knowledge, and present (3.0) examples of each from personal experience.

Sources of Knowledge

It is imperative for teachers to have an understanding of the sources of knowledge. Man has many means of obtaining knowledge. We can identify what is true through *divine revelation.* It can be claimed true because God in His infinite wisdom has willed it so. He has given this knowledge to man. Although many disclaim this method of determining truth, much of what we know is accepted on this basis.

Equally disclaimed, but accepted as knowledge today, is that derived from *appeal to authority*. Something is true because the "great leader" has said it was so. Since he is a knowledgeable man in the field, it must be true.

Knowledge can also be verified through *experimentation*. This is the most accepted way today of obtaining truth. However, this type of knowledge is not infallible because it is based on the world as we can conceptualize it with current methods.

Knowledge is also obtained through *reason*. We begin with premises which we assume to be true. From these premises, we form logical conclusions concerning knowledge otherwise unobtainable through scientific experimentation. These premises are what some scientists would prefer to call "untestable hypotheses." They are based on assumptions which seem reasonable from what we presently know.

There is also knowledge which is based on the shiftiest of sand. This is called *public knowledge* and is verified by asking the individual next to you. He replies, "Yes, everyone knows that." You go on your merry way knowing you have the absolute truth. Public knowledge is what is generally believed to be true. It is often called "hearsay."

Although all of these methods are used to verify knowledge today, some are more popular than others; some more reliable than others. Educated people, which include the authors and the present reader, know that the respectability of these forms of knowledge changes from age to age, time to time, and nation to nation. The sources of knowledge must be considered in any educational program and verification procedures should be identified by the student. In view of the stated purposes of social studies, teachers and students need to know the sources of knowledge from which content is drawn in order to assess its validity. Verification, is the end product of inquiry. It provides a touchstone for the student and the teacher.

Summary

In the beginning of this chapter, a traditional model of curriculum development was examined. Several weaknesses were readily apparent. The model was described as unrealistic in terms of what could be accomplished in educational practice. It failed to assess both student and societal needs. Objectives developed under this model were vague and often unrealistic.

An alternative model of curriculum development was suggested which would take into account the intellectual development of the child, the acts of learning, and the sequence of learning using spiral development. The teacher's role would be that of a manager of means of conveying knowledge, rather than *the* mediator and purveyor of knowledge.

The structure of the disciplines was then examined. Examples were provided to clarify the three components of structure—membership and organization, concepts, and syntax or methods.

Five sources of knowledge were discussed to call attention to the fact that there are ways of obtaining knowledge other than by the scientific method.

References

Benjamin, Harold Raymond Wayne. *The Saber Toothed Curriculum.* New York: McGraw-Hill Book Company, 1939.

Blommers, Paul, and Lindquist, E. F. *Elementary Statistical Methods in Psychology and Education.* Boston: Houghton Mifflin Company, 1960.

Bloom, Benjamin S., et al. *Taxonomy of Educational Objectives, The Classification of Educational Goals, Handbook I: Cognitive Domain.* New York: David McKay Company, Inc., 1956.

Bruner, Jerome S. *The Process of Education.* New York: Random House Inc., Vintage Book Edition, 1960.

Guilford, J. P. "Three Faces of Intellect." *The American Psychologist* 8 (August 1959): 469–79.

King, Arthur R., Jr. "Curriculum Projects: A Perspective." *Educational Leadership* 26 (February 1969): 493–99.

Schwab, Joseph J. "Structure of the Disciplines: Meanings and Significances." *The Structure of Knowledge and the Curriculum.* Edited by G. W. Ford and Lawrence Pugno, pp. 6–30. Chicago: Rand McNally and Company, 1964.

III

The Concepts and Methods of the Social Sciences

Chapter Outline

The Concepts and Methods of the Social Sciences

The purpose of this chapter is to make the structure of the various social sciences meaningful to you. It is organized to follow the major categories of the Structures of the Disciplines Model discussed in Chapter II. We shall analyze each discipline briefly and provide an example of a unit or lesson to illustrate how concepts could be developed. The discussion should help you see the relevance to the elementary school child of the various social science disciplines.

Objectives

After reading the descriptions of the social sciences and the sample units or lessons, the reader will be able to:

Identify (1.0) three to five concepts of each social science.

Describe (1.0) the methods of the various social sciences.

Identify (1.0) the subject matter of each social science.

Discussions of the membership, concepts, and methods presented have been taken from several attempts by various scholars of the particular social sciences. They have attempted to communicate the nature or structure of their sciences to professional educators. Such endeavors have been frustrating to the social scientists and educators alike since members of the same discipline have such different views of their field of knowledge.

The selection of concepts must be evaluated in terms of what is already known about descriptions of the social sciences by educators, and they tend to be invalid. This chapter is important because it allows you to look at a sampling of concepts and methods of the social sciences, briefly, and to see a few of these implemented in classroom instruction. The chapter is *not* intended to be a statement of what should be taught in the social studies. It is merely an attempt to illustrate what has been considered important by a number of social scientists and educators in the curriculum movement of the sixties and seventies. It also shows how innovative teachers have used these concepts and prepared lessons relevant to the lives of children.

Anthropology

Anthropology is the scientific study of man. It attempts to identify the commonalities existing among human beings, the differences which exist, the sources of these differences, and the depth of these differences among the various societies of man. (Kluckhohn, 13)

Methods.

The anthropologist uses both historical and statistical methods. Observing, recording, integrating, and interpretating data are the procedures used in describing primitive, and more recently, complex societies. The data he gathers are generally interpreted by using three major assumptions: all aspects of a problem affect each single element, all data must be seen in its relationship to known data in the same area of study, and both historical and statistical methods are useful in interpreting knowledge about people gathered from the biological, psychological, social, or cultural realms of man's existence.

Concepts.

Some of the important concepts of anthropology are that man must be looked upon as a *social animal* which is a *cultural* being. Man has basic *needs* in each of these capacities which must be met. These needs are satisfied within a *social structure.* This social structure has needs which must be fulfilled if the structure is to continue. Structures have patterned ways of meeting needs which are taught to individuals. These processes become *tradition.* All traditions leave some needs unfilled. Individuals and groups promote changes in tradition to allow better fulfillment of their needs. These *changes* take the form of *innovation* and *borrowing* from other *cultures.* The social structure is either *simplified* or *complicated* by these actions so that further innovation must be accomplished. If the innovation changes man's *behavior* to any great extent, it causes *evolution* in the culture and alters man either physically, socially, or culturally. (Senesh, 34)

A sample unit.

The following lesson was developed for intermediate grade children by a teacher in a small midwestern community. *Change, needs,* and *social structure* were the concepts selected. The methods or processes introduced were field study, recording, organizing, and interpreting. The behavioral objectives of the teacher were as follows:

After observation, the students will be able to discuss the needs encountered by early settlers in providing shelter.
After interpreting the data they gather, the students will be able to write a paragraph indicating the changes that occurred in man's social structure to allow him to meet his needs in a different way.

The data gathering provided was a field trip to an abandoned farm community which is now in a state park. Only a few buildings remain of what once was a small farm village. Several of these remaining buildings show evidence of different levels of civilization. The children were asked to try to find out as much as they could about the people who had lived in one of the dwellings. The following facts were among those recorded by the children.

> An old newspaper had been used to mend a crack in a wall. It was dated 1947.
>
> A mantle and fireplace were covered with boards and plaster. The wall had been papered. In the wall was a hole for a stove pipe.
>
> The dwelling had three separate foundations:
>
> > The outermost building had round nails.
> >
> > An inner building had rough milled lumber with beams made of native trees. The trees still had bark on them.
> >
> > Innermost structure had squared logs with marks of the instrument used to square the logs readily apparent. Nails used on the inner structure were rough and square-headed.
>
> A jug shaped, stone walled hole in the ground was just outside the rear door of the present structure. This was partially filled with tin cans and other refuse. The teacher was afraid to let anyone take things from the well.
>
> The children interpreted the data to mean the following:
>
> The home was occupied at least during the late 1940s. Possible occupancy in the fifties was likely.
>
> The means of central heating had changed from a wood burning fireplace to some other form.
>
> The family or families had grown either in terms of the number of members or in wealth.

The methods of building and obtaining building materials had changed over the years of occupancy.

The availability of sources of water had changed.

After considerable explanation, discussion, and debate, the written statements of the children revealed the following hypotheses:

1. Man had changed his way of obtaining building materials because his society had changed and had become more specialized.
2. Ways of travel had changed because man could buy some things that previously he had to make himself.
3. Man's need for shelter and his means of providing shelter had changed.

In order to check these generalizations, the children felt they needed the following additional information:

What were the dates of the first settlement?

How many families lived in the house?

What was the date of the last occupancy?

What were the occupations of the various dwellers?

Why didn't anyone live there anymore?

What were the changes in transportation and means of obtaining heat during the period of occupancy?

They identified the following sources of information which could be used to determine answers to these questions:

People who had lived in the area for many years.

Library books on travel and fuels.

County records of the area.

Written material from the local historical association.

County maps of the area.

The following means of evaluating the unit were used:

The teacher observed in several class discussions that the students could identify the needs encountered by early settlers in providing shelter.

The teacher collected and read the paragraphs written by the students on the change in man's social structure. These paragraphs indicated that man had changed his social structure through specialization. The specialization was facilitated by improved transportation.

Geography

Geography is concerned with describing how and why one part of the earth's surface differs from another. In order to depict and comprehend the earth's surface, we must understand the role played by nature, as well as the role played by man—the most differentiating factor of all.

Methods.

The geographer's methods are quite similar to those of other social scientists, in terms of historical and statistical methods. As with many other social scientists, the geographer is turning more toward statistical methods in recording, integrating, and interpreting data. One tool the geographer has developed is used by all of the social scientists. This is cartography, the making of maps, which allows the visual comparisons of regions and the establishment of areal associations. This method requires a few concepts useful in the classroom, such as *relative locations, longitude, latitude, scale, distance,* and *direction.* The need for comparison of actual *size* and distance has also produced a model of our world called the *globe,* as well as a number of *projections* which are attempts to replicate specific advantages of the globe by means of a flat map.

Concepts.

To facilitate his study, the geographer has developed or adapted a number of concepts which aid in the indentification of, or differentiation between, regions. The term *region* describes the commonality of one or more factors of places on the face of the earth, as well as the *distribution* of likenesses and differences. Such differences may be in terms of *climate, vegetation, land-use, soil type, topography, animal life,* or *culture.*

The interaction among phenomena in a region is described by geographers as *areal association.* The existence of steel mills in the Chicago area cannot be explained by the presence of water *transportation* alone, nor can it be explained by the location of one of the mineral *resources* adjacent to the area. The location of several resources must be considered along with the level of man's *technology*. In addition to these elements, both the *physical* and *biological* factors of man's habitat must be considered. Man has manipulated his environment to form this habitat, and it must be reappraised with every *change* in his attitudes, purposes, and advance in technical skills. (James, 59)

Earth and sun relationships provide another causal association that must be considered. *Seasons, climate,* and the distribution of phenomena around the earth are products of this relationship.

In recent years, geographers have become increasingly concerned with *population growth* and *population movement* or *mobility*. Interaction between the physical elements of *site* and *situation* must be considered in studying *urbanization* and its relationship to population movement. Major interest has been focused upon the functions of various population centers as *small towns, central cities, wholesale centers, regional centers, national hubs,* and the *megalopolis*. (Brock, 43–49, Getis, 105–106) Of continued interest is the *interdependence* of all men necessitated by the distribution of phenomena over the earth.

A sample unit.

The narration below is one teacher's attempt to prepare realistic materials in geography for young readers. He presented a story about a boy on a shopping trip with his mother. The teacher has integrated several previously mentioned important concepts: climate, soil type, land use, technology, areal association, transportation, and location. The processes used by his students were those of interpreting and inferring. To accomplish these purposes, the teacher prepared a set of guide questions for the children. The questions called for responses on three levels: (1) identifying facts stated explicitly in the text, (2) synthesizing related facts, and (3) making inferences beyond the facts given. The expectations set by the teacher were dependent upon his assessment of the child's ability to function at each of the three levels.

The story was as follows:

> "Mark! Let's go."
>
> Mark dropped his bike. He ran to the family car. Eagerly he climbed into the front seat with his mother. This was the weekly trip to the shopping center. Mark's family lived in a suburb of Chicago.
>
> His mother shopped the same way each week. She began in the bread section. She finished in the produce section. This is where the fruits and vegetables were displayed. The boy who worked in the produce section helped mother weigh and bag the fruit. Today, Mark noticed a box of peaches on a cart. The boy was stacking

the peaches on a counter. The wooden peach box had a label on it. The label read St. Joseph, Michigan.

"Mother, why do those peaches come from Michigan?" Mark asked.

"What?" his mother responded in surprise.

"Why do those peaches come from Michigan?" Mark asked again. He thought to himself, "Why don't mothers ever listen?"

"Oh! Don't be silly. That's where they're grown," his mother replied.

That is where the peaches Mark saw were grown. But can you answer Mark's question? Why are Michigan peaches sold in Chicago, Illinois?

There are two reasons why Michigan peaches are sold in Chicago. First, people want peaches. Second, modern transportation and agriculture enable us to make the product available there.

Growth of cities. Around 1850 there were many jobs in cities. There were few people in the cities to fill these jobs. Workers found out that they could make more money in cities than on the farms. This brought many people into cities like Chicago.

During the horse and buggy days of our nation's past, cities were surrounded by small farms. The farmers brought fresh fruit and vegetables into the cities. As the cities grew, the small farms were sold. Houses were built where the farms had been. More people lived in cities and needed fresh fruits and vegetables. Since the farms that remained near the cities could not raise all of the fresh fruits and vegetables that were needed, cities had to depend upon farms that were located farther away for produce.

Improved transportation. Man has been able to improve transportation. Super highways and railroads have been built. Large refrigerated trucks or trains are now able to transport over long distances products that spoil easily. These products are carried from farms to large refrigerated storage houses. The storehouses are located near cities like Chicago. From the storage houses, the produce is shipped to stores. There it can be placed on cooled counters. People like Mark's mother can buy the fresh fruits and vegetables.

Specialization of regions. These improvements have also enabled regions of our country to specialize. If a region is to specialize, it must have three factors:

First, there must be a demand for a product the region can produce. People must want the product that grows best in that region.

Second, the region must have some natural advantage. That advantage must enable the region to produce a product better than other regions.

Third, people living in the region must use the natural advantage.

To answer Mark's question, let's see why the St. Joseph, Michigan region has been able to specialize in the production of peaches.

Demand for the product. The first advantage St. Joseph has is its location. It is near at least two major metropolitan areas, Chicago and Detroit. Peaches can be shipped by truck or train to these cities. The peaches will not spoil before they can be used by the consumer. The demand is present near the location of the product.

Natural advantages. Besides its location, Michigan has three other natural advantages. First, peaches need water and a well-drained soil in which to grow. Peach trees must have a good supply of water. However, water cannot remain standing around the roots of the trees without damaging them. Sandy soils hold just enough water. The Western portion of Michigan has sandy soil.

Also orchards grow best on gently sloping hills. Western Michigan has these, too.

Climate is a third natural advantage. This natural advantage is due to Lake Michigan. The winter temperature of the East side of Lake Michigan is ten degrees higher than the West side. This protects the peach trees from very cold winters and sudden drops in temperature in the spring and fall.

Sudden temperature changes are common in the upper Midwest. These temperature changes hurt orchards. In the spring and fall of the year, the lake prevents the trees from being warmed or cooled too quickly.

These are the natural advantages of the St. Joseph region—location, climate, and soil. Western Michigan is situated by a large lake; it is near markets, and it has a sandy soil on gentle slopes.

Combining the demand and advantages. Western Michigan is limited in the types of crops it can raise best. Farmers found that orchards did well. They knew peaches could be sold in Chicago and Detroit. So, they began raising peaches.

Nearby universities helped farmers produce better crops. Michigan farmers began using information sent out from these universities. They began to take better care of their trees and remove dead limbs. They removed some of the young green fruit. This made their trees produce larger fruit.

The farmers and the universities began developing better trees. The farmers started using chemical fertilizers to make their trees grow better. The trees were sprayed by machines to kill insects and control diseases.

The Michigan fruit producers saw the demand for fresh fruit. They thought they had the resources needed to produce peaches. The farmers combined the natural advantages with new methods and machines to produce better peaches.

The Michigan peaches Mark found in Chicago were there because people in the city needed fruit. The people in Chicago could not grow their own fruit. The improvement in transportation and farm production helped the city. Chicagoans could get their fruit quickly from farmers in Michigan.

The above, then, is the story which the teacher presented to the children. Based upon the reading of this story, the behavioral objectives for this lesson were as follows:

> The students will indicate comprehension of the written material by answering the guide questions (listed below) at levels appropriate to their ability.

Guide Questions

(1) 1. Why are Michigan peaches sold in Chicago?

(2) 2. Why did workers move to the cities?

(1) 3. What happened to farms as the cities grew?

(1) 4. What types of transportation are available for shipping produce?

(2) 5. In the past, why did fruits and vegetables have to come from nearby areas?

(1) 6. What are the three factors that help a region to specialize?

(2) 7. What are the natural advantages Michigan has for raising peaches?

(3) 8. What is the importance of universities to farmers?

(3) 9. What would limit the raising of certain crops in Western Michigan?

(3) 10. How might improved growing techniques help people like Mark's mother?

(3) 11. If peaches became an unpopular food in Chicago, how might this affect the farmers of Western Michigan?

> The students will be able to summarize in writing the reasons for Western Michigan's specialization in the growing of peaches.
>
> The students will be able to generalize in a class discussion that all regions of our country have natural advantages.

This fifth grade class had been studying the North Central United States in their outdated social studies textbooks. A comment was made about the number of products that were raised in this area. The children seemed amazed at the variety of agricultural commodities and the differences among products of the various regions surrounding Chicago. The teacher capitalized upon this interest.

Since the instructor was not able to find prepared materials to teach the concepts he had selected, he wrote his own. The children were given time to read the narration and answer the study questions. The answers to their questions were later discussed by the class. When the teacher felt that the children were ready, he asked them to prepare a summary on the agricultural specialization of Western Michigan. To capsulate the study, a discussion was planned to guide the children toward a generalization about regional specialization.

The outcomes were evaluated as follows:

1. The teacher collected and examined the answers to the guide questions.
2. The teacher collected and read the written reports on specialization in Western Michigan.
3. The teacher observed the class discussion to determine if the children arrived at a similar generalization to the one he had intended.

Economics

Economics is the study of certain human activities: producing, saving, spending, paying taxes, for the purposes of satisfying their individual wants for food, shelter, and conveniences, as well as their collective wants for such things as protection, education, hospitals, and highways. It includes the study of various ways that people organize in order to satisfy these wants and needs. (Lovenstein, 9–22)

Methods.

Unlike the anthropologist, the field investigations of the economist are apt to be conducted among the advanced societies. His tools are likely to be the computer, charts of trends, or volumes of statistical data, since statistical analysis has become the most popular method of his research. Historical analysis seems to have taken the back seat, except in the study of past events. There are three steps in explaining an economic event. One must identify the event, look for the causes, and explore the possible implications. (Robinson, 45) One of the important methods of the economist is model building. This process is an attempt to construct an economic system through assumptions and conclusions. Given a situation, the economist reasons that if factors A, B, and C are working, D will be the result. Since factors A, B, and C of an economy can effect result D differently, alternative models must be built at the same time. For example, since our economic system follows a free economy model, we would assume that an increase in price would decrease the amount of goods purchased. This is not always the case. The factor of advertising must also be considered in an alternative model. An end of economics is to provide data and principles for making decisions in conducting public policy and predicting the outcome of such policy.

Concepts.

One of the major concerns of economists is the way natural and human *resources* are used to satisfy *wants* and *needs.* These resources are the components or elements from which goods and services are obtained. *Natural resources* include the land, sea, and air from which we extract lumber, minerals, foodstuffs, and energy, while human resources, *labor,* are used to produce products. It takes *capital,* tools, equipment, and machines or the money to buy them plus *management,* an individual or group of individuals who assume risks in the *production* of *goods* and *services.*

As *consumers* we want or need food, clothing, and shelter and a host of conveniences and luxuries; these are called *consumer goods.* Also, because of our *specialization,* we want to buy labor to provide *services.* We obtain these goods and services in the *market place* in exchange for *money* used to facilitate trade.

As producers, we want tools, machines, and factories so that we may supply items for the market place. Through this production, we can provide the consumer goods or services to persons who *demand* them. In turn, we are able to satisfy more of our personal wants and needs.

Scarcity occurs because our resources are not sufficient to satisfy all of our wants and needs, forcing us to make economic choices. What goods and services should be produced? What resources should be used to produce them? Who will produce the goods and services? How will the goods and services be distributed? These decisions are made in different ways by the several *economic systems.*

Society must make its resources stretch as far as possible to get the most output for the least resources. One method of increasing efficiency is through *specialization.* There are several forms of specialization: *geographical,* based on exploration and transportation; *occupational,* based on expanding knowledge and education; *technological,* based on invention and innovation. (Senesh, 25) Another method is through the effective use of *capital.* A third method of increasing efficiency, the goal of specializa-

Second graders discover that toasted jelly sandwiches can be produced more efficiently using the assembly line.

tion, is through *scale* or size. Larger enterprises can take greater advantage of specialization because they can command more capital and can promote research in the use of resources, labor, capital, and management. One of the problems of scale is that of *monopoly*. When industry can corner the market, it often loses the desire to be efficient.

The problem of monopoly is not the only issue faced by an economic system and its people. There is the desire for economic *growth* which allows a better standard of living. However, growth creates possible instability and the desire for *stability*. People also fear the several other hazards of economic change, so they desire some economic *security*. All the people of a society want the profits of the nation's production to be divided fairly and want their children to receive an equal opportunity to share in the products of the future. So, *economic justice* is important. Both producers and consumers desire *economic freedom* to dispose of their *income* as they see fit. All of these interests and demands on the economic system are mediated through *public policy*. This public policy is determined by the *government* which *controls* the economic system. (Senesh, 25)

A sample unit.

A third grade teacher in the Far Western United States was introducing a unit on money as a medium of exchange. The concepts she was developing were *barter, trade, surplus,* and *money*. The behavioral objectives the teacher used were as follows:

> After reading the story, "The Beginning of Trade," the students in a class discussion will be able to suggest reasons for bartering.
> After discussing the story and playing the Trading Game, the students will be able to identify the advantages of money.

The teacher prepared overhead transparencies of the story. Her purpose in presenting this story was to lay the foundation for an understanding of the origin and advantage of trade. Because of the range of reading ability, she selected this method of presentation to gain wide participation from the group. The story that she and the children read follows:

> *The Beginning of Trade*
>
> The earliest traders may have started business in villages where there were markets. It might have happened some thousands of years ago in this way:
>
> Den and his wife sat in the doorway of their hut in the village, watching the market day crowds. The market day was over. People were leaving so they could get home before dark.
>
> "Look at that herdsman," he pointed to a man who was walking up and down. The herdsman was speaking first to one farmer and then to another. The herdsman was offering three sheepskins to the farmers. Every farmer shook his head, "No."
>
> "He must have come in late," said Den's wife. "See, he wants grain for his skins. It's too bad the farmers have traded all their grain or gone home."
>
> "Has old Mel gone home?" asked Den. "He wanted skins and didn't get any."
>
> "Yes, he went home," said Den's wife. "But he'll be back again next market day. He'll try once more to get the skins he wants."
>
> Just then the man from the hills passed the hut. He looked over at Den and his wife and held up his sheepskins.

"Three skins, three fine sheepskins for two measures of grain," he called.

Den shook his head and the man went on.

"Old Mel would give a measure of grain for one skin," said Den. "That would be three measures of grain for three skins."

"We have two measures of grain in the house," said Den's wife. "Let's trade for the skins."

"Why should we trade?" asked Den. "We do not need three sheepskins. Besides we are going to need the grain."

"But if we give two measures of grain to the herdsman, we will have three skins," said Den's wife. "Next market day we will see old Mel and trade him the three skins for grain. He will give us three measures of grain."

"Well, but—" began Den.

"Don't you see? cried his wife. "We will have our two measures back and an extra one as well. Old Mel will give us a measure of grain for each skin. We will have one measure of grain more than we have now. Call the herder!"

Den called after the stranger. They bargained together. The trade was made. But Den was not sure his wife was right. He had to wait until the next market day. Sure enough, he traded the skins to Old Mel for three measures of grain.

After discussing the story the teacher told the children they were going to play a game. She proceeded as follows:

1. Taking 12X18 sheets of construction paper, she cut out a "skin" for each child in one-third of the class and gave these children the following rule: Skins cannot be cut; this ruins their value.

2. Taking other 12X18 sheets of construction paper, she made cutouts to represent bags of grain. She presented these to another third of the class and gave the children these rules: Bags of grain can only be cut into quarters, and quarters of grain cannot be resold without the consumer (the person who plans to use it) being present.

3. Taking more 12X18 sheets of paper, she cut them into the shapes of fish and distributed them to the remaining one third of the class. She gave these children this rule: Fish cannot be divided by fisherman except in the presence of both consumers.

4. She posted this chart before the bartering began:

Beginning Value Chart

1 fish	=	¼ skin
1 fish	=	½ grain
1 grain	=	2 fish
1 grain	=	½ skin
1 skin	=	4 fish
1 skin	=	2 grain

5. Then she issued the following statement: These values can vary with bartering, and price must be agreed upon in the bargain.

After the children had played this game with the rules for several minutes, they found that it was nearly impossible to trade in the bartering system. "If we could use money," the children agreed, "it would be a lot easier for us to trade!"

At this point the teacher helped the children cut out coins from construction paper to represent quarters, half-dollars, and dollars. They agreed on the following value chart:

Exchange Chart

1 fish	=	.50
1 grain	=	$1.00
1 skin	=	$2.00

The children found that trading with money was much easier.

In her evaluation, the teacher observed the class discussion in which the children concluded that bartering was developed because people wanted things they could not raise, hunt, or make themselves. The teacher found that at the conclusion of the game the children easily generalized that the use of money as a medium of exchange facilitated trade.

Political Science

Political science is concerned with understanding how authoritative decisions are made and executed in a society. (Easton, 138) The four basic concerns of this social science are the descriptions of legal governments; the descriptions of what governments should do and how they should do it; the establishment of a means of developing a science that describes governments and their function; and the description of a means of obtaining social action. (Driscoll, 117)

Methods.

Although the historical method is still recognized in political science for the affirming of concepts and forms of analysis, the statistical approach has become the more popular method. In fact, the two basic requirements of the political scientist's research are a specific hypothesis, and rigorous ordering of evidence to substantiate or reject the hypothesis. (Dahl, 130)

Concepts.

Some important concepts of political science include the existence of *institutions* in society—political, economic, social, religious, and educational. *Wants* which cannot be channeled through the other institutions of society are channeled through the *political institution.* Such wants are the result of *external* or *internal pressures* from interactions among men. As wants enter the political institution, they become *demands.*

These demands are screened by *formal* or *informal* organizations. The formal organizations are associations, agencies, or groups which have established means of accomplishing specific tasks. Both within and without these formal organizations are informal means of obtaining wants. Pressure groups, friendships, and status systems allow certain wants to be communicated to the formal political system. Some of these demands vanish; others become *issues* which are debated in the *political community,* a group which operates as a unit to solve political problems. These issues are shaped and reshaped by solicitations from various *interest groups,* and actions by authorities translate resulting demands into final *decisions.* These decisions create both positive and negative support toward a *regime,* a specific form of government which has a definite set of *values* and *goals,* and toward the *authorities* which hold political power within the governmental structure.

Actions on wants generate new wants that must again be channeled through the political institution. Continued *support* for the regime, the political system, and the authorities in power is facilitated by influences from the other institutions of the society through a process of *politicalization.* (Senesh, 28–30)

A sample unit.

In studying the concepts of *wants, issues, support,* and *politicalization* of a totalitarian government, a sixth grade teacher developed a brief unit to capitalize upon the motivation of students before a recent election. The teacher's objectives were as follows:

After having listened to the story, *Animal Farm* (Orwell), the students will be able to identify examples of wants, issues, support, and politicalization.

The students will contrast the means the U.S. government has of dealing with or developing wants, support, and politicalization with that of *Animal Farm.*

After reading the book to the class, the teacher guided the children in identifying and listing the facts as shown below.

Animalism	*Wants*
Major's dream	Better lives
Seven commandments	Retirement
Training of young dogs	Windmill
Training of sheep	House

Support	*Issues*
Squealer's speeches	Windmill
Sheep	Retirement
Force by dogs	Lives of pigs
Snowball common enemy	Boxer's "forced" retirement
	Man
	Snowball
	Killing of animals

After this discussion, the teacher aided the children in developing meaning for the term "politicalization" by discussing the reasons why we believe as we do about our government. This term was substituted for "animalism".

Then, the teacher aided the children in organizing their data on a chart to help them in comparing the totalitarian form of government with our democratic form. A sample chart is given below.

Animal Farm		**U.S. Government**
	Politicalization	
Singing of —"Beasts of England" Slogans: —Four legs good, two legs bad		Singing of —patriotic songs Slogans: —Land of opportunity —Home of the brave and the free —One man, one vote
	Wants	
Retirement Individual rights Better lives Working together		Shorter work week The good life Peace Jobs Equality Individual rights

Support

Squealers' speeches	Speeches
Forced support changed the rules	Support from special people
Snowball bad	Russians

Likenesses

Both teach love of the place where they live in the same way.

The wants of the people of the United States are quite similar to those of *Animal Farm.*

Both use speeches to gain support.

Differences

The pigs changed the wants to fit their own wants.

Our country does not use force to gain support.

Pigs changed the rules to fit their wants.

The animals became worse off as time passed, even though they worked harder.

Generalization

Under totalitarian governments, people actually do not get what they want. The leaders go toward their own goals and force the people to support them.

Evaluation

The teacher evaluated this unit through observation of the class discussion. By asking questions, she determined that the children were able to suggest examples of wants, issues, support, and politicalization. Through careful guidance the children were able to make the comparison between the two forms of government.

Sociology

Sociology is the social science that focuses its interests upon the social processes resulting from the interactions and associations of men under various situations and conditions. The sociologist attempts to answer such questions as: "What are people doing with each other here? What are their relationships to each other? How are these relationships organized in institutions? What are the collective ideas that move men and institutions?" (Berger, 163)

Methods.

Although statistical methods are used to a great extent by sociologists in the accomplishment of surveys, interviews, and observations; the social scientist still makes extensive use of the historical method in making comparisons between groups, case studies, and life histories of individuals. The sociologist performs experimental studies in laboratories, too. But like the anthropologist, most of his work must be accomplished in the observational setting.

Concepts.

In the study of interactions and associations of men, it is important to understand that all individuals belong to *groups.* These groups assign *roles* to their *members* which are expressed in terms of *role expectations.* Groups have sets of *rules* and *values* which the individual learns through some process of *socialization.* Groups enforce rules and values through *sanctions* and *rewards.* All individuals belong to several groups: *primary,* a group like the family, and *secondary,* as association memberships and the like. Since there are several groups and roles within society, individuals must learn to deal with *role conflicts* which often occur.

The term *society,* frequently very confusing to the layman, is comprised of any group which carries on some process of *communication* in their *interaction.* This interaction has some effect upon the *attitudes* of the individual. Groups of societies make up a *culture,* as long as the members of the societies have *shared meanings* and values toward certain objects and other people. (Rose, 43–58)

A sample lesson.

An interesting observational activity for children learning to work in a group situation can be used to illustrate the concepts of role, member, group, and rules. The lesson focuses the attention of the children upon group problem-solving. This will aid them in developing rules for their own behavior for working in groups. The objectives of the activity are the following:

> After observing the nuclear groups at work, the students will be able to identify and describe orally the roles (leader, member, recorder) needed in group problem-solving.
>
> Through class discussion, the students will develop and record a list of rules which will allow them to participate in group problem-solving successfully.

A continuing behavioral objective is that by using the rules as a criterion, the students will be able to evaluate and improve the effectiveness of their group work.

> The teacher forms what is called a nuclear group, three to five children who appear to have the ability to cooperate among themselves. This nuclear group is then presented a simple problem like planning a bulletin board. The other children observe and determine what behaviors help the group to work togethev. They furnish answers to such questions as: What did the group leader do which helped the group? What did the members do that helped the group? What behaviors hindered the group?
>
> After a few minutes of discussing and listing items the children suggest, the teacher moves to aid them in developing a set of general rules to guide the class' group work. The results of such discussion may appear as shown below.
>
> All members should listen to the speaker.
>
> All members should do their jobs.
>
> All members need to have a chance to speak.
>
> All members should contribute to the group progress report.
>
> The group leader can help the group by preventing some members from talking too much.

To evaluate, the teacher will observe the children's discussion to determine whether they identify the roles: leader, member, and recorder, and the tasks of each. He will check the list of rules they have recorded. Periodically, the class will return to the initial set of rules to assess the items as well as their own progress in group problem-solving. The teacher will observe the growth of the class in this area.

Psychology

Psychology is the social science which attempts to predict man's behavior by studying the causes of such behavior. Among the several variables it uses in its research are man's biological nature, the effect of interaction with his physical environment, and the effects of interaction in the social environment.

Methods.

The psychologist, like other social scientists, must use historical as well as statistical methods in his research, but statistical methods dominate this specialized field. Observation, experimentation, and surveys using sophisticated methods of quantification are often used in his theory building. Using man's similarity to lower animals, the psychologist conducts much research with animal subjects. He then makes inferences about human behavior. When possible, laboratory research is also accomplished with human subjects to verify these inferences.

Concepts.

Behavior is one of the fundamental concepts of the psychologist. Both the *biological* and *environmental* factors must be considered in the study of man and his society. This society has a great influence upon man. Through a process of *socialization*, a form of *learning*, the individual gains his *perception* of the world. The *language* of society is an important element of this perception as it controls the way the individual views phenomena, develops *meanings*, and *communicates* with other men.

Motivation is developed through a system of *positive* and *negative rewards*. Although behavior is seen as the result of several motives, it is believed that it must be viewed in its social context. People differ in their *ability* to perform certain tasks as a result of *inherited traits* and *environmental differences*. These differences in *achievements* cause both *conflict* and *frustration* in attempts to gain *acceptance* and *self-fulfillment*. We learn certain *coping behaviors* which reduce our tensions and allow us to function in our society. Failure in the ability to *adapt* emotionally causes *behavior disorders* which may not allow the individual to function in the various *roles* in his society.

Some knowledge of *groups* and the roles individuals play in groups has been gained to explain man's social behavior. This aids us in explaining the ways individuals create *values*, *attitudes*, and *beliefs*. Certain groups, called *reference groups*, influence our lives more than others.

A sample lesson.

The following lesson was developed by an intermediate teacher for a unit in social studies which focused upon the concepts of behavior, perception, and groups. This lesson was one of several which placed the children in conflict situations. They were asked to solve the problem by role-playing how they felt the individual should behave. Discussions were developed after each role-playing situation which asked these kinds of questions: Why do you think the character behaved in this way? Are there alternative ways this problem could be solved?

The behavioral objectives of this lesson were—

> the student will be able to state the way he feels the character perceived the situation before he behaved as he did.

the student will be able to identify the role the group played in influencing the behavior of the individual.

the class will be able to identify alternative ways of solving the problem faced by the character in the story.

The incident the teacher used was as follows:

This fall had been an exceptionally hard one for Ray. Nothing seemed to go right. Two new boys had moved into the neighborhood. He always seemed to be the one-too-many-boy when it came time to play football with the neighbors. Today was no exception.

"You can't play!"

"Why?"

" 'Cause you can't."

"Go home, Ray."

The tousle headed boy dejectedly turned from the group and shuffled painfully over to his bike. "I don't see why I can't play!" he shouted back to his antagonists. Pulling his battered bike from the walk, he stood straddling what he suddenly saw as a weapon. He stood on the pedals, pushed, and hurled the two wheeled missile into the tangled group of football players. All of the players fell safely away except friendly, little Mike, who stood in disbelief; and then suddenly, terror. The blood poured from his mangled forehead.

Fear gripped Ray. He turned. . . .

One child role-played the incident indicating that Ray started to run home. Suddenly, he began to think of little Mike. He turned toward the nearest house, rang the doorbell and told the neighbor about Mike.

The class was quick to point out that this solution would be the best, but many thought that Ray would be more concerned about himself than about little Mike. "After all, he had pulled a pretty stupid stunt," they decided.

The group pointed out that the neighborhood boys had excluded Ray. He would have been hurt, but his behavior was extreme, almost criminal. The discussion brought out live examples of similar "stupid stunts." Since many children had faced the problem of being excluded from groups, they indicated some alternatives:

Play outside of the neighborhood for a while.

Invite single members of the group over to play when the group was not playing together.

Invite friends from school and don't play with the neighborhood children.

The teacher evaluated the activity by observing the children's discussion. She found less participation than she had planned. She voiced some concern that the story, though realistic, was not as effective as she had wished. The group's response to role-playing in this situation seemed stilted.

History

History is the study of the past actions of human beings. It permits man to know himself through the study of what man has done and thus what man is. Although historians are hard pressed to identify the concepts of history, this area of knowledge has three advantages which make it an important subject for social studies classrooms. First, history is the only social science without stated boundaries, therefore, it cuts across all of the social science disciplines. Second, history is the only social science that uses chronology to any great extent. By chronology we do not mean dates, but rather the sequence of events. Third, much of the content of this subject is near at hand and can be illustrated by incidents in the child's community and state.

The author's perspective makes history the core around which concepts of other social sciences can be illustrated and developed.

Methods.

We see history as a social science that uses diaries, letters, secondary accounts, realia, and documents as its tools of inquiry. (Beard) Its methods are those of organizing material into some meaningful interpretation that is controlled, to a degree, by the background, experiences, and biases of the writer, as well as the discovered or "cultural truths" preserved over time. With such prepossessions the historian fabricates generalizations which he uses to write history. The result is not history as "actuality," but simply "written" history (Beard, 5), representing one man's interpretation of history, controlled to some extent by the society and the time in which he lives. Here we have the reason why history has such a great significance in the school curriculum—history, like men, is biased in its views. Even the most carefully controlled research in all the social sciences contains cultural and methodological biases.

Concepts.

Usually concepts have not been identified in the structure of history. The reasoning is that an historian forms concepts and generalizations about materials he gathers. Many of the concepts he uses are borrowed from the other disciplines. Some of the concepts once employed by historians have been formalized and claimed by other disciplines.

We would like to suggest two schemes for teaching concepts borrowed from the other disciplines. The first employs local history to illustrate the relevance of identified concepts to the local community. It utilizes a guided learning approach and presents concrete examples pertinent to the child's community. This approach begins with defined and explained abstract concepts and develops examples of such concepts for children; it utilizes the deductive method of teaching. The second scheme uses concrete examples and asks children to create their own concepts and generalizations. The resulting generalizations are verified with findings in textbooks or other sources. This is an inductive method.

Let's return now to the deductive approach which begins with selected concepts and generalizations. The example we have chosen employs concepts drawn from anthropology and economics. From anthropology, it uses the concept of change. From economics, it uses concepts about specialization, transportation, and communication. The unit might begin with the question: Can we find examples that show the effects that specialization, transportation, and communication have had on our community from 1855 to the present?

What materials are available to classroom teachers that could be used in this type of unit? We would utilize newspaper accounts that present materials of a historical nature. We would use aerial maps showing an area as it is today, as well as reproductions of earlier aerial photographs of the location. County maps of the past and present would also be useful. Often photographs from private collections are available. Interviews with people who have lived in the community for a number of years have value. Some large communities have written histories that can be borrowed from the public library or from the local historical society. Modern methods of reproduction make old, valuable records much more available than they have been in the past. We tend to forget these local sources of materials.

Another teacher created a study similar to the one we discussed under anthropology involving the use of pictures showing the remains of an abandoned farm, now part of a national forest. In a history project, the teacher used a nearby deserted community which once served as the market place for many farms of the area. The marginal farms, abandoned because of low productivity, now serve as recreational areas for metropolitan centers. In the past, the rural area had mines which were abandoned because production costs had risen. At one time, surrounding towns, rural trade centers, were serviced by railroads, but now, they depend on highway and air transportation. New industries are coming to these communities to use available labor supply, and they are willing to pay relatively high costs to transport goods and resources from other areas. By structuring the investigation around questions developed from the study, the teacher was able to identify concepts and to control the direction of the inquiry.

The second example uses the inductive approach. To illustrate this approach, we will use the concepts about change, specialization, transportation, and communication employed earlier in the deductive approach. The example is taken from a larger community that lost a major industry in the early 1950s because of changes in the local and national economy. The industry decided it could no longer afford to operate its factory in that community. After the factory closed, many workers were unemployed for an extended period. Other industries in the community had few openings for these workers.

What teaching materials are available for developing concepts? The local newspaper is a valuable source. Pictures, letters, and diaries which give family accounts of the turmoil caused by forced retraining or job changes supply a wealth of information. Again, interviews with persons who can give both sides of the factory closing issue would offer children interesting value choices. Merchants who were forced out of business or into other businesses provide additional examples of the problems of change. Children could explore the remains of the abandoned factory. A new shopping center that has experienced cycles of boom and bust and back again presents to children interesting possibilities for study.

In presenting these examples we have glossed over the ingredients which need underlining the most. The missing elements are purposes. What are the aims of presenting such units to children in the elementary school? Are we attempting to teach *the method* of the historian or any other social scientist? The answer is a qualified, no. We are interested in teaching children the way some trained scientists organize their data and make interpretations. But as teachers and social studies curriculum developers, we are more interested in teaching children a process by which they can organize data, draw meaningful conclusions, and make decisions from that data.

A Process Model

The method portion of a discipline's structure is the way a social scientist organizes and interprets his data. We are proposing to teach a general process, a way of organizing data generally.

Indeed, we must use the guidance of social scientists to determine the most efficient means of organizing and interpreting data. Many of these methods, such as objective, systematic observation; charting; experimenting; interviewing; measuring; comparing; recording; manipulating;

and classifying are appropriate for use in the elementary classroom. In order to facilitate planning in elementary social studies, the authors propose the following model.

Objectives

After reading the description of the Process Model, the reader will be able to:

Explain (2.0) the steps in the instructional plan.

Suggest (5.0) ways in which process skills might be used to teach concept from one of the social sciences.

The Process Model shown in Figure 3–1 provides a design for instructional planning. Actually, this plan presupposes an examination of the needs of the child and of present society, as well as an understanding of the structure of knowledge. In practice, however, the teacher begins with the selection of a task to be completed by the students. This task becomes the general purpose of the immediate instructional sequence, which may result in one or a series of lesson plans. Local curriculum guides, state courses of study, and teachers' guides for textbooks are generally the sources from which teachers select these tasks.

Once the task has been identified, the teacher surveys the process skills that will be needed to complete the particular task. Having accomplished this, he is ready to diagnose the status of his group with relation to the cognitive and affective areas involved. Based on this information, the teacher selects appropriate teaching strategies, ways of obtaining stated objectives.

One point of clarification is needed. Before appropriate learning experiences can be prescribed, or at least during this process, the teacher must specify the observable changes in student behavior he hopes to achieve during the course of the lessons or unit.

In the prescription of learning experiences, the teacher chooses the materials that will be needed. Multimedia means that the teacher has a variety of ways to convey knowledge to the student. As illustrated earlier in Figure 2–3, the teacher may act as one of the mediating devices, as well as manager of all of them. The result is a plan for instruction.

Returning to the process skills themselves, we would like to emphasize that these skills must be taught directly. Children do not have them when they come to school. Each skill must be developed from less complex skills.

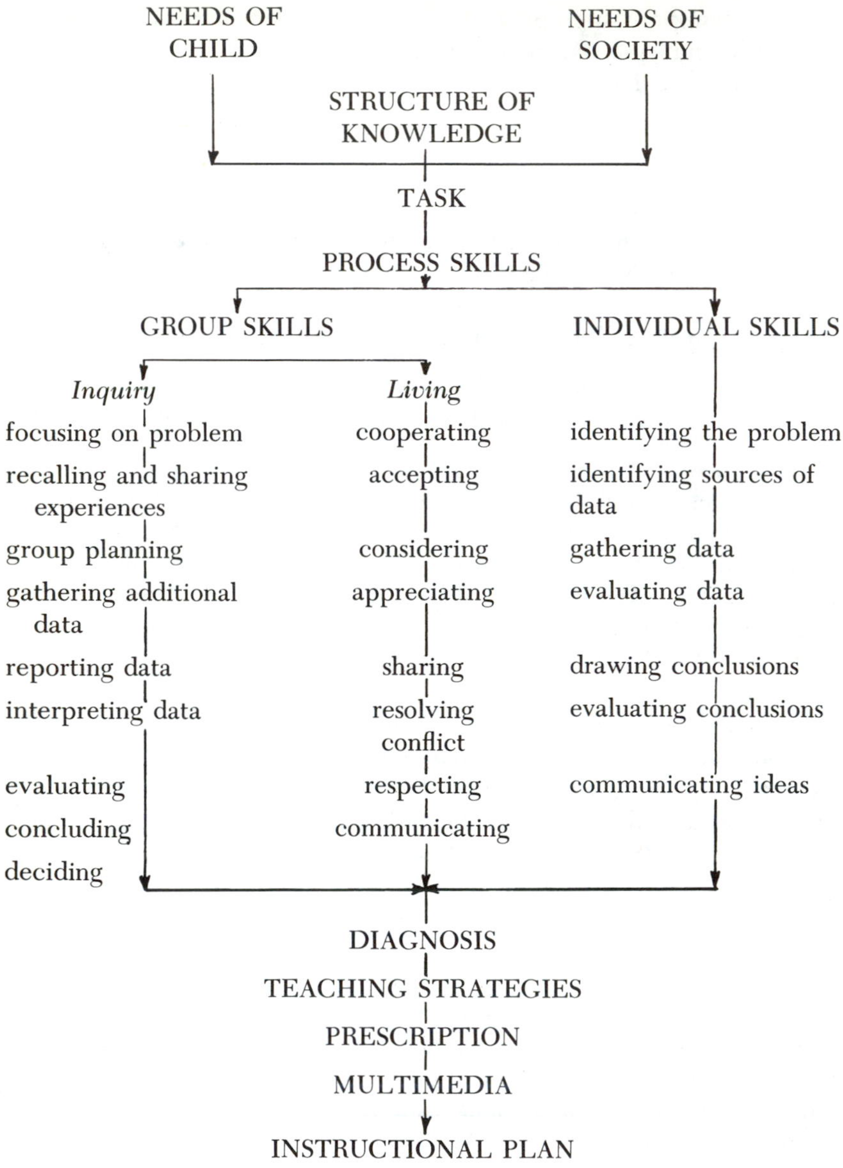

Figure 3–1. *A Process Model*

Summary

In this chapter we have seen examples of concepts taught in *anthropology*, *geography*, *economics*, *political science*, *sociology*, *psychology*, and *history*.

Sample units and lessons showing the development of these concepts by classroom teachers were presented. These were not intended as exemplary samples, but they merely serve as illustrations of the ways some teachers have developed concepts.

Methods were also discussed in the individual descriptions of the social sciences, but the authors feel that some methods of these disciplines are not practicably useful in the classroom. General methods of organizing and interpreting data must be taught to young students.

The authors proposed a process model whereby the teacher can develop a complete instructional plan. This plan begins with the identification of the educational task (purpose) and outlines the process skills which elementary students use in problem-solving. Having assessed the needs and interests of students, the teacher selects teaching strategies and prescribes learning experiences based upon a multimedia approach to accomplish stated objectives.

References

Beard, Charles A. "Grounds for a Reconsideration of Historiography." *Theory and Practice in Historical Study.* A Report to the Committee on Historiography. Bulletin 54. Social Science Research Council, 1946.

Berger, Peter L. "Invitation to Sociology." *The Social Studies: Structure, Models, and Strategies.* Edited by Martin Feldman and Eli Seifman. Englewood Cliffs, New Jersey: Prentice-Hall, Inc., 1969

Brock, Jan O. M. *Geography: Its Scope and Spirit.* Social Science Seminar Series. Edited by Raymond H. Muessig and Vincent R. Rogers. Columbus, Ohio: Charles E. Merrill Books, Inc., 1965.

Dahl, Robert A. "The behavioral Approach in Political Science: Epitaph for a Monument to a Successful Protest." *The Social Studies: Structure, Models, and Strategies.* Edited by Martin Feldman and Eli Seifman. Englewood Cliffs, New Jersey: Prentice-Hall, Inc., 1969

Driscoll, Jean M. "The Nature of Political Science." *The Social Studies: Structure, Models, and Strategies.* Edited by Martin Feldman and Eli Seifman. Englewood Cliffs, New Jersey: Prentice-Hall, Inc., 1969.

Easton, David. "An Approach to the Analysis of Political Systems." *The Social Studies: Structure, Models, and Strategies.* Edited by Martin

Feldman and Eli Seifman. Englewood Cliffs, New Jersey: Prentice-Hall, Inc., 1969.

Getis, Arthur. "Changing Urban Spatial Patterns." *Focus on Geography: Key Concepts and Teaching Strategies.* Fortieth Yearbook of the National Council for the Social Studies. Washington, D.C.: The National Council for the Social Studies, NEA, 1970.

James, Preston E. "A Conceptual Structure for Geography." *The Social Studies: Structure, Models, and Strategies.* Edited by Martin Feldman and Eli Seifman. Englewood Cliffs, New Jersey: Prentice-Hall, Inc., 1969.

Kluckhohn, Clyde. "Queer Customs, Potsherds and Skulls." *The Social Studies: Structure, Models, and Strategies.* Edited by Martin Feldman and Eli Seifman. Englewood Cliffs, New Jersey: Prentice-Hall, Inc., 1969.

Lovenstein, Meno. *Studies in Economic Issues.* Minneapolis, Minnesota: Curriculum Resources, Inc., 1962.

Orwell, George. *Animal Farm.* New York: The New American Library, Inc., A Signet Classic, 1954.

Robinson, Marshall A., Morton, Herbert C., and Calderwood, James D. "Problems and Goals." *The Social Studies: Structure, Models, and Strategies.* Edited by Martin Feldman and Eli Seifman. Englewood Cliffs, New Jersey: Prentice-Hall, Inc., 1969.

Rose, Caroline B. *Sociology: The Study of Man in Society.* Social Science Seminar Series. Edited by Raymond H. Muessig and Vincent R. Rogers. Columbus, Ohio: Charles E. Merrill Books, Inc., 1965.

Senesh, Lawrence. "Organizing a Curriculum around Social Science Concepts." *Concepts and Structure in the New Social Science Curricula.* Edited by Irving Morrissett. West Lafayette, Indiana: Social Science Education Consortium, Inc., 1966.

IV

Building Concepts, Generalizations, and Constructs

Chapter Outline

Building Concepts, Generalizations, and Constructs

Communication is possible to the extent that two fields of experience overlap. As teachers, we assume children have the same fields of experience, the same depth and breadth of a concept and have organized their experiences in the same way as adults. In our haste, we often fail to test this seemingly harmless assumption. We would like to share with you one of our experiences to show what can happen when we fail to assess the experiences of children.

One day, while working with a first grade reading lesson, one of the authors was confronted with the phrase "at the foot of the hill," which played an important role in the plot. The children's oral reading seemed to indicate satisfactory comprehension.

At the close of the group reading session, I sent the children back to their desks with this assignment: draw a picture of your favorite part of the story.

Checking Mike's drawing, I observed a large hump with a protruding, human-like foot. "Mike," I inquired, "why did you put a giant in your picture? There was no giant in this story."

Mike blithely replied, "Teacher, that's a hill and that's the foot!"

It is very obvious that there was a communication barrier in this case. The fields of experience of the teacher and child did not overlap!

Objectives

The reader will be able to:

Define (1.0) the term "concept" and list (1.0) the three components of a concept.

Give an example (2.0) of a concept and delimit (4.0) attributes, distinguish (4.0) classes and suggest (2.0) symbols.

Concepts

"Concepts are abstractions which refer to a class or group of objects, all of which have characteristics in common." (Fancett, 6) The incident above arises because the individual perceives his world as he has experienced it. The concepts he develops, the meanings he places upon his world, are woven into his existing cognitive structure—the way he has organized his experiences. Although some meanings are universal within a culture, others are not. They can be highly personal and dependent upon the individual's cognitive framework. Consider, for example, the concept of *bullfight.* To one person it may call to mind gore, dirt, horror, revulsion, and baseness, yet to another, it might connote bravado, courage, triumph, and pageantry.

There are some learned commonalities, or universalities within concepts, however, that make them useful in communication. Let us try an experiment with you. Quickly write the names of all the natural resources that come to your mind. Take about a minute. Now let's take a look at some of the examples other students have given.

water	silver	iron ore
timber	gold	uranium
copper	fish	plants
sulfur	gas (natural)	birds
air	furs	tin
soil	game	vegetation
limestone	animals	nickel

Well, how did you do? Chances are that you listed several of the items given above. This is to be expected. Somewhere in your formal or informal education you have acquired a means for identifying natural resources. What caused you to identify the items you recorded? What do these items have in common? Think a minute.

Attributes.

When the students who contributed to the list above were asked the same question, they responded as follows:

> I listed these because they are made in the earth and are there for man to take out and use for his benefit. They are not man made; they come from nature.
>
> They are raw materials that man can use to make his life easier. He takes the raw materials and converts them to another form for his use.
>
> These items are not man made; they are here naturally. They are used by man productively.

What these contributors and you have done is to identify the characteristics of natural resources. These characteristics can be called attributes of the concept, natural resources. Attributes are really nothing more than distinctive characteristics of things, events, or ideas.

What are the attributes of this concept? First, they are things provided by nature, but there are other attributes. These resources must be useable by man; otherwise, they are not resources. The early American Indian did not use uranium. He did not have the technical knowledge required to utilize this mineral; so it was not a resource to him. Many years ago the iron ore limonite was not employed by our industries because we had neither the need for it nor the knowledge that would allow us to use this relatively low grade iron ore. During that time it was not a resource. Since our technology has changed and our needs for iron have increased, limonite has become an important resource.

All concepts have attributes which make them useful to us, but knowledge of these attributes varies among people because of the breadth of their experiences. A geologist, because of his background and experience, would insist that we record the three types of iron ore, magnetite, hematite, and limonite, instead of the more general term "iron ore" in our list of natural resources. Iron ore has many attributes for the geologist. The term is not specific enough for his purposes. Since most of us have more limited experiences in this area, it seems adequate for us.

Concrete experiences provide common meanings for concepts. Because they can be experienced through our senses, rain and snow are concrete concepts; they are common to most environments. Abstract concepts, on the other hand, can not be experienced directly through our senses. The more abstract the concepts are, the more diverse the meanings become. For example, the concept "beauty" varies widely among individuals and cultures: Beauty is in the eye of the beholder. Examples of this difference are obvious when we compare women's fashions over a fifty year period.

Classes.

The second component of a concept is the category or class in which we group things, events, or ideas having the same or similar attributes. There are several classes that could be included under natural resources, such as *animal, plant,* or *mineral* resources. Returning to our earlier listing, now we can classify our natural resources as shown below.

Concept:	Natural Resources		
Classes:	*animal resources*	*plant resources*	*mineral resources*
Items:	furs	vegetation	water
	game	plants	copper
	birds	timber	sulfur
	fish		

animal resources	*plant resources*	*mineral resources*
		air
		soil
		limestone
		gold
		iron ore
		uranium
		tin
		nickle
		gas

Categories are important because they permit us to communicate by referring to large classes of things without enumerating every item.

A concept is dependent upon the context in which it is used. Although animal resources are one of the classes under natural resources, in another context, it might be used as a concept as shown below.

Concept: Animal Resources

Classes:

Furs	Game	Birds	Fish
mink	deer	duck	sardine
beaver	bear	geese	salmon
marten	moose	wild turkey	tuna
ermine	duck	bobwhite	white fish
rabbit	geese		halibut
	rabbit		

Each of the items in the above listing may, in certain contexts, be used as concepts. If birds were the concept under consideration, the concept label for the classes might include listings by types of beaks, feet, wings, or natural habitat. It would seem that this branching could go to infinity, but actually, it stops at the experiential limit of the individual. When an item cannot be further divided into classes, it remains an item for that individual.

Concepts are important because they allow us to communicate a large amount of information efficiently. They help us capsulize and categorize meanings. Meanings are recalled by the labels given these individual categories or classes. Such labels, we will refer to as symbols.

Symbols.

Symbols are another component of concepts. They give us the ability to communicate concepts readily to others. Some symbols are verbal labels, words, or numerals which stand for words. Some are pictorial, such as the heart, symbol for love. There are nonverbal visual concepts, such as the shoulder shrug, while a nonverbal auditory one would be the scream which communicates fright or emotion. Most of the symbols we deal with in social studies are verbal, but the symbol alone is not the concept. It is an agreed upon way of referring to the concept. The meaning it recalls depends on both the real and vicarious experiences of the receiver. Real experiences are those in which we have direct involvement, such as a field trip to the airport. Vicarious experiences are secondary experiences, such as reading a book or seeing a film about an airport.

Objective

The reader will be able to:

Distinguish (2.0) between concepts and facts.

Facts

Facts are related to concepts because they are the information or bits of data upon which the concept was developed initially and subsequently verified.

Facts, according to Fancett (5), are items of information and data which can be checked for accuracy and which are generally accepted to be true. Facts are basic to the development of concepts. In order to clarify the relationship between facts and concepts, let us summarize what we have discussed to this point. First, we have said that concepts are used to organize and communicate our experiences. Concepts are delimited by attributes. These limits or parameters vary according to our experiences. Concepts are recalled through verbal, nonverbal, pictorial, or auditory symbols which allow us to retrieve meanings.

Concepts, attributes, classes, facts, and symbols have a close affiliation. Perhaps an example showing their association will help. The concept of intelligence, which we use in Figure 4–1, shows the various components we have discussed and illustrates the relationship of facts as well. "Intelligence" recalls the attributes of the ability to achieve, capacity to learn, ability to profit from experience, and learning rate. The symbols that produce these meanings are the pictorial symbol of a mortar board, the nonverbal symbol of pointing to one's head and closing the right eye, and the verbal symbols of "intelligence" or "IQ." The several classifications under this concept are verbal, nonverbal, high intelligence, average intelligence, and low intelligence. You will recall that we also make groupings

Concepts	Attributes	Symbols	Classes	Facts
Intelligence	Ability to achieve in school	IQ	Verbal	Standardized scores
	Capacity to learn	Intelligence	Nonverbal	Quotient of mental age over chronological age
	Learning rate	"smarts"	High intelligence	
	Ability to profit from experience		Average intelligence	Results of tests
			Low intelligence	Responses to questions Responses to problems

Figure 4–1. *Components of the Concept and Relationship to Facts*

under these areas. The facts we accept in the verification of the concept of intelligence are sets of standardized scores, an individual's quotient of mental age over his chronological age, and the results of several tests of intelligence which reflect his responses to certain questions and problems.

Objectives

The reader will be able to:

Apply (3.0) the steps in developing concepts in a role playing situation with a group of his peers.

Assisting Children in Concept Formation

The writings of Snygg (87) indicate that if we are to assist children in the formation of concepts, we must formulate experiences which lead them to reexamine their present knowledge. We must cause them to be dissatisfied with their present cognitive structure.

Perhaps the most carefully researched method for allowing children to reexamine their knowledge is that devised by the late Hilda Taba, a recognized theorist and researcher in the area of school curriculum. Professor Taba also conducted one of the Project Social Studies programs in the 1960s which focused upon teacher behavior in the development of concepts. Her research indicated that teacher behavior determined the level of thinking in the classroom. As a result of this research, her staff developed procedures which facilitate concept development. The following material has been adapted from her findings. Figure 4–2 is a simplification of the steps which she identified in the cognitive task of concept formation. (Taba, 92)

The advantages of guiding children's thinking in this way are that (1) it gives the teacher some insight into the conceptions of the children; (2) the child is encouraged to examine his own thinking, and (3) he is taught a process of manipulating information. The teacher begins by focusing attention of the children upon a problem or situation and lists items contributed by the children in the class. Children are encouraged to participate since there are no incorrect responses. As indicated in the illustration below, the pupils are actually differentiating various items of information because of teacher questions, such as what did you see on our visit to the abandoned community?

Teacher's Question	Child's Mental Operation	Observable Activity
What do you see, hear, or think?	Differentiating items	Listing
What things seem to belong together? Why do you place them together?	Identifying common properties	Grouping items
What can you call these groups?	Determining and justifying labels	Labeling

Taba, *Teachers' Handbook for Elementary Social Studies*, Introductory Edition, 1967, Addison-Wesley, Reading, Mass.

Figure 4–2. *Developing Concepts*

Returning to Chapter III, you will recall that a group of intermediate grade children had visited such a community in their study of the concepts *change*, *needs*, and *social structure*, taken from the discipline of anthropology. A listing of items might be developed as indicated below.

fireplace	stove pipe	native floor beams
shaped logs	plastered walls	new well
square nails	papered walls	
stone well	larger houses	
newspaper	round nails	

There is a natural advantage to such a listing. It has the built-in motivational device of being the product of the children themselves. They don't need "a new word" list. As each word is recorded, the child who is contributing the word explains what it means to him. Yes, there are mistakes at times among the children, but each can be corrected in an accepting way by the group, not the teacher. After the listing and explanation has taken place, the teacher asks, "Do *you* see some items that seem to go together?"

Let us illustrate this process by allowing you to respond as the student. Return to the listing above and attempt to make some groupings. We will continue with the conversation of the hypothetical class. This will give you some idea of the way a teacher might accomplish the task.

"Yes, Allan?"

"I'd like to put fireplace, stone well, newspaper, and new well together."

"That's good, Allan," the teacher encourages. "Would you tell us why you placed those things together?"

"Well, they seem to show us some of the needs that the people had. The fireplace was for warmth and cooking, the newspaper was so they knew what was happening. . . ."

After several such lists have been made, the teacher asks the children to perform the next step—supplying labels for the lists of items. Allan might suggest *needs* as the label for his list. This could be challenged by the group, "Aren't all of these needs?"

"Do you have a different label?" the teacher might ask. (You see there are several possible ways the listing can be grouped.) The teacher listens as the children supply the labels. The result is active learning in which the communication gap between teacher and pupils is narrowed.

Objective

The reader will be able to:

List (1.0) the steps to plan for expanding children's conceptions.

Expanding Children's Conceptions

Determining the conceptions of children is only one step in concept formation. In working with children's concepts through listing, grouping, and labeling of events, ideas, and facts, we confront children with conceptualizations which they have not previously considered. This confrontation can be used to expand the child's conceptual field. In such situations, teachers find opportunities to clarify misconceptions or to introduce new word labels. The task from the teacher's point of view is to begin at the child's present conceptual level and attempt to expand the number of attributes or possibly delineate them more precisely, as our geologist friend would have us do in the case of iron ore. As our teacher, he could accomplish this through giving us experiences with the color, hardness, magnetic qualities, or color streaks that hunks of the mineral produce on a porcelain plate. Possibly, the importance of each mineral in the production of iron could be illustrated by films showing the processing of these iron-bearing minerals. Field trips might also be useful. A study of the geographic distribution of the various ores could prove helpful.

Basically, the procedure the teacher uses has three steps. First, discover the student's level of conceptualization; second, determine what the children need to know about this concept. A more useful label, more distinct attributes, more relevant facts, or broader classes of things, events, or ideas may help them to understand the concept. Third, identify experiences which will allow the students opportunity to gain additional insights.

The procedure we have outlined, adapted from Taba, helps the teacher discover and use the conceptual framework of the child. Often neglected, although implied in this strategy, is the embellishment of the concept that exists in the child's conceptual field. When we involve children in listing, grouping, and labeling, there will be a great amount of embellishment. The teacher must see the other dimension that of broadening present conceptions and correcting misconceptions. A word of caution. Teachers must refrain from correcting conceptions during the listing, labeling, and grouping activities. If the children do not correct the error, make a note of it and continue gathering their responses. Nothing destroys the participation of children more than the domination of the teacher. The assumption is that the teacher can maintain a helping atmosphere among members of the group so that they can feel free enough to make mistakes and receive assistance from their peers.

Objectives

The reader will be able to:

Define (1.0) the term "generalization."

Give an example (2.0) of a generalization, and identify (1.0) the concepts contained in the generalization.

Demonstrate (3.0) the use of the developing and testing of generalizations procedures in a role playing situation with his peers when given a teaching topic.

Developing Generalizations

Generalizations are statements of relationships among concepts which have predictive validity in time and space. Generalizations are important to us because they afford a means of transferring past experience, either real or vicarious, to new experiences. In order to generalize, we must have sufficient meaning built around the concepts used in the generalization. The generalization that man uses the resources of the place where he lives is meaningful to the extent that the cognitive structure of the individual contains the concepts: man, uses, resources, place, and lives.

In this instance, the word "man" must recall the abstraction of all humans, past, present, and future. Similarly, "use" must bring to mind that man changes natural resources to meet his needs. The child must remember what resources are. The geographical meaning collected around the term "habitat," discussed in Chapter III, must be substituted for "place".

To aid the child in developing generalizations, we must insure that he has formed the concepts upon which the generalization is based. In other words, he must have identified the attributes, classified items according to certain attributes, and developed or accepted a symbol that recalls specific meanings from his past experiences. We inventory the child's experiences to develop the generalization. (Taba, 101) Again, we will use an adaptation of Taba's work to accomplish this task. The steps in the process are listed in Figure 4–3.

Teacher's Question	Child's Mental Operation	Observable Activity
What did you read, hear, or see?	Differentiating facts	Identifying facts
Why did ______ happen? What similarities (differences) did you see? (Durkin and Hardy),	Relating facts in terms of cause and effect, similarities and differences	Explaining facts
What does ______ mean?	Going beyond what is given and finding implications	Making inferences
What can we conclude generally?	Finding relations of facts and attempting to predict	Making generalizations

Taba, *Teachers' Handbook for Elementary Social Studies*, Introductory Edition, 1967, Addison-Wesley, Reading, Mass.

Figure 4–3. *Developing Generalizations*

In order to illustrate the use of this process, let's pretend that we have made a careful study of Brazil and have listed the following facts:

Many resources in Brazil are developed.

Mineral resources are difficult to extract.

There are shortages of coal and petroleum.

Ownership of land is in the hands of the wealthy.

Although there is a great deal of land, only two percent is used in food production.

Only one-half of its food is produced in the country.

Ninety per cent of Brazil's exports are agricultural. One crop, coffee, is the most important.

Most labor is concentrated in the cities.

Many people are unemployed.

Over fifty per cent of the population is illiterate.

Inflation absorbs the savings of people.

Importation is greater than exportation.

Investments are primarily in real estate.

Heavy investment is in coffee.

Transportation is poorly developed in areas where resources are located.

There is a small middle class, and a large lower class.

The government is relatively unstable.

The government has seized property of foreign investors.

Many people in the country invest their money in other nations.

Now let us look at some of these facts in order to reach conclusions about Brazil's economy. What is the effect of the situation found in Brazil in which only a relatively small amount of land is used for food production?

"This is obvious," you might respond. "There would be little food available in the country."

"Why do you think that?" we might ask.

You could reply, "That's what we found. We've listed the fact that the country imports a great amount of food. We know that cities need food and can't produce their own."

Since we seem to be going a bit astray, let us refocus the discussion and ask, "What is the result of the country's use of so little land in its own food production?"

"The effect is that they have to buy their food from other countries," you might answer.

"What does this cause?" is the next query.

"This forces the country to spend its money for food, rather than for other things like roads, factories, and schools."

"What is the effect of that?"

"The country can't develop its own industry to use some of its resources."

At this point we could ask you to make a conclusion.

You might reply, "Brazil can not become a developed nation until she can control her own food supply."

We would continue our data gathering and organizing by relating the following facts:

> There is little savings in the country because of inflation, poor education, investment in foreign countries, and investment in one crop which competes with several other countries. These things prevent Brazil from becoming wealthy.
>
> Transportation is poorly developed; there is a lack of money to develop transportation because of the lack of savings. Without the money to develop transportation, little can be done to develop resources.
>
> Government instability, confiscation of foreign owned industry, long terms of inflation, lack of education, concentration of wealth among a few, and high unemployment are all things that cause people to distrust their government.

All of these facts must be explained as they are related. It does little good for us to talk about inflation if no one really understands how this affects savings of people. Stability might mean very little to a group of fifth grade children. These are concepts, uncovered in our data, that must be clarified. The communication gap must be closed among the children, as well as between the teacher and the children.

From these inferences, we could draw the conclusions: (1) Brazil must develop a more stable government which can capture the confidence of her people. (2) Brazil must increase her savings and invest them in the development of transportation, which will allow her to use her resources and develop industry within the nation. These conclusions are elicited by such questions as: What can we say generally? Does this data give you some idea about ________ that we might test? Can anyone give us an idea that explains all these inferences?

The process we have discussed asks children what information they have discovered about ________. Then, the teacher lists the ideas as the children relate the individual pieces of data. He asks the children to explain relationships they see. The teacher encourages, probes for meaning, gathers additional ideas, encourages the discussion of relationships. He guides learning and facilitates thinking. During the discussion he encourages cause and effect thinking or probes for likenesses and differences which we will discuss later.

After such a probing discussion, the teacher asks the children to generalize. Notice that no generalizations were provided at the beginning of our example above. These were arrived at through the discussion. One point that must be clarified is the relationship of assumptions to inferences. As teachers, we neglect to ask of ourselves or our students what the assumptions are. Let us illustrate what we mean.

Suppose we were discussing the plight of Appalachian Whites who moved from the hills of Eastern Kentucky to the teeming metropolis of Chicago. One student infers that the family would have to get more education in order to find a job. "What are the assumptions you are making?" asks the astute teacher.

"What do you mean?" is the usual reply.

"Well, what do you think the family's occupation is?"

"They are probably miners, or they have had no jobs at all. They might also be farmers," the harrassed student continues.

"That's what I mean by assumptions," the teacher explains. "They might also be mountain folk artists. Such persons might fit very well into the metropolitan culture."

Examining assumptions is an important part of this strategy. After making several inferences, some of the children should be ready to suggest a generalization that could be tested for instance, about developing nations.

To insure that the children could generalize about developing nations, we might use another means of deriving generalization, such as the comparison of likenesses and differences. Our stated purpose in this activity is to allow the children to generalize about the factors nations must have to develop economically. After the study of Brazil, the teacher might turn to the growth of our own country. A list of similar to that completed on Brazil might look like the one below.

Resources are available because of development of transportation.

Land ownership is in the hands of people who use it.

Technology is developed to make use of resources.

Products are manufactured from several resources.

There is an adequate supply of skilled labor.

Attitudes of the work force are similar to those of management.

Education supplies new sources of labor.

Some inflation exists from time to time causing decreases in savings.

The government attempts to control the amount of inflation.

The balance between exports and imports is decreasing; the government periodically inserts control to restore some balance.

Investments are made at home and in some foreign markets.

The government is relatively stable.

Sources of capital for transportation, hospitals, communication, and public services are available.

People and groups of people in the country are willing to risk their savings in enterprises.

Government attitude encourages business.

After the listing has been accomplished, we would ask the children to find likenesses and differences between a developed nation such as the United States and a developing nation like Brazil. The children might list the following likenesses:

There is some inflation in both countries.

Both have resources.

There is money in both countries.

Labor is mostly in the large cities.

Inflation absorbs savings in both countries.

Each country has some import problems.

As these likenesses were listed, the teacher would ask the children to explain and clarify their listing. In a similar manner she would continue by asking for differences.

Investments are made by United States citizens in their country and in foreign markets.

Brazil does not use much of her savings at home.

Transportation is more highly developed in the United States, and she can get to her resources.

Coal and petroleum are available in the United States for manufacturing. We can also use electricity, but the Brazilians have not developed theirs.

Public education is readily available in the United States but not in Brazil.

More people have jobs in the United States.

The United States produces more than one product; Brazil depends mainly upon one.

> Inflation is less severe in the United States, and it lasts for shorter periods.
> Government action in the United States encourages industry. Actions of the Brazilian government have discouraged industry.
>
> The United States is able to feed her people from her own production. Brazil can not.

After we had checked the assumptions implied by these listings, we would be ready to accomplish our stated task of allowing the children to generalize about the factors needed for economic development. Below are some statements which might result.

> Developing nations must have savings which they can use to tap their resources.
>
> Developing nations must have some people or organization of people who are willing to take risks and invest in the country's future.
>
> Developing nations must use their own resources to increase savings. People are resources which need to be taught new skills.
>
> Developing nations must have stable governments which encourage people to invest in the country and make use of the resources for the good of the country.

Again let us state that we are attempting to allow children to generalize from their own experiences. It is true that we must provide some of the experiences for them, but in providing these experiences, we must use the conceptions they have or the ones they develop during classroom activities.

Arriving at the generalization is not enough. Often, as educators, we stop at this point. Although the generalization has been made by the child, it is not a useable generalization for him. It is, in reality, in the child's cognitive field merely a testable hypothesis. The task facing the teacher who attempts to aid the child in generalizing is to present him with situations which allow the testing of the generalization. In order to accomplish this task, we will use a method based on the work of Taba (109). This strategy allows children to apply their generalizations in a new context. This was accomplished by one teacher through the use of the following teacher prepared article which places the child in a problem-solving situation intended to test the following generalizations:

> Developing nations must use their own resources to increase savings. People are resources which need to be taught new skills.

Developing nations must have stable governments which encourage people to invest in the country and make use of the resources for the good of the country.

The teacher asked the children to determine whether the generalizations they had made applied to Japan, which has recently become a developed nation.

THE FARMER—MODERN JAPAN

Japan has a limited amount of farm land. Therefore, she has had to develop methods of increasing her food supply. Rice was once grown in Japan in the same way it is grown in the rest of Asia today. In the following article, you will see the importance of rice. You will be told how it is grown in Asia. Then you will be able to see how Japan has increased production. You will try to answer this question: How did Japan increase the production of rice?

Rice: The Food of Asia. Most of Asia has a very large population. It also has very little farm land. This is one reason rice is raised. The rice plant produces a great deal of grain. No other grain produces as much food per plant.

Rice is easy to store, too. It has a tight jacket on the kernel. Moisture and insects that would destroy the grain cannot get into the kernel. Rice can be stored in sacks on the ground. Most grains would spoil very quickly if they were stored this way.

There are thousands of varieties of rice. It has been grown in Asia for many centuries. Rice can be classified in two ways: lowland rice and highland rice.

Lowland rice requires a lot of water. It is best because it produces the most grain. Highland rice is better where irrigation is difficult.

The lowland rice needs the delta or river valley soils. These soils hold water. Here water is easy to get. The river valleys and deltas are flat. Water can be moved easily on flat land by the use of irrigation canals. Rice needs a lot of water. It must be raised in water. The river valleys are also fertile.

Much of Southern Asia has a warm humid climate. There is a large amount of rainfall. No other crop will produce as much food under these conditions.

Old Methods of Production. Rice is planted in Asia today in the same way it was centuries ago. It is planted in seed beds for about two months. Here it is allowed to sprout. This permits wheat or vegetables to be raised on the land where rice will be planted. Rice could be planted directly in the fields. This, however, would not allow enough time for a second crop to ripen. Since land is scarce, second crops are needed for food too.

This method of planting takes a great deal of labor. The transplanting must be done by hand. Labor is cheap in Asia. There has always been a large number of people. They are used in the fields.

The rice is transplanted when the seedlings are about two months old. Rice must be planted in fields that have about four inches of water in them. This means that the fields must be surrounded by levies. They are plowed by hand with a hoe or with a crude plow pulled by an ox or buffalo.

The plants are replanted in groups of two to five plants and placed in rows about eighteen inches apart. Fertilizers, human, animal, and plant, are placed on the plants. Often the use of these fertilizers causes diseases. Thousands of Asians have died from the use of human fertilizers which have not been treated to kill dangerous germs.

The fields must remain flooded during the growing season. A field of about two and one-half acres requires 10,000 tons of water. This water must be pumped or scooped by hand. A primitive water wheel is still used in Asia for pumping water.

During the growing season, the plants must be cultivated and protected. Insects and birds cause a great amount of damage to rice crops. Little flags are often tied on lines which run across the fields. Often these little flags have writing on them to frighten away evil spirits. The fields are drained before the harvest. This allows the fields to dry. It helps ripen the grain.

Rice is harvested by hand. A knife or sickle is used to cut the grain. The plants are left in the fields to dry. Sometimes they are hung from poles. After a few days the dried plants are spread on a hard surface. The grain is either trampled out by cattle or pounded out by the use of the flail. The flail is a hinged stick. It is nearly as old as the sickle.

When the rice is knocked from the stem, pieces of stem and the chaff are removed by winnowing. This means that the grain is tossed in the air. The wind separates the lighter stems and chaff from the heavier grain.

Rice Farming in Japan. Japan is a mountainous country with little farmland. River valleys make up about half of the useable farmland in Japan. Only 15 per cent of the land can be farmed. This makes farmland very valuable. Nearly half of Japan's population lives on these farms too.

Japan has been able to increase production a great deal. Actually, she produces more grain per plant than any other country.

Rice is planted in Japan in the same way it is in the rest of Asia. It is planted in seed beds until the plants are about two months old. These seeds have been carefully selected.

This selection is made in each district where rice is raised. A government agent aids the farmer in selecting the best seed for his soil.

Most of Japan's rice is raised in the lowland areas. Here the fertile river valleys make irrigation possible. Levies are carefully maintained.

The government's development of electricity has brought electrical power to Japanese farmers. Water can be pumped into the fields with electric pumps. Many of these pumps are being used today. This brings water to the fields quickly and easily.

Japan has never been able to use much animal power for plowing. The animals are very costly to feed. Pasture land has always been hard to find around farming areas. Every available field must be used for food. Hoes were once used to plow most fields.

Today plowing is done by the use of two-wheeled tractors. These tractors are used for both plowing and cultivating. Weeds are a constant threat to rice.

Transplanting is done by hand. Japan still has a great number of people living on the farms. They commute, by public buses, to cities to work in the factories. Women do much of the work in transplanting.

Fertilizers are applied by hand. Both animal and plant refuse is used. These fertilizers are carefully treated to prevent diseases. Chemical fertilizers are becoming popular in Japan. This is possible because Japan has developed a large chemical industry. These chemical industries are able to produce fertilizers cheaply.

Insecticides are also produced by the chemical industries. These are used by the farmers. Bug catchers, run by electrical current, are also used to protect rice plants from insects.

The fields are drained before harvest. This allows the fields to dry. The plants also ripen more quickly. The grain is cut by hand sickles. It is dried in the sun after it is cut. The grain is then threshed by a portable, motor-driven thresher. The grain is usually sacked in the field.

New Trade and Agricultural Products. Japan's agriculture still cannot supply all the food her people need. Before World War II, Taiwan and Korea supplied much of Japan's rice imports. Today Japan can receive rice from Europe and the United States. She trades silk, electronic equipment, cameras, textiles, and some manufactured clothing.

Wheat was once Japan's most important second crop. Today, vegetables are becoming important. The improvement in transportation has allowed cities to get fresh vegetables. Many farmers are now turning to the production of vegetables.

Dairy farming and cattle raising have also developed since World War II. Many acres of land that were once unused can be utilized for pastures. The products can be shipped to the growing urban areas using improved methods of transportation.

Let us examine the article using the strategy of testing generalizations. The first question we must pose according to Figure 4–4 is, What has happened here?

Obviously, Japan has been able to increase the amount of rice she could produce through the use of modern machinery and methods. You will recall that our task was to test the hypothesis which had been developed in the previous task, the hypothesis stating that a nation must develop her resources including people.

"What data do we have to show that this has happened?" we might ask.

"The government has agricultural agents who advise the farmers on the types of grain to use. Also, someone has taught the farmers to use tractors, chemical fertilizers, and threshing machines."

"Yes, this is possible. What conditions would have to exist for this to be true?" the wise teacher might ask.

"Well, we can assume that someone taught the people how to use machines in place of the methods formerly used. We might guess that it was the government or other farmers."

"Since this article indicates that the government aids in the selection of seeds, this could be assumed."

Someone might also state, "The government has developed electricity, at least the people in the country have; this would help us verify the fact that the country has made use of its resources."

"Yes, but they also buy their food from foreign nations," a participant counters. "We found that this decreased the wealth of Brazil."

"But Japan also uses other resources," you might reply.

"What other resources?" the teacher asks.

"She exports electronic equipment, cameras, and textiles. These are industries that require a great amount of technical skill. In order for one to have these skills, he must have been trained in some way. This proves that the country has developed her human resources. We can assume that other resources have been developed when we look at agriculture, electricity, and the chemical industry."

At this point the teacher might focus the conversation on the last step. "Let's examine our generalization. Do you think that it is a good one?"

"I think we have proved the last part; people are resources that need to be taught new skills," you wisely point out. "But we have not said much about the first part of it, that developing nations must use their own resources to increase savings."

It is necessary that we point out two things about the procedure outlined in Figure 4–4. First, the questions are given only as suggested phrasings. Second, the steps indicate somewhat artificial separations which teachers should understand as necessary procedural steps in aiding thinking. Many times, especially with more mature children, the thought process proceeds in this direction. In some situations, the teacher must refocus the attention of the group to the business at hand. This is actually the purpose of the steps and the questions.

Teacher's Question	Child's Mental Operation	Observable Activity
What has happened here?	Analyzes problem or situation	Makes predictions Hypothesizes
What data do you have that would indicate what happened?	Retrives relevant data Relates causal links	Explains relationships he sees
Under what conditions would that generally be true?	Identifies conditions	Supports Prediction
Does the data collected support the generalization?	Compares data, conditions, and causal links	Accepts, revises, or rejects generalization or hypothesis

Taba, *Teachers' Handbook for Elementary Social Studies*, Introductory Edition, 1967, Addison-Wesley, Reading, Mass.

Figure 4–4. *Testing of Generalizations*

Objective

The reader will be able to:

Apply (3.0) the concept development, developing generalizations, and testing generalizations procedures to the teaching of a social studies topic in the early grades.

Strategies for Early Grades

The methods we have illustrated in this chapter are applicable to any grade level. The example given earlier applied to grades three or above; we would like to provide an example showing the use of the same strategies with younger children. There will be certain modifications because these children are not as mature intellectually, physically, and emotionally.

In the early primary grades, pictures can be used as the children may not have acquired skill in reading. Rather than grouping the verbal symbols, words, the children will group and label pictures. Since the children's attention span is much shorter, the teacher will design instruction for shorter periods.

One first grade class was studying animals. The teacher had a picture collection of several animals which she placed along the chalk tray. The purpose of this lesson was to introduce the children to categorization. The dialogue ran as follows:

"What do you see, boys and girls?" the teacher asked.

The children named lion, cow, bird (parakeet) elephant, tiger, duck, horse, dog, chicken, turtle, and cat.

"Do you see some animals that you think go together?"

Here are some of the responses the children gave.

"The lion and tiger go together," Billy said.

"Why did you put those animals together, Billy?" the teacher asked.

"I've seen them at the zoo," Billy explained.

"The elephant too," Marsha chimed. "I saw one at the zoo once."

"I've got a dog and a cat at home," added Jerry.

"Why would you put the dog and cat together, Jerry?"

"Because I play with them."

The discussion continued resulting in the grouping of animal pictures as follows:

lion	cow	dog
tiger	duck	cat
elephant	horse	bird
	chicken	turtle

The children, after discussing the reasons why they grouped as they did, decided upon the following labels:

zoo animals	farm animals	pets

At this point, the teacher stopped the discussion and left the pictures grouped and labeled as the children indicated.

The next day, the teacher encouraged the children to reconsider their groupings.

Joe, noting that the horse was grouped with farm animals protested, "My uncle has a horse for a pet. He keeps it in his back yard. Horses are pets, too."

Then Marsha volunteered, "My big sister got a baby chicken for Easter last year. It was a pet."

"I've seen horses, chickens, ducks, and cows at the zoo, too," Phillip insisted. "Why aren't they zoo animals, too?"

The discussion ensued, and the children concluded that the animals could be put together and labeled in different ways. This example gives you an idea of how the concept development strategy can be utilized in the primary grades. Now let us look at developing generalizations.

The teacher's purpose in this lesson was to encourage the children to generalize that man uses animals in many ways. Referring to data the children had gathered from the two previous lessons, the teacher asked, "What have we done here?"

Juan replied, "We put the pictures together."

"Well, why did we put the dog, cat, and bird together, Juan?"

"Because we play with them."

"What did we call this group of animals?"

"Pets."

"What makes an animal a pet, boys and girls?" the teacher asked.

"We play with them," several children answered.

"Don't we play with some animals on the farm? You can play with the animals in the Petting Zoo."

"But that's not the same, teacher," Phillip protested.

"Why not?" the teacher probed.

"Well . . . those animals don't live with us."

"Why do pets live with us? What do we get from pets?"

The discussion continued. The children concluded that people have fun with pets. They love us, and keep us company. In similar discussions, the children examined the function of the other groups of animals to man. They concluded that zoo animals allow us to see and learn about animals most people would not have available. They concluded that "Farm animals were kept by the farmer because he made money from them." They generalized that "People use animals for many things."

Objectives

The reader will be able to:

Identify (1.0) the three steps in the development of a construct with children.

Work with a group of his peers to organize (3.0) a teaching sequence from a social science construct.

Constructs

At the apex of the process of thinking is the development of constructs. "A construct is an organization of interrelated generalizations and concepts." (Tanck, 109) It represents a complex organization of ideas placed together because of their usefulness in explaining specific phenomena. It is a model, which allows us to relate both concepts and generalizations in a meaningful unit. A construct is shown below which illustrates the knowledge developed in this chapter. The phenomenon it attempts to explain is children's thinking. We have discussed three basic elements, concepts, generalizations, and constructs, which organize thinking. These elements function within what we call a "cognitive structure."

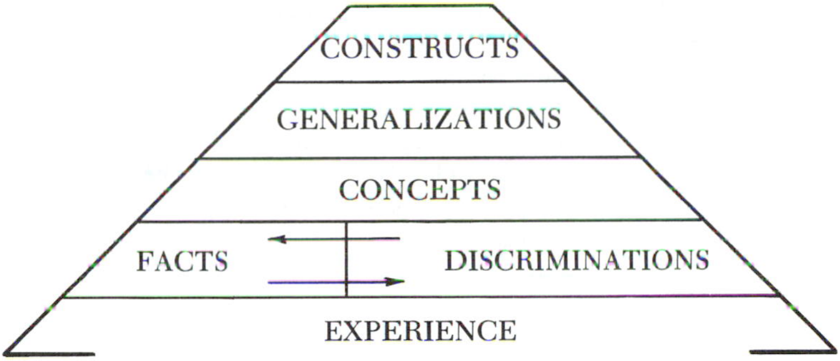

Figure 4–5.

The elements are hierarchically arranged because each higher element is based on the learnings attained at the lower levels. Unless a child has used or been presented facts which allow him to make discriminations between further facts presented to him, the child can not use a concept. Concepts, you will recall, must be drawn from such facts and discriminations as exist in or can be placed within the child's experience. Generalizations also become mere verbalizations unless children build them from their own concepts.

Constructs, too, must be built on the concepts and generalizations developed from the experiences which children have had. Although articles appear in educational literature concerning the value of promoting higher levels of thinking in children, little research exists on the development of constructs or models. Tanck (127–34) identifies a sequence for building these problem-solving devices which includes advanced organizing, cumulative structuring, and periodic augmentation. To illustrate these three steps, the authors must rely upon personal experiences.

Advanced organizing is simply a process in which the teacher structures an experience which reveals to the children the major concepts and generalizations in the construct he is developing. This can be accomplished through telling a story to children or through an open discussion. We have selected the former to introduce the construct of *productivity*.

> Man is limited by the number of resources he has. There are never enough resources to supply all of his needs, so he must make choices to obtain as many of his wants and needs as he can. Man does this

> by combining things in his environment to produce goods in the best possible ways. In order to understand this, we must identify all of the things used in fulfilling our wants and needs.
>
> First of all, we need some natural resources—something that is provided by nature that we can use. The soil we use to grow our food is a natural resource. So are the seeds we plant. There are many other kinds of resources, such as water, air, fish, and other animals, trees and other plants, and minerals from the earth. Man can use all of these things to fulfill his wants and needs.
>
> But merely having the resources available is not enough. Rocks could be used by ancient man as crude tools, but they didn't work as well as he wanted. He had to change them. Some food he gathered or hunted was edible raw, but he found that cooking made it more tasteful. Man has to change resources to make them more useful. This takes time and work we call "labor."
>
> He has also found ways to produce more by dividing his labor with other men. Some men today are carpenters, bakers, barbers, factory workers, and salesmen. They work for money with which they buy things to satisfy their wants and needs. They can do this because others are making the things they need and want.
>
> Some work man does not have the strength to do. So he has trained animals to perform specific tasks. As man has learned more about his world, he has also found that he could build machines to do work he could not or did not want to do. But these means of sharing labor can not be obtained by merely wishing for them. Man must have some means of obtaining them.

These various things—animals, special tools or machines—or the money which can be used to obtain these things, are called "capital." Capital is gained through savings, through borrowing from the savings of others or through the production of more things than we need. When we produce more than we need, we call this a "surplus." This surplus can be traded for capital.

The fourth thing we need in order to satisfy more of our wants and needs is the careful management of resources, labor, and capital. Here we can use new methods. Ancient man developed a new method when he found he could sharpen stones. This improved his tools.

Man, then, has four basic ways to increase production to fulfill his wants and needs: (1) He can find new resources or improve the use of those he has. (2) Capital can be utilized to produce the required changes. (3) Man can increase the supply of labor by training people or animals to do tasks. (4) New methods of combining the above factors can be designed to provide us with more of what we want or need—this is management.

During the story the children are encouraged to share their experiences and knowledge. This aids in the acceptance of the ideas presented. Remember, these concepts and generalizations must be related to children's experiences.

Through this simple discussion, the children have been introduced to the elementary concepts and generalizations of the construct we are developing. The construct, prepared in advance by the teacher, is then placed on the board or chart for further use. The model looks like this.

Resources

Man has limited resources.
Man changes resources to fit his wants and needs.

Labor

Man divides his labor with other men.
Man divides his labor with animals.
Man divides his labor with machines.

Capital

Man must have a surplus before he can divide his labor.

Management

Man combines the other factors in many ways.

The next step is building upon the initial construct. Of course, there must be several experiences for the members of the class before this construct becomes their own. After studying several units—Grasslands of the World, Farming Around the World, and The Development of Industry—the construct developed by one fifth grade class looked like this.

Resources

Man has limited resources.
Man changes resources to fit his wants and needs.
Man improves resources to make them more useful.

Labor

Man divides his labor with animals, machines, and other men.
Man's basic needs can be met more easily if he cooperates with other men.
Specialization causes man to become more dependent upon other men.

Capital

Man increases the amount of work he can do by improving his tools.

Improvements in transportation and communication have allowed man to increase his markets.

Man must produce a surplus before he can trade.

Management

Man can combine resources, labor, and capital in many ways.

Man has made laws and agreements to assure cooperation of other men.

Man's beliefs about himself and his world affect the ways he combines resources, labor, and capital.

The teacher began with a simple construct which contained the basic concepts and generalizations. As the experiences of the children grew, the teacher asked them to evaluate and add to this construct. This is the last step—augmentation.

As in the case of generalizations, the students must be encouraged to test this model. The following activity partially achieved this purpose for the teacher who wrote the article, "Farming in Modern Japan." He simply added the following introduction to the article: Use the model we have developed to analyze how the Japanese have increased there production.

The paper below is an example of one student's response. The reader may wish to return to that article beginning on page 96 to see how well this fifth grade student did.

Social Studies Test
The Farmer

Production of Rice in Japan

The production of rice in Japan was increased in many ways. Japan takes more grain from its plants than any other country does. Every field has something growing in it so that no land is wasted. Machines plow and cultivate the land. Electricity is used and water can be brought to fields faster because of it.

Japan has improved its methods of production by using such things as fertilization and irrigation. They also use insecticides and bug catchers. Plowing is done by tractors. And the grains are threshed by machines.

The teacher considered a child should be able to identify 50% of the items correctly. His analysis appears below.

Resources

Expansion of pasture land

Use of chemical fertilizers
Seed selection
Use of insecticides

Labor

Use of tractors for plowing and cultivating
Women used in transplanting

Capital

Electrical pumps used for water
Improved transportation
Tractors
Threshers
Chemical industry

Management

Maintenance of levies
Trade for some needs
Use of agricultural agents
Development of electricity

In attempting to aid the children in the development of a construct, the teacher first helped the children to identify basic elements of such a construct. Second, through several experiences, he guided the children to add to the basic model, and third, to evaluate their own additions to or deletions from the construct. The fourth step, illustrated above, allows the children to test the model and tests each pupil's grasp of the model which the class had developed.

Summary

In this chapter, we have stated that in order to aid children in the thinking process we must communicate with them through their own meanings and experiences. These meanings and experiences are capsulized in concepts which are developed through a process of discriminating between bits of information we call "facts." The higher levels of thinking, generalizing, and the building of constructs are dependent upon such conceptualizations.

We have explored processes developed for aiding children in the building of concepts and generalizations. These were examined through classroom situations. The teacher's role in these processes was one of probing and supporting. Although no researched process for the development of constructs was given, an experientially based process was explored.

References

Durkin, Mary C., and Hardy, Patricia. *Teaching Strategies for Developing Children's Thinking: The Taba In-Service Education Program, Interpretation of Data.* Palo Alto, California: Institute for Staff Development, 1969.

Fancett, Verna S. *Social Science Concepts and the Classroom.* Syracuse, New York: The Social Studies Curriculum Center, Syracuse University, 1968.

Snygg, Donald. "A Cognitive Field Theory of Learning." *Learning and Mental Health in the School.* 1966 Yearbook of the Association for Supervision and Curriculum Development. Washington, D.C.: Association for Supervision and Curriculum Development, NEA, 1966.

Taba, Hilda. *Teachers' Handbook For Elementary Social Studies.* Introductory Edition. Reading, Massachusetts: Addison-Wesley Publishing Company, 1967.

Tanck, Marlin L. "Teaching Concepts, Generalizations, and Constructs." *Social Studies Curriculum Development: Prospects and Problems.* Thirty-ninth Yearbook of the National Council for the Social Studies. Washington, D.C.: National Council for the Social Studies, NEA, 1969.

V

Components of Instruction

Chapter Outline

Components of Instruction

In the preceding chapters we have discussed ways of teaching children to think effectively, but we have said little about the ways in which instruction can be analyzed or how the teacher can systematically design instruction. In the next five chapters, we shall concentrate upon a way of dividing the instructional process into its various parts. This chapter will show you components of a model which will help us examine instructional design. Later, we will show the interrelationships of these components.

Objective

The reader will be able to:

Identify (1.0) the five major components in the Model for Instructional Design (MID).

Components of a Model for Instructional Design

The Model for Instructional Design (MID), which will be discussed in these chapters is an adaptation of a General Model of Instruction (GMI), developed by several individuals. The GMI has been fully explained by Kibler, Barker, and Miles (1–27). The MID was adapted as a procedural guide for teachers attempting to prepare instruction for children. It differs from the GMI because its starting point is usually a curriculum guide, teacher's guide, or prepared unit of study. As with the GMI, the MID is based on the premise that the goal of instruction is to enable the student to achieve specific objectives in the least amount of time. To accomplish this purpose, those involved in teaching must focus upon the five major components illustrated in Figure 5–1. They are given as the *instructional purposes* for which the teacher is attempting to design the sequence of experiences; the *behavioral objectives* which state the behaviors the teacher is attempting to obtain; *pretesting* which tells the teacher the present knowledge, skills, or attitudes of her students; the *learning area* consisting of teacher actions, student actions, and mediating devices; and *evaluation* which assesses the degree of achievement of the assigned objectives. We will analyze each of these components separately. This chapter will focus upon instructional purposes, behavioral objectives, and pretesting.

Objective

The reader will be able to:

Identify (1.0) the sources of instructional purposes in social studies.

Sources of Instructional Purposes

As beginning teachers, often we are placed in the position of implementing an instructional design, rather than initially designing instruction. Often, in social studies, we are provided with a curriculum guide which has been prepared by social studies specialists or, more frequently today, a group of experienced teachers from our own school district. This guide may be extensive enough to contain sample units; or it may be merely an outline of the content we are requested to cover at each grade level. In some districts, teachers are provided with only a textbook series and a teacher's manual. In this case, the curriculum is the textbook; the teacher takes the content from suggestions given in the manual.

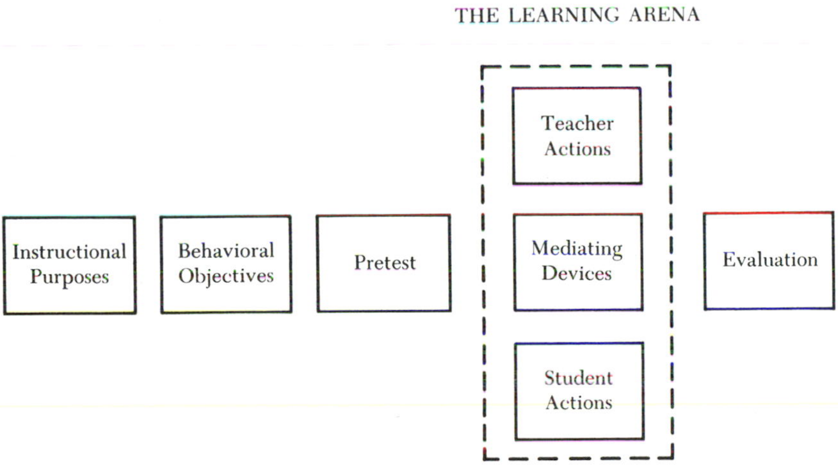

Figure 5–1. *Components of a Model for Instructional Design (MID)*

Commonly included in curriculum guides are the purposes for instruction in each of the suggested units or topics. The teacher's task becomes one of selecting the purposes which best suit his group and teaching situation. These purposes are the source from which the teacher prepares his behavioral objectives. At times, the teacher is unable to adopt purposes directly from the curriculum guide. Nevertheless, the purposes provided in the guides give direction to classroom instruction. Currently, teacher's guides may include behavioral objectives which have been derived from stated purposes. Such statements give more specific direction to the teacher.

A second source of instructional purposes is found in the teacher's manuals of textbook series. Although some educators are extremely critical of these manuals, when used judiciously, they remain a valuable tool for planning instruction. "Judiciously" in this instance means adapting and supplementing to fit your teaching situation. Some textbook manuals now provide behavioral objectives, as well as purposes.

Social studies lessons or units can also be taken from current events or local issues and happenings. Other lessons may result from the needs and interests of students. In these cases, the teacher cannot depend upon a guide or manual for suggestions; he will have to develop his own purposes or plan them cooperatively with his students. If the purposes are determined by the teacher, it is essential that he communicate them to his students. Children learn more effectively when they understand the purposes for instruction and perceive the relationship between the learning experiences and those purposes.

Objectives

The reader will be able to:

Describe (1.0) the three elements of a behavioral objective.

Defend (2.0) the use of behavioral objectives.

Design (5.0) behavioral objectives for a given lesson.

Focusing on Behavior

Although the purposes of instruction direct our attention to things we want to teach, they are not sufficient for identifying suitable learning activities. They are too broad or general for this purpose. Let us assume, for example, that one of our purposes is to have the students understand the Constitution of the United States. This is a worthy goal, but unfortunately, this objective is open to various interpretations. Further, it does not focus upon the behavior required of the student.

Behavioral objectives.

Although we believe we can describe the cognitive functioning of the human being, this is of little help to the classroom teacher unless he has some way of telling when the child has produced a cognitive product. Perhaps this is what makes teaching so challenging. It is difficult to determine when a child "understands" what we have attempted to teach. How do we know that the learner understands the Constitution? A related problem is determining the extent of a student's understanding.

Our first step is to translate this instructional purpose into student behaviors that we can observe. The result will be the first step in creating a behavioral objective. Such an objective has three parts. It states the desired change of behavior we hope to elicit from students as a result of instruction; it tells the conditions during which we expect the behavior to occur, as well as the level of success (criterion) we expect our students to attain.

Returning to our example of understanding the Constitution, let us translate our purpose into an observable behavior. Perhaps if we say "the child will show his understanding of the Constitution by stating the governmental branches it establishes," we can communicate what we mean by "understanding." This helps somewhat, but we still have not determined the specific student behavior. Is the child going to state *orally* the names of the governmental bodies, or should we have him *write* the answer? It is important that we state the objective in such a way that the behavior is clearly identified.

If we revise our behavioral objective to read "the student will identify, in writing, the branches of government established by the Constitution of the United States," we state precisely what we want the child to do. We can observe the performance of this behavior. We have completed the first step in developing our behavioral objective.

Our objective lacks two important elements, the conditions and criterion. Without a statement of conditions, we don't know when we can expect this behavior to take place. Are we to hand the child a piece of paper and a pencil and allow him to write all day, or does he have two seconds to complete the task? Again, let us clarify our objective: "On a unit test the student will identify, in writing, the branches of government established by the Constitution of the United States." Now we know exactly when the desired behavior will occur.

The above statement is still lacking one element. What is the level of success we expect the student to attain? In other words, how many branches of government will the student be required to identify for successful completion of the task? From the way the objective is stated, we might infer that the child would have to identify the legislative, judicial, and administrative branches. To clarify, we could insert a number in our objective which would serve as a criterion against which we can assess achievement. Now our objective would read, "On a unit test the student will identify, in writing, the three branches of government established by the Constitution of the United States."

Why behavioral objectives?

The first major reason for the use of behavioral objectives is that they allow us to communicate our objectives to others interested in education. This includes our students, parents of our children, and the administrators and supervisors of our schools. We improve communication by stating the behaviors we seek along with the level of achievement (criterion) we expect and the situation in which we plan for the behavior to be displayed (conditions).

Behavioral objectives act as a guide for the teacher in developing activities that lead toward the end behavior. This is the second important reason for using behaviorally stated objectives. Our task is to take the children from where they are to the point at which they should be at the end of the learning sequence. We state the end behavior and then design the activities that will result in this behavior.

Thirdly, behavioral objectives enable the teacher to select appropriate evaluation techniques. Teacher made tests, for example, have a notorious reputation for dealing with facts or details totally irrelevant to the purposes of instruction. If the teacher's purpose were to have the students understand the Constitution of the United States, than a test question, such as Who wrote the Constitution? or In what year was the Constitution ratified? might seem extraneous. However, if the teacher assumed that understanding the Constitution would include knowledge about the times and the authors' background, then such questions would be appropriate. Without behaviorally stated objectives, writing test questions is difficult, if not impossible.

The last and perhaps the most important reason for using behaviorally stated objectives is for the improvement of instruction. Behavioral objectives force the teacher to analyze his objectives and procedures in the teaching act. We humans are notoriously fuzzy thinkers. Unless we consciously place ourselves in the situation where we must answer the questions: "What do I want students to accomplish?" "Did my procedures allow the children to reach the desired behavior?" our objectives and activities may appear compatible, but they may not produce the intended results.

In order for us to communicate our intentions, determine the previous learnings, select appropriate evaluation techniques, and improve instruction; we use behaviorally stated objectives.

Writing behavioral objectives.

In the preparation of objectives, you will be concerned with three factors: the past experiences of your students, the experiences you plan to provide them in the future, and the means of instruction you have at your command. (Kibler, 3–5) This last factor includes your teaching skills, available materials, and, in some instances, equipment. Let us analyze an actual teaching situation to illustrate what we are attempting to say. We will use the "Developing of Concepts" procedure discussed in Chapter IV. This procedure, you will recall, asked children specific questions that elicited certain observable behaviors. For your convenience, the questions and behaviors are listed below.

Teacher's Question	Observable Behavior
What do you see, hear, or think?	Children list items
What things seem to belong together?	Children group items
Why do you place them together?	Children explain groupings
What can you call these groups?	Children label the groups

If we were to select this set of procedures for introducing children to categorization, it would be necessary first to determine whether the children had ever experienced this concept development procedure. Several persons who have used this technique report that students who have never been exposed to this teaching method attempt to find out what the teacher wants them to say. They will ask, "What's the right answer?" In the first encounter with any teaching procedure, children will require more guidance than a group which has been through the procedure before. Your students' previous experiences are a factor you must consider before any objective.

The next factor to be considered is the future experiences you plan to provide for the children. In order to illustrate this, we shall return to the sample primary lesson in Chapter IV which used the above teaching procedure. You will recall that the teacher's purpose was to introduce the children to categorizing. This teacher's reason for using categorization was that it would aid her children in developing concepts. Since we know that the process of categorization requires the act of labeling and the evaluation of that label, we know that this is a sound procedure. The skill of categorizing can also be used by children in math, language, and science activities. Since our future units or lesson plans require this skill, it is a useful experience for the group.

Part of the third concern is the teacher's skill. This does not mean that you as a teacher should not try new things. It does mean, however, that if you are a novice at a certain procedure, you must evaluate the achievement of an objective in that light. Many a teacher has refused to use group activities with his children because his first experience resulted in what the teacher considered a noisy class or an uncompleted project. Actually, the problem may have been that the teacher lacked experience in classroom management. Possibly, he failed to communicate assigned roles, neglected to state explicitly what was to be accomplished, failed to provide one group with the resources needed, or forgot one of the many seemingly small details that permit groups of children to work productively.

Your behavior is only one concern in what we shall call the "delivery of instruction." Also, you must be concerned with the equipment and materials you have available for the completion of an objective. We will not elaborate on this point now, except to say that the objective the teacher prepares must take into account the means he has for accomplishing this objective.

Now that we have alerted you to the three items with which you must be concerned in the preparation of objectives, let us construct a few. We will set the stage by saying that you are faced with a racially integrated group of effervescent first graders. One of the skills you are responsible for teaching in social studies is categorization. Your stated purpose for this lesson is "to introduce the children to categorization." It is time for you to begin preparing your behavioral objectives for this lesson. You will recall that your first task is to translate this purpose into behavioral objectives. Return to the listing we provide for you earlier in this chapter, and attempt to develop your objectives. After you have a set of behaviorally stated objectives containing specific behaviors, conditions, and criteria, return to this page and check yours against ours.

(1) In an oral discussion using pictures, the children will list animals they recognize.

(2) In a class discussion, the children will group the animals they have named.

(3) As individual students group items, they will explain their reasons for the groupings they make.

(4) After all the items have been grouped, the children will label the groups they have formed.

Let's look at the behaviors stated in our objectives.

list group explain label

Can these be observed? It appears so. Are conditions given for these behaviors? In an oral discussion, as individual students group, and after the items have been grouped, are all contexts in which the behaviors are to be displayed. It does appear that these are precise objectives which can be used to determine whether specific behaviors are achieved. You will note that the objectives in our example lack stated criteria. In some objectives, criteria are implied because the outcomes must remain flexible. The teacher can not tell how many items the children will list.

Objectives

The reader will be able to:

Evaluate (6.0) the authors' suggested classification of cognitive objectives using Gronlund's Tables 5–1 and 5–2.

Explain (2.0) the rationale for classifying objectives.

Explain (2.0) the hierarchical arrangement of the major categories in the cognitive domain.

Analyzing and Classifying Cognitive Objectives

Merely stating a set of objectives is not enough. Our real concern is whether these objectives will get us to the point we want to go with the children. To accomplish this, we must analyze each objective critically and attempt to answer the questions: "What kind of thinking am I asking the child to perform?" "What am I asking the child to do?" Through this process, we can ensure that we reach our stated purposes. This procedure calls for a specialized tool, the *Taxonomy of Educational Objectives: Handbook I* (Bloom). This Taxonomy is a means of classifying cognitive instructional objectives according to levels of complexity in thinking. The major purpose of this Taxonomy is to facilitate the communication of educational outcomes among educators and laymen. Although it can be used to analyze questions, as well as objectives, the latter will be illustrated here. This tool has been placed in an exceptionally useful format by Gronlund (20–21), a Professor of Educational Psychology who has made many contributions to educational measurement and evaluation. His Tables 5–1 and 5–2 can be used for the classification of objectives and questions. We shall use them in the analysis of our objectives.

Let us review the four behaviors: list, group, explain, and label. We can enter Gronlund's tables in the column titled "Illustrative Behavioral Terms for Stating Specific Learning Outcomes." You will note that our term "list" is entered under the category "Knowledge." Under this category, all the student is required to do is to call forth specific information or data. Since this fits our objective, we can be satisfied that this is what we intend to have students do.

Our second term is "group." This term cannot be found in the column showing behavioral terms. Perhaps we can find a similar objective in the column marked "Illustrative General Instructional Objectives." This doesn't seem to help us either. Let's examine the "Descriptions of the Major Categories in the Cognitive Domain." Maybe the phrase "application of such things as rules, methods, concepts" may help us classify this behavior. Is there a synonym in the list of terms? Not really, but the three terms "produce," "prepares," and "relates" state more or less what we intend.

Table 5–1. Major Categories in the Cognitive Domain of the Taxonomy of Educational Objectives (Bloom, 1956) [1]

Descriptions of the Major Categories in the Cognitive Domain
1. **Knowledge.** Knowledge is defined as the remembering of previously learned material. This may involve the recall of a wide range of material, from specific facts to complete theories, but all that is required is the bringing to mind of the appropriate information. Knowledge represents the lowest level of learning outcomes in the cognitive domain.
2. **Comprehension.** Comprehension is defined as the ability to grasp the meaning of material. This may be shown by translating material from one form to another (words to numbers), by interpreting material (explaining or summarizing), and by estimating future trends (predicting consequences or effects). These learning outcomes go one step beyond the simple remembering of material, and represent the lowest level of understanding.
3. **Application.** Application refers to the ability to use learned material in new and concrete situations. This may include the application of such things as rules, methods, concepts, principles, laws, and theories. Learning outcomes in this area require a higher level of understanding than those under comprehension.

[1] Reprinted with permission of the Macmillan Company from *Stating Behavioral Objectives for Classroom Instruction* by Norman E. Gronlund. Copyright © 1970 by Norman E. Gronlund.

4. **Analysis.** Analysis refers to the ability to break down material into its component parts so that its organizational structure may be understood. This may include the identification of the parts, analysis of the relationships between parts, and recognition of the organizational principles involved. Learning outcomes here represent a higher intellectual level than comprehension and application because they require an understanding of both the content and the structural form of the material.

5. **Synthesis.** Synthesis refers to the ability to put parts together to form a new whole. This may involve the production of a unique communication (theme or speech), a plan of operations (research proposal), or a set of abstract relations (scheme for classifying information). Learning outcomes in this area stress creative behaviors, with major emphasis on the formulation of *new* patterns or structures.

6. **Evaluation.** Evaluation is concerned with the ability to judge the value of material (statement, novel, poem, research report) for a given purpose. The judgments are to be based on definite criteria. These may be internal criteria (organization) or external criteria (relevance to the purpose) and the student may determine the criteria or be given them. Learning outcomes in this area are highest in the cognitive hierarchy because they contain elements of all of the other categories, plus conscious value judgments based on clearly defined criteria.

If we agree upon these verbs, then we can classify "group" under "Application" which is the third level of the taxonomy.

The next term we are interested in analyzing is "explain." Actually, we are examining more than the term. We are attempting to determine the cognitive level of the activity we are asking the children to perform. "Explains" is listed at the "Comprehension" level under the second column in Table 5–2, but this is not exactly what we want. The child is asked to do more than to repeat an act in a new situation. The term is also listed under category 5, "Synthesis," which as indicated in Table 5–1, "refers to the ability to put parts together to form a new whole." Most of the groups the child will produce would be of this nature. He might perceive relationships he had not considered. At times, members of the group would help individual children discover relations they had not seen. Our analysis would categorize this behavior as one of "synthesizing."

Although the term "label" is listed at the lowest level in the taxonomy, this is not the level we are asking the child to accomplish. In this objective, we are requesting the children to label the groups they have formed. Actually, the student summarizes the discussion of the listing he has created. Some questioning of this classification is justified. In noting the sequence of the discussion, however, you will recall that the child has already explained his reason for placing some items together. The discussion which

Table 5–2.

Examples of General Instructional Objectives and Behavioral Terms for the Cognitive Domain of the Taxonomy [2]

Illustrative General Instructional Objectives	*Illustrative Behavioral Terms for Stating Specific Learning Outcomes*
Knows common terms Knows specific facts Knows methods and procedures Knows basic concepts Knows principles	Defines, describes, identifies, labels, lists, matches, names, outlines, reproduces, selects, states
Understands facts and principles Interprets verbal material Interprets charts and graphs Translates verbal material to mathematical formulas Estimates future consequences implied in data Justifies methods and procedures	Converts, defends, distinguishes, estimates, explains, extends, generalizes, gives examples, infers, paraphrases, predicts, rewrites, summarizes
Applies concepts and principles to new situations Applies laws and theories to practical situations Solves mathematical problems Constructs charts and graphs Demonstrates correct usage of a method or procedure	Changes, computes, demonstrates, discovers, manipulates, modifies, operates, predicts, prepares, produces, relates, shows, solves, uses
Recognizes unstated assumptions Recognizes logical fallacies in reasoning Distinguishes between facts and inferences Evaluates the relevancy of data Analyzes the organizational structure of a work (art, music, writing)	Breaks down, diagrams, differentiates, discriminates, distinguishes, identifies, illustrates, infers, outlines, points out, relates, selects, separates, subdivides
Writes a well organized theme Gives a well organized speech Writes a creative short story (or poem, or music) Proposes a plan for an experiment	Categorizes, combines, compiles, composes, creates, devises, designs, explains, generates, modifies, organizes, plans, rearranges, reconstructs, relates, reorganizes, re-

[2] Reprinted with permission of the Macmillan Company from *Stating Behavioral Objectives for Classroom Instruction* by Norman E. Gronlund. Copyright © 1970 by Norman E. Gronlund.

Illustrative General Instructional Objectives	*Illustrative Behavioral Terms for Stating Specific Learning Outcomes*
Integrates learning from different areas into a plan for solving a problem Formulates a new scheme for classifying objects (or events, or ideas)	vises, rewrites, summarizes, tells, writes
Judges the logical consistency of written material Judges the adequacy with which conclusions are supported by data Judges the value of a work (art, music, writing) by use of internal criteria Judges the value of a work (art, music, writing) by use of external standards of excellence	Appraises, compares, concludes, contrasts, criticizes, describes, discriminates explains, justifies, interprets, relates, summarizes, supports

ensues often broadens meaning. The label becomes merely the capstone in the process. This act requires "comprehension" only.

You are aware that we have mentioned classification as we analyzed our terms. It should be apparent to you that the acts of analysis and classification cannot be separated; as you do one, you accomplish the other. What we have accomplished is the classification of the objectives we have selected. The result of this classification is a list of objectives which state our intentions clearly. As in so many cases, the process is more important than the product. We see our instructional objectives more clearly. As a result, we know what the children must be able to do. It will be easier for us to identify the prerequisite learnings required. In order for you to recall your intentions the next time you refer to this lesson, as a teacher you may want to record the objectives as follows:

(1) In an oral discussion, the children will list (1.0) the animals they identify.

(2) In a discussion, the children will group (3.0) the items they have listed.

(3) As individual students group items, they will explain (5.0) their reasons for the groupings they make.

(4) After all the items have been grouped, the children will label (2.0) the groups they have formed.

Perhaps the illustration above is not sufficient to clarify this very important process of classifying objectives. To provide you with a similar experience, we shall explain why we have classified the behavioral objectives on page 114 in the manner that we did.

You will note that our first objective asked the reader to "describe the three elements of a behavioral objective." Notice that we classified this objective (1.0) according to the Taxonomy listed in Tables 5–1 and 5–2. Obviously, this behavior is at the lowest level of the Taxonomy because it merely requires the reader to recall specific information which has been set forth in the text.

The next objective called upon the reader to "defend the use of behavioral objectives." This objective was classified (2.0) because we felt that the reader would need some understanding or comprehension of behavioral objectives if he were to defend them. Comprehension, you will recall, is the second level of the Taxonomy.

The third objective for the reader required that he "design behavioral objectives for a given lesson." This behavior would demand much more of the reader than either of the preceeding objectives. Because it would call for the synthesis of information found in that section of the chapter, as well as the production of a unique communication, we labeled this objective (5.0).

We would like to repeat a statement which was made earlier. The use of one category of the Taxonomy implies the use of all appearing above it. If the child is to synthesize, he must of necessity use the categories of knowledge, comprehension, application, and analysis. This is important to consider in sequencing instruction. For example, what would be the sequence required for teaching a child to summarize an article? The student would have to be able to read the article, to identify the words, and identify the main points in the presentation. This latter task requires that the child know such conventions as topic sentences, paragraphs, and details. Then, the child would be requested to apply these knowledges in another setting. Identifying the main points is a process of analysis, separating a whole into its composite parts. Then, one might ask the child to combine these main ideas into a summary. Thus, in this simple illustration, we have covered much of the cognitive domain in which each level builds upon the skills of the previous levels.

Objectives

The reader will be able to:

Evaluate (6.0) the authors' suggested classification of affective objectives using Gronlund's Tables 5-3 and 5-4.

Explain (2.0) the hierarchical arrangement of the major categories in the Affective Domain.

Analyzing and Classifying Affective Objectives

We have discussed the analysis of cognitive objectives, but there are other objectives that we need to consider in the teaching act. These objectives relate to the feelings, attitudes, and values of our students. Krathwohl and others continued the study of objectives beyond the cognitive area and produced the *Taxonomy of Educational Objectives Handbook II: Affective Domain* in 1964. As in the cognitive domain, the behaviors are listed in hierarchical form. The behaviors represent a continuum of an internalization process. To illustrate what we mean, let us assume that we are attempting to teach an individual cooperation in group activities. Again, the work of Grondlund (22–23), as shown in Tables 5–3 and 5–4 will be useful.

Table 5–3.

Major Categories in the Affective Domain of the Taxonomy of Educational Objectives (Krathwohl, 1964) [3]

Descriptions of the Major Categories in the Affective Domain
1. **Receiving.** Receiving refers to the student's willingness to attend to particular phenomena or stimuli (classroom activities, textbook, music, etc.). From a teaching standpoint, it is concerned with getting, holding, and directing the student's attention. Learning outcomes in this area range from the simple awareness that a thing exists to selective attention on the part of the learner. Receiving represents the lowest level of learning outcomes in the affective domain.
2. **Responding.** Responding refers to active participation on the part of the student. At this level he not only attends to a particular phenomenon but also reacts to it in some way. Learning outcomes in this area may emphasize acquiescence in responding (reads assigned material), willingness to respond (voluntarily reads beyond assignment), or satisfaction in responding (reads for pleasure or enjoyment). The higher levels of this category include those instructional objectives that are commonly classified under "interests"; that is, those that stress the seeking out and enjoyment of particular activities.
3. **Valuing.** Valuing is concerned with the worth or value a student attaches to a particular object, phenomenon, or behavior. This ranges in degree from the more simple acceptance of a value (desires to improve group

[3] Reprinted with permission of the Macmillan Company from *Stating Behavioral Objectives for Classroom Instruction* by Norman E. Gronlund. Copyright © 1970 by Norman E. Gronlund.

skills) to the more complex level of commitment (assumes responsibility for the effective functioning of the group). Valuing is based on the internalization of a set of specified values, but clues to these values are expressed in the student's overt behavior. Learning outcomes in this area are concerned with behavior that is consistent and stable enough to make the value clearly identifiable. Instructional objectives that are commonly classified under "attitudes" and "appreciation" would fall into this category.

---

4. **Organization.** Organization is concerned with bringing together different values, resolving conflicts between them, and beginning the building of an internally consistent value system. Thus the emphasis is on comparing, relating, and synthesizing values. Learning outcomes may be concerned with the conceptualization of a value (recognizes the responsibility of each individual for improving human relations) or with the organization of a value system (develops a vocational plan that satisfies his need for both economic security and social service). Instructional objectives relating to the development of a philosophy of life would fall into this category.

---

5. **Characterization by a Value or Value Complex.** At this level of the affective domain, the individual has a value system that has controlled his behavior for a sufficiently long time for him to have developed a characteristic "life style." Thus the behavior is pervasive, consistent, and predictable. Learning outcomes at this level cover a broad range of activities, but the major emphasis is on the fact that the behavior is typical or characteristic of the student. Instructional objectives that are concerned with the student's general patterns of adjustment (personal, social, emotional) would be appropriate here.

Table 5–4.

Examples of General Instructional Objectives and Behavioral Terms for the Affective Domain of the Taxonomy [4]

Illustrative General Instructional Objectives	*Illustrative Behavioral Terms for Stating Specific Learning Outcomes*
Listens attentively Shows awareness of the importance of learning	Asks, chooses, describes, follows, gives, holds, identifies, locates, names, points to, selects, sits erect,

[4] Reprinted with permission of the Macmillan Company from *Stating Behavioral Objectives for Classroom Instruction* by Norman E. Gronlund. Copyright © 1970 by Norman E. Gronlund.

Illustrative General Instructional Objectives	*Illustrative Behavioral Terms for Stating Specific Learning Outcomes*
Shows sensitivity to human needs and social problems Accepts differences of race and culture Attends closely to the classroom activities	replies, uses
Completes assigned homework Obeys school rules Participates in class discussion Completes laboratory work Volunteers for special tasks Shows intergst in subject Enjoys helping others	Answers, assists, complies, conforms, discusses, greets, helps, labels, performs, practices, presents, reads, recites, reports, selects, tells, writes
Demonstrates belief in the democratic process Appreciates good literature (art or music) Appreciates the role of science (or other subjects) in everyday life Shows concern for the welfare of others Demonstrates problem-solving attitude Demonstrates commitment to social improvement	Completes, describes, differentiates, explains, follows, forms, initiates, invites, joins, justifies, proposes, reads, reports, selects, shares, studies, works
Recognizes the need for balance between freedom and responsibility in a democracy Recognizes the role of systematic planning in solving problems Accepts responsibility for his own behavior Understands and accepts his own strengths and limitations Formulates a life plan in harmony with his abilities, interests, and beliefs	Adheres, alters, arranges, combines, compares, completes, defends, explains, generalizes, identifies, integrates, modifies, orders, organizes, prepares, relates, synthesizes
Displays safety consciousness Demonstrates self-reliance in working independently Practices cooperation in group activities Uses objective approach in problem solving Demonstrates industry, punctuality and self-discipline Maintains good health habits	Acts, discriminates, displays influences, listens, modifies, performs, practices, proposes, qualifies, questions, revises, serves, solves, uses, verifies

In the lowest category, "receiving," the student would be shown what was meant by cooperation. He would be aware that cooperation could be expected. Also, at this level, the individual might be asked to observe how a situation was improved through cooperation. The child would choose the better of two solutions: One would include cooperation, the other, non-cooperation.

"Responding," might involve the individual in a group situation. At this level, he would merely meet our requirements, but as this type of experience is repeated, his behavior should become more voluntary. The child would begin receiving some satisfaction in cooperating with others.

As the child reached the "valuing" level, we might expect the student to place some value upon cooperation. He would accept cooperation as an important behavior. He would show some preference for this behavior when given a choice between situations. At this level, we would expect a degree of commitment to the concept of cooperation, and we could find him attempting to help others cooperate with the group.

At the level of "organization," the child goes through a process of integration. Here, he weighs such values as competitiveness and cooperation in the accomplishment of a task. He evaluates his responsibility in a specific task. The major difference between this level and the last, "characterization," is that cooperation would be the child's expected way of behaving. At this point, he has more or less become a "missionary" for the cause. He would be interested only in the problem facing the group and would attempt to work toward a solution in light of the opinions of others.

A list of objectives which described the above sequence might appear as the one given below.

(1) After observing a group of children preparing a bulletin board, the class will be able to describe (A1) behaviors which facilitated or inhibited the group from achieving its goal.

(2) Working (A2) in groups of three, the children will assist in the development of a list of rules which will help them work in groups.

(3) After working in groups (A2) of three, individuals will be able to tell the teacher ways they helped the small group.

(4) Working as a class, the children will select (A2) the rules they feel should be followed by groups.

(5) After a two day group assignment, the individual groups will evaluate (A3) the list of rules and suggest revisions.

(6) After a group assignment, individual students will identify (A4) ways each has changed his behavior to help the group.

(7) In group activities, individual students will display (A5) cooperativeness.

In summary, we begin the act of designing instruction by deciding upon a set of purposes. From the stated purposes, we develop a set of objectives which translate these purposes into behaviors which we can observe. To ensure that we focus our instruction in the intended direction, we must analyze these objectives. This analysis results in a classification which allows us to remember our exact objectives and to communicate these objectives to those interested in our instruction.

Objectives

The reader will be able to:

Identify (1.0) the reasons for pretesting.

Explain (2.0) how pretesting can help teachers individualize instruction.

Pretesting

After delineating our purposes and specific objectives, it is necessary for us to determine (1) the knowledge or attitudes the children possess that are related to the subject to be studied; (2) the prerequisite skills upon which the unit of study is built; and (3) the degree of mastery of the skills individuals possess so that progress in these skills can be maintained.

Why pretest?

We have stated that knowledge and attitudes along with their concomitant skills are hierarchically arranged. Children cannot reach higher levels of knowledge or attitudes unless they have attained lower levels. This is illustrated in Figure 5–2 showing the "Developing of Concepts" procedure discussed in the previous example.

It is obvious, if you reread the objectives on page 118, that objectives two through four are based upon the children's knowledge of the animals pictured. All of these objectives depend upon the earlier experiences of the children involved. They had to know the names of the animals and,

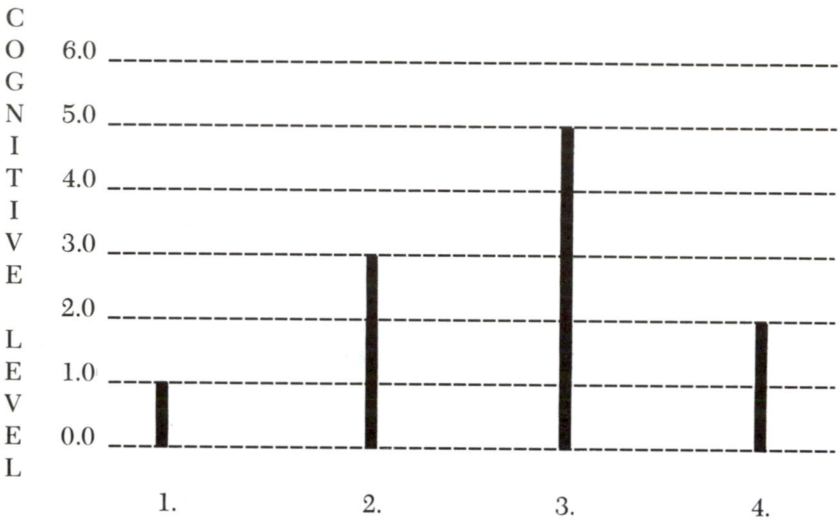

Figure 5–2. *Number of the Objective*

also, the characteristics of the animals in the pictures. If these children had been limited in experiences, the teacher could not have started at this point. Knowledge of the background of students is an important ingredient of a successful unit. To obtain such knowledge about his students, the teacher must pretest.

This leads us to the next consideration, prerequisite skills. It is believed today that if a child has the prerequisite skills for a behavior, he can easily learn the terminal behavior. (Gagné, 471) The Terminal behavior is the behavior we are seeking. It becomes important, then, that we direct the child through the proper sequence of skills. This can be illustrated by analyzing possibly the most used, but least understood, skill in social studies—reporting.

Let us assume that our purpose is to teach children to prepare reports. We can translate this purpose into the objective: "Given several sources of information on a topic, the child will prepare (5.0) a two page report which contains eighty per cent of the main ideas presented." Let us further assume that this is an objective for fifth grade children. Our pretesting task is to measure the present ability level of our students in the skills of reporting. In order to prepare a valid pretest, one that really tests children's skill level in reporting, we need to determine the prerequisite skills. Remember that our terminal behavior is the objective we have stated. When the children have accomplished this skill or behavior, they have completed one sequence in our plan for the year. In order to determine where the children are at the beginning of this teaching sequence, we must test them for the prerequisite skills. Here is a second reason for pretesting.

The diagram below attempts to delimit these skills. It shows five possible points of entry into the learning sequence. The lowest level of complexity is represented by point one which involves identifying topic sentences.

The next level requires the identification of main ideas, entry point two. Summarizing, point three and outlining, point four, represent higher skill levels contained in our terminal behavior of reporting. Various individuals, because of their previous experiences, will begin at different points in the diagram. Our initial pretest for the skill portion of our unit must include some means of evaluating whether children have mastered each of the prerequisite skills: identifying topic sentences, identifying main ideas, combining these main ideas into summaries, preparing summaries from several sources, and combining these through the use of outlines into reports.

We use this information as data which allows us to prescribe instruction for each of our students. This is the third reason for pretesting. At the fifth grade level, we would expect most of the children to begin at entry points three and four. There might be a few children who had difficulty

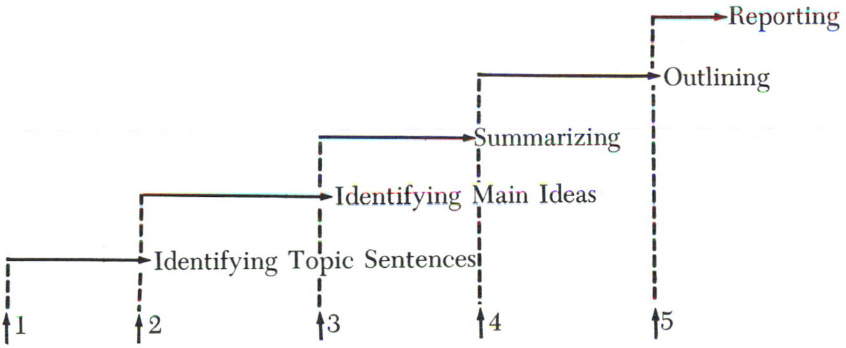

Figure 5–3. *Points of Entry for Terminal Behavior—Reporting*

identifying topic sentences, entry point one. It is also conceivable that some children entering at point five would profit from review of more complex lessons in the teaching sequence for entry point two. This, too, can be determined by the carefully designed pretest.

How pretests help teachers individualize instruction

Pretesting is not a new idea. Educators have talked about the usefulness of this procedure for decades. Perhaps the present impetus is the product of our desire to individualize instruction. First, the results of a pretest can indicate if children are able to skip some of the lessons we have designed. The determination of prerequisites allows us to do this. If the child already has the behavior for which a sequence is designed, it is ridiculous and self-defeating to place him in the sequence. This destroys motivation.

Perhaps certain students do not possess the entry behaviors that allow them to begin a teaching sequence. This is detrimental to motivation, also. If the child can not possibly succeed in the sequence, he has no business in it. Think how hopeless it is for the fifth grader who can't read to enter the teaching sequence we illustrated above. A well designed pretest allows us to prevent such disasters. This is the second way pretests help us successfully individualize instruction.

Pretesting, thirdly, tells us the point of entry for each child in the sequence of instruction. Beginning here, they can progress at their own speed through the series of lessons we have designed.

Summary

In this chapter we have introduced you to the basic elements of a Model for Instructional Design (MID). Three components of the MID have been isolated for examination. They are given as, instructional purposes, behavioral objectives, and pretesting.

We began by discussing instructional purposes because this is where planning is initiated. Through a process of translation, the teacher then specifies his objectives behaviorally. The product of this translation must be carefully analyzed using either the cognitive or affective domains as tools. The result is a classified objective which communicates our intent in instruction.

Before we can continue designing instruction for children, we must pretest them to determine the knowledge or attitudes they possess, as well as their level of mastery of prerequisite skills. Pretests help us individualize instruction by indicating the entry level of students in the teaching sequence.

References

Bloom, Benjamin S., et al. *Taxonomy of Educational Objectives. The Classification of Educational Goals, Handbook I: Cognitive Domain.* New York: David McKay Company, Inc., 1956.

Gagné, Robert M. "Some New Views of Learning and Instruction." *Phi Delta Kappan* 51 (May 1970): 468-472.

Gronlund, Norman E. *Stating Behavioral Objectives for Classroom Instruction.* New York: The MacMillan Company, 1970.

Kibler, Robert J., et al. *Behavioral Objectives and Instructon.* Boston: Allyn and Bacon, Inc., 1970.

Krathwohl, David R., et al. *Taxonomy of Educational Objectives. The Classification of Educational Goals, Handbook II: Affective Domain.* New York: David McKay Company, Inc., 1964.

VI

Examining the Learning Arena

Chapter Outline

Examining the Learning Arena

In Chapter V, we examined three components of the Model for Instructional Design (MID). In this chapter, we will analyze another component of this model, the learning arena. The focus of our discussion will be on the interactions of the participants in the learning arena—the teacher and the students.

Much confusion exists among educators concerning this component of instructional design. We have acted as though instruction were something that was done *to* someone. Instruction is an interactive process in which the actions of both the student and the teacher must be considered carefully. These actions are focused upon content—knowledge, skills, and values—toward which the teacher is attempting to direct the child's learning. In our MID, content is represented by the purposes and objectives. The intent of our first analysis in this chapter is to examine the actions the teacher can take to facilitate the communication of this content. Later in the chapter, we will focus upon an analysis of student actions.

Objective

The reader will be able to:

Identify (1.0) the four reasons the authors give for pretesting.

The Reevaluation of Purposes and Objectives

You will recall that the last topic discussed in Chapter V was the pretesting of children. We concluded that the results of a pretest tell us (1) if some children can skip a portion of the lessons we have designed or plan to design, (2) if some children have the prerequisite skills or knowledge required by our design, and (3) the point of entry for each child for which the lesson or unit is being planned.

Another significant point we should add is that pretesting enables the teacher to reexamine his purposes and objectives in the light of this additional data on his students. Often, only minor adjustments must be made in our objectives. This is especially true toward the end of the year when we know our students well. However, at times, even experienced teachers can underestimate or overestimate the abilities of their students. If our error of estimation has been great, we may have to revise both our purposes and objectives for individuals, small groups, or the whole class.

Objectives

The reader will be able to:

Arrange (2.0) the elements of the "Cone of Experience" in correct sequence from least to most abstract and suggest (2.0) experiences for children at each level.

Give the rationale (2.0) for utilizing a variety of experiences for children.

Contrast (2.0) the deductive and inductive teaching methods.

Suggest (4.0) ways of using selected techniques for motivation, given a teaching situation.

Suggest (5.0) ways of developing a model of mastery, given a specific social studies skill.

Identify (3.0) three types of models of mastery.

Suggest (5.0) ways of providing active responses in a lecture situation.

Identify (1.0) the three segments in the guidance process.

Give (1.0) the steps in the guided discovery technique and apply (3.0) this model when given a social studies concept or generalization.

Give (1.0) the steps in the group inquiry technique.

Select (3.0) a problem and suggest (3.0) appropriate activities for each step in the group inquiry sequence.

Explain (1.0) the teaching strategy model presented by the authors.

Rank (1.0) the roles of the teacher from least to greatest involvement.

The Identification of Teacher Actions in the Learning Arena

After reevaluation of objectives, the teacher is ready to consider the purposeful actions he will take in the learning arena illustrated in Figure 6–1. These considerations determine the success or failure of instruction. They include selecting experiences for children, and teaching methods, as well as the role the teacher will play.

Selecting experiences for children.

One of the first tasks of the teacher in the learning arena is the selection of experiences for children. In Chapter II, we alluded to the fact that there are many ways of conveying knowledge to the student through purposeful experiences. We did not attempt to rank these experiences at that time. This has been done by several individuals. Perhaps the most productive model is that originally produced by Edgar Dale, a leader in audiovisual education. The adaptation made by Sowards and Scobey (378), leaders in elementary school curriculum, is presented in Figure 6–2.

Levels of experience. It will be recalled from our earlier discussion that the most meaningful and impressive experiences are real ones, those in which the person is a direct participant. You will note that these experiences form the base of Dale's cone.

The next level is called contrived experiences. These experiences are used because it is too expensive, dangerous, or time consuming for students to have the real experience. The simulation lesson on the manufacturing of automobiles used in Chapter I is one of these contrived experiences for children. The advantage of this technique is that it requires a very low degree of abstraction.

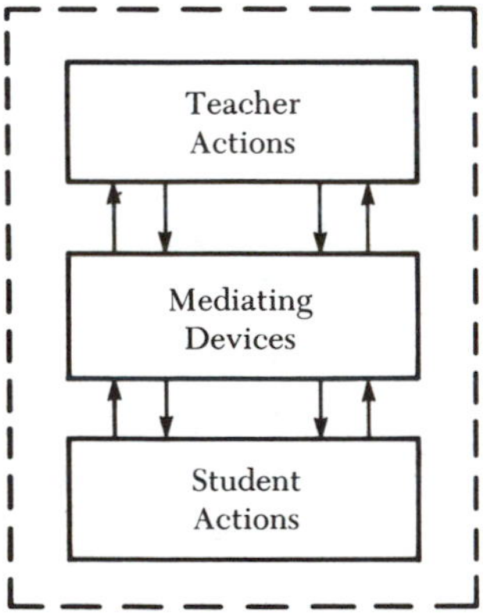

Figure 6–1. *The Learning Arena*

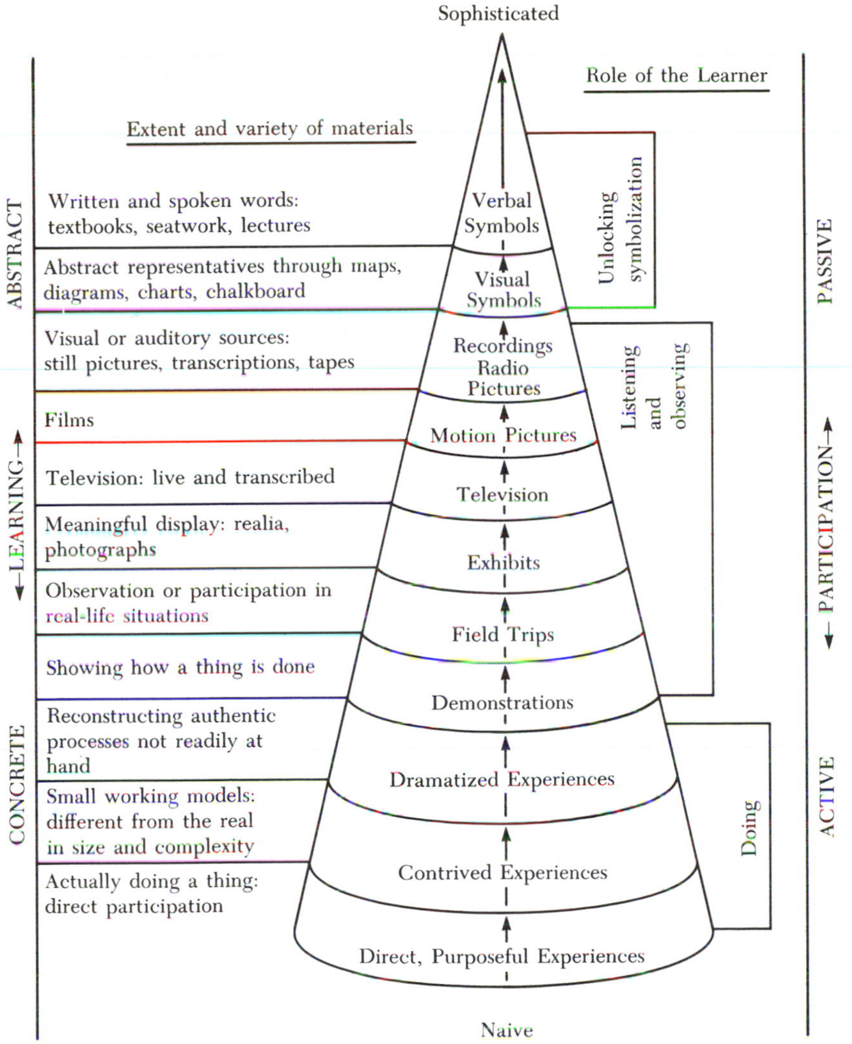

From *Audiovisual Methods in Teaching* (Third Edition, 1969) by Edgar Dale. Copyright © 1969 by The Dryden Press Inc. Reprinted by permission of the Dryden Press Inc.

Figure 6–2. *The Cone of Experience*

Another type of activity which involves the child in "doing," as illustrated in Figure 6–2, is dramatization. Possibly the greatest advantage of dramatization is that it allows the child to experience behaviors which he cannot try out in any other way. Yet the feelings the child has in role-playing or in the production of plays are vital enough to allow him some semblance of the real world. Beyond this level of the cone, the activities become more abstract.

At the lower levels of the next section of the cone, demonstrations and field trips offer the child various sensory inputs. These activities involve the student in listening and observing. Many demonstrations are given in such a manner that the child is able to touch, taste, smell, see, and hear. A field trip to a truck farm, an egg factory, or a steel mill permits the child to perceive the environment of each more fully because several of his senses are utilized. Recordings or films are less dimensional in character. They limit the child to one or two sensory inputs, unless the individual can combine the recorded or filmed experience with a real one. The latter is evident in the following example:

> After a primary class had viewed a film about an egg farm, one child made this statement. "My uncle's chicken house didn't smell very good. I had to hold my nose when I went after the eggs!" In this incident, the child was adding the olfactory (smelling) dimension to the verbal classroom conversation, the latter being one of the most abstract of experiences in the cone.

Although prepared maps, charts, and chalk-talks add dimension to the more abstract symbols used in textbooks and classroom discussions, they are inadequate for providing experiences to children who need vivid images—preschool and early primary children. For example, division of labor is going to be meaningless to the upper primary child unless it can be related to an area in which he has had some concrete experiences. If the teacher enters an abstract area in which intermediate grade children have not had an opportunity to have real experiences, an automobile factory for example, he would be wise to provide the class with at least a contrived experience similar to that shown in Chapter I.

The value of this cone is that it provides a tool the teacher can use in evaluating the level of abstraction as he designs learning activities. It also permits the teacher to determine where selected activities lie on a continuum from active to passive student response.

The need for a variety of experiences It is important that a variety of activities be provided and that lessons enable the student to build on concrete experiences. Variety is essential for at least four reasons. *First,* if the learner has mastered the skill we are teaching, he needs additional activities to maintain his learning. Do you remember how to take the square root of a number? Chances are that unless you are a math specialist, you have not maintained this skill. The *second* involves the improvement of skills. When you were taught handwriting, the teacher may have given you a model by holding your hand and guiding it through the construction of the letter B. However, it took many experiences before you were able to approach this model on your own. At a certain point in your learning, you developed the intuitive feel for B. You knew when you made a good B and a bad B.

A *third* reason involves the transfer of learning. A variety of experiences affords the student greater opportunity to relate the learning to *his* world. Thus, transfer of what is learned in school is more likely to be made to out-of-school experiences when learning becomes personally meaningful to the student. Finally, the importance of individual learning styles necessitates a variety of activities.

We have been aware of differences in learning styles for many years. Undoubtedly, you have experienced this phenomenon when you have been in a tight spot in a learning situation. Perhaps you are a person who must draw a picture of something you don't understand. Maybe you can't comprehend something if it is read orally to you, and you must read it yourself. Perhaps you can read directions and put things together; perhaps you can't. These are examples of learning styles. The greater the variety of experiences we provide for a group of children, the more likely we are to reach *all* of our students. Discussion of various mediating devices will be left for the next chapter.

Selecting teaching methods.

The following section will demonstrate two types of teaching methods which are frequently used in social studies. They are the deductive and inductive sequences. Guided discovery and group inquiry will be used as examples of inductive sequences.

A deductive method As we pointed out in Chapter II, the current trend in education is to select inductive methods, but there are many situations in which these methods are too time consuming or impractical. It may be more efficient and, therefore, less expensive to depend upon a deductive method. The identifying characteristic of this type of sequence is that the concept, generalization, or construct is given to the child in the beginning of the instructional sequence. Examples are then provided to allow verification in given situations. The steps in this model are discussed on the following pages.

1. Motivation of the student. Motivation is an important concern of the teacher. It is motivation which focuses and increases the pupils' interest in a given experience or event. There is a popular story which illustrates this aspect of teaching. It appears below.

> Jed, a farmer, needed a good mule. A neighbor, Ollie, had an animal which seemed to fill the bill. So they struck a bargain. Ollie cautioned

Jed, "The only way you can get this mule to work is to be kind to him."

"Oh, you can be sure I will," Jed promptly replied, feeling that he had finally received a good deal from Ol' Ollie. Since it was still early in the day, Jed decided to put his new mule to work and break him in right. He walked the mule home to the barn, rigged him for work, took him out to a field, and hitched the handsome animal to a plow.

"Giddap mule," the farmer called. The mule started forward, but upon feeling the strain of the plow, he promptly sat down.

"Giddap mule," the farmer commanded. He was ready to reach for his whip when he recalled his neighbor's caution about kindness.

Getting off the plow, Jed walked to the mule, scratched the mule's ears, rubbed his muzzle, and even fed him a couple of cubes of sugar which Jed normally reserved for his favorite mare. The mule rose to his feet, with this the farmer expectantly crawled back onto his seat and gave an encouraging, "Giddap mule." The cantankerous animal took two steps and returned to his seated position.

The frustrated farmer jumped from his perch, whip in hand, and started toward the mule when he noticed that Ol' Ollie had happened by and was standing near the fence.

"I thought you said if I was kind to this animal he'd work."

Ollie reassured Jed that this was so.

Jed carefully related his treatment of the animal and implied that Ollie was something other than an honest agrarian.

"I know just what's wrong," Ollie countered. Picking up a broken rail from the fence, Ol' Ollie told Jed to get back on the plow. Ollie strode deliberately to where the defiant animal sprawled and administered a jolting blow to the culprit's head yelling, "Giddap mule." With this the mule rose promptly to his feet and started off down the row.

"I thought you said you had to be kind to this mule," Jed shouted back as the plow jumped and jerked down the field.

"Ya do," Ollie called ahead, "but ya got to git his attention first."

Although jolting blows to the head are frowned upon, teachers must get the attention of their protégés. Surveys of beginning teachers indicate that motivation is one of their greatest concerns. Experienced teachers are likely to counsel that motivation is one of the spices, as well as challenges, of the profession. It is extremely rewarding to see the spark of enthusiasm in the eyes of children or to hear it in the hum of active involvement in classroom activity. After their words of reassurance, even experienced teachers will admit that obtaining the required level of motivation is difficult, at times.

There are at least four means the teacher can use to motivate children. He can make use of their interests, teachable moments, or discrepant situations. He can also set the needs and purposes for learning with his students.

a. Interests of the child—The child who is self-motivated can be the easiest child to teach *if* the teacher builds on this motivation to achieve his own purposes. Perhaps an example will help.

Steven was an extremely bright boy who loved biographies. In fact, it was difficult for the teacher or Steve's parents to get him to do anything except read biographies. As in many fifth grade classes, the major topic for the year was the study of the United States. Steve's teacher decided that the boy could learn as much about the United States through reading and reporting about the lives of some of its great men, as through the study of the social studies textbook. Steve and his teacher worked together developing a list of names of great men and identifying the era and place in which they lived. Several types of questions used to direct the young reader through selected books follow.

What was the contribution of this man to the United States?

What were the special conditions of the period in which he lived?

How was life different from the way you live?

In your opinion, what were the important times in his life?

These questions were changed from time to time to fit the person about whom the report was being made. This was accomplished through pupil-teacher planning. The important element in this example is that the teacher used the natural interests of the child to achieve his purposes.

Previously, Steven had been a behavior problem because he refused to conform to the teacher's direction. Other teachers had fought this strong will and had lost the battle. As teachers, we must remember, it is our goal to develop self-directing children, not to subdue them.

b. Teachable moments—Teachers, like comedians, must develop a great sense of timing. Sometimes it is more profitable to teach something that is not in the lesson plan, than to proceed with a lesson that has the children moaning and groaning. Tragic, delightful, ecstatic, debilitating, mundane days happen in classrooms all the time. The tragic day, perhaps when a student in the school has a serious accident with his bicycle, may offer the opportune time to discuss the importance of rules, laws, caution, and the avoidance of extremes. The delight filled day, after the class returns from presenting a play to the parents, may be the time to "enjoy" because it aids in the development of class unity. The ecstatic day, with vacation around the corner and an egg hunt planned for the afternoon, may be the best time to stay on the planned unit to prevent the roof from coming off the building! The point is simply this, if it's a good day to teach ________, then hang the lesson plan; teach what can be most effectively taught at that time.

c. Discrepant events—The use of discrepant events is taken from the work of Suchman (95–100), a psychologist who has developed a strategy for teaching inquiry procedures to upper grade elementary children. His strategy differs from Taba's approach in that the teacher's role is changed. Suchman's Inquiry Development Program places the teacher in the role of question answerer. After viewing a discrepant event on film, the children ask questions to which the teacher responds, "Yes" or "No."

In a recent tour to a local museum, a fourth grade class spotted a mental arrowhead among the relics found in an Indian burial display. The children's curiosity was immediately aroused. Inquiry led them to request the museum curator to visit their classroom as a resource person. In the process of questioning and discussion, they found that white traders had traveled in that region long before settlement. The traders had bartered a few of these precious arrowheads for desired pelts.

The importance of the discrepant event to motivation is that something happens which seems contrary to what the student would normally expect. This helps to trigger interest and arouses curiosity.

d. Establishing needs and purposes—One of the most commonly used methods of building motivation involves establishing needs and purposes with the children. This is a technique which every salesman is taught—create a need which previously did not exist. Witness the TV set which blares that unless we use a certain mouthwash, we shall be doomed to a lonely, loveless existence. The teacher, at times, sells his "wares" as he cleverly sets the stage so that students feel the need for skills or information he is going to teach. Then the purposes for the lesson can be established with students.

Two teachers collaborated to create a need for reporting. The teachers and their respective students developed an interclass competition to propose solutions to the environmental crises brought about by present means of transportation. It was determined that the class which presented the most feasible solution, as judged by two respected teachers and the principal, would be given a field trip to the National Museum of Transportation near St. Louis. To this point, nothing had been mentioned about reports, although the teachers obviously had this activity in mind. How do you convince an intermediate grade child that he needs to learn to prepare a report? The simplest way is to have him convince you.

After the competition was arranged, the teachers and the children formulated a plan so that they could present the best possible solution. The discussion went something like this.

The teacher asked, "How shall we begin?

"We need to find out as much as we can about pollution caused by transportation," a child responded.

"How can we do that?" the teacher queried. After a short discussion, the children decided to divide the labor among appointed groups.

"How are we going to share our information?" the teacher questioned. In the ensuing discussion, the children decided that each group would need to make a report from which the final presentation would be prepared. The teacher probed, "Do you know how to prepare a report?" There were several negative nods:

"What kinds of difficulties have you had?" the teacher queried.

"I never know what to write down," a conscientious little girl replied.

"Lots of times I can't find any information," another child offered.

"After I get my notes, I can never seem to get them together right," a boy complained. "Mother says I copy down too much information."

"Are there ways to solve some of these problems?" the teacher asked, as comments began to ebb.

The teacher beguiled the group into a natural opening for teaching main ideas, short summaries, and outlining, as well as the terminal objective of reporting.

Consumers will not buy things they feel they don't need. Good salesmen spend a great amount of time developing these needs. As teachers, we must spend some time creating in the student a feeling of need for our products, if they are to be motivated to learn.

If the need cannot be created, discuss your purpose for entering the teaching sequence you have selected. You can prepare yourself for this discussion by attempting to answer the question: Why does this child or these children need this lesson? If you can't honestly justify the teaching of it, forget it.

2. Model of mastery. It is important for the student to have some idea of what he is attempting to achieve. Perhaps this becomes more evident in the area of physical skills: throwing a ball, jumping a hurdle, or flying an airplane. Let's use the latter example.

After the flight instructor has given you a few lessons in the basic maneuvers, such as turning the airplane, stalling it, and flying it at low speeds, he begins to teach you to land the aircraft. He approaches the airfield's pattern and says, "Now, place your hands and feet on the controls, and I'll show you how to land."

Together, you approach the landing strip as the instructor points out various speeds, approach altitudes, the pitch, and controls of the aircraft. You continue the descent and find that the aircraft is more difficult to handle. The instructor continues in control, but you are feeling the reactions of the craft as you near the ground. Just before contact, the instructor gently pulls back on the wheel and explains that this maneuver further decreases the speed of the aircraft so that it settles to the ground gently. The aircraft touches to earth smoothly and continues straight down the runway.

The instructor says, "It's yours." You push in the throttle slowly as you have been taught; you feel the surge of power and notice the slight sway of the aircraft as less inept hands take control.

The instructor has provided you with a model of mastery. Now you know how the aircraft is landed. It will take many landings before you are able to do as well, but you have been shown how it is done. Children need such models, too. As students, you have felt the panic when an instructor at the piano, on the archery range, the golf couse, or in the swimming pool has said, "Now you do it." Your mind races to remember how to perform the demonstrated task.

Let's examine a few types of models that we can provide for children in social studies. The most common models used are informational, skill, and attitudinal. Let's consider the differences among these three types. When a model is used to direct the child in the retrieval or use of specific information, it is conceived as being an informational model. If the child is able to use the model for general purposes, then it is a skill model; it is a generalized tool. Attitudinal models demonstrate how people who hold certain attitudes behave in selected situations.

a. Informational models—Models aren't as difficult to create as one might expect. You have many in mind that you use without thinking. Perhaps the most common one will be recalled when we ask this question: What kinds of information are included in a newspaper article? The answer was taught to most of us in the upper elementary grades—who, what, when, where, why, and how.

Outlines are informational models also. Many teachers provide outlines for children when they ask them to prepare reports.

b. Skill models—Using the above working definitions, the outlining models often seen in intermediate classrooms on charts similar to the one shown below are skill models.

I. The first main idea
    A. The first subtopic
    B. The second subtopic

II. The second main idea
    A. The first subtopic under the second main idea
    B. The second main topic under the second main idea

Another skill model which is common to many classrooms is the proofreading model or checklist. Teachers who use this device focus the children's attention upon this model before papers are handed in. Letter writing models which illustrate the heading, salutation, body, closing, and signature are another type of the many skill models used today.

c. Attitudinal models—You will recall that the purpose of the model of mastery is to give the student some idea of what is expected of him. Although it may be difficult to perceive the presentation of an attitudinal model, you may recall that we discussed having children observe a group working together cooperatively. Actually, what we are doing is supplying an attitudinal model which the children can observe.

Another type of attitudinal model which the authors have not illustrated to this point is the model of alternative behaviors. This model is the product of answering the question: How would a person behave who believed __________? There is no reason to assume that all such models would be prepared by the teacher. Children can plan and demonstrate these models themselves. Such models can provide excellent problem-solving devices in the area of values.

3. Providing for active responding. In order to explain what we mean by active responding, let's return to the airfield where you had just given the aircraft power for another takeoff. You will recall that during the last approach, the instructor had control of the aircraft. He was giving you a model you could follow to make a landing. The plane is yours this time around, but the instructor will be helping you.

You climb the aircraft to the approach altitude. You've done *this* since your first day of instruction. Your instructor says, "All right, we are going to land again. What is the first thing you must do?"

Your mind races through the seemingly endless amount of detail you have learned and retrieves the answer, "I must slow the aircraft."

"Right," is the immediate response. As you continue your approach, the instructor provides you information he feels you need. "You're a little high. You need less power. Relax. All you need is the right speed, and the aircraft will land itself."

You really can't believe him at this point, but because you don't know what else to do, you continue the approach. Just as you are about to reach the ground, you pull a little too hard on the wheel, and you make three landings on that first approach—kabump, kabump, kabump.

"That's not bad for the first time!" your instructor encourages.

During this sequence of instruction, the instructor was doing several things. First, let's focus on the fact that you were actively responding. The instructor asked what you needed to do first. You responded to this question and performed the act. In fact, you were actively involved on the first landing when the instructor asked you to follow him through with your hands and feet on the controls. Active responding is not necessarily physical. Much of our active response in learning is mental. Identifying the themes in a musical selection you enjoy is one example of active cognitive response. Children can make active mental responses while the teacher addresses questions to the class or to other children. This is often evident in class discussions when you see children "mouth" answers to questions their classmates are attempting to answer.

As teachers, we must plan for the active response of children. After we provide them a model of mastery, we may break down the teaching sequence into steps in order to encourage response on the part of the student. The lesson on outlining is an example. After you have shown students that an outline is a model of mastery, you ask them to identify the first main idea in the material you are using for the lesson.

"What is the first main idea?" you ask after the children have had a chance to study the material. "Can you tell us, Gilberto?"

"I think it is in the second paragraph," the boy replies.

"Does anyone else have a suggestion?" you continue.

The children agree, finally, with Gilberto, and you go to the second main idea. You use the same procedure of allowing the children to identify it and discuss differences of opinion. In this way, there is active involvement both physical and mental. During the discussion, you walk around the room checking the written responses of individuals. This technique helps you individualize instruction more effectively. The product of this active responding is that the child has some knowledge of his results in the learning of information, skills, and attitudes.

4. Providing for knowledge of results. Knowledge of results enables the child to compare his understanding of the learning sequence against a model. Again, in our flying example, the instructor pilot might tell you, "The aircraft bounced because you pulled the wheel back too quickly. Next time ease the wheel back slowly." You had knowledge of results when the aircraft bounced. The children had knowledge of results in outlining when Gilberto suggested a main idea, and they compared their selection with his.

5. Guidance. The reason for providing knowledge of results is to guide the student toward achieving the established objective. With knowledge of results, the student is able to continue progress toward his goal with the guidance of the teacher. There are segments in the guidance process that may not be readily apparent. First, the teacher must be able to diagnose the student's difficulty. Second, he must be able to identify some means of correcting the pupil's error, and third, he will supply additional information as he feels the student can handle it.

In our flying example, in the go around when the instructor asked you to land the aircraft, he was observing your approach and analyzing the situation in exactly the same way you must do on all approaches to landings. You must carefully control your speed and altitude. The instructor pilot was giving guidance to aid you in your approach. He was providing you with a feel you had not yet developed. You will notice that the instructor did not provide you with too much information. He gave you only what he thought you could use. Although the instructor did not attempt to correct all of your errors, he was going through a diagnosis process. The result of this process is the next lesson.

This lesson starts on the ground. After a careful preflight inspection, you both enter the aircraft. The instructor begins, "You will recall when we were approaching the landing yesterday you had trouble because you were too high. Remember this simple rule, altitude is controlled by the throttle; speed is controlled by pitch, the attitude of the nose. If you are too high, pull back the power. If you are too low, add some power."

In providing you this information, the instructor carefully deals with the problem you encountered yesterday. Note, although he provided you with another principle, the speed of the aircraft, he did not dwell on this. He was afraid of giving you too much information; information you may not need. This confuses any learner. You will also note that he said nothing more about the bouncy finish to yesterday's lesson. He'll deal with that in time. The most important part in the act of landing is the approach. When the student has that mastered, the touchdown will come along better. The important instructional principle here is to give the student *only* the information he needs to complete the task or problem he has encountered. The guidance you provide is the instruction the child needs at that point.

Let's apply what we have learned to a school situation: teaching children to identify topic sentences. The teaching sequence you have developed includes these steps: (1) an overview, (2) topic sentences at the beginning of the paragraph, (3) topic sentences at the end of the paragraph, (4) topic sentences in the middle of the paragraph, and (5) introductory paragraphs without topic sentences. This last step is needed because materials for children are often written with introductory paragraphs intended to motivate the reader.

The procedure you use to accomplish this teaching sequence is to begin with an explanation of topic sentences. You work with the children in identifying topic sentences located in one of these positions at a time. The teaching sequence is spelled out in detail below to illustrate the process. Although teachers will agree with the procedure listed below, few would ever produce such a listing for classroom use. The important element contained in Table 6–1 is the breaking down of a skill into its component parts. Every teacher is involved in this act in his attempts to diagnose the problems encountered by his students. Such an analysis is required to correct learning difficulties experienced at some point by every child.

Table 6–1

Teaching Sequence for Identifying Topic Sentences

Series 1:	Overview—Importance of topic sentences
Series 2:	Topic sentences in initial position—model
	Experiences in identifying topic sentences—initial position
	Check mastery level
	Guidance
	Check mastery level
Series 3:	Topic sentences in final position—model
	Experiences—final position
	Check mastery level
	Guidance
	Check mastery level
Series 4:	Topic sentences in medial position—model
	Experiences—medial position
	Check mastery level
	Guidance
	Check mastery level
Series 5:	Topic sentences in random position—model
	Experiences—random position
	Check mastery level
	Guidance
	Check mastery level
Series 6:	Paragraphs without topic sentences—model
	Experiences
	Check mastery level

You will note that the first step in each lesson series listed in Table 6–1 is the provision of a model of mastery. After this model has been presented, you give the student experiences which enable him to actively respond to problem situations. These experiences should be constructed so that children know as quickly as possible, how well they are achieving. In certain instances, because of past experiences, some children will master the series on their first attempt. Such children are ready for the next series of lessons.

Others in the group will require more guidance. Perhaps, using the second series of lessons as an example, the children select the very first sentence in a paragraph. Such children have a misunderstanding. You point out to them that they must look at the paragraph as a whole and identify the sentence that tells what the paragraph is about. Although the first sentence is most often the topic sentence, the second sentence may possibly be the topic sentence. You remind such students that you are attempting to show them that the topic sentence *most often* appears in the beginning part of the paragraph. At this point, you present another set of exercises to this group of children. Again, some of this smaller group will attain mastery. Others will require additional experiences.

Two inductive methods Inductive methods are sequences which begin with examples of experiences from which the learner forms conclusions or generalizations. As you will recall, in the deductive sequence, the student begins with the general and moves to the specific. Inductive methods take the student from the specific to the general. The two inductive methods we will discuss here are guided discovery and group inquiry.

1. Guided discovery. The guided discovery technique is inductive in nature. It has as its purpose the teaching of a concept, generalization, or construct to help children develop a basic understanding. The steps in this teaching sequence are as follows:

a. Select the concept, generalization, or construct you want the children to learn.

b. Flood the children with examples of this concept, generalization, or construct.

c. Guide the children to "discover" the understanding you have selected.

d. Guide the children in testing the concept, generalization, or construct.

e. Help them revise if necessary.

Perhaps a look at an example of this strategy will help you understand how it may be used.

In a school district in the Southwestern United States, the social studies curriculum guide suggested that the third grade should focus upon the basic needs of man for food, clothing, and shelter. The children had already done some work in the area of shelter. For the following lesson, Miss Schwartz, the teacher, had selected this concept as the focus of her students' learning—people solve their need for shelter in many ways. In making this selection, she had completed the first step in the teaching sequence.

Next, she prepared and assembled learning aids which would show many different types of shelter used by people all over the world. At the beginning of the lesson, the teacher asked her group, "What kind of shelter does your family have?" Most of the children responded that they lived in houses made for a single family. Then she queried, "What other kinds of homes are there?" After some discussion, the children decided that the single family dwelling was one kind of home (shelter) for people. But, as a few of the children insisted, apartments or apartment houses are homes for people, too. One child added that she lived in a duplex, where two families make their homes. A couple of the children said that trailers or mobile homes provide shelter for many families, too.

Thus, through a discussion of examples near at hand, the children were beginning to grasp the concept which the teacher had chosen. Miss Schwartz ended this lesson with an art experience in which each child drew a picture of the home in which he lived. The children helped the teacher arrange their drawings on one side of the bulletin board under this caption: How Our Families Meet the Need for Shelter. Miss Schwartz, however, wanted to extend the children's understanding, so she planned a follow-up lesson.

The next day, the teacher turned the discussion from the immediate environment to a discussion of a nearby Indian reservation. The children talked about the hogans, made of earth and branches and covered with mud or sod, which provide shelter for the Navajo families living on the reservation. Miss Schwartz called their attention to a film the class had seen earlier in the year. They recalled the igloos which were "home"

Primary children exploring the ways people meet their need for shelter.

for early Eskimo families. The teacher then brought out her picture collection which showed examples of many different types of homes used by people around the world. At the end of the discussion, the children were ready to form their conclusion which was a statement similar to the one which the teacher had set out to have the children "discover." They concluded that people solve their need for shelter in many ways.

At the end of this lesson, the children drew pictures of the many different types of homes found across the world and placed them on the other side of the bulletin board under the caption: How Families in Other Parts of the World Meet the Need for Shelter.

The teaching sequence was not complete, however. The following day's lesson was planned to guide the children in testing the generalization about shelter. Miss Schwartz initiated the lesson by saying, "Yesterday, boys and girls, we decided that people meet their need for shelter in many different ways. But do you suppose that this was true back in primitive times—the days of the cave man?" The children were uncertain. So, they went to their reference materials and found out that even primitive man met his needs for shelter in different ways. In fact, how he met this need appeared to be related to the topography and climate of the area in which he dwelled. They decided that this would be a good topic for further study at a later time.

Since no revision of this generalization seemed necessary, the teacher concluded this learning sequence and went on to a related topic the next day.

The preceding example should provide some insight into the "guided discovery" strategy. Depending upon the complexity of the concept, generalization, or construct, the length of time needed for the completion of the sequence may be as short as one class period, or it may extend over many days. Some lessons may require a great deal of mediated experiences. In the lesson above, however, the teacher used the experiences of the children and a set of pictures which she had collected. In guiding the children to "discover" or formulate the conclusion, the teacher will rely on asking questions of the children. These questions will aim at helping students think critically, reason, and make discriminations. These are skills which children must have if they are to acquire a stock of concepts and generalizations through which they may filter their world. Not all of our teaching lends itself to the use of this strategy, however. Another useful inductive strategy will be explained below.

2. Group Inquiry. The group inquiry strategy is a problem-solving model. This teaching sequence is used most appropriately when there is a problem situation in the classroom arising out of either natural conditions or conditions set or contrived by the teacher. The steps in this sequence are the following:

a. Focus on a problem to be examined.

b. Formulate a plan of action for attacking the problem.

c. Gather data.

d. Analyze data.

e. Synthesize data.

f. Formulate conclusions and recommendations.

g. Evaluate these conclusions and recommendations.

This sequence is basically a group strategy. However, it can be used for individual inquiry as well. The following example may help you understand how this sequence might work.

> The scene is a middle-sized city in the South. A fifth grade class has made a science study trip to the nearby park. The children are students in a school located in an economically depressed area of the city. It is difficult to get them interested in school. Let's see what happened.
>
> The science study trip to the park was quite a learning experience for these students but not in the way that the teacher Mrs. Whyte had planned. The first inkling of what was to come greeted the lively group as they entered the park, it was the stench of death. There was a stillness all about them that captured their immediate attention and quieted the most boisterous of the group. Instead of a park filled with creatures of many kinds which they had expected to observe, they found a nightmare. There were dead birds around the trees and dead fish floating in what not too long ago had been a lovely pond. Litter and debris were in evidence everywhere. Hardly a scenic spot for the picnic they had planned to have later in the morning. Mrs. Whyte had not been to the park in quite some time. She, too, was shocked by what she saw, as well as depressed. Flora, as well as fauna, presented the group with a dismal sight. Some of the children decided to take samples of the stagnant water back to class with them. Quickly, they recorded their science observations and chose to return to school to eat lunch there. No one felt like eating anyway. At this point, the teacher was unaware that her next social studies unit was on the brink of its conception.
>
> That afternoon during social studies, the children couldn't keep their attention on the textbook lesson Mrs. Whyte was presenting. All they wanted to talk about was the pollution they had seen in the park. At once it struck the teacher that here was a "teachable moment" at hand, a situation of such vital concern to the children that it could be tapped profitably and turned into worthwhile inquiry. She asked the children to put away their books and encouraged them

to discuss what they had seen that morning in the park. By guiding their discussion, Mrs. Whyte helped them develop a two-faceted problem which they wanted to study. The children formulated two questions: What is causing the pollution in the park? What action can be taken by citizens to clean up the city's parks and prevent further pollution? Step one in this teaching sequence had been completed.

Perhaps it should be noted here that this teaching strategy requires a longer period of time. It is more suitable for unit teaching. Many blocks of time will be needed in order to accomplish the activities involved in this inquiry model.

On the following two days, the children, with the help of their teacher, formulated a plan of action for attacking the problem. They determined the kinds of information that would be required, trips that could be useful, committees which they would need, and the like. Mrs. Whyte was amazed at the intrinsic motivation involved in these preliminary activities. Previously, she had had a most difficult time getting this group of children interested in anything which had to do with social studies. Now her problem was prying them away to move on to other things during the day!

Approximately a week was spent on the data gathering and recording activities. Several days were needed to analyze the data which they had gathered from many sources both within and outside of the school. The teacher helped the children eliminate the extraneous and organize the pertinent information. The class decided upon the most effective means for each group to share data with the others. It took two class periods for the children to synthesize the material they had gathered. On the following day, the teacher guided the discussion as the children formulated their conclusions and made some tentative recommendations. It was obvious to the teacher that some of their recommendations were not very practical, but she accepted all responses at this time. Later, each conclusion and recommendation would be examined in greater detail. She would help them weed out recommendations that might not be economically feasible or practical for one reason or another.

The interest of the children was high throughout the entire teaching sequence. In fact, this inquiry led to some related problems which the children wanted to study. They wanted to know the answers to these questions: What are the methods commonly used for purifying water? What can be done to encourage people to deposit litter in trash containers? What are the fines for littering? What action can students take to help the city clean up its parks? What began as a "ruined" field trip turned into a set of valuable learning experiences for these children.

Perhaps it should be noted here that this strategy is not dependent upon a pressing need for inquiry based upon certain natural conditions which make their appearance. The teacher can set the conditions in the classroom in such a way that a problem or need will arise.

Sometimes it is difficult for children to trim the problem to manageable size so that they can make a thorough inquiry. This is somewhat similar to the dilemma that the college student faces in attempting to settle upon a topic for a term paper. Once the topic has been selected, it seems as if the task is half-completed! If the problem or topic is too broad, the ensuing inquiry will be of unmanageable size and the resulting data gathering, analyzing, and synthesizing experiences will result in frustration and failure for students.

If the children are not skilled in group work or if they lack the necessary study skills, additional guidance from the teacher will be essential.

The group inquiry model is adaptable to any curriculum area in which there are problems to be solved. It is a particularly valuable strategy for social studies because of the nature of the content involved, and the practice it provides in utilizing study skills and thinking skills, as well as group processes.

We have examined a deductive strategy and two inductive strategies. It is important to note that there are significant similarities in actions the teacher must take. For example, motivation is vital in every effective teaching sequence. Students must, also, have knowledge of results in such sequences if learning is to take place. The importance of this presentation is not the order in which it is given, but the elements included in the presentation.

Selecting a role.

The teacher's involvement in the learning arena depends primarily upon the objective he is attempting to achieve. Illustrated below is one way of viewing the interrelated components we are discussing.

Behavioral Objective
↓
MMI + TA + SA ⟶ Teaching Strategy

By analyzing his objective, the teacher identifies the means of mediating instruction required, the type of teacher involvement needed, and the type of student involvement which will allow the fulfillment of the objective. Out of these selections, the teaching strategy develops. Given the means of mediating instruction, let's examine a few types of involvement which the teacher might consider. We will attempt to move from a role of least teacher involvement to one of greatest involvement.

Observer In some situations, the teacher takes the part of the observer.

This type of involvement requires the most constraint of all. A principal was overheard telling a supervisor as they were observing a fifth grade class in the process of role playing, "The teacher isn't doing much in this lesson."

"Oh yes, she is," the supervisor replied. "She is keeping her mouth shut!" This is especially vital when children are exploring in the realm of values. Students will not reveal their feelings if they are going to be criticized by the teacher. It is difficult enough for them to explore their feelings in front of their peers. The role of the observer is one of observation; it's that simple.

Traditionally, children expect teachers to play the dominant role in every lesson. How many teachers have you had who could observe without interfering? Students will not expect you to stay out of the interaction the first few times you assume this role. You must develop their confidence in you. You can begin by creating situations which call for role playing. The first few times, discussion or participation may be restrained. As children become accustomed to your role as observer, they will change their expectations of what teachers should do.

Facilitatior The role of the facilitator calls for a little more active participation. Observation is a part of this role, too, but the primary reason for observation in this case is to help groups or individuals find a solution to a problem.

Let us assume you are walking into a classroom where the teacher is acting as facilitator. You notice the hum of activity. The teacher sees you and recognizes that you are the visitor to whom she was introduced earlier. She goes on about her business. One small group of children working with a film is having difficulty focusing a projector. The teacher starts in their direction. She is stopped en route by a child who needs posterboard. Mrs. Hitt, the teacher, reminds the child where to find such supplies. As she nears the group with the projector problem, they focus the film properly. They smile sheepishly. Mrs. Hitt smiles back; she passes on to a small group working on the floor.

This group is building a model of a steamship. A couple of the boys have made a smokestack that hasn't met the approval of the girls in the group. Mrs. Hitt asks, "Do you girls know a better way to make the smokestacks?"

"No." The young ladies readily admit.

"A paper towel roll would work," a husky little fellow responds.

"There are a couple in the back cabinet," the teachers offers. She moves to where you are seated.

Mrs. Hitt's work seems, perhaps, unorganized, but she is prepared to probe, suggest, run errands, or propose additional resources. Her role is one of facilitating the work of the groups during this part of the lesson.

Guide The teacher assumes the role of guide when he directs children's thinking through the use of questions. Such queries can be informal kinds of questions or written questions which the children answer. A guide is someone who helps you through the unknown. It is a more structured role than that of facilitator. In most cases, the student lacks a structured set of procedures which he can use independently.

Perhaps the most common example of this role can be seen as the teacher directs a class discussion about transportation. This second grade class is studying ways in which products are brought into their community. Things seem to be going well until Johnny starts talking about the number of wheels he saw on a big truck.

The teacher asks, "Johnny, are you saying that trucks bring things to our town?"

"Yeah! I see trucks at the grocery store near my house all the time," Johnny adds enthusiastically.

Without criticizing Johnny's irrelevant point, the teacher directs the discussion back to the matter at hand. The teacher has prepared a set of questions which he can use to initiate and channel the discussion. Perhaps the teacher's set of questions might look like this.

(1) What are some ways in which things are brought to our city?

(2) Why are things brought in these ways?

(3) What are the fastest means of transportation?

(4) Why would some products be sent in this way?

(5) What are some products that would be sent by slower means of transportation?

In this role the teacher has a preplanned purpose for the discussion. He works toward this goal and plays a more dominant role in the lesson.

Demonstrator Just before recess, Mrs. Byrd, a third grade teacher, told the children that they could expect a special visitor when they returned. She scurried to the teacher's lounge where she had secretly hidden trappings borrowed from a local historical society. Donning the garb, she transformed herself into pioneer woman of about 1880. She crammed her feet into the high buttoned shoes, put on her bonnet, picked up a few kitchen utensils, and strode back to the classroom in time to meet her shocked class.

Mrs. Byrd introduced herself as a pioneer woman who had come to tell the children of her life on the prairie. As her class asked questions, she told them about her garb and demonstrated the use of several of the utensils she had brought to show them. Also, she showed them how she spun yarn from the cotton fiber which she grew.

In this case, the focus of the lesson was on the teacher. She played the dominant role. Although this lesson called for interaction with students, nevertheless she played a more active part than in the previous examples.

Coordinator As coordinator, the teacher is attempting to merge the efforts of several groups involved in differing activities. One teacher designed a unit focusing on the life style of primitive man for a fifth grade class of children with a wide range of reading abilities. The work sessions had covered approximately a week. Five groups had been encouraged in the following activities:

> Group I had been constructing a time line using simple materials written by the teacher. These children were reading below grade level and were unable to use materials written for the fifth grade.
>
> Group II had been preparing reports and drawing illustrations of the types of tools used by primitive man in Europe and Asia.
>
> Group III, utilizing advanced reference materials, had prepared a pamphlet illustrating tools of contemporary primitives.
>
> Group IV had constructed a primitive village showing forms of specialization among Masai peoples of Africa.
>
> Group V had written a skit about an imaginary visit of primitive man to our modern culture, comparing life styles of his culture with ours.

In the role of coordinator, the teacher helped the children to see relationships among the endeavors of all the groups. The focus of activity was on the teacher. The children were dependent upon him (the teacher) putting the pieces together to form the whole, the structure from which the teacher had originally designed the unit.

Lecturer The lecture is extremely useful in providing knowledge input to children when time is the critical factor or when children lack procedural models which enable them to get information independently. For example, it is pointless to have children "discover" how to make reports. There are several established procedures for such efforts. The lecture method can be used to provide children with this procedure in an efficient and effective manner.

A slight modification of an old model for the lecture can be utilized as a guide: Tell them what you are going to tell them. Tell them, and then, tell them what you have told them. We would suggest this model:

1. Provide an overview (What you are going to tell them).
2. Present a segment of the information (Tell them).
3. Ask questions to check comprehension.
4. Summarize, allowing the children to check their own understanding, and solicit student responses. (Tell them what you told them.)
5. Correct misunderstandings.
6. Return to number two and present the next portion.

The lecturer role requires the greatest involvement on the part of the teacher. As such, it is at the opposite end of the continuum from the role of observer. It should be noted that the teacher plays many roles during the school day and even in one lesson. The important point is that the selected role should be compatible with the means of mediating instruction and the actions required of the students.

Objective

The reader will be able to:

Explain (2.0) the relationship between teacher involvement and student involvement in the learning arena.

The Identification of Student Actions

Student actions are the things that students do in the instructional setting which should result in the terminal behaviors. You will recall that the terminal behavior is stated in your behavioral objective. We have indicated that the behavioral objective is used in the selection of the planned activities for the unit or lesson. Let's return to Dale's cone illustrated in Figure 6–2 to describe student participation.

Looking at the right-hand side of the cone, you will note that the activities at the base of the cone require the greatest amount of motor involvement. In direct experiences, for example, the learner is totally involved with his body, as well as his intellect. This is also true for contrived and dramatic experiences. These experiences are essential for the less mature child, as well as the child with a meager experiential background.

Moving up the cone, we find less motor involvement on the part of the student but more complex cognitive skills. Listening and observing are contingent upon the sensory apparatus of the individual, as well as his ability to attend. The skills involved in listening will be discussed in Chapter X. Listening and observing require the child to gain meaning from auditory and visual stimuli.

At the apex of the cone, the student is required to unlock visual and verbal symbols. There is relatively little motor involvement compared with the base of the cone.

Perhaps one confusing point in the model should be clarified. The experiences in the cone appear to be arranged hierarchically from active to passive participation of the learner. This refers to *physical* involvement of the child only. In actuality, as the child is required to unlock symbols at the top of the cone, he must be an active participant in the learning situation. However, this activity is cognitive, rather than motor.

One example of this is the child who is so completely involved in finding the answer for a math problem that he "tunes out" the rest of the world and remains fastened to his seat oblivious to the fact that the rest of the class has already left for lunch.

The task of the teacher is to maintain active involvement in learning. Unless there is active involvement, there is no learning, at least in intended directions. It is naive to assume that all of the student actions in the instructional setting are preplanned by the teacher. There are the teachable moments which we discussed previously. We have unteachable ones, too—the child who becomes ill and requires our immediate attention. There is the clown who breaks up the class at the most inopportune time. Since these moments cannot be foreseen, we must attempt to meet each situation judiciously as it arises.

In considering student actions, we need to mention emotions with which the teacher must deal in the learning environment. Perhaps the most frustrating emotion for the teacher is learner anxiety. Anxious behavior can be identified in a class as children begin asking questions which have been answered previously. Individuals often complain that they don't know what you want them to do, although you have explained the assignment carefully and fully.

This behavior can be alleviated by involving the group or individual in the task itself.

Ask the child, "What do you think you are supposed to do?"

If he responds, "But I don't know."

Then ask, "What do you think your first step is?"

Often the child will answer this simple question. If he can't, possibly he doesn't know. If he answers the question, then ask him about the second step. At this point usually the youngster will decide he is able to go ahead on his own.

Summary

In this chapter, we have examined the actions of the participants in the learning arena, the fourth component of the MID. We have pointed out that there is an interactive process among the participants in the learning setting. After the reevaluation of his purposes and objectives and the result of pretesting, we saw that the teacher turns to selecting experiences. The Cone of Experience was presented as a model which can be used to select differing levels of experiences for children. The need for a variety of such experiences was established.

Two distinctly different teaching methods, the deductive and inductive, were explored. A sequence was given for one deductive method and two inductive methods. The teacher's role was seen as a variable one. It vacillates between active and passive involvement, according to the media selected and the student role intended.

References

Sowards, G. Wesley, and Mary-Margaret Scobey. *The Changing Curriculum and the Elementary Teacher.* 2nd edition. Belmont: Wadsworth Publishing Company, Inc., 1968.

Suchman, Richard J. "Inquiry Training." *Conceptual Models in Teacher Education.* Edited by John R. Verduin, Jr. Washington, D.C.: The American Association of Colleges for Teacher Education, 1967.

VII

Mediating Instruction in Social Studies: Doing, Observing, and Listening

Chapter Outline

Mediating Instruction in Social Studies: Doing, Observing, and Listening

In previous chapters, we have stated that the teacher may be considered one of the mediating devices in social studies education or the manager of them all. The purpose of mediating devices is to provide children with experiences which are real or vicarious. The question faced by the teacher is "What type of experience should I give my students?" This chapter will attempt to provide some guidelines which you as a teacher can use to select and utilize specific experiences.

In order to accomplish this task, we will discuss general procedures the teacher can employ in using all mediating devices. Then, we will discuss the characteristics of each of the devices, provide examples, point out advantages and limitations of each, and present specific procedures for their successful use.

Objective

The reader will be able to:

Identify (1.0) the major determinant for the selection of media.

Generalizations Concerning Methods

Perhaps the most common error committed by educators at all levels is asking themselves the question: "What am I going to do with my class this morning?" We often fail to find the right answer because we are asking the wrong question. This should be the question: "Why am I going to meet my class this morning?"

"To make the payments on my car isn't the right *answer* either!"

You'll recall in Chapter VI we discussed the model listed below. At that time, we indicated that the selection of media was dependent upon our objectives.

Behavioral Objective
↓
MMI + TA + SA ⟶ Teaching Strategy

We should determine what we want the student to do. When we have made this decision, it is much easier to identify what the teacher must do. Although the roles the teacher plays differ, generally, the actions followed are similar to those used in the deductive and inductive models discussed in Chapter VI. You'll recall that in the deductive model we do the following:

(1) Establish the purpose for attending to the activity.

(2) Provide a model if the students are to perform a precise task.

(3) Give the students an opportunity to respond actively.

(4) Allow a means for the student to gain some knowledge of his results.

(5) Guide individuals toward achievement of stated goals.

In the inductive model, we do thus:

(1) Focus the students attention upon the information or events to which you wish them to attend.

(2) Present several examples which contain the necessary elements of the concept, generalization, or construct, and focus children's attention on these elements.

(3) Guide the children to discover the concept, generalization, or construct.

(4) Allow the children to test this concept, generalization, or construct.

(5) Aid the children in revising if necessary.

Also, there are instances when we will select the media first. Perhaps you have only one choice of mediation in some situations. If this is true, the type of teacher actions you can select will be limited.

The two models above provide a general guide for employing media. Although these models will have to be adapted somewhat in specific situations, the teacher should attempt to follow these guides and revise them where it is necessary.

Objectives

The reader will be able to:

Identify (1.0) the advantages and disadvantages of direct experiences.

Suggest (3.0) an appropriate direct experience when given a topic in social studies.

Direct Experiences

Returning to Chapter III, we have an example of a direct experience in which an intermediate class engaged in the inquiry of social scientists. You will recall that the children examined an abandoned farm house to gather data on the needs of people and the ways these needs had changed. Their data-gathering was a productive and real experience.

Another example, taken from the primary grades is one in which children became engrossed in the process of making butter. They had been studying dairy products and were curious about how butter came from the cow. They saw little connection between yellow butter and white milk.

The alert teacher posed the question: If we had some cream, do you think we could change it into butter? The children were incredulous. Shortly, the teacher managed to obtain some whipping cream from a local dairy. She divided it into four quart jars and allowed each member in four groups to shake the contents. You can imagine the look of surprise on the young faces when yellow globs began appearing on the sides of the jar. The contents were combined, salted, and served on crackers to the wonder-struck youngsters. The impression which remained in the minds of the neophytes was one which would not be forgotten soon.

Here is a list of some real experiences that can be created for children.

candlemaking	preparing maps	various crafts
baking bread	constructions	sewing
making tools	making murals	making pottery
cooking	weaving	basketry
picking fruit	picking cotton	making dye

Such activities allow insights because they build a foundation of experiences upon which verbal learning can be based. Remember, most learning obtained in school comes through the verbal channel; unless there are meaningful concrete experiences to which the child can attach verbal labels, his learning is mere verbalization.

The first advantage of real experiences is that they allow several sensory inputs. The children are able to smell the baking bread, taste the salted butter, smell and hear the popcorn popping, or experience the frustration of breaking the tool they worked so hard making. Second, it is easier for them to recall such experiences and to form abstract generalizations because of the multiple inputs.

Third, real experiences are a boon for teachers working with students of low reading ability. Reading skills are not required to gather the information needed to establish a generalization. These direct experiences can accommodate students with widely differing communication skills and learning styles.

Although many teachers fail to see the significance of cohesive groups, our teaching task becomes more rewarding when we gain group unity. One means of promoting such unity is through creating common enjoyable experiences for children. This is the fourth reason for using real experiences in the classroom. It allows all of the children to play a part in learning. When all can take part, there are no outsiders.

We must also mention two disadvantages of direct experiences. The first of these is that the teacher cannot control the informational inputs as carefully in the area of real experiences as he can with other activities. There is the chick that dies shortly after being hatched, the dog that runs into the middle of the group breaking the class made transit just as a child is about to read the last elevation on the hill, or the bread that fails to rise. These are irrelevant bits of information which inhibit you from fulfilling your purposes. They distract the students from intended learnings and interfere with the impact of necessary information. The teacher may wish to capitalize on these situations, but this forces a change of purposes.

The second disadvantage of such experiences is that they require a great deal of preplanning on the part of the teacher. There may be a variety of materials to secure, equipment to gather, or the classroom to rearrange. Often school schedules make such planning difficult. There are special music, physical education, speech, and reading classes which children may miss. Professional and personal relations among the faculty usually allow cooperation, but such cooperation must be sought. All of these things take time from the busy day.

Objective

The reader will be able to:

Identify (1.0) the advantages and disadvantages of simulated experiences.

Simulated Experiences

Control of the learning environment can be obtained by bringing the important elements of the real experience into the classroom. Here the student's attention can be directed to essential elements. Confusing and irrelevant data can be eliminated. This process is called simulation because it provides an operating model of a physical or social situation (Nesbitt, 4). Perhaps the simulation with which you are most familiar is the game of Monopoly. This is an economic game which simulates the free enterprise system without government controls.

At the beginning of Chapter I, there is an example of a simulation game created by a teacher. Nesbitt (137–44) lists several commercial games which are available for the elementary schools. Selected ones are given below.

BUSHMAN EXPLORING AND GATHERING—Fifth grade

This two-phase board game is designed to teach the concept of cultural adaptation to a harsh environment. These are ways in which man deals with his environment. The game illustrates the subsistence economy of Bushmen in the Kalahari desert of Southwest Africa.

CARIBOU HUNTING—Fifth grade

This is a board game simulating some of the difficulties Eskimos experience in hunting caribou on Canada's Simpson Peninsula. Players represent the family of hunters and the forces of nature. The children learn the Eskimo's way of thinking about his world and the way he organizes his society.

SEAL HUNTING—Fifth grade

This is a board game simulating some Eskimo strategies and means of cooperation for securing seals. It demonstrates the role of chance in this activity.

The above games were developed by Education Development Center, 15 Miflin Place, Cambridge, Massachusetts 02138, as part of their fifth grade course, "Man: A Course of Study."

THE COLUMBIA RIVER GAME—Fourth and fifth grades

This game builds an understanding of the industries, agencies, and farming interests along the Columbia River as well as their relationships to each other and to the river. It is available from Teaching Research, A Division of the Oregon State System of Higher Education, Monmouth, Oregon 97361.

GITHAKA—Fourth grade

This is a game which introduces children to the settlement pattern of the Kikuyu tribe of East Africa. It is one of ten games developed by Abt Associates for EDCOM systems. This fourth grade program is available from EDCOM Systems, Inc., Witherspoon Street, Princeton, New Jersey 08540.

MARKET—Sixth grade

This game fosters an understanding of our economic system—the laws of supply and demand. The game was originally developed by the Industrial Relations Center, University of Chicago. It is now available from Benefic Press, 10300 W. Roosevelt Road, Westchester, Illinois 60153.

POLLUTION—Elementary

This games teaches students the technical and economic causes of pollution and the social, political, and economic problems involved in attempts to control pollution. The game can be obtained from Wellesley Schools Curriculum Center, Seawood Road, Wellesley, Massachusetts 02181.

There are several other advantages to simulation. First, as in the case of direct experiences, the level of abstraction is quite low. Although the actual concept the student is dealing with may be very abstract, he is directly involved in the activity.

One important finding of recent research on games indicates that these games must be discussed by the teacher and the players after play has been completed. Merely playing the game alone is not sufficient. Generalizations must be established and tested, possibly by further play if these generalizations are to be developed in the minds of participants. Basically, you are attempting to focus the thinking of the student upon elements of the game.

A second advantage of the simulated experience is that it does not usually require the student to have sophisticated communicative skills. In many cases, the child must read only simple directions. The importance of this is not apparent until you've sweated through most of the school year with a small boy or girl who has met with little success all year in spite of a great deal of expended effort. After spending several, unsuccessful days with the class studying the concept of specialization, you give the children a game. Before anyone else sees through it, the little redhead comes running up, almost shouting, "Mr. ______, that's specialization!"

As in the case of direct experiences, simulation requires the type of interaction that is conducive to class unity. Also, it allows a type of experimentation which cannot take place in the real environment. A third advantage is that games are *fun*. Children are naturally motivated to participate in such simulated experiences.

Perhaps the most disappointing feature of simulation is that the research of antagonists and protagonists fails to establish whether this method of mediating instruction is more or less effective than other means. Supporters are quick to refer to the amount of positive motivation generated during sessions of simulation. Since most commercial games are expensive, opponents ask whether a mere increase in motivation is sufficient to justify extensive use of this procedure. The expense is minimal when teachers design their own simulations, however. Many experts encourage teachers to develop their own.

The most important consideration in terms of the disadvantages of simulation is the question of their validity. How real is the model of the physical or social situation? This is an important question when it comes to training drivers and pilots. Sometimes, simulation screens out important elements like traffic, noise, and the need for considering others on the road or in the air. Are such questions applicable to *all* simulation? The answer seems to be yes. How real then should simulation be? The answer appears to be—as real as one can make it. Designers, including classroom teachers, should eliminate only those portions which are irrelevant to the basic process being studied.

Objectives

The reader will be able to:

Identify (1.0) the purposes for using dramatic techniques.

Suggest (1.0) the advantages and disadvantages of dramatic techniques.

Compare (4.0) the guidelines suggested by Means with the inductive and deductive models provided by the authors.

Dramatic Techniques

Dramatic techniques appear to come naturally to children. Walk around any playground during a free play period, and you are likely to see a little boy in a swing making the sound of an airplane. A group of little girls and, maybe, a boy or two will be playing house or school. There will be some kind of a ball game where you might find a Bart Starr, Lew Alcindor, or Johnny Bench. If the game is tag, there may even be a Frankenstein, not necessarily by consent!

The value of such activities has long been recognized by teachers and children's writers. Although we will explore many of the dramatic activities in Chapter X, we would like to discuss the characteristics of these activities in this chapter. Dramatic techniques can be used to transmit information, explore values, release feelings, stimulate student participation, and entertain. As with simulation, dramatic activities do not require prerequisite advanced skills in communication. Also, they allow individual participation in the group or classroom which facilitates unity. A high level of physical and mental involvement is required of participants to maintain the activity.

Unlike real experiences and simulated experiences, dramatic techniques may lose reality. In creative experiences this is beneficial. In others, children must be brought back to earth either by the group or as a last resort, by the teacher asking, "Do you really think that could happen?" Remember, however, you might have to agree once in a while that it could possibly happen.

There is a very wide range of dramatic activities from the least structured, such as dramatic play, to the most structured, dramatizations. For this reason, it is difficult to develop a set of general procedures which would be applicable to all dramatic techniques. Means (28) has presented some guidelines for the use of dramatizations which might prove helpful in implementing this technique.

> Plan the dramatization so that it progresses logically and smoothly for the period of time designated.
>
> Tie the content or subject matter into other work under study and to problems of real-life value.
>
> Actively involve as many participants as possible in different dramatizations which might be developed over a period of time.
>
> Create an active interest on the part of the observers as well as the participants.
>
> Avoid busy-work type activities, such as the construction of elaborate scenery or costumes, unless they can be justified as meaningful educational experiences.

The greatest disadvantage of some dramatic techniques is that the amount of motivation can cause children to get out of hand unless the teacher plans well. The reason for confusion may be that the students do not understand why they are participating in the activity, or perhaps they are not well enough acquainted with the technique to use it successfully.

Since examples of the various types of dramatic activities are offered in Chapter X, it would be more appropriate to present suggested ways to use such activities here. These are listed below.

exploring value choices	sharing information
learning social skills	reporting to parents
examining alternative behaviors	recreation
	observation of behavior

Demonstrations

The demonstration combines an oral explanation with the handling or operating of materials or equipment. This technique is particularly useful in those situations where materials are small and relatively valuable; in situations in which there are too few materials for the entire class; or when items are too dangerous for the class to handle at that point in their training. The fourth purpose for selecting this technique is that you can control the amount of information and the pacing of the presentation so that it can be absorbed by the students.

A major disadvantage of this technique is that it limits student involvement to a degree that they often lose interest. Because of this, the teacher must prepare the demonstration very carefully. Basically, the deductive model must be followed. Since this is a difficult technique, let's adapt our previous model to fit the demonstration. We will have to add a couple of steps at the beginning.

(1) Specify your objectives for the activity.

(2) Have the materials you need laid out in the sequence in which you plan to make the presentation. It's a good idea to practice the presentation. Make sure all the class can see important parts. If they can't, make an illustration on the board or on a poster.

(3) Set purposes for the presentation with the students.

(4) If you expect them to do something after the demonstration, provide a model.

(5) Give the students opportunities to respond. Asking individual students questions is not sufficient to guarantee the attention of the entire class. You may want to prepare response sheets for the group.

(6) Check the responses of students to questions on point *one* before continuing to point *two*.

(7) Provide individual guidance as much as possible. Pick up stragglers later if some are lagging behind the rest of the group. Moving too slowly causes the loss of interest.

(8) Retest the entire group for comprehension. Individualize to meet the needs of the students if your objectives require mastery.

Let's look at an example of a well planned demonstration. One teacher initiated a social studies-science unit in her third grade classroom. She had selected a field trip to continue development of elementary map skills. In preparation for the trip, she presented the demonstration below. Her objectives were stated as follows:

(1) Looking at a simple compass card, the student will be able to identify the four cardinal directions.

(2) Looking at a compass needle, the student will be able to read each of the indicated cardinal directions.

(3) When asked, each student will be able to explain why he must make sure that there are no metal objects nearby when taking a compass reading.

Before the children came into the room, Miss Allen had brought in an opaque projector and set up a screen. Turning around, she bent down beside the projector and plugged it into an outlet. Then, she pushed the projector far enough from the screen and set the focus for her demonstration as the morning bell rang. Walking to her desk, she picked up some dittoed papers and asked the first child who came in the door to pass them out. After completing a few routine items, she began.

"Boys and girls, I would like for you to list on the top four lines of your papers the compass directions we have studied." As the children started to work she began walking from seat to seat checking the children's papers as she went. What was she doing? Naturally, she was taking a pretest to determine whether the children knew this fact. This is a prerequisite task, isn't it? If the children don't know what the directions are, they can't very well identify them! Finding that two of the children didn't know these facts, she sent them to a tape recorder on which she had recorded a programmed lesson she had adapted from a children's publication. She continued with the rest of the children.

"This morning we are going to learn to read a compass." She picked up a brass, watch-like object, opened the lamp door and set it on the projection stage of the opaque projector where the entire class was able to see the object enlarged on the screen. "By the time we are finished this morning, most of you will be able to show me North, South, East, and West on a compass. You will all be able to find these directions for yourself from compass readings."

Miss Allen used the pointer in the machine to indicate the cardinal directions marked on the compass card. "I'd like you to mark these directions on the compass I've drawn on your papers. Would you do that for me, please?" Again, the teacher moved around the room checking papers as she went.

One of the two children working at the recorder had finished. She briefly checked his paper and asked him to begin the same task the other children were now doing.

Assured that she could continue, Miss Allen proceeded. "That's very good! Reading the compass simply means that we say or write down what the compass shows us with its needle." By this time, the teacher had moved to the projector pointer.

"Notice, boys and girls, that this needle is made like an arrow."

A few of the class answered aloud, "Yes."

"In order to read the compass correctly, we must place North under the head of the arrow." The teacher reached in the projector and turned the body of the compass to align the needle and the North marking on the compass card. "Now the arrow is pointing North."

"But that's North," little black haired Bobby stated, as he pointed a determined finger toward an opposing direction.

"That is North, Bobby," Miss Allen smiled. "I'm making my compass read incorrectly by placing it in this metal projector. Watch what happens when I place this metal weight in the projector, too." As the needle swung, the teacher focused the attention of the students to the new compass reading. "Which way does our compass say North is now? Please draw a needle on the second compass on your papers. Be sure to draw it in the same direction as the one on the screen. Since you can not turn the compasses on your papers, draw the four directions as they appear when I turn my compass to the proper directions." Again, she walked around the room correcting mistakes as she proceeded.

"Who can tell us why this metal weight and this projector make my compass read incorrectly?"

"Because they are metal," Jimmy replied.

"That's partly true," the teacher encouraged. "Is that the only reason?"

"Is the metal weight a magnet?" Ralph asked.

"No, it isn't, but that's a very good question."

"Is the compass a magnet?" Ralph queries.

"Yes, it is." The teacher paused to see whether Ralph could continue the analysis alone. After quite a long pause, the teacher posed another question. "What part of the compass is a magnet?"

"It must be the needle," Jerry offered and the other children agreed.

The teacher continued with the demonstration. She provided several opportunities for the children to find the other three directions when the compass needle indicated different directions. Later, she provided the children opportunities to practice reading a compass on their own. We will return to Miss Allen's class when we discuss study trips.

You will recall that we stated earlier that, as teachers, we must choose the means of mediating instruction which best accomplishes our purposes. In this case, Miss Allen chose a demonstration because she did not have enough compasses for the entire class. Since all of the children could not have the real object, she had to do the next best thing. She could have accomplished the objective by using small groups, but this would have taken a great deal of her time which she could use more effectively in working with small groups *after* the initial demonstration was completed. In order for this activity to be successful, the teacher had to select a means of actively involving her students to prevent them from losing interest.

One point should be made concerning logical sequencing. Many inexperienced teachers become thrown when children interrupt their planned sequence as you can be sure little Bobby did in Miss Allen's lesson plan above. Although she had arranged to tell the children how metals affect the magnetic compass readings, it was not in her lesson plan to do it at the time Bobby changed her presentation. You'll notice, however, that this became a natural place for the discussion after the interjection was made. Lesson planning must remain flexible enough to allow a few diversions from the intended route.

Objectives

The reader will be able to:

Identify (1.0) two major determinants of the selection of a field trip.

Identify (1.0) the steps in planning and conducting a field trip.

Identify (1.0) the steps necessary in the development of a successful field trip.

Suggest (3.0) a productive field trip for a group of children, when given a grade level and subject.

Study Trips

Study trips or field trips can be useful to the classroom teacher in providing experiences which are not available through other means of mediation. It should be noted that this method is extremely expensive because of the amount of student and teacher time involved. Cost should be one of the major determinants of whether a field trip should be taken. The second major consideration should be whether the planned field trip is actually appropriate for the grade level and the age of the children.

The major advantage of such trips is that they provide many experiences which children can obtain in no other way. This is especially true for disadvantaged children. Such activities can also allow students to show levels of responsibility uncommonly tested in the school environment.

A great amount of planning must go into the arrangement of a study trip. Planning can be divided into three distinct phases: preliminary planning, the trip itself, and follow-up activities. Preplanning should include an actual tour by the teacher or teams of teachers involved. During this preplanning, information should be sought concerning places buses can load and unload, location of restrooms and lunch facilities, availability of first aid facilities, as well as information on the responsibilities of guides.

After the teacher has made his tour, he should meet with the principal to discuss such details as a time table for the trip, transportation, tour fees, schedule conflicts, and to obtain permission slips which will be sent home for parent signatures. Be prepared to state the objectives and to answer questions, such as what the children are going to do after the field trip.

The class must be prepared for the field trip, too. The general guides given earlier should be considered carefully. It is extremely important that the children understand the objectives they are attempting to fulfill through this activity. Trips for fun require a different response than trips for learning. Planning, beforehand, should include some specification of how the children are going to combine the information they receive. This is extremely important because it allows the students to start summarizing their experiences on the way home. It takes many field trips before teachers learn that the noise level on a bus of thirty to sixty children can be controlled simply by providing something constructive for the children to accomplish during this travel time. It can be used quite constructively in synthesizing what children have seen. They can draw conclusions from their synthesis, too.

Two other items that must be discussed with children seem rather mundane, but they are extremely important. Students must know how you expect them to behave. Children need guidelines to meet new or unusual situations. They become insecure without them; you must meet this insecurity with positive suggestions. The second procedure you must establish is what is done in an emergency. Usually, this emergency is a child becoming separated from the group. Determine a place where stragglers can go if they "misplace the group."

The study trip must be conducted in the way it was planned with the class. Unnecessary changes should be avoided because this creates confusion. Constantly check to be sure all of the children are physically present. Often buddy systems—having one child responsible for another member of the group—are helpful. An obvious place to check roll is before you leave to return home. Let's look at an innovative example of a study trip.

Miss Allen, the third grade teacher referred to in the section on demonstrations, utilized four senior high school students on a unique field trip to a forest preserve. The trip combined a science unit on plant identification with a social studies unit on the use of the compass. The weekend before the planned field trip, the teacher and the high school students went to the nearby forest preserve and planned, with the help of the ranger, a treasure hunt identifying edible, poisonous, and useful plants in the forest.

The morning before the field trip, the high school students preceded the third grade class to the forest and placed directional notes at designated points along the various trails. These notes provided the children with compass directions and point descriptions which led them on a treasure hunt.

Polaroid Colorpack cameras, operated by the student guides, were used to document the finds by the teams of five children. These pictures were to be used that day, and, also, during the development of the science unit.

After the treasure hunt, the forest ranger explained the various plants. This presentation was tape recorded for later reference in the classroom. On the trip home the children from the various teams were asked to group specific plants they had found and to develop specific questions they could use for further research. The advantages to motivation, experience, and the application of previously learned skills on such a field trip are obvious.

Objectives

The reader will be able to:

Identify (1.0) the three uses for exhibits listed by the authors.

Suggest (3.0) a specific display, given a classroom problem.

Identify (1.0) the factors one must consider in developing a display.

Exhibits

The use of real things, objects, specimens, samples, and models are valuable resources for expanding children's learnings. Such displays can be used to dress up a room, to share what is being learned with parents and other school children, as thematic organizers for units of work developed around concepts or generalizations, and as models—informational, skill, and attitudinal. Let's illustrate the first use described, to show how and why displays are used to dress up rooms.

The setting is a Midwestern classroom in October. Indian summer with its bright hues and warm sun is upon us. We walk into the neat, austere school and enter an upper primary classroom. Witches and goblins adorn the walls. A corn shock with a homemade jack-o-lantern for a head smiles at us from a corner. A ghostlike sheet dangles from the clearstory. Children's creative stories of characters which abound at this time of year adorn the bulletin board. We have come to see the children perform a puppet show. The room is an example of an exhibit which creates a mood in us. It is very obvious, if you have ever had a similar experience, that the exhibits were there to create a mood. The environment is motivating; it even seems to catch us up in this joyous fantasy. Perhaps you say this is decoration. In some classrooms, it could be. In the one which we discussed above, the teacher was using the excitement of the moment to motivate her teaching. To these children, at this time, learning was indeed enjoyable.

There are a few general principles which the teacher can use in the development of exhibits. (Haney and Ullmer, 91–96) Let's explore these general principles in a simulated classroom environment.

We'll pretend that you are a student teacher in one of our classrooms. We are going to prepare a display which illustrates the concept "production." The generalization we want the children to make in the unit we are developing is: man has increased his production in many ways. Remember that in order for us to communicate the idea, our message must be obvious; this is the first principle in the development of good displays.

The class we are working with is a fifth grade group of children living in an agricultural marketing community of about 20,000 people. In other words, most of our children know something about farming. Since it is important for us to cmmunicate with children through something in their background, we will use agriculture as the context through which we shall communicate. This principle is the second important consideration in developing displays. We will use the caption: How Has Man Increased His Production of Wheat?

"Where are we going to put the display?" you ask.

"Well, it has to be someplace where it will attract the children's attention," I reply.

"Although these children's eyes are sharp, they seem never to see what you want them to."

I laugh. You are aware that this is another of the important elements of a good display. "I think we ought to put our masterpiece in the showcase by the door. We have finished the art perspective unit. That display should come down." I move toward the display case and begin removing the blocks used in that display.

"We will want something to show primitive farming," I mutter.

"There's a colorful 12x18 picture of a primitive woman using a sicklelike instrument to cut wheat in my picture collection," you offer. "We could use that."

"We've got an old scythe in the shed at home," I recall. Then I continue, "Say! I know an agricultural equipment dealer who would loan us a metal model of a combine."

"In our picture file, we have a picture of an early manure spreader," you add as the ideas begin to come. "We can use one of the flasks from the chemistry experiment to illustrate the preparation of chemical fertilizers. That might not get our idea over, though," you decide and nearly reject the idea because communication is the major purpose of a display.

"Maybe we could find a small picture of a bag of commercial fertilizer and place it in the flask. That would help," I suggest.

Now that we have the display planned, all we have to do is select the proper colors, provide some type of pedestals for the objects so that the children's eyes will be led around the display. In this way, they can get the ideas we are attempting to communicate. Using little pieces of yarn connecting such things as the sickle, scythe, and combine is an excellent way to tie ideas together, too.

Reviewing, then, we selected a topic and objective. Considering the background of the children, we isolated a means of communicating the idea to them. Then, we selected a caption which would capture their attention and placed the display where the students would be sure to see it. We designed the display in such a way that the children's eyes would be led in the intended direction. With this visual display, we can motivate some questions on production, the concept upon which our teaching unit will focus.

Perhaps it would be useful to demonstrate how models can be developed using the exhibit technique. For this example, we will use a fifth grade teacher's method of guiding children to read factual material, an important skill that has been allotted to both social studies and science programs. This teacher adapted the familiar SQ3R system of reading—survey, question, read, review, and recite—for use in his classroom. Along the back bulletin board, he had a sequence of four very large charts tied together with the caption, "Steps to Reading for Facts." Various size bookworms with comical, but relevant, expressions on their faces aided in the transition from chart to chart.

The first chart was subtitled, "Preview the Material." Under this heading were samples of charts, graphs, boldface headings, and picture captions; these are the things a student looks at when he is trying to find out what a chapter of a book or article is about. The second chart took the same boldface headings, picture captions, chart captions and headings and made questions out of them. This portion of the display was subtitled, "Prepare or Read Questions."

"Read," was the caption of the third portion. In another color and much smaller than the subtitle, the caption continued "to Answer Questions." Here, a very diligent bookworm with a sweaty brow was pouring over a very large book.

The last chart contained elements of the other three in an attempt to communicate that the final step was a combination of all three other acts. Here, another bookworm with a professor's scholarly headdress sternly demanded, "Review," which was posted in large letters followed by "to See What You've Missed," written in smaller letters.

This bulletin board display was a teaching tool. The children learned to use it in both social studies and science. The students were often amazed to find that it also worked in other areas.

Objective

The reader will be able to:

Identify (1.0) and explain (2.0) the useful functions of television.

Television

An educator once referred to television as the educational boom that "busted." Perhaps this is not true, but it certainly *is* true that this medium has not fulfilled its educational potential. One of the few exceptions to this statement is the program, "Sesame Street," produced by Children's Television Workshop. It has changed many conceptions of what education generally and, especially, educational television should be.

Haney and Ullmer (74) identify five functions of television which seem useful in social studies education. Television "multiplies images." This function of television has several advantages which are beneficial. Within one school system or building, many students can receive the same image. This is important when the image being sent is of a demonstration or presentation which cannot be done as well in the classroom.

An example of such a demonstration was employed in one school system. The Director of Outdoor Education conducted a videotaped presentation which showed how early man made his weapons from flint. Few teachers have the skill required to give such a demonstration. Even if the demonstration could have been done live in the classroom, few children would have been able to see the important concept of pressure flaking and would have lost the appreciation of man's early techniques.

If the act can be completed in the classroom live, then that is where it should be performed. If the same type of teaching behavior and content is telecast as is traditionally presented in the classroom, then the medium is being misused.

As illustrated above, this medium also "magnifies images." The process of pressure flaking, a means early man used to place sharp edges on his flint tools, is lost unless the child can see a close-up of the process. A skilled technician with a television camera can easily catch a close-up so that every child can see the skilled fingers at work.

Television also "transports images" across our nation, world, and even through space to bring the child visual experiences which he can view during or shortly after the actual happening.

Many school systems now have videotape recorders which teachers or technicians can utilize to record evening and weekend programs for use in the classroom. This technique makes use of television's propensity for the "storage of images" which has many classroom applications, including the observation and evaluation of the children's own performances.

Teachers feel that the greatest disadvantage of using television is that one can't prepare a class for the program before it begins. This is not necessarily true. Educational television provides lesson guides which can be utilized by schools. These can be obtained from local stations if you ask that your school be placed on the mailing list.

The topics on nationally televised programs can also be obtained from the major networks. This type of information is valuable to a teacher who uses a specific program to study, for example, the family. For such studies, a schedule is needed well in advance. The networks have this information, although they do not necessarily have the schedule of the exact days such programs will be given. The local newspapers provide this information.

Objectives

The reader will be able to:

Identify (4.0) the likenesses and differences among slides, filmstrips, and films.

Analyze (6.0) mediation problems and select a viable means of presenting experiences to children using slides, filmstrips, or films.

Slides, Filmstrips and Films

Although slides have become rather commonplace since the development of automatic 35mm cameras, the filmstrip and the film are still very confusing to the beginning teacher. Possibly this confusion exists because filmstrips are not used by the general public. Although there is some similarity among these three separate means of mediating instruction, there are distinct differences in the benefits to be derived from each.

Slides.

Although slides can be purchased in many multimedia kits, packages which usually teach a concept or generalization, they are more often private collections made by the school, teacher, a friend, or by technicians in the local district.

Slides are useful because they can be employed in many different teaching episodes. A picture of the Grand Canyon can be used in a unit teaching about national parks, or it can be utilized to show the geological formations of the earth. Since a single slide can have multiple uses, the teacher can compose his own program or sequence of pictures.

Another advantage of slides is that they can be used independently by children. There is no need for the teacher to operate the simple projectors that show such slides. The preparation of slides is described in several media production books. Two examples of such books are listed below.

Nelson, Leslie W. *Instructional Aids: How to Make and Use Them.* Dubuque, Iowa: Wm. C. Brown Company Publishers, 1970.

Kemp, Jerrold E. *Planning and Producing Audiovisual Materials.* Second Edition. Scranton, Pennsylvania: Chandler Publishing Company, 1968.

The first of these books is more general in nature and covers classroom use and development of many simple aids. The latter is a little more technical, but it tells you exactly how to do things you want to do, from planning to preparation.

Filmstrips.

Filmstrips are not quite as flexible as the slide in terms of use. They can be employed similarly by the teacher operating the projector on the frame the single picture she wants to show. Filmstrips are generally developed on topics, concepts, generalizations, or specific skills. They can be used to teach these things to an individual or group. The major advantage of the filmstrip, however, is that the individual can pace his own learning. This implies that the student, himself, will operate the projector. This projector is not usually the same type the teacher uses with the class.

One problem encountered with filmstrips, however, is that children must read the captions to get the information they provide. There are some filmstrips available which have sound tracks on records. While this solves one problem, it decreases the flexibility of the device. Again, we must remind you that the reason for choosing one means of mediating instruction over another is determined by the objective you are attempting to reach.

Another advantage of the filmstrip is that it can be developed by children in the classroom. If the objective is one in which a group of children are attempting to communicate information, concepts, or generalizations to other children or to parents in a Parent Teacher Association meeting, and it is impossible to show the actual objects or products; then, you could help the group or entire class prepare a filmstrip. We will not explain this procedure here. Such an explanation is available in the two references listed above. We will only report the fact that teachers are beginning to develop their own filmstrips to fulfill specific classroom purposes.

Films.

The major weakness of the filmstrip is that it cannot provide the motion needed to represent reality. Films allow this motion. However, again, it must be pointed out that unless this motion is required by the objective, there is question of whether a film should be used. As with the filmstrip, the objective should be considered before the teacher shows the complete film. If there is only one portion of the film that meets the objective, that alone is the portion which should be used.

Another procedure which has been questioned is the periodic reuse of films for the second or third showing. Recent research evidence indicates that students receive more information from repeated showing of audiovisual presentations. Although, as teachers, we may understand the information the first time through because we are familiar with the content, we should not place this expectation upon children. This is especially true if they are to perform a task using the information presented.

Often the same film can be used to attain different objectives. This can be illustrated by an example taken from a fifth grade classroom. During an early part of a unit on the North Central United States, the teacher used a film and called the attention of the children to the resources of this region. Later in the unit, the teacher used the same film and focused the children's attention upon industries in the region. The children expressed the fact that they had missed the latter information the first time through the film. This emphasizes the importance of the teacher guiding the children in what to look for in a film. Recent research also indicates that motivation to see a film is not sufficient to communicate the content presented. Restating, just because children are interested in a film, it does not mean that they will learn the content which is carried in the film presentation. The children need to be prepared to view a film.

The addition of color to a film does not increase learning unless that color is needed to complete the objective assigned to the presentation. This generalization is somewhat related to the idea above. Just because a film looks "good" to a child, it does not guarantee learning of the content.

In addition to the above cautions on films, the teacher must carefully consider the background of the children to whom he is showing the film. Although we indicated when we discussed real experiences that many sensory inputs aided learning, there is evidence that too many sensory inputs may impede learning. This seems especially true in the use of audiovisual materials and, particularly, in films where the level of difficulty in narration and visual content is high. This suggests that in some film presentations one of the channels of input can be eliminated while using the other. Perhaps you will show the film without the narration the first time. After students have succeeded in comprehending what has been presented visually, the other channel can be added profitably.

The reintroduction of the 8mm motion picture film into educational media allows the student to use films independently. The employment of "single concept" 8mm film loops has the advantage of enabling the learner to pace himself. It is necessary to provide the student a means of checking on his own learning. This can be accomplished by having the child answer written questions on the content or by asking him questions orally. Nonreaders can use the tape recorder along with the silent 8mm film loop to check their comprehension.

Another advantage of the 8mm film loop is that teachers can produce their own films. In fact, many classes are preparing films for their social studies projects. The results have been surprising.

Objectives

The reader will be able to:

Identify (1.0) from his own experience instances where recordings and still pictures, in his opinion, have been used successfully.

Identify (1.0) the criteria for selecting good still pictures for classroom use.

Analyze (6.0) a teaching mediation problem and select a viable means of presenting experiences to children, using the material presented in this chapter.

Recordings and Still Pictures

Both of these methods of recording or retrieving data are extremely useful in social studies education today. In terms of audio recordings, either disc or tape, it is relatively difficult to pace the medium to fit the needs of the individual. In contrast, the still picture, whether in slide, flat picture, or transparency format, is rather easily paced to the individual.

The media discussed under this heading have an element in common which make them appealing for use in schools. They are relatively inexpensive and available. Although record players and records are still widely used in classrooms, tape recorders are now the most populár recording device. This is especially true since the introduction of inexpensive cassette recorders which all children and even the most mechanically inept teacher can operate with ease.

Using the Tape Recorder.

One of the most common uses of the tape recorder in the classroom today is in student self-analysis. The advantage is two-fold. In the first place, there is little that is more motivating to the child than hearing his own voice. In the second place, the child is listening to *his* presentation. He is likely to be more vitally interested in the content of that presentation. It must be pointed out, however, that children need training to accomplish the latter. When first using the tape recorder, the student is interested only in the sound of his voice. In the same manner, the tape recorder can be employed to evaluate group participation and presentations.

Tape recorders can also be utilized by students in the gathering of information. This is especially important in the recording of interviews with resource persons who cannot visit the classroom.

Students can be given directions through the use of the tape recorder. One teacher used this device as an aid to individualizing the teaching of study skills which we have previously discussed in the area of reporting. Two children still lagged far behind the group in identifying topic sentences at mid-year. It was important for these children to continue the sequence since they were, at last, making progress. By this time, the teacher felt as if he were conducting a three-ring circus with the tent on fire.

Before class, he recorded the instructions for these children on his portable cassette. At the end of his initial instruction he directed the students, "Please turn off the tape recorder and identify the main ideas in this article. After you are satisfied that you have selected the proper ideas, restart the tape and check your answers against the ones I will give you."

The children began work. At the end of the taped lesson they were instructed to join another group to continue the morning's work. This type of technique can be used in many ways in the classroom.

Perhaps the greatest disadvantage of the tape recorder is that you must spend the same amount of time retrieving information as it took to record the information in the first place. You simply cannot hasten this retrieval process in the same way you skim a paper. Perhaps this will be possible in a few years. At least, we have learned that we can listen faster than people can speak.

Using still pictures.

Still pictures are possibly more useable in the classroom today than at any time in educational history. Unfortunately, teachers have not discovered this fact to any great extent. It comes as a shock to most of us to realize that many of the children in our classrooms own and can operate cameras quite skillfully. Inventive teachers often find ways to put the photographic skills of their students to creative use in social studies projects. Maybe the most relevant use of still pictures in the classroom is illustrated by the social studies-science field trip we discussed earlier. The teacher used an inexpensive Polaroid camera to extend the experiences of her children. This is the real value of pictures.

This mediating device can also provide vicarious visual experiences. Unfortunately, these pictures, unless carefully chosen, may present misconceptions. The best example of such misconceptions is the distortion of size relationships.

Good pictures eliminate distortion by providing the viewer with some size referent. This is not as important for adults, who have had a wide range of experiences, but children are easily confused by such little things as cows being larger than houses. There are other criteria: a picture should catch and hold interest; it should be large enough to be seen clearly; its content should be relevant; its information must be accurate; it should be realistic and attractive.

Another kind of still picture which should not be ignored is the transparency. Nearly every classroom has an overhead projector available to it. Perhaps the area of social studies could make better use of this device. In the last five years, publishers have developed map transparencies of reasonably good quality. This is extremely important in the classroom because wall maps are notoriously small when they are used in classroom lectures. The overhead projector and transparency have aided in this respect because moving the projector varies the map size to some degree. We shall continue discussing this useful device in the next chapter.

Summary

In this chapter, we have set forth some general guidelines for the use of mediating devices. Some of the advantages and disadvantages of devices which involve the student in doing, observing, and listening were discussed. Examples were given illustrating how some of these means of mediating instruction have been used successfully.

References

Haney, John E., and Ullmer, Eldon J. *Educational Media and the Teacher.* Issues and Innovations in Education Series. Dubuque, Iowa: Wm. C. Brown Company Publications, 1970.

Means, Richard K. *Methodology in Education.* Merrill's Foundations of Education Series. Columbus, Ohio: Charles E. Merrill Publishing Company, 1968.

Nesbitt, William A. *Simulation Games for the Social Studies Classroom.* 2nd ed. New York: Foreign Policy Association, 1971.

VIII

Mediating Instruction: Using Visual and Verbal Symbols

Chapter Outline

Mediating Instruction: Using Visual and Verbal Symbols

As we indicated in Chapter VI, visual and verbal symbols represent the highest level of abstraction in the mediation of instruction. These levels place the student in a physically passive role in the learning arena. The learner is required to attend to and interpret visual or verbal symbols in order to obtain the message which is being communicated. Only after the symbol is identified and related to the experience of the receiver is meaning obtained from the message. On the receiving end, there are three possible points of error: the symbol may be misinterpreted, it may be unknown to the receiver, and, also, it is possible that the receiver's level of experience is insufficient to allow understanding of conventional meaning.

Perhaps an example will help. If you have never encountered the word symbol "corona" and have not observed this brilliant ring through a telescope or have not seen pictures of this phenomenon caused by the moon's total eclipse of the sun, it would be difficult for you to understand a communication containing this word. You'd have to hustle off to a dictionary or encyclopedia to provide yourself with a vicarious experience. As adults, we can depend upon these supplements to our experiences because of our ability to abstract. Children have not developed this ability.

In this chapter, we shall discuss, first, the use of visual symbols and, second, the use of verbal symbols. Our discussion of verbal symbols will be limited to printed materials. Listening, also a part of verbal communication, will be discussed in Chapter X. The central focus will be to provide guidelines which you can utilize in preparing experiences for children. Since the discussion of symbolization will touch on the development of certain skills, some of these skills will be listed for you. Again, let us remind you that there are both inductive and deductive procedures for using mediating devices. We have discussed these procedures in Chapter VI.

Objectives

The reader will be able to:

Restate (1.0) the principle required for the successful use of visual symbols by children.

Explain (5.0) how five different visual devices could

be used in the study of population growth in the United States.

Prepare (5.0) a lesson sequence utilizing the MID which will teach a map skill at a grade level of his choice.

Visual Symbols

The child comes into contact with many types of visual symbols in his educational experience. In the area of social studies, these visual symbols usually are in the form of maps, diagrams, charts, graphs, and cartoons.

Maps and the skills children need.

Since the trend is away from geography as the central discipline of social studies, you might ask: "Why should we bother with the teaching of maps and map skills?" This seems to be a reasonable question, but the authors feel that such a question is based on a limited understanding of maps.

Maps are an abstract symbolization representing certain factors of relationships of a defined area. In social studies, we are usually talking about the earth, while the sciences map other objects, such as the moon.

Although maps are considered to be the tools of geographers, they are a means of abstraction used in all the social sciences. Anthropologists use maps to show relationships between ancient cities and people, movement of ancient peoples, present locations of people being studied, or even the distribution of animal societies. Sociologists, also, make use of maps. Political scientists are likely to use maps to show voting patterns. If this doesn't convince you, how many times have you used a map in the last week? Think carefully. What about road maps? Campus maps? Building layouts? The point is simply that maps are used in many ways.

For most teachers, justification for teaching map skills is an academic exercise because these skills are a part of most social studies programs. However, teachers face the problem of determining what children need to know in order to use maps. In other words, a teacher must ask himself, what map skills do children need; at what grade or experience level should certain skills be taught?

In his survey of recent research on map skills, Rushdoony concluded that much of the study completed in this area has focused on what students knew about maps, rather than what they could learn. Although he found a grade to grade progression in children's ability to use maps, children's errors seemed to be the result of a lack of training. (Rushdoony, 214) Children are simply not taught the skills they need to read maps. While it is true that some students seem to learn these skills by osmosis, most children must be taught the skills in a carefully planned program. Unfortunately, there are a number of questions regarding the "best" methods of teaching map skills in the elementary school. Most practitioners seem to agree that map making should precede map reading.

This generalization is based on the same principle which we have discussed during these three chapters on mediating instruction—abstract learnings must be based on real experiences. Children should begin with real experiences and progress toward abstraction. The suggested sequence of map skills presented attempts to accomplish this sequencing. It is based on the list developed from Rushdoony's research (215–18) and a sequence chart published by The Geographical Research Institute (see References). You will note that the skills have been presented in behavioral phrases. These phrases have been divided under the major map concepts and, then, by grade level. The major map concepts are size and shape, orientation and direction, location, distance, symbols, and interpretation.

Size and shape Perhaps the most complicated of the skills in mapping are the understandings of size and shape relationships. It may be difficult for the sophisticated undergraduate to appreciate the complexity of this concept. Perhaps we can motivate you by focusing on some problems which will uncover misconceptions in your own mind. Which has the greatest land area, Greenland or Mexico? Honduras or Indiana? We're not asking for figures. Just guess which is larger.

If you selected Greenland and Honduras as the larger, you are correct. Actually there is little difference between these areas. If you chose Greenland because of the error learned through your experiences with the Mercator projection, the size reference you used is grossly incorrect. You may have selected Mexico because you were aware of this problem, but why in the world would one pick Indiana over Honduras? "Countries are larger than states, aren't they?" you might reply.

Strange that we should make such generalizations. Another error may exist because you are familiar with maps of the United States which are drawn on a larger scale than classroom maps of Central and South America. We have not made much use of the globe in our teaching in the past. We make such strange generalizations because of errors in our experiences or possibly because we have not thought about or otherwise encountered such things. They are not in our range of experience. Perhaps such gaps can be filled if children can accomplish the following behaviors:

Preschool

Identifies the differences in size of known objects

Kindergarten
- States that the globe and earth are round
- Identifies the fact that the earth turns
- States that the earth is very large

Grade 1
- States that the globe is a model of the earth
- States that the earth is made of land, water, and air
- Makes pictures showing the relative size of known objects

Grade 2
- Compares the earth with a ball
- Identifies the concept of sphere
- Can divide the earth into hemispheres
- Can demonstrate the rotation of the earth from west to east using a globe

Grade 3
- Uses the globe to show correct shape, size, distance, and location
- Identifies that changes of the earth's position in relation to the sun causes seasons

Grade 4
- Identifies distortion on flat maps
- Compares the size of states, nations, and continents
- States the reasons for night and day

Grade 5
- Compares various map projections
- Explains the earth's orbit around the sun and the moon's orbit around the earth
- Explains the significance of the analemma

Grade 6
- Relates the earth's shape and the sun's position to animal and vegetable life on earth

Let's try another interesting problem related to the size and shape of the earth, which many sixth grade pupils can answer. Suppose upon graduation in January that you and your young husband are being transferred to Buenos Aires, Argentina, by his corporation for a two year stint. Are you going to prepare summer or winter clothing? What city in the United States would have a similar climate? Why?

In order to accomplish the conceptualizations required to understand this problem, a slide projector or flashlight can be aligned so that it will focus on the globe in approximately the same way the sun shines upon the earth. The 23½° slant of the earth is maintained to present the visual perspective required. Of course, the shape and slant of the earth are not the only relevant considerations. Buenos Aires' orientation to the sun and the surrounding land and water forms also must be taken into account. This demonstration would enable you to discover that the seasons south of the equator are opposite those experienced in the Northern Hemisphere.

Orientation and direction Many fail to appreciate knowledge about direction and orientation until they build a house or work in an office with large plate glass windows which face the west. The results can be sunburned eyeballs and overheated secretaries.

In order to stir your imagination somewhat, let's return to your hypothetical move to Argentina. Would you want to consider an apartment on the north or south side of the building in which the company arranged for you to stay? Pictures of the building show you that there are large, plate glass windows placed flush to the outside walls. You and your husband will be paying the utilities which include both heating and air-conditioning. Actually, we are asking you to consider which side of the apartment building will receive the most sun and why.

Research does indicate a few guidelines for teaching cardinal directions. Howe's (421–24) work with primary children indicates that students can acquire clear conceptions of direction as early as grade two. His research also indicated that the most favorable place to teach the cardinal directions is out-of-doors, to prevent associations with objects in the classroom. The directions in Howe's study were taught according to sun positions. The authors recommend the instructional sequence listed below.

Preschool

Can direct persons to home, school, theater, grocery, and other places he has experienced

Kindergarten

Can trace routes of activities of people to places he knows or stories he has had read to him

Grade 1

Differentiates between the concepts of up and down

Uses "left" and "right" correctly

Identifies cardinal directions

Maps his community

Uses maps to show simple distance and direction

Grade 2

- Finds the cardinal directions in relation to the sun
- Explains the concepts of equator, hemisphere, North Pole and South Pole
- Begins to use a simple compass

Grade 3

- Can associate the North Star with North direction
- Identifies the compass rose
- Identifies North on a map
- Uses intermediate directions

Grade 4

- Identifies the purpose of longitude and latitude grid lines
- Identifies the concept of Prime Meridian and the International Date Line
- Finds proper routes on road maps

Grade 5

- Uses intermediate directions accurately
- Uses parallels and meridians correctly
- Explains the concept of Great Circle
- Compares routes plotted on a flat map with those plotted on a globe

Grade 6

- Explains the flowing of rivers in terms of elevation
- Extends the use of longitude and latitude to the interpolation of positions

It is readily apparent that you will begin in preschool and early primary with the personal experiences of your children and extend their knowledge with experiences which you can provide for them. Although skills are initiated at one grade level, you will notice that meaning is expanded at higher grade levels. This is true of cardinal directions which are mentioned at grades 1 and 2. You will also note that elements of this concept continue up the sequence. This skill is combined with the concepts of longitude and latitude for fourth grade children. Teachers at higher grade levels should not be led into thinking that skills assigned to lower levels have been mastered. The only way to determine what your children know is to pretest them on such skills. Then, you will know where to begin.

Location The concept we are discussing under this heading is relative location, as opposed to distance and direction. What important understandings come from this concept? Are you near one of the earth's major fault lines which are prone to earthquakes? What about the paths of tornadoes? In case of a tidal wave, are you on safe ground? How about risks from hurricanes, forest fires, or urban riots? If you don't know the answers to these questions, you can bet your insurance company does.

If such concerns don't phase you, think about the possibilities for obtaining teaching positions in the area where you are planning to live. What about the supply of eligible young men? Our physical location is a prime determinant of our livelihood, life style, and, even, life span.

Perhaps, the most important reason for teaching location to children is to enable them to relate elements meaningfully. We begin with the familiar, pointing out factors in the environment, as early as second grade. In the intermediate grades, the interrelationships of seemingly independent factors are underlined.

Preschool

- States the location of known objects referring to pictures

Kindergarten

- Points to approximate locations around the world on a simple globe
- Locates specific areas in the school building

Grade 1

- Can describe his physical environment: mountainous, hilly, level
- Uses simple street maps
- Locates his city, state, and nation on a globe

Grade 2

- Can identify city, state, North America
- Locates major natural features
- Locates areas in the news

Grade 3

- Identifies continents
- Identifies such features as peninsula, bay, river, isthmus, island, and delta.
- Uses grid system to locate places

Grade 4

- Locates countries in the Northern and Southern hemispheres
- Identifies natural and man-made features on maps

Grade 5

- Relates the United States to other parts of the world
- Locates important physical features on maps
- Locates and compares areas of resources and population density

Grade 6

- Locates and uses the International Date Line

Translates time in his time zone to others
Explains wind belts
Explains air circulation in the atmosphere

Distance Most adults seem to have a pretty good sense of distance, or do we? An experience recalled by one of the authors leads us to question this, at least in terms of interpreting road maps.

> After an interesting evening in Juarez, Mexico, my family and a guest crossed the Rio Grande into El Paso and began what normally would have been a six hour drive to Lubbock, Texas. The area was new to the author, and he was not familiar with the roads or road maps of Texas. Since the traffic was heavy, and it was nearing dark, the author never bothered to calculate the distance. He asked his wife which way she would like to go. Quickly, she flashed a map in his direction, pointing out the fact that there were two possible routes. It was evident that one led through mountains the family had never seen. The foolish choice was made to take the El Paso-to-Pecos-to-Midland-to-Lubbock route. The actual distance was never calculated. It was estimated. This minor error cost five extra hours and some loss of family stature.

Preschool
- Differentiates between the concepts of near and far.

Kindergarten
- Determines near-far relation to parks, downtown, and homes of individuals in the class

Grade 1
- States distance in terms of blocks or streets

Grade 2
- Estimates short distances in the environment
- Explains use of the distance scale
- Recognizes the distance scale on a legend
- Associates distance and time in travel

Grade 3
- Uses distance scale to compare distances on maps
- Makes maps of familiar areas

Grade 4
- Identifies the differences between large and small scale maps
- States relationships between elevation and climate

e as degrees north and south
nputes distances
tical areas but different scales

s of scale unit for measurement
of various routes traveled

Map concepts presented at the fifth grade level can be introduced through a bulletin board display which uses a city map, a road map, a state map, and topographical maps of the area in which the children live. Such a caption as "Maps Use Different Scales" or "Is Our City Sanforized?" might call seemingly discrepant data to the attention of the children.

Symbols Map symbols are extremely useful to the student who has learned to interpret them. They are the shorthand which supplies him with pages of information or the symbolization that allows him to accumulate and organize data. The teacher must realize that symbols vary. Although there is an internationally accepted symbol and color system, every map maker meets situations in which he must improvise. Many times he is limited to specific colors; at times, certain symbols become confusing because of their similarity to other symbols. The best guide for the teacher and the student is the map legend. Although, often, we become familiar with map symbols through their use, there is little need for having children commit them to memory.

As with the other map skills we have presented, the interpretation of symbols progresses from real objects toward abstractions of real objects. Real objects become pictures; pictures become combinations of pictorial symbols and symbols; these are abstracted further to become combinations of color, lines, and abstract symbols of the most sophisticated type. The identification of these symbols is developed from the third grade on. The ultimate goal is to encourage the child to use special purpose maps which will permit him the flexibility he needs to make and use a variety of maps for interpretation and communication. During the later elementary years, children should be encouraged to develop and use their own maps as data-recording and data-reporting devices.

Preschool
- Identifies symbols resembling real objects

Kindergarten
- Identifies symbols for land, water, and cardinal directions
- Makes three dimensional maps of known areas

Grade 1
- Recognizes pictorial symbols on commercial maps

Grade 2
- Makes and uses his own symbols
- Associates common symbols for items in the environment

Grade 3
- Uses special map symbols, such as those for railroads, highways, airports, and cities
- Develops his own map legends
- Identifies color as a symbol on a map

Grade 4
- Can read color symbols to show elevation
- Can explain the use of color on relief maps
- Recognizes boundary lines

Grade 5
- Identifies correct symbols on maps
- Uses a variety of his own symbols

Grade 6
- Compares aerial photos with relief and contour maps of the same area
- Reads maps using colors as symbols for production, resources, and precipitation

Interpretation of maps and globes One technique used in teaching fifth and sixth grade children to interpret maps and globes is to use such special purpose maps as growing seasons, rainfall, vegetation, land utilization, and population distribution in the study of areas. Students are asked to find relationships among the factors illustrated on these maps. After the study of one area, you might ask children to find similar areas in the world where such conditions exist and have them predict the economic activities of people who live there. This teaching procedure presupposes a carefully laid foundation of subskills.

Symbolization at these grade levels progresses to an abstract level. Each of the symbols is considered separately to prevent confusion. Mere reading of symbols is not the task, however; it is the patterning of these symbols that provides essential information. For example, what does it mean when railroads travel along rather straight lines? What would it mean to have a road and railroad running side by side along a rather crooked route? In the first instance, the railroad is probably in a plains area. In the second, the two roadbeds are probably following a river through a mountainous or hilly area. As illustrated below, this set of skills begins with the interpretation of pictures in early learning experiences. Pictorial symbols and simple maps are introduced next. Gradually children learn to use maps for a variety of purposes.

Preschool
- Uses pictures to make inferences

Kindergarten
- Interprets pictures and simple picture maps
- States the purpose of maps and globes

Grade 1
- Interprets a diagram of the classroom correctly
- Uses simple maps as a source of information

Grade 2
- States that maps can be used in many ways
- Uses wall maps and relates size to maps
- Uses simple map terms such as equator, poles, continents, oceans, lakes

Grade 3
- Uses commercial, highway, and special purpose maps
- Uses maps in textbooks
- Compares maps and infers from information presented: population, rainfall, crops

Grade 4
- Identifies low, middle, and high latitudes
- Interprets resource, rainfall, and land-use maps
- Plans trips using road maps

Grade 5
- Makes inferences about such relationships as livestock production and corn and grain production
- Translates information from maps and globes to bar graphs

Grade 6
- Consults several maps in obtaining information
- Compares old maps and new maps of the same area
- Compares distances of various trips on road maps

Each of these relationships takes time to develop. These skills are developed in sequence and undergird the student's ability to make optimum use of maps and globes.

Diagrams.

Many early maps produced by children could fit the category of diagrams more easily then maps. The reason for this statement comes from the view that a line drawing which shows line and space relationships is technically a diagram. (McCune, 222) The usefulness of this mediating device is that it reduces reality to its simplest form. The purpose of a diagram is to produce a skeletal simplification of real objects. Of course, diagrams can range from simple line drawings of the barest essentials to detailed manufacturing specifications.

In order to understand diagrams, the child must be able to visualize the real object and perceive that the line drawing is an abstraction of that object. Perhaps the best way to teach the student to use diagrams is to present both the picture of the real object and the drawing together. This same procedure can be employed to teach children how to draw diagrams. Use a picture of a real object, such as a pulley, and ask a child to draw an abstraction which would show how the pulley works. Such diagrams are useful to children in the late primary grades.

Charts.

Charts are often mistakenly called diagrams. Therefore, we have difficulty separating the two media. Charts contain a greater amount of verbal symbolization. Most of us have seen charts in government textbooks illustrating how a bill becomes a law. Jarolimek (417) would classify these charts as "narrative charts." The tables containing the cognitive and affective domains presented in Chapter V could be considered charts. Although these charts contain a great amount of verbal information, they condense the original works, two volumes, into the two sets of tables presented.

Another type of chart is the Structure of the Disciplines Model developed in Chapter II. This model shows the relationship of the elements of knowledge. The chart summarizes an article which is difficult for the student to read. It presents data in a useable form. These illustrations are good communication devices; also, they accomplish another purpose we teachers have failed to reach to the fullest extent—to enable children to organize information effectively.

Most of us have been taught to use the outline as an organizational tool. There is nothing wrong with the outline; it has served a useful purpose for those of us who are verbally oriented. But what about those who are pictorially or logically oriented? In this case, logically oriented is intended to mean step by step.

Actually, the Structure of the Disciplines Model is nothing more than a visual outline of ideas. The boxes at the top of the chart are main topics; the rectangles falling below are subtopics. To some individuals, this device communicates more effectively than an outline; it holds their attention. Others immediately turn the page. The point is simply that charts are efficient ways to organize data. They are more useful to some individuals than to others.

Although many teachers are frightened by flow charting, children have found this technique quite useful in communication. Kessler (220–24) illustrates the successful use of this procedure with intermediate grade students. The process for initiating this skill is to introduce a simple flow chart to children. Either one of the flow charts shown in Figures 8–1 and 8–2 could be used. Figure 8–1 was developed by a sixth grade child on how to use a Polaroid camera. Figure 8–2 is the product of a fourth grader's thinking on how to use a tape recorder. Have the children tell you what the symbols seem to mean. They will discover that the boxes with rounded corners mean beginnings and ends. The rectangles are descriptions of actions to be performed. Diamond shaped symbols are decisions. The lines and arrows show the direction to go through the flow chart.

Another type of chart which is useful to the student is what we shall call a data-organizing chart. Such charts allow children to list their findings. Figure 8–3, a data-organizing chart, is the result of one fifth grade's study of herding on the Great Plains. This chart remained in front of the group for several days. Finally, they were ready to settle on three to four generalizations which they felt could be used to predict what they would find in other regions in the world. Again, the value of this chart was that it allowed children to organize and manipulate their data.

In addition to such data charts, children also develop procedural charts. We mentioned these previously when we discussed models for children in Chapter VI. These charts can provide the group with models for guiding their behavior, proofreading their papers, preparing outlines, or behaving on field trips.

Basically, charts serve the student through informational presentation, storage, and organization. Also, charts can permit children to communicate their ideas in a succinct manner. Our failure in education is that we have focused on teaching children to consume charts, rather than having children produce charts to organize their own information. Let's see if we can't reverse the trend.

Graphs.

Graphs, like charts, are intended to communicate information quickly and fairly accurately. Until the last ten years, graphs have been neglected in the primary grades of the elementary school. Little attempt was made

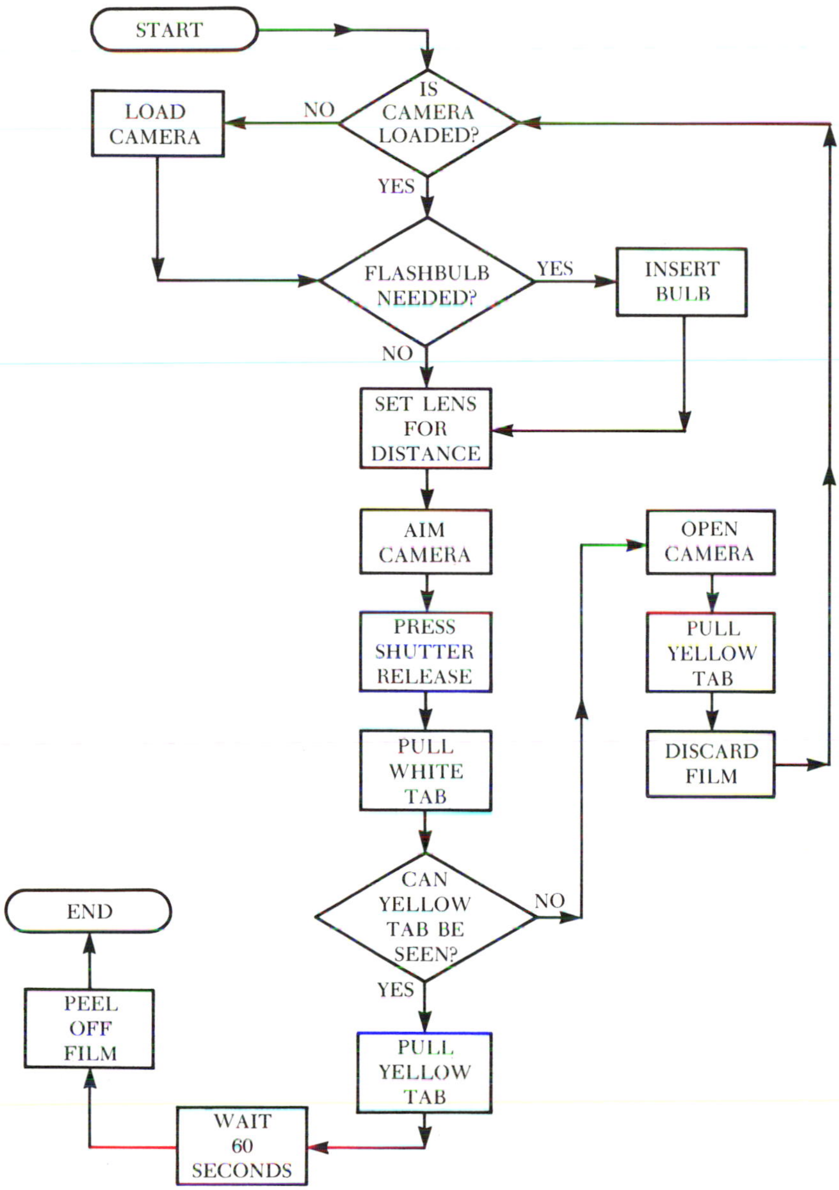
START
IS CAMERA LOADED?
NO
LOAD CAMERA
YES
FLASHBULB NEEDED?
YES
INSERT BULB
NO
SET LENS FOR DISTANCE
AIM CAMERA
PRESS SHUTTER RELEASE
PULL WHITE TAB
CAN YELLOW TAB BE SEEN?
NO
OPEN CAMERA
PULL YELLOW TAB
DISCARD FILM
YES
PULL YELLOW TAB
WAIT 60 SECONDS
PEEL OFF FILM
END

Figure 8–1.

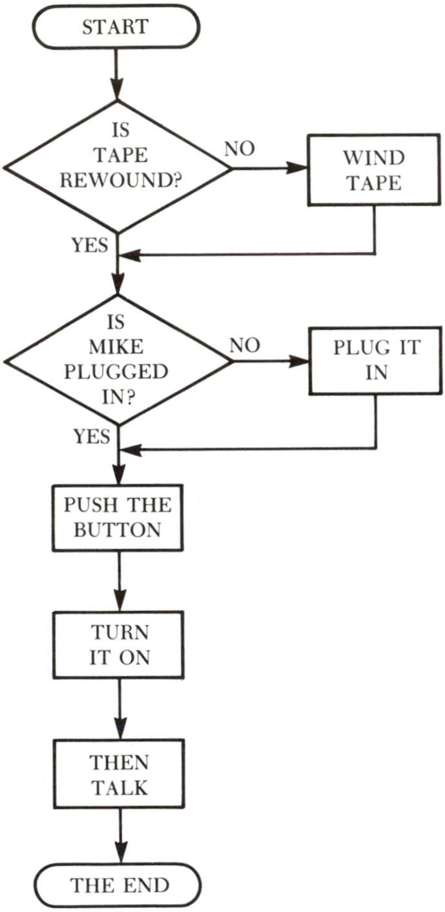

Figure 8–2.

to have children use this device until the new math programs began utilizing the number line extensively to teach number concepts. It is a very small step from the number line concept to some simple questions: Which line is longer? shorter? about the same? The simple bar graph is the next step.

There are presently used in social studies materials in the elementary school several types of graphs: line, bar, circle, and pictographs. Preparation for graph reading experiences begins as children learn to record daily temperatures, days of rain during the month, daily attendance or birthdays.

Another form of graphic representation which aids young minds with the elusive concept of time is the time line. In the early primary grades,

Results of classroom discussion on Herding in the United States.

		Yes	No
L A N D	Resources: steppe region (great plain) short grass		
	Use: grazing of cattle, sheep, and goats		
	Improvement: developed new grasses, used irrigation, fertilization, control wind erosion		
L A B O R	Source: Very little labor available		
	Skill: Special skills are required though many do not need a lot of education		
	Improvement: Division of labor with both machines (trucks, tractor, aircraft, special machinery) other people and animals		
C A P I T A L	Source: personal savings account for most of the capital supplied. There are some corporations.		
	Accumulation: Machines listed above, various buildings, irrigation equipment, building stock		
M A N A G E M E N T	Ranchers: Many receive very good educations and use organizations for raisers: most modern methods of raising and selling cattle		
	Government Aids: Rents, grazing lands, loans money supports prices, irrigation projects, support colleges and universities in research on product and giving information on selling product		

Figure 8–3

this technique records what happened during grandfather's life, daddy's life, and the child's own life, in a systematic way. Time lines are discussed further in Chapter XIII.

It should be apparent by now that the first principle of graphing is that graphs must be created from real experiences—the things that happen in the child's life. In this way, horizontal and vertical scales take on real meaning. "This is me; this is what I did." The second principle is that the understanding of scale comes in the early intermediate grades after size comparisons and proportion are understood. Even in late intermediate years, graphs should remain simple and uncluttered. Content should require only simple comparisons, trends, and in the upper grade levels, proportion. Precise statistical analyses should not be required.

In addition to *reading* graphs, children should learn that they are communication devices. This means that as early as third grade, children should be encouraged to communicate their statistical data to their classmates through the use of graphs.

The chart below illustrates the types of graphs, their use, and grade level for introduction, as well as the reason for introducing a specific technique at that time.

Type	Use	Level for introduction
Line graph	Connects points to indicate trends.	Fourth to fifth grade level since children need to understand that the placement of points shows quantity.
Bar graph	Shows increases and decreases of quantity. There are both vertical and horizontal types.	Primary and early primary. Concepts of real quantity must be introduced.
Pictograph	Usually used to hold attention. Symbols not as precise as other forms.	All grade levels. Inaccuracy must be underlined.
Circle graph	Used to show proportion.	Upper intermediate because of the need to understand proportion.

Cartoons.

Cartoons are complicated simplicity. The cartoonist captures life in a few, simple well-chosen strokes, but you must have some understanding of the topic he is communicating, or his subtleness will cover his meaning. The cartoon below is a good example.

It would be easy for us to miss the time and temperature sign with its usual advertisement. In fact, we nearly miss the "Quality of Life." This may not be meaningful to someone in 1990. He may not have experienced or might have forgotten the decline in our standard of living common in the last decade.

The stock symbols of the cartoonist are often meaningless to the elementary school child. Some fourth grade children may fail to see the humor in cartoons which set their peers "on their ears."

One fourth grade teacher met this problem through the use of reproductions of magazine covers drawn by Norman Rockwell. She called the children's attention to facial expressions, postures, and gestures to help them see that these were exaggerations of expressions we use everyday. Similar expressions were abstracted further in cartoon examples she had collected. This familiarized the children with the use of exaggeration. Capitalizing on her students' interest in an election, she displayed the symbols of political parties and caricatures of famous people in the election. One art period was employed in the production of such drawings. She encouraged the children to begin developing their own cartoons.

During the time that interest remained alive, which was most of the year, a special place was allotted on the bulletin board where children could share their own cartoons or interesting cartoons they found. Often artists and collectors had to explain the meaning of displayed cartoons. These students had become alerted to another medium of communication. On occasion the teacher was stumped by cartoons the children brought in. The point is simply that children can enjoy cartoons, but like the other visual symbolizations we have discussed, they must be taught to use the medium or there will be no message received.

Objectives

The reader will be able to:

List (1.0) three ways materials can be constructed to fit the reading levels of children.

Explain (5.0) the reason for integrating current events into social studies programs.

Prepare (5.0) ten guide questions on this chapter, at various levels of Bloom's taxonomy, which will aid his peers in identifying the significant points in the chapter.

Verbal symbols: Written Materials

Verbal symbols are both oral and written. Since we shall discuss listening in the section on language arts in the social studies, we shall limit this section to the use of reading in social studies.

For many years, reading has been the primary source of data-gathering in our schools. This is unfortunate since we realize now that it has deprived many children of the benefits of using their experiences as a source of information. It is essential that we place reading in its proper perspective. Children must learn to use reading materials as *a* source of data which communicates through both time and space. Teachers must realize that books are not the *only* sources of information. Many teachers would like to see the old standard version of the textbook disappear. Realists must face the fact that it is still the cheapest instructional device available to the classroom teacher, even if it is not the most effective. We can discuss individual pacing a great deal. Still, when one carefully selects written material, it is as individualized as any known form of media. The point is that it is not the use of the reading material that has failed us; it is its misuse.

There are two major principles that we would like to discuss in this section. The first is that no single set of material, textbook, or the like can be used by *every* learner in a typical classroom, and the second is that every learner in a typical classroom must be taught to read "factual" material. We often mistake indications of a child's ability to read fictional material as evidence of his ability to read factual material. Such an assumption is invalid.

Making material fit the child.

In Chapter III, we presented one way of individualizing reading material for children. In this example, guide questions were prepared for students to read at three response levels: identify facts stated explicitly in the text, synthesizing related facts, and making inferences beyond the facts given. The expectations the teacher placed on the children were based on these three levels. In other words, the teacher did not expect every member of his class to do the same things with the assigned material. In his assignments, he attempted use the material he had. Also, you will recall that he prepared some material himself when the available material did not complete the intended objective. You may be asking, "You don't expect me to write my own textbook do you?"

No, at least not the first year, but writing your own materials will allow you additional flexibility. Bloom's Taxonomy can be used to set the response levels. If you examine the questions in Chapter III, you will note that some of these questions require synthesis. The first means of making the material fit the child is to allow several levels of possible performance.

Another means of individualizing a textbook-oriented program is to assign the reading to be accomplished in the text to certain readers. Other data can be taken from children's periodicals. Four such periodical sources are listed below:

American Education Publications, Education Center, Columbus, Ohio 43216: *My Weekly Reader,* grades K-6; *Current Events,* grades 7 and 8.

Scholastic Magazine, 50 W. 44th Street, New York, N.Y. 10036: *Let's Find Out,* Kindergarten; *News Pilot,* grade 1; *News Ranger,* grade 2; *News Trails,* grade 3; *News Explorer,* grade 4; *Young Citizen,* grade 5; *Newstime,* grades 5 and 6; *Junior Scholastic,* grades 7 and 8.

National Geographic Society, 17 and N Streets, N.W., Washington, D.C. 20036: *School Bulletin,* grades 4-8.

The American Museum of Natural History, Central Park West at 79th Street, New York, New York 10024: *Nature and Science,* grades 4-8.

Most of these periodicals print a planned schedule of articles for the year. The resourceful teacher usually subscribes to more than one level of at least one series. Since there are enticing inducements to subscribe for the next year, often teachers order individual class copies at the end of the year. When class takes up in the fall, copies for those levels for which you haven't subscribed can be obtained through supplemental orders. Often, teachers trade copies. With several copies and the publishing schedule, the teacher can plan to supplement his text with current material at several reading levels. The teacher can organize his units so that there are topics which certain students can develop individually. In this way, all of the children are placed in material they can read. They have data to contribute to the class project or unit.

The periodicals listed above are of different types, too. *My Weekly Reader* tends to be a current events type magazine which deals with timely topics. This material can be used to underline important issues. Scholastic magazines are similar, but they contain articles on states and topics of a general nature, as well as current events. The *School Bulletin* and *Nature and Science* are special feature materials which are useful in several ways. One topic which has been common to both magazines in the past is the contribution of underwater exploration to our future life on earth. Items of a travel nature are likely to appear in the *School Bulletin,* not dry old travelogs though. *Nature and Science* has highly motivating material on social, biological, and physical science subjects. Although both of these magazines are written for upper intermediate level children, often students can read the material because it is highly motivating. A second method of individualizing written material, then, is to use a variety. The textbook is only one of several resources.

Perhaps you have been surprised to see current events integrated directly into the social studies program. This can be accomplished because the newer programs are focused on concepts. These concepts are alive; they describe man, his environment, that environment's relationship to man, and man's relationship to man. The events are the things that are happening on this spaceship, Earth.

The third solution for poor readers, and this suggestion applies at all levels, is to let them write their own material. It is much more motivating to read material written by someone you know. This is especially true if everyone helped to write it. You may recognize this as the Experience Chart Approach to reading. It is, but the content has changed from fictional or creative materials to recordings about man and his world of which the child is a part.

The following photograph shows an experience chart which one second grade class composed after a trip to the fire station. This chart was a recording of the children's observations during their trip. The teacher recorded information as the children presented it—in their language. From this chart generalizations could be developed concerning the daily routine at the fire station, as well as the equipment firemen use in their work.

Drawings and an experience chart help this second grade class recall their trip to the fire station and provide a springboard for discussion.

Teaching children to read for facts.

Children must be taught to read factual material. Perhaps their inability to read for facts is a result of being taught to read fictional material in reading programs. When they encounter factual material, they tend to read it in the same way. Consequently, they can not retrieve the data teachers expect them to find in their texts, magazines, or informational library books. How can we help them? The first task is to teach them to read for a purpose.

Analyzing the group In the beginning of a planned teaching sequence, the teacher attempts to identify those children who can pick out details. Again, you are pretesting to see which children can skip the teaching sequence. We would use Bloom's Taxonomy to design the levels of the sequence. Supply individual children material designed at their level. Various articles from back copies of the aforementioned magazines are excellent testing devices. Have the students read to identify information stated in the material, interpret graphs presented, indicate relationships they find, and categorize elements presented. If they can do these things, they are pretty good readers of factual material. Guide these boys and girls into selection of identified problems and give them a free rein. For those who can't accomplish these tasks, begin by aiding them in establishing purposes for their reading of factual material.

Although we have been punching textual material pretty hard, it is time to build your trust in some of the newer materials which have been published in the seventies. The major publishers have taken criticism to heart. Many of the materials they are producing are valid in terms of content and teaching methods. These books have been prepared by teams of social scientists and professional educators—qualified public school teachers and professors of education. Teachers can trust such materials to a greater extent than previously. Critical appraisal must be the watchword.

Developing a purpose through surveying Using this textual material, you can develop purposes for studying the text. After you and the children have designed the purposes, find questions the text authors suggest that meet your needs. You can also begin teaching the children to develop questions from the boldface type chapter headings and design questions which will unlock data from pictures, graphs, and charts. You are beginning to focus the children on reading for a purpose.

After you have developed a set of questions, stop. Ask the children to evaluate whether these questions will provide them with the data they need to accomplish the purposes they have established. There *should* be some doubt because they haven't read the material. However, they have a purpose to begin with, and they have developed some questions. They have surveyed the material so that they know some possible places to look for answers.

Teaching the reading of materials At this point, one might turn the children loose with the material. This would depend upon the group. Also, one might teach them to scan the printed pages looking only for the facts they need. After some students have mastered this skill, one might teach them to skim to get only a general idea of what is presented. Smith (359–83) suggests that this is an intermediate grade skill. Scanning, she feels, can be used in the primary grades.

Aiding in the development of conclusions After the children have obtained the information through reading the material, they can combine what they have found to determine whether they have answered all of their questions. This, too, is a valuable step in reading for facts. Many times, children find they have failed to obtain the answer they desired. Obviously, this requires further reading. In some cases, the children could return to the text. In others, they must seek other sources. Such a process emphasizes the importance of the text as *a* resource and not *the* resource.

The steps in this suggested procedure to teach children to read for facts are having the children (1) survey the material; (2) form questions to guide their reading; (3) read the material to answer specific questions, and (4) evaluate the answers they have received to determine whether further reading is necessary. After this data-gathering has been completed, the children can use the Developing of Generalizations Procedure described in Chapter IV to aid them in drawing conclusions.

It will be apparent to you that the textbook is cast in a different role in this chapter. Even the newer, bound materials don't fill the bill as the only source of information. They become outdated too quickly for that. They are a source from which inquiry can begin. They aid in teaching some inquiry skills. Textbooks present a bias which children should be taught to recognize. Perhaps, the most important point is that textbooks will fill a specific role, the one which is defined by the teacher, the manager of all media.

Using free and inexpensive materials as kits

Free and inexpensive materials can be used in many ways by teachers. Two major cautions must be advised, however. The first is that some of the material is difficult for children to understand. Secondly, critical reading must be used with most of the material. This latter statement can be softened, somewhat, because many companies have become more aware of their responsibility to education. These companies produce excellent material, in good taste.

Although free and inexpensive materials are both visual and verbal, they are presented in this section because the authors have used them to individualize their instruction. Since the children, given the packages, have to read the instructions that guide them through the kits, we have placed them here. In order to explain this procedure, let us use a kit distributed by United States Steel.

This particular kit provides four small plastic bottles which contain limestone, iron ore, coke, and a sample of pig iron. It has a colorful filmstrip which explains, through the use of excellent maps, photographs, diagrams, and charts, the processing of iron ore into steel. The filmstrip contains factually oriented guide questions to aid the student in getting meaning from it. The kit, then, contains real objects, as well as visual materials children can use.

One fifth grade teacher used this kit and several others as inquiry units to supplement and provide materials which either advanced or low-skilled readers could use independently. Each box contained the samples various distributors provided, as well as a teacher-developed booklet offering guide questions, projects, experiments, and suggestions for presentations individuals could plan for the entire class. Each of these kits could be integrated into the year's study of the United States in at least one way. This is only one of many ways thoughtful teachers can use the wealth of free materials available.

The most extensive source of such kits is given below.

Educator's Progress Service, Randolph, Wisconsin 53956:
Guide to Free Curriculum Materials
Educators' Guide to Free Films
Educators' Guide to Free Filmstrips
Educators' Guide to Free Tapes, Scripts, and Transcriptions

There are many such sources today. Book stores carry paperbacks listing free and inexpensive materials for the teacher. One of these is Thomas J. Pepe's, *Free and Inexpensive Educational Aids,* Fourth Revised Edition, New York: Dover Publications, 1970.

Summary

Mediating instruction through the use of visual and verbal symbols was the topic of this chapter. Map skills for preschool through grade six were provided to guide the reader in the selection of experiences for children. Diagrams, charts, graphs, and cartoons were the other types of visual symbols presented.

Written materials were the only verbal symbols discussed in this chapter. Suggestions were given for individualizing material for children. The importance of teaching pupils to read for facts was stressed. Finally, the use of free and inexpensive materials as social studies kits was explored.

References

The Geographical Research Institute. *Sequence Chart of Map and Globe Skills and Understanding: Kindergarten Through Grade Six.* Chicago: Denoyer-Geppert Company, 1966

Howe, George F. "The Teaching of Directions in Space."*Current Research in Elementary School Social Studies.* Edited by Wayne L. Herman, Jr. New York: The Macmillan Company, 1969.

Jarolimek, John. *Social Studies in Elementary Education.* 4th ed. New York: The Macmillan Company, 1971.

Kessler, Bernard M. "A Discovery Approach to the Introduction of Flow-charting in the Elementary Grades." *The Arithmetic Teacher* 17 (March 1970): 220-24.

McCune, George H.,and Pearson, Neville. "Interpreting Material Presented in Graphic Form." *Skill Development in the Social Studies.* Washington, D.C.: The National Council for the Social Studies, NEA, 1963.

Rushdooney, Haig A. "A Child's Ability to Read Maps: Summary of the Research. "*Journal of Geography* 67 (April 1968): 213–19.

Smith, Nila Banton. *Reading Instruction for Today's Children.* Englewood Cliffs, New Jersey: Prentice Hall, Inc., 1963.

IX

Effective Evaluation in Social Studies

Chapter Outline

Effective Evaluation in Social Studies

This chapter deals with evaluation, the last component of the Model for Instructional Design (MID). In one respect, evaluation is a continuous process throughout the model, which is illustrated in Figure 9–1 showing the lines of interaction among the components. As the teacher prepares behavioral objectives, he is constantly focusing back to the instructional purpose he is attempting to accomplish. We have stated, previously, the importance of adjusting our behavioral objectives using the results of pretest data. In the learning arena, too, evaluation is inherent in the interaction of teacher, media, and student. The evaluation component of the MID, however, refers to the assessment of student progress toward stated objectives, the efficacy of our teaching, as well as the effectiveness of the curriculum. Thus, we shall see that assessment has three foci: the student, the teacher, and the curriculum.

In Figure 9–2, the interaction among the teacher, student, and the curriculum is shown as a triad. You will note that teacher-student evaluation is reciprocal. The teacher evaluates the student, as the student evaluates the effectiveness of the teacher. Also, these participants perform self-evaluations. Each of the facets of evaluation has its own purposes and techniques. These will be discussed later. Both the teacher and the student evaluate the curriculum, each from his own vantage point. Utilization of the evaluation triad should result in a more satisfactory program.

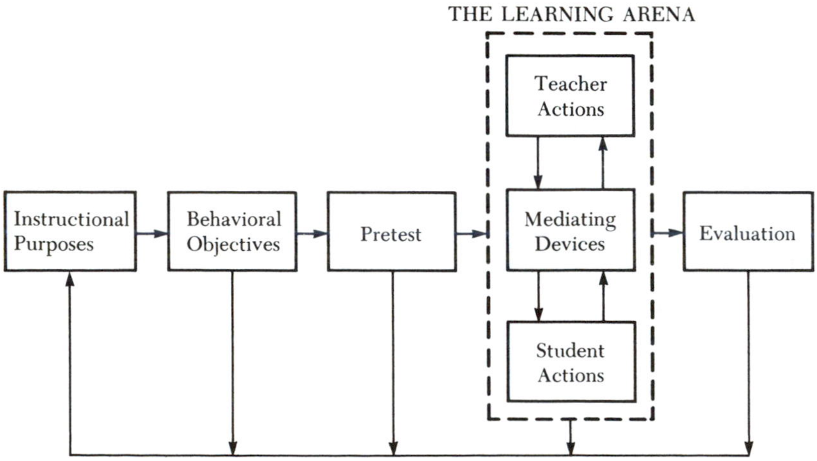

Figure 9–1. ***Model for Instructional Design (MID)***

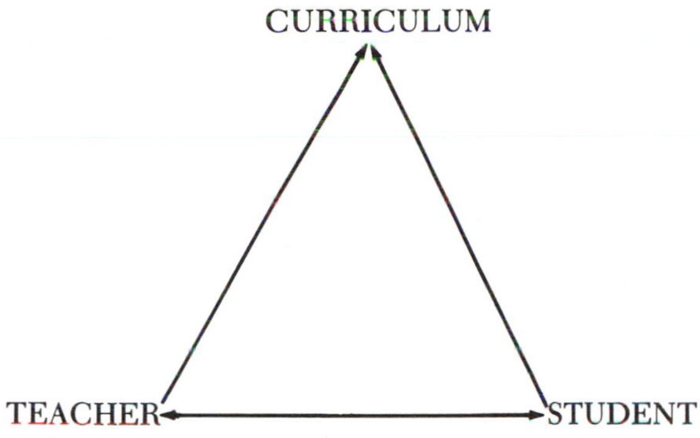

Figure 9–2. *The Evaluation Triad.*

Objective

The reader will be able to:

Describe (1.0) the pitfalls in evaluation offered in this section.

Pitfalls in Evaluation

Evaluation is typically considered the weakest component in the MID. Although the use of the triad can help strengthen evaluation, the unwary can be trapped in at least three pitfalls: limiting evaluation to teacher assessment of pupil progress, confusing evaluation with grading, and stressing lower levels of cognition in appraising pupil growth.

Limiting evaluation to teacher assessment of pupil progress.

As we have stated, the evaluation triad has three focal points: the teacher, student, and curriculum. Although a vital part of the evaluation process, teacher appraisal of pupil growth is only one consideration. There are two other facets, the teacher's behavior and the quality of the curriculum, which must be considered before complete assessment has been accomplished.

There are several reasons for this narrow view of evaluation. The first stems from an authoritarian philosophy. The institution of education was considered guardian of knowledge. Knowledge was purveyed to the student through the teacher whose wisdom and authority went unquestioned. Evaluation was the teacher's subjective judgement of pupils' progress toward meeting teacher demands. Purposes for learning were basically unknown to the student. He learned because the teacher said this was to be learned. Those of us who have been raised under this philosophy tend to perpetuate a similar orientation, unless somewhere in our professional growth we begin to question the worth of knowledge learned for its own sake. We feel that the student should be able to use knowledge obtained in the learning arena, and we view him as an active participant with differing needs, feelings, and abilities.

A second point concerns our effectiveness as teachers. It is always less painful to judge and find fault with the actions of others. It is difficult to look at oneself and ask these questions: Did I handle that situation effectively? Did I select appropriate experiences to teach that skill? Are my actions impeding student progress? Many times you can hear teachers making such statements: "I can't get Steve to do a thing! He's the laziest child I've ever seen." When visitors come to a classroom, a teacher may comment, "This is one of our *slower* groups. They are so unmotivated!" Perhaps the problem is that such *teachers* are unmotivating. They are quick to blame the students, instead of analyzing their own actions in the learning arena.

Confusing grading with evaluation.

Grading usually refers to the assigning of marks to pupils' daily work and tests. Using such grades, the teacher places an evaluation mark on a report form. Evaluation, on the other hand, is related to grading since the teacher uses methods of appraising pupil progress which result in a final grade. One of the continuing controversies in education is grading.

There are several differing philosophies of grading which we will examine briefly. The *absolute* philosophy holds that all children must be able to achieve given standards of performance. In practice, this philosophy has been translated into arbitrary standards for each grade level. Teachers are caught in this trap because they don't know, for example, what third grade children "should" do. Since they must assign a grade, they may employ one of the several kinds of absolute grading systems.

Some teachers assign grades using a fixed percentage. This is often called grading on the curve. This technique is not sound when used with small groups of students. For example, in a class of 30 very capable students, all of whom are working at grade level or above, ten percent are doomed to failure at the outset. On the other hand, in a class of slow learners who are working considerably below grade level, ten percent of these students will receive *A*'s. Obviously, the *A*'s assigned to the radically different groups will mean different things.

Percent of Pupils	Letter Grade
10	A
15	B
50	C
15	D
10	F

Another absolute means of grading is employing a percentage system. The teacher gives the children who achieve 90% and above on a test an *A*, while those who receive 80 to 89% get a *B*, and so forth. The success of this system is based upon superior test construction. Test items would have to be well written. The test would have to contain a sufficient number of "easy" items to permit the average student to achieve between 70 and 79%. Obviously, these are unrealistic assumptions; few teacher-made tests are that well constructed. Later in the chapter, we will discuss test construction in the social studies.

Another philosophy of grading advocates that we assess children only on what we think they are capable of doing. Employing this philosophy, a child in the fifth grade reading at first grade level could conceivably get an *A* in reading on his report card if the teacher feels he is making satisfactory progress at his reading level. This view of grading may be called the *relative* approach since it sets standards relative to the abilities of each child.

Some school districts have combined these two approaches: teachers assign dual grades on report cards in each of the subject areas. One is given on the basis of absolute grade level standards and the other is relative to the abilities and efforts of the child.

There is no simple answer to the complex practice of assigning grades. Teachers must apply the philosophy of the school system in which they teach. Many schools are moving away from both of the philosophies stated above. They are abolishing report cards and letter grades. Some schools have moved toward continuous progress reports. Often, such reports are combined with parent conferences or letters to parents which tell specific objectives the child has completed. Behavioral objectives are used in such programs and aid in communicating the accomplishments of children. One caution which must be noted is that behavioral objectives can become absolute standards, unless they are individualized.

Social studies has been one of the most difficult areas to grade in the elementary school. The reasons for this are multiple. In the first place, social studies includes a broad range of goals. Goals, such as the teaching of citizenship, are not readily translated into behavioral objectives which would generally be accepted. Also, the skill areas of social studies have remained nebulous until recently. Teachers have had difficulty identifying appropriate skill objectives. In the past, they have relied heavily upon reading from a single textbook in social studies. Grading became an analysis of reading comprehension in the social studies text. This is related to the problem of evaluation we will discuss below.

Stressing lower levels of cognition.

"What is the capital of ________?" "Where was George Washington born?" "Who is buried in Grant's tomb?" Unfortunately, these are not unusual questions in some social studies classrooms. You will note that these questions are the lowest level of the hierarchy in Bloom's taxonomy. We have stated that this taxonomy provides us with a means of analyzing and classifying cognitive objectives. We would like to mention here that this same tool can be used to construct or analyze discussion questions or test items. The taxonomy can be utilized to achieve a balance of discussion questions or test items which range from the lowest to highest levels of cognition. This application of the taxonomy will be discussed in the test construction section of this chapter.

Objectives

The reader will be able to:

Explain (2.0) the methods commonly used for teacher self-evaluation.

Explain (2.0) the ways informal and formal devices can be used to evaluate student progress.

List (1.0) the sequence of steps the authors suggest for the development of effective tests.

Contrast (2.0) the two major classifications of test items.

Prepare (5.0) sample test items from selected portions of this text.

Suggest (5.0) ways to encourage student assessment of teacher effectiveness.

Establish (5.0) personal goals for the remainder of this book.

Describe (1.0) the teacher's role in aiding student self-evaluation.

Interactive Evaluation—The Base of the Triad

There are three elements we must consider in discussing the base of the triad. *First*, is the teacher's evaluation of his actions in designing and implementing instruction. *Second*, we shall consider teacher-pupil assessment of progress, the cooperative venture in evaluation. *Thirdly*, we will discuss student self-evaluation in which the student assesses his personal growth.

Teacher self-evaluation.

Many times, a teacher finds himself faced with perhaps the most plaguing of questions: How good a teacher am I? We all have days in which we feel that we own the world; also, there are those days in which we wonder whether we have selected the "right" profession. The fact is that the good teacher is one who constantly seeks out better ways of doing things. Poor teachers refuse to examine their own teaching; they make scapegoats of the children, the administration, or the weather.

What is teaching, after all? It is setting the conditions which allow learning to take place. We can't "teach" anyone anything. We merely facilitate learning. This, then, is the approach we need to take in evaluating our teaching. We must ask ourselves these questions: Are my actions causing children to learn? Where can I improve?

The checklist One of the most common devices used for self-evaluation is the checklist. Such a checklist provides a useful guide in assessing our teaching effectiveness. It is especially helpful for the beginning teacher who is in the process of discovering what teaching is all about. Here is a suggested checklist that may prove valuable to you. It has been organized according to the Model for Instructional Design.

This checklist is a product of our feelings and experiences in the area of teacher self-evaluation. It is only as valid as our beliefs about teaching are accurate. Persons using this checklist should revise it from time to time as they feel it necessary to fit their teaching situation.

The conference Conferences can be a useful self-evaluation technique. The success of the conference is contingent upon the skill of the supervisor in guiding the teacher to examine his teaching. Current philosophies of supervision place the supervisor in a helping capacity, rather than the former role of critic. You can expect supervisors and principals to come into your room, from time to time, to observe your teaching, especially, if you are a beginning teacher. These observations are generally followed by a conference. If you view the conference as a device to improve your teaching, which it is in reality, then, it will not be perceived as a threat to your ego.

SELF-EVALUATION CHECKLIST

	Satisfactory	Needs Improvement	Unsatisfactory
Overall Planning			
Have I read the course of study for my level?			
Have I prepared an outline for the year's program in social studies?			
Is daily and weekly planning adequate?			
Have I included students in my planning?			
Have I used a systematic procedure for designing instruction? (e.g. MID)			
Have I sufficient background to teach each segment of study?			
Am I familiar with the neighborhood setting of the school?			
Do I know my students well?			
Have I met the parents or visited children's homes?			
Do I accept my students?			
Purposes			
Are my purposes consistent with the course of study for this level?			
Are my purposes cohesive?			
Are purposes stated clearly and concisely?			
Have I set purposes with my students?			
Are my purposes consistent with those of others teaching at this level?			
Behavioral Objectives			
Have I translated my purposes into behavioral objectives?			
Are my behavioral objectives stated clearly and concisely?			
Does each behavioral objective contain an observable behavior?			
Have I set a level of success, criterion, for each objective?			
Have I adjusted my objectives to accommodate individual differences?			
Pretesting			
Are my pretests valid? Do they test for the objectives I intend?			
Have I used a variety of pretest devices?			
Have I used the results of pretests to guide my planning?			
Have I used pretesting to individualize my instruction?			

The Learning Arena

Have I used a variety of levels of experience?			
Have I selected experiences appropriate for the age and background of my students?			
Have the experiences I have used considered the learning styles of my children?			
Have I used both inductive and deductive methods?			
Have I considered the motivation of my students?			
Have I provided adequate knowledge of results?			
Have I provided adequate guidance?			
Am I flexible enough to handle the unexpected?			
Have I arranged my room as a learning laboratory?			
Have I provided adequate resources for children?			
Is my room attractive to children?			
Do I place enough attention on the physical aspects of the classroom—heat, light, furniture, ventilation?			
Do I offer students a good example in dress, manners, speech?			
Do I praise my students?			
Is the rapport of the classroom conducive to learning?			
Have I selected a variety of means for mediating instruction?			
Have I provided recognition for each student?			
Do students trust me?			
Have I given children opportunities to carry out responsibilities?			
Are my students actively involved in learning?			

Evaluation

Do I use a variety of means of evaluation?			
Are my tests valid? Do they test what I intend for them to test?			
Have I included higher levels of cognition?			
Do I use tests as a diagnostic tool?			
Do I use my tests as a teaching technique?			
Have I provided for student self-evaluation?			
Do I use results of evaluation techniques to improve my program?			

Audio and video techniques Media devices can be used to help the teacher evaluate his own performance and the behavior of students in the classroom. The tape recorder is an effective instrument for monitoring the verbal interaction between teacher and pupils. It is one way to determine whether we are talking too much and the children too little. It is also useful in checking on voice quality, speaking rate, language usage, and speaking mannerisms.

The video tape provides even more information about our teaching performance. In the art of teaching, it is surprising what one can overlook that will appear on the video tape recorder. During a taping session in an intermediate classroom, a teacher was engrossed in lecturing to the children about one of his favorite topics. It became obvious to the teacher reviewing the tape of his morning lesson that many of the children were politely listening to the obviously boring presentation. One little girl simply had endured more than she could take. Placing her hands on the tail of her sweater, she pulled it over her head and totally disengaged her being from the classroom. You can imagine the teacher's shock at seeing the self-made cocoon appear on the screen. No other form of evaluation could have been more revealing.

Video taping allows us to check voice, too. However, it also enables us to view the unconcious, nonverbal communication we emit. At times, the verbal and nonverbal message is incongruent and interferes with our communication. While viewing her performance on video tape, one teacher discovered that she inclined her body forward about thirty degrees from the upright position whenever she really wanted to stress a point. Annoying mannerisms, such as pacing the floor, tugging on one's ear, and biting one's nails are extremely obvious on a television monitor. Perhaps these recording devices are most useful because they present a completely unbiased feedback.

Interaction analysis One of the most researched techniques for the analysis of verbal interaction in the classroom has been developed by Ned A. Flanders, a prominent educational sociologist. The Flanders system divides the verbal interaction in the classroom into ten categories for classification and tabulation. This behavior is divided into teacher talk, student talk, and silence. Teacher talk is further divided into these traits: accepts feelings, praises or encourages, accepts ideas, and asks questions. These represent indirect influences of the teacher on pupils. Direct influences include lecturing, giving directions, and criticizing. The next two categories are divisions of student talk: response and initiation. The tenth category is listed as confusion or silence.

The teacher can use a tape recorder to obtain a sample of classroom interaction. By playing back the recording, he is able to determine his pattern of the interaction which he promotes in the classroom. An optional means of using this method is to have a fellow teacher observe and tabulate a sample of our teaching. The disadvantage of this system of analysis is that approximately nine to twelve hours of training is required for one to become proficient enough to use the tool effectively.

Teacher-pupil assessment of progress.

We have noted earlier that the appraisal of student progress is a task which the teacher shares with students. Often, teachers feel that they alone must assess everything the child produces. When specific objectives have been established with students, they are the best evaluators of their progress toward these objectives. The teacher facilitates feedback by asking the student questions about his achievement. The answers the student gives provide him with the guide for continuing progress. The time the teacher spends at his kitchen table arduously pouring over piles of papers, muttering to himself, is wasted if the students are not present to benefit from these verbal outbursts.

Although educators have been reluctant to evaluate children's growth in affective areas of learning, this growth can be evaluated effectively. We refer the reader to Chapter V where an example was presented illustrating how cooperation in group activities could be developed. A teacher might use the following checklist to assess pupil growth in cooperative behavior.

___ 1. Discriminates between behaviors which facilitate and inhibit group cooperation.

___ 2. Assists in the development of group rules.

___ 3. Identifies his behaviors which aid the group in accomplishing a task.

___ 4. Evaluates rules and suggests revisions which facilitate group cooperation.

___ 5. Identifies changes in his behavior which enable him to work more effectively in groups.

___ 6. Displays cooperative behavior in group assignments.

In many instances the Affective taxonomy itself can be used as an evaluative checklist. As you read through the remainder of the chapter, you will note that many of the informal and formal devices suggested can be utilized to assess affective learning as well as cognitive learning.

Informal devices Evaluation is a continuous process and an integral part of the instructional program. We tend to think of evaluation in terms of tests. However, some of the most effective techniques for evaluation are the informal devices that the teacher uses throughout the day. Three of the most common of these devices are observation, class discussion, and individual and group conferences.

1. Observation. Even in the area of observation, our central focus is what we want the child to attain. Observational techniques are particularly

useful for the evaluation of skills, as well as objectives, in the affective domain. Observation is also useful in supplementing data gathered through evaluation techniques. There are several ways to make our observations more reliable and valid. The methods discussed below help us to focus on specific behaviors and permit us to record data objectively. This will aid us in designing and individualizing our instruction.

2. Checklists. You will recall that in Chapter V we discussed the points of entry for the terminal behavior of reporting. We identified a hierarchy of subskills which would be required for children to reach the terminal behavior. From one of these subskills, we developed a series of lessons in Chapter VI. The following is a checklist which would show the progress of students through this series of lessons:

Topic Sentence Sequence   Student's Name ____________

✓ indicates completion

Identifies topic sentence in

Initial position ____
Final position ____
Medial position ____
Random position ____

Identifies paragraphs that do not have topic sentences ____

3. Rating scales. Rating scales provide an excellent means of recording evaluative data on individuals or groups. Generally, the rating scale contains a list of behaviors relating to specific objectives. It has some type of scale which can be used to record judgements concerning the degree of achievement of this behavior. We have discussed, previously, that

a. When asked, does the child attempt to work with a group?

1 2 3 4 5

b. Does he share materials with others?

1 2 3 4 5

c. Does he volunteer for routine housekeeping duties?

1 2 3 4 5

d. Does he carry out responsibilities?

1 2 3 4 5

cooperation is one value which we wish to promote in our classrooms. The preceding is a checklist developed by a teacher to evaluate growth of children in displaying cooperative behavior. Using a numerical rating scale, the teacher circled the number representing his judgement as follows: 1 was considered unsatisfactory performance, 2 below average, 3 average, 4 above average, and 5 outstanding.

4. Work samples. Collecting samples of children's work throughout the year allows the teacher and the student to review progress in skill development. Early in the year, many teachers set up file folders for each child and begin collecting samples of work in each of the skill areas. These folders can be used diagnostically to detect strengths and weaknesses. Often, the child is guided in analyzing his own problems so that the additional time spent on learning a skill becomes meaningful to him.

For example, some of the behaviors in social studies which can be assessed in this way are the answers to cognitive levels of questions the child gives on worksheets. Also, such items as vocabulary, sentence construction, paragraphing, outlining, summarizing, plus his ability to use reference materials, and to follow directions can be checked. An important advantage of work samples is that they are readily accessible to parents in their visits to the classroom. They provide teachers something concrete to show parents during parent-teacher conferences.

To improve the use of work samples as a diagnostic tool, some teachers note patterns of strengths and weaknesses in children's work. They place these on individual 3 × 5 index cards for each child and place them in file boxes. Other teachers make notes on the folders so that children have access to this information. Such techniques save the teacher and children the time usually required to rummage through the voluminous amounts of work which accrue toward the latter part of the school year.

There are other forms of work samples which the teacher can use to appraise pupil growth. Some examples are scrapbooks, collections, dioramas, models, murals, and the like. Sometimes, misconceptions can be detected in the products of children's endeavors. An example of this happened in one classroom in which a group of children had been working on a mural for several days. When they displayed the finished product to the teacher, she was shocked to discover an electric lamp resting on a table in a pioneer family's log cabin.

A more subtle example was discovered by a teacher in another classroom. Her children were studying the people of the Navajo nation. She found one group using the tepee to illustrate the home of a Navajo family. The teacher quickly recognized that this group had not learned that the Navajo lived in mud covered huts called *hogans*.

5. Class discussion. Class discussions provide another useful means of obtaining data on the progress of individuals and groups. In a class discussion, the teacher can determine how well children understand and use

new vocabulary. Valuable insights into the concepts, generalizations, feelings, attitudes, and values of children may be obtained through careful observations of classroom discussions. Such discussions can show types of social interaction among class members, which reveal the social structures within the group.

6. Individual and group conferences. As we indicated above, children should be encouraged to evaluate their own work. This task can be accomplished through careful teacher guidance in the individual conference. Here is how one teacher used this device in working with a student. One morning, while most of the class was busily working on a group project, the teacher decided that she should work individually with Ben who had trouble in writing descriptive sentences. Since social studies is one of the content areas in which Ben seemed especially strong, the teacher decided to use this content to help Ben write more expressive sentences. The paper she had selected was one which Ben had recently written about his imaginary trip to California, a culminating activity to the study of the gold rush. Ben read his paper to Mrs. Martinez.

My Trip to California

> We left St. Louis. The trip was very rough. Our wagon broke down twice. We saw Indians. We were very scared. We crossed the mountains, and it was very cold. We were all happy to get to California.

"Ben, let's look at the first sentence," Mrs. Martinez requested. "Can you tell me more about St. Louis? How did you feel when you left? What kind of day was it?" As Ben responded, Mrs. Martinez noted his answers on a piece of paper. "Look what you have told me, Ben. Can you place these things in that sentence?" the teacher asked.

At first Ben looked puzzled. Then he started to respond. Mrs. Martinez helped him juggle the words and phrases. Eventually, Ben came up with the following sentence: "One sunny spring day our family eagerly departed St. Louis, located on the banks of the Mississippi River."

Mrs. Martinez continued guiding Ben through the rest of the story. Obviously, one conference is not sufficient to correct Ben's language problem, but the conference may begin to focus his attention on expanding his sentences.

Group conferences can be used in much the same way as individual conferences, in assisting groups or entire classes in determining progress toward goals. The authors have had the experience of publishing elementary school newspapers in their classrooms. These newspapers were developed by the children to fulfill certain stated goals in the school. Periodically, the entire class would focus its attention on the original goals or purposes to assess whether they were accomplishing, in the newspaper, what they had set out to do.

Formal devices There are many formal devices which are appropriate for use in evaluation. These devices range from narrative descriptions of the performances of children to quantitative devices which measure the accomplishment of specific objectives.

1. Anecdotal records. Anecdotal records are brief-descriptions of the school behavior of individuals or groups of children. Usually, they are employed when the teacher perceives the need to monitor certain aspects of behavior which require systematic study. The most frequent use of this method is for the recording of anti-social behavior. These behavioral descriptions are only useful to the degree that the record describes what actually has happened. Although many people record their interpretations of specific situations as they occur, the value of this technique is that over a period of time, a pattern of behavior can be observed. This allows more insight for interpretation.

Some teachers keep a notebook; others record observations on slips of paper which they place in confidential folders. Children are not provided access to this type of information. Anecdotal records are helpful in communicating pupil progress to parents concerning the affective domain. For example, it is one thing to say to a parent "Your son is a bully." Since this is a value judgement which may be open to questioning by parents, it is much easier for the parent to see Johnny's problem if the teacher can produce a record of specific instances which describe the child's behavior.

Such recordings also become useful when teachers are asked to prepare case studies of specific pupils. The case study is an intensive analysis of a child with serious problems in school. Since data must be gathered from many sources in such a study, this technique is very time consuming for the teacher. The analysis of anecdotal records may reveal the need for a case study.

2. Diaries and logs. If there is a distinction to be made between diaries and logs, perhaps it is on the basis of the focus of these two instruments. The former is usually a more general, narrative account, sometimes over a longer period of time. Logs, on the other hand, usually cover one activity, skill, or specific span of time.

A class diary might be used to record events in which the class had participated throughout the year. A group log might be employed to note the process of the production of a play. A review of this log would allow the group to analyze the problems they had encountered during the development of the presentation and to note the growth of group skills. Such logs are useful to children when groups are involved in differing activities. They help groups of children keep the major problem in focus and to communicate their progress to other groups.

Individual student logs may help pupils keep track of reference materials they have used in a study project, as well as the personal problems they have encountered in using reference materials.

3. Inventories. There are, basically, three inventories which are useful to the social studies teacher, the attitudinal, interest, and skill inventory. Very simply, an inventory consists of a list of questions for which students are asked to provide answers which best typify their feelings about, their knowledge of, or interest in a subject or situation.

4. Sociometric techniques. Knowledge of the social group represented by children in the classroom is often essential. The teacher can work effectively with individuals if he knows with whom these individuals identify, with whom they are at odds, and who the isolates and leaders are. Such considerations are especially important in the intermediate grades and the upper primary levels because of the growth of peer influence. There are a number of ways this information can be obtained. Lee and Lee (276–88) suggest several. Perhaps the simplest way is to tell the children that you are going to work in groups during the year, and you need to know the classmates they would like to have in their group.

Give the children a list of classmates' names with the boys and girls separated in different columns. Ask the students to place the numeral 1 by the names of children they would select as their first choice. After the students have recorded a 1 beside all the names of the children they would choose first, you ask them to record their second choices in the same manner. You continue by asking them to record 3 by the names of all the children with whom they don't think they could work successfully.

The teacher must assure the class that their choices will be confidential. After they have made their choices, the teacher must collect the papers. It's a good idea to have the children fold the papers to prevent accidental embarrassment.

We will use the classroom survey presented in Figure 9–3, which illustrates the way a teacher organizes the data he collects. Since this type of tool takes six to eight hours to develop, it is best prepared on a weekend when there are few interruptions.

a. Ruling the chart. Some time can be saved by using Dietzgen's Planning Profile graph paper, available from engineering supply stores or bookstores carrying engineering supplies. You can, also, prepare the ruled charts yourself. Notice that the lines are drawn so the squares developed by the vertical and horizontal are divided diagonally, as shown in Figure 9–3. This is extremely important because it allows you to read the chart more easily. The shaded boxes are important, too, as we will illustrate below. Record the children's names, boys and girls separately along the side and the top. Be sure that you record them in the same order in both places.

b. Recording choices. From the class lists on which the children have indicated their choices, record the information as illustrated in Figure

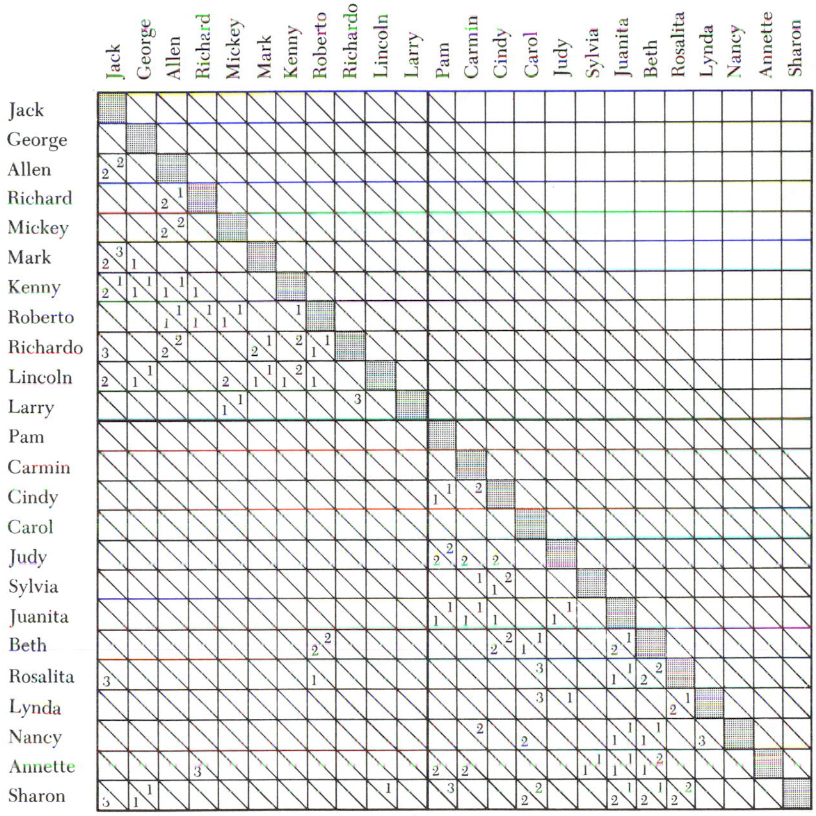

Chosen 1st	1	3	3	3	2	1	4	7	2	2	1	2	1	3	1	1	2	6	4	1	2	2	2	4
Chosen 2nd	4	2	3	0	2	1	0	1	2	1	0	2	1	3	2	1	1	2	4	3	0	1	1	2
Total	5	5	6	3	4	3	4	8	4	3	1	4	2	6	3	2	3	8	8	4	2	3	3	6

Mutual	2	3	6	1	3	2	4	6	3	3	1	3	1	3	2	2	2	8	8	4	1	2	3	5
Reject Made	1	0	0	0	0	0	0	0	2	0	0	0	0	0	2	0	0	0	0	0	0	0	0	1
Reject Rec'd	3	0	0	1	0	1	0	0	0	0	1	1	0	0	0	0	0	0	0	1	1	0	0	1

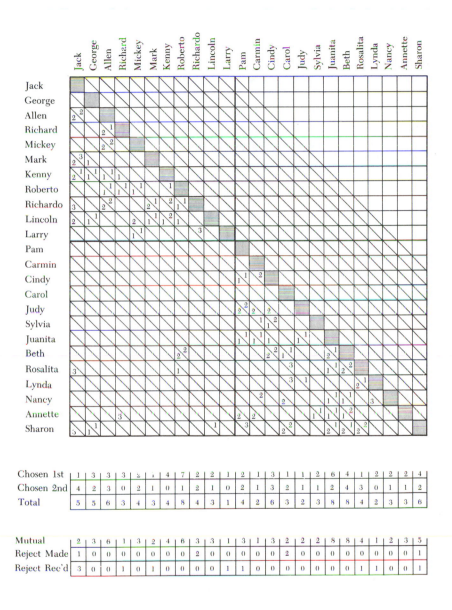

Figure 9–3. *Data Chart for Sociogram*

9–3. In our sample class, look at Mickey's choices. Proceeding out from his name we have recorded his second choice for Allen in the lower half of the box. Note that the 90° angle is always toward the line on which the name of the person making the choice is placed. Proceed, then, to the right, and you will note that you enter the shaded square. In this square, you turn and go down the chart. Mickey gives a first choice to Roberto and to Larry. Note that these choices are recorded again in the triangle with the 90° angle on the line on which Mickey's name is placed, this time on the top of the chart. Kenny's choices are recorded in the same manner. He chooses Jack second; and George, Allen, and Richard, first. Continuing to and coming out of the shaded square on the bottom, we find that Kenny gave Roberto a first choice and Richardo and Lincoln a second choice.

After you have recorded all the boys' choices, you can begin with the girls'. In our example, Pam's choices are all recorded going down the table. The recording for the girls, you will note, is all done in the right hand lower squares, formed by the intersecting lines dividing the lists of boys and girls. Choices between boys and girls are recorded in the left hand, lower square. The tallies at the bottom of the chart indicate the more popular children. These are useful in preparing the next step. Group interactions are shown more easily through the development of a sociogram. This is a tedious but rewarding task.

c. Preparing the sociogram. There are a number of ways this can be accomplished. Begin with the boys, by placing the most popular children in the center of three concentric circles. Place the less popular children in the next circle or band and the least popular on the outer band. Now establish linkage between the mutual choices. After this has been accomplished, identify the isolates—the children rejected by members in the group. Place these on the sides so that polarizations within the group can be established.

In Figure 9–4, notice that Ricardo rejects both Larry and Jack. Jack has rejected Mark. These children have mutual choices in this rather well integrated group. There appear to be few closed cliques, possibly, because of such children as Kenny and Roberto. Closed cliques are those mutual choices in which the members of the group choose only each other. All children in our illustration have at least one mutual choice. Larry's position in this group would cause a teacher some concern. Although rejections within integrated groups are not uncommon, the teacher must form his groups so that such rejections are considered. These children can rarely work well together. Children's choices do change. Evidence for such changes are found through observation.

Cleavage also exists among girls in our sample group. Carol could not work with Lynda or Rosalita. Nancy and Sharon obviously reject Lynda, too. Lynda might be integrated successfully into a group including Judy, Pam, and Cindy. Juanita could be used as the social center of several

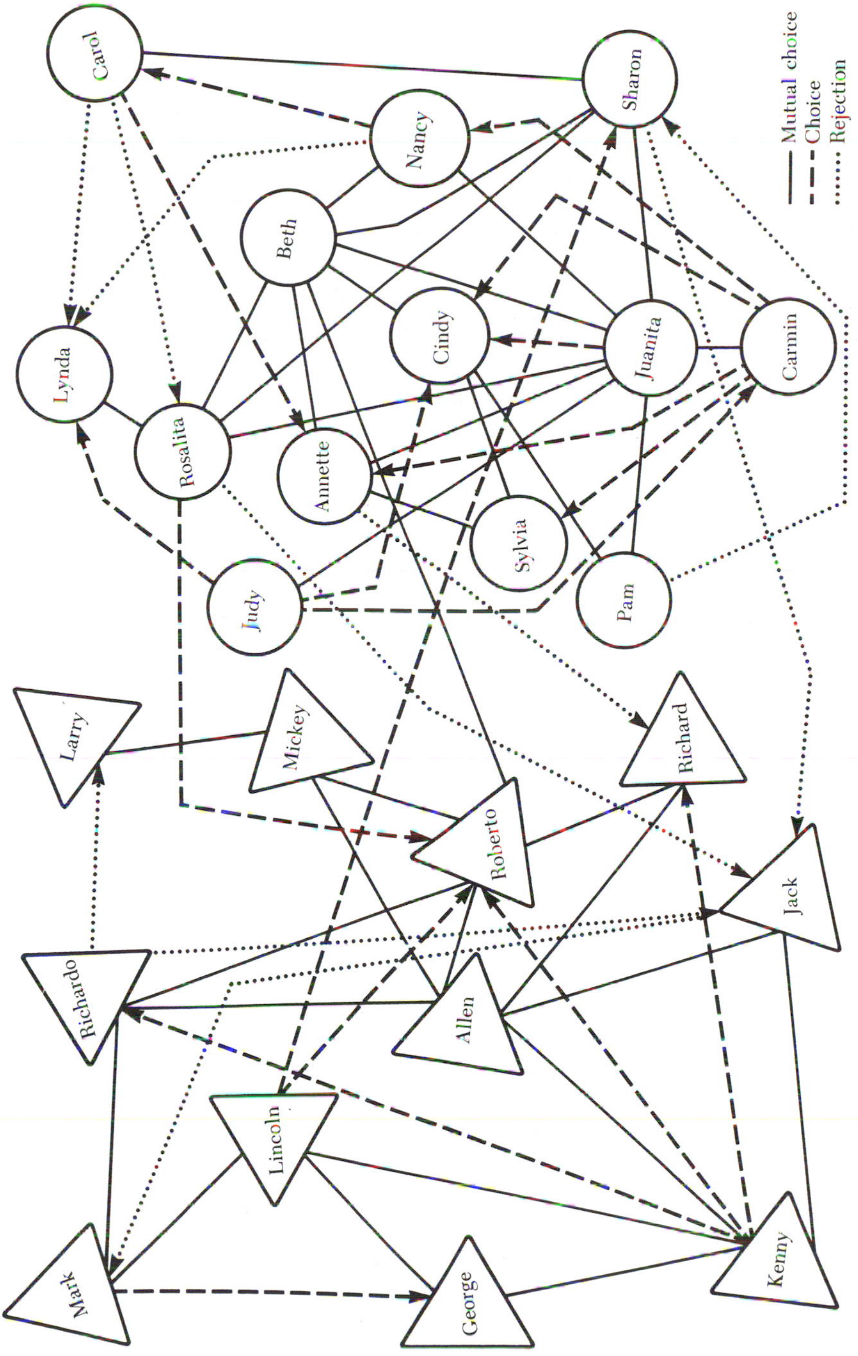

Figure 9–4. *Sociogram*

groups. Rosalita could be placed with Sharon, Beth, Nancy, and, possibly, Annette.

In the intermediate grades, it is expected that one will find an absence of choices between boys and girls, or it is possible that the age phenomenon will produce a large number of rejections. The only way to decipher the data is through observation. Some rejections are real; others are peer fads. The teacher must remember that the sociogram is only one tool which he can employ to *help* him observe group interaction. Although it has aided teachers in solving preplexing classroom interaction problems, good judgement is required to prevent misuse of this tool.

5. Teacher-made tests. Test construction in social studies has been a thorn in the side of many teachers. This is so because of the spectrum of objectives in social studies learning, and because teachers are often ill-equipped for the task. They simply do not know where to begin in building a "good" test.

Frequently, teachers put the cart before the horse and make "grading" the main reason for giving tests. Actually, the only justifiable reason for giving a test is to improve instruction. The "grading" element should not enter, except as a by-product of our testing.

We should use the results of tests to improve instruction in various ways. First, test results provide necessary feedback on the effectiveness of our own actions in the learning arena. Have we helped children learn? Next, such results allow us to individualize our instruction, when used to pinpoint the strengths and weaknesses of each student. How well is each child progressing? Thirdly, test results are useful in evaluating the curriculum. What learning experiences need to be changed if our purposes are to be met?

In this section, we shall look at some basic considerations in test construction. Then, we shall offer some steps in test construction which we hope will prove useful to you in your teaching. Finally, we shall provide information concerning different types of test items.

a. Basic considerations. Constructing a "good" test is not an easy task. As a college student, undoubtedly you have become disgruntled by your exposure to poorly constructed tests: items that were poorly written and vague; tests that were too long and too difficult; questions which did not apply to what was stressed in the course; and a sampling of test items which did not allow you to demonstrate what you had learned in the course. All of us have had similar experiences.

One of the most important of the basic considerations in test construction is the validity of our tests. Test experts have identified various types of validity. However, it is not the purpose of this section to make a test expert of you. We shall discuss only those aspects of test construction which are most appropriate for the classroom teacher and applicable to the elementary school. This means that our major concern will be with the content validity of our tests. Content validity means that the test actually measures what it purports to measure in terms of content learned or other behavioral changes. We might ask ourselves when considering the content validity of a test we have built, "Does this test provide ample opportunity for my students to demonstrate what they have learned in the unit or lesson?" When we offer our steps for test construction, we shall provide you with a means for assuring that your tests will have content validity.

Reliability is another term which you will hear in connection with tests. A reliable test is one which consistently produces the same results. Obviously, it would appear that the only way one could determine the reliability of a test would be to administer the same test to the same set of children more than once. However, this is not possible since once the test is administered the children would have been exposed to the items, and, thus, the following administrations of the tests would be affected. Reliability, therefore, is more the concern of standardized test makers than classroom teachers. In this sense, it is a statistical concept There are statistical methods of computing the various kinds of reliability. You may find a reliability coefficient in the manual for a standardized test that you administer.

Economy is another important consideration in constructing tests. Here, we are referring, mainly, to economy of time. Frankly, teachers do not have a lot of time to spend on test construction. Good teaching involves a considerable amount of time spent in planning and organizing of learning activities for students. If evaluation, including provisions for testing, is part of our overall planning, we can save ourselves time, as well as produce better tests. Our behavioral objectives, precisely stated, will help us determine the best means for assessing progress toward desired goals.

Sometimes, teachers run out of time and look to the tests offered at the end of chapters and units in textbooks. This would be a reasonable course of action to take if the teacher were basing the learning experiences of his students on parts of textbooks. However, the use of a multimedia approach makes this procedure unsuitable. It is rare that commercial materials can be incorporated totally into the learning environment. Generally, the teacher selects segments of these materials and combines them in various ways in the learning arena to suit the needs and purposes of instruction and the individual differences of his students. Test items offered in the teacher's guides of commercial materials may be utilized by the teacher if he is careful to select items which will have content validity for his program. Often, these items are carefully constructed and represent various levels of cognition and affection. They may provide the teacher with helpful insight for the construction of high quality test items.

b. Steps in test construction. You will recall that in the Model for Instructional Design (MID) the teacher translates purposes into behavioral objectives which will guide the selection of learning experiences. When we are formulating our behavioral objectives, we are actually completing the first step in test construction—*identify the expected changes of observable student behavior.*

Again, returning to the MID, when we identify the content which will provide the vehicle for student learning, we are completing the next step in test construction—*identify the content which will be employed to meet the selected objectives.*

Now we will need some systematic way of assuring that our tests have content validity and a balance in the included levels of cognition. In other words, we need a way to make certain that we are testing the content which we have selected, and that we are not restricting test items to the lowest level of cognition—simple recall of information. Gronlund (49–50) suggests constructing a Table of Specifications so that the test maker will have "greater assurance that his test will measure the learning outcomes and course content in a balanced manner."

In the sample unit on geography presented in Chapter III, you will recall that the children were engaged in inquiry into why Michigan peaches were found in Chicago. The table of specifications which the teacher had prepared for this unit of study is presented in Table 9–1. This presentation is an adaptation of one prepared by Gronlund (49).

The teacher used the following steps in constructing this table: After writing behavioral objectives and selecting content and experiences for the unit, he determined the amount of time which the class would spend on each of the concepts contained in the unit. This figure appears as a total in the second column of our table. The numbers in this column represent percentages of time the teacher plans to spend on the concepts presented in the unit. For example, 10% of the unit teaching time will be spent on climate. Area association will take approximately 20% of the time required. The total for this column is always 100%. Next, the teacher determined what portion of time would be spent in the various cognitive levels for each concept. For example, 10% of the total instructional time will be spent on soil-types at the following cognitive levels: knowledge, 3%; comprehension, 2%; application, 3%; and analysis, 2%. These figures total 10%. You will note that the teacher did not plan to spend time at the synthesis and evaluation levels for this concept, in this unit.

After completing the table of specifications in this manner, the teacher summed each column. These figures helped the teacher to balance the cognitive levels of learning presented to his children. For example, 25% of his time would be spent in the knowledge level; 21%, comprehension;

TABLE 9–1

Table of Specifications for Michigan Peaches Unit

Concepts	Knowledge	Comprehension	Application	Analysis	Synthesis	Evaluation
Climates	2	3	1	2	2	–
Soil types	3	2	3	2	–	–
Land-use	5	3	2	–	–	–
Technology	–	3	2	3	2	–
Areal association	5	3	3	4	3	2
Transportation	7	2	1	4	4	2
Location	3	5	2	4	4	2
Total	25	21	14	19	15	6

14%, application; 19%, analysis; 15%, synthesis; and 6%, evaluation. You will note that these figures, also, total 100%. The table of specifications helps the teacher in budgeting his time for instruction, as well as determining the relative stress which will be placed on each concept. This provides useful information for test construction. Utilizing the table assures content validity, as well as balance, in terms of the questions asked.

The table should be open to modification during the instructional process. Often, through pretesting, we find that children already know what we intend to teach. If this is true, then, it is wasteful to spend time on the identified concept. This time can be spent teaching a concept the children do not know. There is a third step in test construction which we have just described—*make a table of specifications.*

The fourth step in the construction of tests is to *prepare test items suitable for measuring progress toward stated objectives.* The various types of test items will be discussed in the next section of this chapter. The process you go through in determining the type of item involves an analysis of the behavior specified in the objective. Are you asking the child to list facts he has been presented? Do you intend for him to use a skill which he has learned? Are you asking him to evaluate a situation with some external criterion? The answer to such questions will provide a guide for you to use in the selection of the type of test item.

The fifth step is to *write and assemble the test items.* The writers have found that test items are more useful if they place them on 3x5 cards. This facilitates the assembling of the test because the items can be easily rearranged or discarded.

The last step is to *compare items with behavioral objectives.* Before putting your test in final form, it is important to return to your behavioral objectives in order to determine if test items will assess the desired changes of behavior. Take each of your behavioral objectives and go through your test, checking the items which relate to the objective under consideration. This step provides the teacher with another opportunity for changing or deleting items before finalizing the test.

The steps we have suggested for the construction of tests are summarized below.

1. Identify the expected changes of observable student behavior.
2. Identify the content which will be employed to meet the selected objectives.
3. Make a table of specifications.
4. Prepare test items suitable for measuring progress toward stated objectives.

5. Write and assemble the test items.

6. Compare items with behavioral objectives.

c. Types of test items. Basically, there are two major classifications of test items: essay items and objective items. The essay item is not generally used for testing the simple recall of information. Because it requires a response from the student in narrative form, it is particularly valuable when the student is called upon to demonstrate his comprehension, make inferences, organize thoughts, compare and contrast, analyze, synthesize, and evaluate material. An essay test usually requires that the teacher prepare only a small number of test items. At first, it may sound like an easy way to construct a test. However, since tests of this type are often most laborious to score, teachers may be reluctant to utilize essay items.

Essay items must be constructed carefully so that the student is provided with sufficient freedom of response but, nevertheless, is given some direction in making his response. Items which are too broad and general will be very difficult for students to answer and even more difficult for the teacher to score. Obviously, a question such as "What caused the Civil War?" would be placed in the "too vague" category. It would be better to structure students' responses to some extent. The following are examples of such essay questions: "What role did slavery play in precipitating the Civil War?" "What factors caused the South to secede from the Union?" "Contrast the economy of the North with the economy of the South at the beginning of the Civil War?" If you formulate your essay items with the precise changes of behavior you are helping children achieve, you are less likely to write vague items which have little content validity and relevance for the program of instruction.

Objective items, on the other hand, are more difficult to construct but are more easily scored. There are many kinds of objective test items which are appropriate for classroom test construction. We shall describe, briefly, the main types of objective items used in tests for elementary school children.

A true-false or alternative response item is a statement to which the student responds by marking it true or false, agree or disagree, correct or incorrect, or a similar response. Such an item can be used to assess a variety of objectives ranging from simple recall of information to the higher cognitive levels of analysis, synthesis, or evaluation. Although very easy to score, the true-false item is difficult to construct because the statement must be precise without "giving away" the correct response. The statement must be simple and clear so that it is not open to more than one interpretation. Often, the writer of the item will have his interpretation in mind and cannot perceive that the reader may misinterpret the statement. It has been said that the very bright or creative student may "read more" into the item than the writer intended and, thus, may score lower on a true-false test than is indicative of his understanding of the subject matter. Whether this is true or not is a matter for debate. However, it is up to the test writer to prevent the inclusion of ambiguous statements.

There is the possibility, too, that a "test-wise" student may get clues from the manner in which the statement is written. You probably have learned that true-false items which are strongly "for" or "against" with no exceptions most often are not "true." For example, without any knowledge of the subject at all, you would be reluctant to respond affirmatively to these statements: "All rivers flow from north to south." "Policemen never break the law." "All Eskimos live in igloos." "George Washington never told a lie." "Specific determiners," such as "always", "never," and "all," should be avoided in writing items.

A serious disadvantage of the true-false item is that it encourages guessing. It is possible that the "lucky guesser" can score higher on this type of test than a child who has a much better grasp of the material. In order to avoid this particular trap, some teachers include a penalty for guessing. This is accomplished by subtracting the number of incorrect responses from the number of correct responses ("rights" minus "wrongs"). The result is that the student has a double penalty for marking a response incorrectly. If the statement is left unmarked, obviously, this statement has not been marked correctly. Thus, the teacher cautions the student to guess only if he is certain that his will be an "educated" guess—he has some basis in fact for his response. He is discouraged from guessing by the double penalty.

Let's see how this example might work using a 50 item true–false test. Student A responds to each item although he is not sure of six of the items. Of these, he has responded incorrectly to five and misses three additional items. Thus, he has answered 42 items correctly. He has answered eight items incorrectly, and 42 - 8 = 34. His score, then, is 34. Student B, on the other hand, is not sure of six items but responds to only two of these. He gets one of these right and misses the other. In addition, he, too, misses three other items. He has answered 42 items correctly. He has answered only four items incorrectly, and 42 – 4 = 38. Thus, student B was better off by not guessing.

The true-false item has another serious limitation since it does not permit the student to express himself—to demonstrate his command of the subject matter. This is particularly true when teachers select insignificant bits of information from a text book and convert these into true-false items. An example of this might be, "Abraham Lincoln took a long walk each day before he went to work." Obviously, an understanding of our heritage is not based upon a knowledge of unimportant items such as this!

In order to produce true-false items that are well-worded and which have content validity, it may be necessary to rewrite the items several times. Having a colleague read your items before you insert them in a test is a profitable course of action. Perhaps you can do the same for him. In this way you have greater assurance that the items you produce will be of high quality.

Multiple–choice items, too, can assess a range of cognitive levels. A multiple–choice item consists of a "stem," which may be either a question or an unfinished statement of some kind, followed by four or five alternative choices—the correct response plus several distracters. In writing the stem, the teacher must avoid nebulous statements and the inclusion of irrelevant material. The problem or question should be clearly and concisely stated. The alternatives must all be plausible. Too often, teachers, for lack of more than two or three plausible distracters, will include a distracter or two which are obviously incorrect. The "test wise" student is aware of this flaw. In responding to multiple–choice items, he looks for the response which is obviously incorrect. Perhaps, he can eliminate another of the distracters, too. Thus, he can skillfully narrow down the choices to maybe two. The multiple–choice item is not effective when alternatives are poorly written. If there are only two logical alternatives, then, it would be better to use a true–false item instead.

Also, the use of "all of the above" or "none of the above" is not considered good practice. Often, these distracters are included as "fillers" when the teacher is unable to construct sufficient suitable distracters.

The experienced test constructor is wary of grammatical inconsistencies in the wording of the alternatives which may help the student eliminate several of the distracters on that basis. The stem and all of the alternatives must be grammatically consistent. It is wise to construct all of the alternatives in a parallel fashion. For example, it is obvious that two of the distracters in the following question don't fit the stem.

Chicago is located in:

A. Wisconsin
B. Illinois
C. near the Mississippi
D. by Lake Erie

Examine this multiple–choice item.

Fifty years ago, the typical Eskimo family lived in an

A. tepee
B. house
C. cabin
D. igloo

Obviously, usage tells us that "D. igloo" has to be the correct response because "an" is used before vowels. An alternative way to word this item might be as follows:

Fifty years ago, Eskimo families typically lived in

A. tepees
B. houses
C. cabins
D. igloos

Another pitfall of writing multiple–choice items concerns the inclusion of more than one distracter which will complete the stem correctly. For example, if we were to reword the item concerning the location of Chicago, we might come out with this.

Chicago is located

A. in Wisconsin
B. in Illinois
C. near the Mississippi
D. by Lake Erie

The best choice would be "B. in Illinois." However, depending upon the reader's interpretation of "near," "C. near the Mississippi" might also be considered correct. Chicago is certainly closer to the Mississippi than New York or Los Angeles.

When students are asked to select the "best" alternative, confusion can arise unless it is clear what "best" in this instance means. For example, look at the following multiple-choice item:

The best way to travel across the country is by

A. auto
B. train
C. bus
D. airplane

The reader has no way of determining what the writer had in mind by "best." Best in terms of cost? This might be contingent upon the number of passengers who would be traveling together. If "best" means most economical in terms of time, then "airplane" is the correct response. However, if "best" refers to the ability to plan a personal itinerary and see the most sights, the automobile may be the answer.

Another way teachers "give away" multiple–choice items is through making the correct response longer than the distracters. The test-wise student soon learns that teachers tend to include more information in the correct response. The item below is a glaring example.

> Studies of children who learn to read early show that early reading tends to
>
> A. interfere with subsequent progress in reading at school.
>
> B. be associated with parents' exerting considerable pressure on the child to achieve.
>
> C. contribute to the child's developing a positive self-image and favorable attitudes toward learning.
>
> D. be associated with high achievement during subsequent years in school.

Scoring of multiple–choice items is quick and accurate. Many teachers feel it worthwhile to take the time to construct quality multiple–choice items which can be reused. If your objectives remain the same, this appears to be the sensible thing to do. Placing your items on index cards as we have suggested earlier, can help you collect and file the items which appear to be of sufficient quality to retain in your files.

A third type of objective test item involves the matching of two sets of data. Matching items are most often used at the lower cognitive levels, particularly for recall of information. An example of a matching exercise follows:

> Match dates to events by placing the letter of the correct date in front of each event.

A. 1620	__________1. Columbus discovered America
B. 1776	__________2. The Declaration of Independence
C. 1492	__________3. The Magna Carta
D. 1536	__________4. Pilgrims land at Plymouth Rock
E. 1215	__________5. The First Continental Congress
D. 1774	

What criticisms do you have of the matching exercise above? Take a minute and list what you think is objectionable in this exercise.

Perhaps these are some of your criticisms: If the point of the exercise is to have students recall key dates in American history, why include the Magna Carta? Also, perhaps you felt that the two dates 1774 and

1776 are too close together and, thus, easily confused. Maybe you questioned the need for recalling the dates at all.

Matching tests are fairly easy to construct; they are compact, and scored quickly. They are most appropriately used when it is your purpose to strengthen students' association of related sets of data. The major difficulty lies in assuring that the correct response for one item of your data can logically serve as the correct response for all of the other items. In our matching exercise above, we see that this has been violated. The date 1215 stands out immediately as having occurred before the beginning of America, even before Columbus' discovery. The very sequence of events in our history "gives away" the responses to several of the events.

It is best to confine matching exercises to a single topic or theme. The above item is good from the standpoint that all possible responses are dates. Avoid irrelevant data and make your statements brief. Include an extra response or two such as was done above. Make sure that the material really lends itself to this type of item.

If it is the sequence of events you wish your students to retain, perhaps a different type of exercise would suffice. You might construct an item like this one.

> Arrange the following events in chronological order by placing the numeral in the sequence appropriate for each event.
>
> _____ The First Continental Congress
>
> _____ The Magna Carta
>
> _____ Pilgrims land at Plymouth Rock
>
> _____ The Declaration of Independence
>
> _____ Columbus discovers America

Listing exercises are another type of objective item which are utilized when simple recall of information is the task you wish to require of your students. These items are easy to construct and score. However, the major drawback stems from the limited learning outcomes which can be assessed in this way. For example, you might require the following of your students:

> List the four cardinal directions.
>
> 1. __________
>
> 2. __________
>
> 3. __________
>
> 4. __________

Or perhaps:

Name the first five presidents of the United States.

1. ________
2. ________
3. ________
4. ________
5. ________

Perhaps we should note once more that social studies testing has been criticized in the past for relying too heavily on items of this type which require only simple recall of information. There is a place for these items. There will be times when we shall want our students to recall certain information on tests. However, this is only a small portion of the learning in social studies. Our tests can and should assess learning at all cognitive levels, as evidenced by the many and varied tests and test items we would include in any evaluation program in social studies.

Student assessment of teacher effectiveness.

Returning for a moment to the evaluation triad, you will recall that teacher-student evaluation is reciprocal. In the previous section, we offered many means, both informal and formal, of obtaining data on the progress of students toward stated objectives. Use of the triad will remind us that students are our most effective source of obtaining information about our own teaching effectiveness.

We mentioned previously that this facet of evaluation is often overlooked. Beginning teachers, particularly, may be reluctant to provide opportunities for students to offer feedback on the effectiveness of their teaching. With experience comes an increase in confidence. It is this confidence which allows us to open the door to student evaluation of our actions. Fledgling teachers cannot expect to have acquired the same degree of confidence which the "old hand" may possess. This is understandable.

Both of the authors encourage their students in college classes to complete evaluation forms relating to each course they teach. An analysis of the results is sometimes ego-enhancing, sometimes shattering, but always enlightening! You can't please everybody, it is true, but patterns of responses can provide helpful clues in modifying content and experiences.

It isn't likely that as an elementary school teacher you will devise a paper-and-pencil instrument to help students assess your teaching effectiveness. This kind of evaluation will take place continously, as you search for clues in the faces of your students and the remarks they make. At times you may ask directly, such questions as "Did you enjoy the field trip we took yesterday?" "Is there any portion of this experience that you would change?" "Which of the activities in this unit did you feel were most worthwhile for you?" "Why?" "What part of the lesson was most difficult for you?" "Are there any suggestions that you have for my helping you?"

Letting students know that they will have many opportunities for evaluating your actions in the learning arena helps them view you as a human being. It is more likely that you will be able to meet students on a person-to-person basis and develop the type of rapport in the classroom which makes it a helping experience for all. You can see how the classroom can become a battleground in which the teacher faces students in a real power struggle. When a warm, accepting atmosphere permeates everything that is done, the situation is not likely to deteriorate in this way. All are working toward the same goals, and these goals are known and accepted by the students.

Student self-evaluation.

Much of the student self-evaluation which we would encourage is in the realm of personal-social goals and interpersonal relationships. In addition, there may be some skill goals which the student sets for himself, either with or without your help. Part of the task of the teacher is to help the child understand, accept, and think well of himself. The classroom atmosphere in which the student feels secure enough to engage in self-exploration is of the type we have described earlier. The democratic classroom in which the worth of every individual is respected should produce the helping atmosphere which will allow the individual child to set personal goals for himself and work toward the accomplishment of these goals.

The teacher's main function in the students' assessment of progress toward personal goals is generally one of providing feedback and encouragement. Here, the teacher takes his cues from the student and only enters the child's private world when he is invited.

The following are some of the personal goals which students in one fifth grade class set for themselves:

I want to control my temper better.

I need to learn to listen to others.

I have to speak up more in class.

I want to make more friends this year.

I'm going to try to be neater in my work this year.

I'm going to study harder.

I've got to stop trying to be the center of attention all the time.

Some of their skill goals included the following:

I'm going to use the dictionary to check the spelling of some words. When I guess, I get them wrong.

I want to learn to write more legibly this year.

I want to learn to take notes from references.

In addition to acting as a sounding board for students in helping evaluate their own progress, the teacher may encourage children to keep private diaries or at least notes on changes in their own behavior. The teacher may want to stress that the personal records the children keep are shared with the teacher only if, and when, the student desires.

Informal individual conferences with students initiated at odd periods during the day can be used by the teacher to help students assess their own progress, as well as to aid them in setting realistic, attainable goals for themselves. Helping students adjust levels of aspiration should result in increasing the likelihood of success-oriented experiences. This will occur if the teacher is willing to individualize his program to accommodate differing levels of aspiration, as well as previous achievement.

Objectives

The reader will be able to:

Describe (1.0) curriculum evaluation from the vantage point of the student and the teacher.

Explain (2.0) the use of the triad to improve evaluation.

Curriculum Evaluation

Evaluation of the effectiveness of the curriculum is too often left to supervisors and administrators. However, it is the teacher, in his daily implementation of the curriculum, who can observe the program in action and note its strengths, as well as its weaknesses. Current trends in supervision and administration offer the teacher a greater share of responsibility in curriculum evaluation.

On the other hand, it is the student whose behavior is supposed to be affected by the curriculum. The student views the curriculum from a different vantage point or frame of reference. Therefore, it is essential that students, too, play a role in this most important facet of evaluation. Currently, students in secondary schools and in higher education are pushing for a greater voice in determining policies and programs. In the past, educators have made faulty assumptions concerning the interests and needs of students. Perhaps if we had listened more to students, we would not face as much of the turmoil in education as we have now. Even elementary students are pleading to be heard. We must listen, but let's go a step further and solicit feedback from our students concerning the worth of what we are doing in schools.

Thus, we view curriculum evaluation as a two-sided affair. It is hoped that the discussion which follows will shed some light on this often neglected phase of evaluation, that of dealing with the curriculum itself.

The teacher's view.

The teacher's view of curriculum effectiveness can be most effectively communicated to the school system if the teacher has a set of questions to which he may respond. The authors suggest the following questions which may be used to guide your thinking in evaluating the social studies curriculum. This list is far from exhaustive. However, it may provide you with some insight with which you might go about this task. May we also state that such a list of questions could well be used to evaluate any curriculum.

THE TEACHER'S GUIDE TO CURRICULUM EVALUATION

What are the goals of the curriculum?

Are these goals realistically attainable?

Are the goals true to the disciplines, the needs, and interests of students, and the needs of the community, state, and nation?

Who formulated these goals?

Are the goals stated clearly enough so that they can be translated into purposes which can be utilized to design instruction?

How flexible is the curriculum?

Does the teacher have freedom in implementing the curriculum in terms of selection of strategies?

What provisions are there for modifications?

Is the scope of the curriculum too broad or too limited?

Is the sequence of topics logical?

How do I communicate suggestions for revision to supervisors and administrators?

How helpful is the curriculum guide?

The curriculum, indeed any curriculum, should be perceived as fluid and ever changing. It is constantly open to modification. The teacher can and should play a vital role in improving the curriculum and, hence, improving the quality of education for students.

The student's view.

The student views the curriculum from a different vantage point. Whereas the teacher sees the curriculum as something to be implemented or brought to life in the classroom, the student perceives the curriculum as an opportunity to learn about life and living. We hear numerous complaints, many of which are justified, from today's students concerning the lack of relevance in what goes on in schools. Often, students see little relationship between what is being offered in school and their own lives. This is sad. Not only that, it violates a basic principle of learning—that for learning to be retained and applied, the learner must understand the purposes and objectives for the learning and perceive the relationship between what is taught and those purposes and objectives. Perhaps there remains a teacher here and there who still teaches saber-tooth-tiger-scaring-by-fire because that's what he was taught. This same teacher would view any learning as an end in itself. Students just don't hold to this view. They want to see the "payoff." They want and need to know not only why something is to be learned, but how they can apply this learning in their daily lives.

We can make our curriculum more relevant and meaningful for students by providing them with an opportunity to assess the worth of the program. Again, this is a continuous process throughout the course of the school year when we ask students for their opinions and feelings about daily experiences in the classroom. At first, students may be reluctant to make such comments unless they are sure that what they say won't be held against them. The free and open classroom climate which we have described throughout this book should be conducive to the type of communication which will result in improvement of the curriculum.

One of our failings as teachers has been to get students excited about what we want them to learn and, then, to expect them to make the applications of what they learn with little or no help from us. We need to allot more time for guiding students in applying what they have learned so that in-school learning will have relevance and meaning for them.

Students vary widely in their ability to make such applications. Some pupils may be able to show the teacher certain applications which had eluded him. Other students will have great difficulty in transferring learning from one simple situation to another. It is the latter group of students with which we must spend the most time.

Eliciting comments from students about events in the learning arena can help us make modifications in the curriculum which will make it more relevant for them. The so-called generation gap is more a communication problem than anything else. It has little to do with age. If we take the time to listen to our students, we will have gone a long way in preventing a communication bloc. If we take what we hear from students and use it to modify, to innovate, or, perhaps, even delete parts of the curriculum, we will have taken a mighty leap toward relevance.

Summary

Evaluation, the last component of the Model for Instructional Design (MID), was the subject of this chapter. The evaluation triad shown in Figure 9–2 was offered by the writers as a means for assuring better balance in evaluation. We discussed three pitfalls in evaluation: limiting evaluation to teacher assessment of pupil progress; confusing evaluation with grading; and stressing lower levels of cognition in appraising pupil growth.

The remainder of the chapter focused upon a description of evaluation according to the triad. Teacher self-evaluation was given attention first. The cooperative venture in evaluation—teacher-pupil assessment of progress—was discussed next. In this part of the chapter, a myriad of formal and informal devices for evaluation was examined. Then, student assessment of teacher effectiveness and student self-evaluation were discussed. The chapter concluded with a section on curriculum evaluation by the teacher, as well as the student.

References

Gronlund, Norman E. *Measurement and Evaluation in Teaching.* New York: The Macmillan Co., 1965.

Lee, J. Murray, and Lee, Doris May. *The Child and His Development.* New York: Appleton-Century-Crofts, Inc., 1958.

X

Communication Skills in the Social Studies

Chapter Outline

Communication Skills in the Social Studies

If you couldn't read or listen, how would you "learn" in social studies? If you couldn't speak or write, how would you share with others what you have learned in social studies? Obviously, communication skills are crucial to social studies education.

The English language arts are considered by some to have no body of content. (Smith, 42) They are the *tools* of communication. Language arts and mathematics are the two basic skill areas in the elementary school curriculum (see Table 10–1). They are not content subjects at this stage, but they do permit us to manipulate thoughts and ideas. Both have a code. The language arts are concerned with our language as a code for dealing with ideas. Mathematics utilizes our number system for the same purpose. The subject areas in the elementary school curriculum, namely, science and social studies, provide the content or "meat" to be used for the development of these vital skills. The correlation of language arts and social studies, therefore, is a "natural." The expressive-aesthetic areas of the curriculum, art, music, and physical education, also play an important part in the total experience of the child in the elementary school.

The language arts are made up of the four modes of communication through human speech: listening, speaking, reading, and writing, plus certain mechanical skills, such as handwriting, spelling, punctuation, capitalization, grammar, and usage. Mechanics aid the communication process.

Table 10–1

The Elementary School Curriculum

Skill Areas	Content Areas	Aesthetic-Expressive Areas
Language Arts	Social Studies	Art
Mathematics	Science (Health-Safety)	Music
		Physical Education

The United States needs a literate citizenry—people who can communicate precisely and evaluate carefully what they see and hear. Never before have communication skills been more crucial to our very survival as a nation or even as a planet. A common complaint of social studies teachers is that, frequently, students are not able to read and understand the social studies materials suggested for their grade level. This means that many children in a typical third grade class will not be able to read "third grade" material. The problem may not lie with the material itself but with children's communication skills. The social studies teacher must help children develop skills, many of which are directly related to language. Let's take a look at the way in which language develops in children. This will aid us in focusing on language skills, as they relate to social studies.

Objectives

The reader will be able to:

Summarize (1.0) the sequence of language development in children, and explain (2.0) the skills in each phase.

The Origin and Natural Sequence of Language Development

We don't really know what triggers the development of language in humans. Some experts in the field of language study believe that we are born with an innate capacity to learn language, and that this capacity is what sets us apart from the animal world. Others reject this view, however, and hold that we are born *tabula rasa,* a blank tablet, or, in other words, with no innate disposition toward language learning. They feel that language is developed by receiving stimuli from the environment, responding vocally to the stimuli, and obtaining positive reinforcement for these responses, which ensures that this vocalization will be repeated.

Children are born with the physical apparatus for producing sounds. However, it is interesting to note that we have no "organs of speech"—organs used exclusively for the production of speech sounds. Humans have adapted certain groups of muscles which aid in the production of these sounds but which are also utilized for other purposes. These are the muscles of respiration, muscles which control the vocal cords, and muscles of the tongue and jaws. We share all of these physical attributes with other mammals.

At first, the infant elicits cries which call attention to certain physical needs. He receives stimuli through his sensory organs but has not learned to distinguish among the stimuli. Infants vocalize vowel sounds before consonants and, in fact, may not be able to produce all of the consonant sounds well until they are of school age. Consonant substitutions are common, and first grade teachers struggle to get some children to say *"Run, rabbit, run"* instead of *"Wun, wabbit, wun!"; father and mother,* instead of *faver* and *muvver. Valentines* may be *balemtimes* and *sandwiches, sammiches. Spaghetti* often comes out more like *pasghetti!*

Infants are intrigued with their own bodies and delight in discovering their power over parts of their bodies. They enjoy producing sounds, just for the sake of producing them, as they gain control over their vocal apparatus. This stage of development has been called the "babbling period" and consists of repeating certain syllables such as *mama*, *dada*, *bye-bye*, and the like.

As the child passes his first birthday, the babbling period gives way to the jargon stage. He probably has uttered his first word by now or will soon. During this period, the child appears to be speaking in a conversational way, except that early in this stage his speech doesn't make much sense. Gradually, the child learns that he can satisfy his wants and needs through the use of certain words, and he makes rapid progress in control of speech.

Jargon diminishes as the child's vocabulary grows, and there is an increase in the amount of talking. Children often move out of the jargon stage at age two, or a little older, and may begin to carry on lengthy monologues, while speech will accompany most actions. Linguistic abilities continue to increase at such a rapid rate that most preschool children are considered to be "linguistically sophisticated." This does not mean that they have an advanced command of the language, but rather that they are able to use the language fluently, effectively, and confidently to communicate thoughts and needs.

The four year old talks a great deal and loves the sound of Dr. Suess' silly language. Nonsense words like "supercalifragilisticexpialadocious," of Mary Poppins fame, really intrigue him. At age five, he still has difficulty between the real and the fanciful but continues to be a "talker." As he enters kindergarten, the child has a sizeable vocabulary and enjoys his power of speech.

Language develops in an orderly sequence (see Table 10–2). Basic to language development, of course, is experience. When children are deprived of sensory experiences early in life, they do not develop normally and may become linguistically handicapped. An extreme case of this is the supposedly true story of a "wolf boy" who as a small tot had wandered away from his parents in the woods, and was subsequently found and raised by a family of wolves. For years, he had no contact with humans and, hence, no opportunity to develop human speech. The sounds he uttered were wolf-like sounds. He was discovered and captured at long last, but rehabilitation was slow and not too successful.

The child deprived of experiences will not develop language normally. He may never completely recover from this lack of cognitive stimulation in these formative years. Thus, rich and varied experiences form a solid foundation on which the building blocks of language are laid.

Table 10–2

Natural Order of Language Development[*]

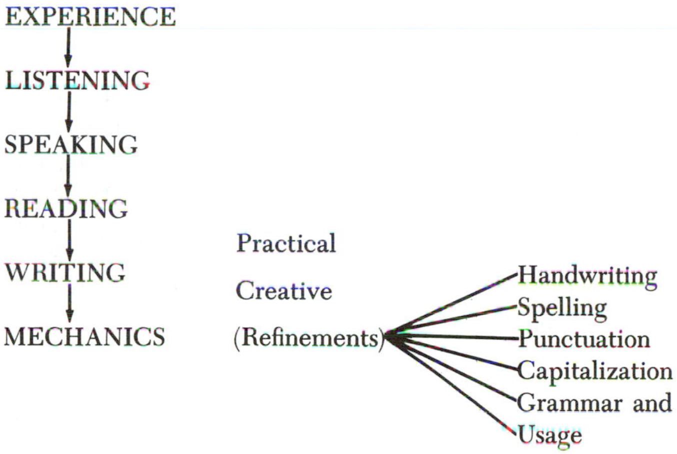

Listening is next in the sequence of language development. Of course, listening is a part of experiencing, since without experiences, there would be nothing to listen to. Children learn language by listening to it as it is used in the total environment. Imitation and association play important roles in acquiring a stock of words—speech sounds which convey meaning. For words to be meaningful, the child must have had some experience with them, either direct or vicarious.

The terms *listening* and *auding* may be used interchangeably. Both consist of two phases—hearing or decoding the spoken message and then comprehending. If you cannot or do not understand the communication you are receiving, you may be hearing but not listening. Too often in social studies this is what happens to students. "Paying attention" is the first step, but we cannot assume that because our students are attentive, they are "getting the message." Perhaps there are some learning gaps which will need to be closed in order for the material to be meaningful for our students. An oral question, here and there, by the teacher can help to determine if our assumptions are correct.

Listening, as a skill to be taught, is a fairly recent addition to the language arts curriculum of the elementary school. There are several reasons for this. In the past, children were supposed to be seen and not heard. When this philosophy prevailed, children were expected to sit passively for long hours in school and soak up wisdom like little sponges. Even in this "enlightened age" of ours, one occasionally runs across a teacher or prin-

[*]Modified from Smith (55).

cipal who will tolerate no noise in the classroom! (By noise is meant anything above a whisper.) Before much research was accomplished in the area of listening, teachers underestimated the demands they put on students for attentive listening during each school day. Also, it was not recognized that listening is a developmental skill which can and *should* be taught.

Speaking or oral expression follows listening in this sequence. The child learns to discriminate sounds—to listen—before he is able to reproduce sounds which bear meaning. Deaf children can be taught to talk, but it is a long and arduous process, and their speech has a different quality. The preschool years are a time for development of oral language patterns. Kindergarten experiences often have oral language development as a prime goal, especially, for the child who is bilingual or whose language development has been retarded for some reason.

Reading appears on the scene as the child enters first grade. It is an expectation of our culture that children learn to read during this year. Yet, this is contrary to what we know about individual differences. On the one hand, we are aware that children can learn to read before age six. This has been proven in many studies particularly in England, as well as on the Continent. Many children come to school knowing how to read, either having taught themselves or due to the efforts of well-meaning parents who want their child to "get ahead." Television has helped to introduce the printed word to small fry at an early age and to make them aware of the importance of written language in the communicative process. On the other hand, there are many six year olds who are not "ready to read" in the first grade for one or several of many reasons. Learning to read is a complex process which we still don't know very much about.

We are just barely beginning to scratch the surface in discovering how the individual learns to read. This process is not unlike that of listening. We stated earlier that listening is a two phase process consisting of decoding (hearing) and comprehending. Reading consists of the same two phases—decoding and comprehending. However, in reading, decoding involves the additional step of translating written symbols back into the speech they represent before meaning can be derived.

Decoding is made more difficult by the lack of one to one correspondence between graphic symbols and speech sounds. For example, the words *dough, blow, sew,* and *hoe* all rhyme, ending in what we call the long *o* sound. These sound-spelling inconsistencies help to make the task of acquiring skill in learning to read a very difficult one. On the other hand, Spanish may be termed a phonetically regular language because there is almost perfect correspondence between graphic (written) and speech (oral) symbols. Once the child has "cracked the code," that is, he has mastered these sound-symbol relationships, he can read with ease, providing the material is within his realm of meaning. Those lucky Spanish-speaking children, in schools in Mexico and Spain, do not have to cram for weekly spelling tests because spelling is not taught in their schools! It is not necessary, since spellings follow regular patterns. In our country, spelling remains a problem throughout the years in school and is troublesome for college students and professors alike!

When one tampers with the natural sequence of language development, there may be disastrous results. For example, when children are forced into a formal reading situation before they have a good command of oral language, the results are frustrating and defeating for the child and teacher, alike. This is often the case with children who speak a tongue other than English, as a native language, or who speak a non-standard dialect of English. More attention will be given to problems of the linguistically different learner in Chapter XIII.

Writing, both practical and creative, follows reading in the natural sequence. It is not until the child has acquired some facility in reading and understands that words represent thoughts, that he is able to do much writing on his own. Even the most simple writing assignment may be a monumental task to a beginner who is unable to spell many words and has not developed "sentence sense." The first step in getting children interested in writing is by recording their dictation—a word or phrase at the start—usually about a picture they have drawn. Most children need many dictation and chart story experiences before they are ready to write on their own. Chart stories or experience charts are often composed after the group has shared a common experience, such as a trip to the fire station. The children contribute the sentences for the chart story as the teacher records them on a chart tablet or the chalkboard. They may be reread many times during the year.

Writing or written expression should not be forced upon a child until he feels a real need to communicate in this manner. Fledgling writers will need to be given immediate individual help with such mechanics as capitalization, punctuation, and spelling so as not to interrupt their trains of thought. The child who has poor manual coordination may learn to use the typewriter for his stories. We are beginning to see more and more typewriters used by elementary school children.

Mechanics are not given great stress until the intermediate grades. Such things as punctuation, capitalization, and spelling are refinements and conventions which, if given too much stress in the early grades, can cause communication blocs in children. It is true that these skills are introduced informally in the first grade or even kindergarten. Although children's writing provides a meaningful context for the teaching of these mechanical skills, the mechanics must remain of secondary importance to the message.

Handwriting requires control of the small muscles of the hand. It is no longer looked upon as an end in itself but rather as a means to an end—communication. In days of yore, a delicate, flowery "hand" was cultivated as a thing of beauty. It was regarded more as an art form, than a medium of communication. Some children easily acquire a very legible hand. College students blame professors who lecture a "mile-a-minute" for their handwriting illegibility. "I could write pretty well until I came to college," is a common lament. And speaking of college professors, some are noted for their extreme illegibility coupled with the ability to erase what they have written before the student has hardly a glimpse of it! Thus, we should not be too harsh in evaluating the handwriting of elementary students, as long as it has a reasonable degree of legibility and fluency. Again, it is recommended that handwriting assignments be incorporated into the many aspects of the curriculum which require written communication, rather than isolating this skill from the communication process.

Grammar and usage are important to communication, also. They are not the same, however. Grammar refers to the structural principles underlying a language, including its phonology or sound system, morphology or forms of words, and syntax or word order (the latter not referring to a tax placed upon wrongdoing, although it might be next!).

Usage, on the other hand, deals with lexicon—word choice. The appropriateness of usage is judged on the basis of the context or situation in which the communication takes place. There is no absolute "right" or "wrong" usage. It depends upon the situation. The college professor who speaks to his friends with the erudite usage appropriate for his English class, but not for this informal situation, is a clod. On the other hand, an individual who addresses a college class using the "folksy expressions" of his locale may be well received. The former has had the benefit of many years of education and should know how to adjust his level of usage. The latter individual may not have had the benefit of higher education and may be severely limited in his range of usage.

Traditional grammar confused grammar and usage, tended to be prescriptive of good usage, and stressed memorizing lists of rules relating to language. The "new grammars" currently being taught in our schools are the product of recent linguistic findings and are eclectic in nature. Elements of structural and transformational grammar have been added to portions of the older, traditional grammar. The "new grammars" separate grammar from usage. They recognize varying levels of appropriate usage and are descriptive, rather than prescriptive, of language usage. Further, they enable students to arrive at concepts and generalizations about language using inductive processes.

Objectives

The reader will be able to:

Explain (2.0) the interrelationships of the language arts, using the chart in Figure 10–3; differentiate (2.0) among the four vocabularies each individual possesses; describe (1.0) the differences which occur in command of vocabulary from childhood to adulthood.

The Interrelationships of the Language Arts

"The language arts are interrelated in developmental sequence, reciprocity of communication, and relationship to mental processes and behavior." (Michaelis, et al, 54) We have already seen how language develops in the individual (see Table 10–2). We experience, learn to listen and speak, then, as we enter school, to read and write. Last of all, we are concerned with the mechanics and refinements of language. Linguists stress the primacy of oral language over the written. Most of us will deal more with the spoken word than with written language in our lifetime. The impact of mass media has increased our need for critical listening skills.

Now let's examine the reciprocity of communication. Listening and speaking are both phonological in nature. In other words, both are concerned with the sound symbols of our language. Speakers need listeners, unless they enjoy talking to themselves! Listeners are listening to speakers, unless, of course, they are "tuned in" to a musical experience. Reading and writing are both graphological in nature. They are concerned with the written symbols of our language. Readers read the writing of others. Writers, except for entries in a most personal "secret" diary, are writing with the expectation that their communication will be read by someone. This is especially true for textbook writers!

Listening and speaking usually take place concurrently unless the message is being preserved on audio tape. However, reading and writing do not have to take place at the same time, and, most often, they do not. We can read the writing in books, such as the Bible, which originated many centuries ago.

Lastly, the language arts are related with respect to the individual's behavioral and mental processes. In both listening and reading, the person is receiving the communication, gaining information. Many of the same comprehension skills are needed in both listening and reading. Poorly organized discourse makes communication just as difficult as poorly or-

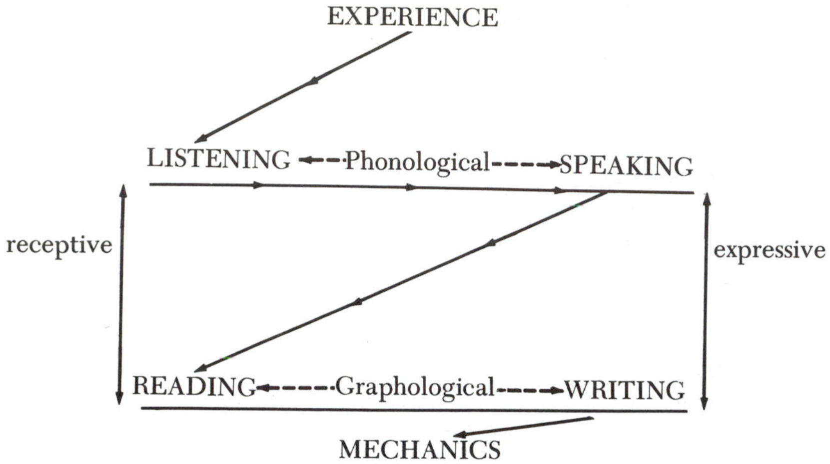

Figure 10–3. *The Interrelationships of the Language Arts*

ganized writing. Both are hard to follow. The listener, however, has the additional problem of being at the mercy of the speaker. He cannot set his own pace for listening as he can for reading. Reading is more permanent. When reading, one can go back and reread passages to clarify the writer's intention. Speech, on the other hand, is fleeting. Unless recorded, words and the thoughts they represent may be lost forever after the communication. The listener does have one advantage over the speaker, however. If he is able to engage in conversation or discussion with the speaker, he may be able to draw much more from the communication than the reader who probably will not have the opportunity for such give-and-take with the writer.

Speaking and writing are related. Both are expressive arts since the speaker or writer is getting across a message of some sort. Both types of communication require organizational sequencing. Speaking comes more easily to most people than writing, because we do more of it, and, also, as speakers, we don't have to concern ourselves with such mechanics as paragraphing, spelling, punctuation, and capitalization. If we feel we are not getting our message across to our listeners, we can repeat, rephrase, try again. Many people do very little writing in their lifetimes, except for personal correspondence or communications required in their occupations. Writing is an arduous task. Not only must the mechanical skills be mastered, but, because the writer has to get his message across the very first time, he must be concerned with logical organization and sequence, word choice, precision, and clarity.

There is one major point of difference among the language arts—size of vocabulary. In the case of the preschool child, the listening vocabulary is the largest. By vocabulary, we mean the words which he receives and understands. The speaking vocabulary lags behind the listening vocabulary. It is easier to receive than express thoughts. Young children understand many more words than they are able to use meaningfully in their oral discourse. Preschoolers, for the most part, have negligible reading vocabularies, and except, perhaps, for a budding genius here and there, they don't write! Children learn to read in the primary grades and make great gains in acquiring a reading vocabulary.

The child's writing vocabulary grows much more slowly. This is due partly to spelling and composition problems. Elementary children differ widely in their writing abilities, making the evaluation of their work a difficult task for the teacher.

By the time the child reaches adolescence or a little later, his reading vocabulary begins to surpass his speaking vocabulary. Thus, in adulthood, the two receptive vocabularies, listening and reading, generally exceed the two expressive vocabularies, speaking and writing. Except for people who do a lot of writing as a vocation or hobby, the writing vocabulary probably will remain the smallest of all. By writing vocabulary, we mean the vocabulary which the person can and does use in his writing—not all the words in the dictionary which he may have at his disposal!

Objectives

The reader will be able to:

Give examples (2.0) showing the use of each language area in the social studies from their own past experiences.

Distinguish (2.0) among the five levels of listening and give an example (2.0) of each in the social studies.

Identify (1.0) six purposes for attentive and analytical listening.

Language in the Social Studies Program

Let's review the steps in the natural sequence of language development and relate these to social studies.

Experience.

Experiences in social studies give children something to talk about and write about. They create a need for self-expression. We can't talk talking or write writing. (Michaelis, et al, 42) We talk *about* something or write *about* something. Social studies programs in the primary grades rely to a great extent on firsthand, real experiences. The trip to the airport taken to initiate a transportation unit; the policeman who visits the classroom to explain the parts of his uniform, to talk about his job, and to answer questions about his duties, perhaps as part of a "Community Helpers" unit; the experiences children have who attempt to make beeswax candles in the same way that pioneers of days gone by did, as part of a unit on "Westward Expansion"—all such experiences provide food for thought for children and opportunities to express themselves orally or in writing. Indeed, unless experiences like these are "milked dry" languagewise by the teacher, the children will not be getting full benefit from them. Greater use is made of vicarious experiences in the later grades, but these, too, can be the basis for many fruitful language experiences.

The communications of children can help teachers evaluate the learning which has taken place. Misconceptions and learning gaps may be uncovered which will help the teacher adjust her program and select future learning experiences.

Listening.

Listening plays an important role in social studies. Children listen to the teacher and other resource persons; they listen to other students as they present reports. Students listen to themselves as they replay tapes which they have made; they listen to records, audio and video tapes, films, sound filmstrips, and the like.

Marginal listening Different levels of listening are utilized in the curriculum. Marginal listening (Smith, 91) requires the least involvement of students. It may be called "half listening" because, usually, there are two or more distractions present. The importance of this type of listening is seen as we view television programs or films in which music is skillfully used to set the mood of the story. At times, we are almost unaware of this mood creating device. To set the stage for "Indian Day" activities, the third grade classes in one school played tapes on which an astute teacher had recorded Indian ceremonial music while on a summer's trip to New Mexico.

Attentive listening Attentive listening requires greater involvement of the listener as he tunes in, intently, to one form of communication. There are many instances which call for this form of listening: following directions, gathering data, participating in group discussions, listening to demonstrations, stories, plays, and films. It is important, therefore, that we set the purposes for attentive listening with our students. The following lessons illustrate three purposes teachers can set for attentive listening.

1. Listening for Details

The teacher asks the children to listen for details about what Father and Mother do and then reads the following paragraph:

Every morning Father goes to work by bus. He usually leaves the house about seven o'clock. In rainy weather Mother drives him to the bus station. When the bus reaches the city at seven forty-five, Father goes to the general office of his company. An elevator carries him to the eighth floor. His important job takes hours of extra time, and many evenings he doesn't arrive home until late. Joe and Betty are disappointed when he works at night, for he frequently helps them with their lessons. Then, too, if there is time after dinner for games, he often plays with them before they begin to study.

Following the reading the teacher asks questions such as these:

(1) What time does Father leave the house in the morning?
(2) What does Mother do for Father when it is raining?
(3) On what floor is Father's office?
(4) How does Father help Joe and Betty when he is home?
(5) When does Father play games with them?

2. Listening for the Main Idea

The teacher writes these sentences on the board and covers them.

(1) The burro is a very gentle animal.
(2) Children ride on their burros.
(3) The burro is a favorite pet in Mexico.
(4) The children give names to their burros.

The teacher asks the children to listen carefully to what they are about to hear and to think of the one thing it tells about. This paragraph is then read:

Many children in Mexico have burros for pets. The burro is so gentle that a small child can take care of him. The children enjoy riding on their burros. Sometimes the children ride them in parades. They call their pet burros by name, and talk to them just as they talk to one another. Often a boy will carry sugar in his pocket. His burro will follow him, sniffing in his pocket to get the sugar.

The teacher then uncovers the sentences and reads then aloud. He then asks the children to write the sentence which is the main idea of the paragraph.

3. Listening to Follow Directions

The teacher distributes to each pupil one sheet of lined paper and says, "Today we are going to have a game to see how well you can listen to directions. Have your pencils ready, and be sure to do exactly what my directions say. I shall give each direction only once." The following is then read:

(1) Write your first and last name in the upper right-hand corner of the paper.
(2) At the left-hand margin, on every other line, write the numbers from one to ten for answers to ten directions.
(3) After number 1 write the words *from, with, at.*
(4) If California is south of Oregon, write the word *south.*
(5) Listen to these numbers and write the largest of them: 6—2—7—5—1—8—3.
(6) Draw a square and put the number 3 in the lower right hand corner of it.

The directions could be continued for as long as the teacher wishes, and the pupils are motivated to listen. Answers should be checked. (Green and Petty, 174-77)

Analytical listening This level of listening demands attentive listening but, in addition, calls for an analysis and at times a critical evaluation of the communication. The prime example of this type of listening is asking our children to analyze a political telecast. In consumer education, students enjoy evaluating the validity of commercial advertisments. Again, illustrations from Greene and Petty can be used to show three different purposes for this type of listening.

4. Listening for Word Meaning from Context

The teacher writes the following words on the board: *exalt* and *ravine.* He asks the pupils if they know the meanings of them. He writes the meanings they give and then asks them to listen to the following to find out if they were right:

A little way off, to the left, stood a small house; and to the right was another, before which stood the wagons belonging to his father. Directly in front was a wide expanse of rolling prairie, cut by a deep ravine. To the north, beyond the small farm which was fenced, a still wider region rolled away into unexplored and marvelous distance. Altogether it was a land to exalt a boy who had lived all his life in thickly settled Wisconsin.

Following the reading the meanings of the words should again be discussed and looked for in a dictionary if necessary.

5. Listening to Distinguish the Relevant from the Irrelevant

The teacher asks the pupils to listen to a selection and to be ready to tell which sentences are needed to gain the meaning and which do not really relate to the remainder of the selection. The following is read:

> There were six boys beside the campfire. The dry sticks blazed and the heavy logs glowed with the heat. It was almost time to put the fish in the frying pan. Already they had poked the potatoes in their foil wrappings and they were softening. Jim's older brother had stayed at home. He was going to college this fall. All the boys were hungry and were anxious to eat. Bill put on more wood and Bob got the frying pan.

The teacher asks the pupils to tell which sentences do not relate to the remainder of the paragraph and why they are not relevant.

6. Listening to Draw Inferences

The teacher tells the pupils to listen to the following to answer some questions which can only be answered by listening "between the lines."

> The air was crisp and clear but a wet snow had pelted the windows last night. I breathed deeply, glanced toward the snow-covered cars parked along the curbing, and thought "What a beautiful day." Suddenly I came down with a bump on the sidewalk.

The teacher then asks these question and the meaning of making inferences is discussed:

(1) Why did the speaker fall?
(2) Does the speaker live in town or in the country?
(3) Has the snowing stopped? (Green and Petty, 174-77)

Creative listening Creative listening differs from analytical listening only in that creative listening goes a step beyond analytical listening because the listener must use elements of his past experiences to add to the original communication. In a unit of transportation, one fourth grade class had listened enchantedly as a pilot from a nearby air base explained jet flying. He demonstrated the use of his special suit, helment, and oxygen equipment. He showed slides of his needle-nosed aircraft, photographs of the earth from high altitudes, and explained the utility of high altitude supersonic transportation. As part of a follow-up activity, several of the children wrote stories describing interplanetary transportation. They utilized parts of the pilot's presentation, as well as their own experiences with science fiction in completing their imaginative stories.

Creative listening need not result in a written communication. A kindergarten class was engaged in the exploration of feelings. They had been discussing how music affects the way we feel. The children moved imaginatively as they listened to "Peter and the Wolf." This was a creative listening experience because each child was reacting to the changes in sound and rhythm according to his individual interpretation.

Appreciative listening If the only purpose for listening is enjoyment, it is appreciative listening. Activities such as listening to records and stories are often used for this purpose. Many times the sharing of such creative stories as "My Life as George Washington's Horse" or "The Day I Interviewed Benjamin Franklin" provides pleasure for the listener and writer alike. Interludes like these provide a welcome change in the daily routine of any classroom.

Another element, often overlooked, is the group unity derived from the sharing of such pleasurable experiences. The rapport within the group and the cohesiveness created allow greater productivity from individual members. Also, group production is facilitated.

Speaking.

Activities involving oral language are numerous in the social studies. Group work would be impossible without oral communication among members. To a large extent, it is through speaking that we share information with others. There are many techniques ranging from brainstorming, which is a highly unstructured activity, to a pageant, which may be used to culminate a social studies unit. The latter activity would be considered highly structured. No longer do we feel that children "should be seen and not heard." They learn by active involvement.

Another aspect of oral language activities, such as conversations and discussions, is that the teacher can evaluate children's progress in language and thinking skills by listening and observation. As we have discussed earlier, this is an important means of determining what children know and what concepts or misconceptions they may have. Also, we can gain valuable insight into the feelings, attitudes, and values of our students.

Reading.

When many of us were in elementary school, reading was confined to textbooks. Social studies meant reading the assigned pages in the textbook and answering the questions at the end of the chapter. The trend now is toward the use of a variety of textbooks, as well as other resource materials.

No, books aren't everything. They are only one means of allowing the child to gain specific information. Included in social studies reading materials are magazines, pamphlets, newspapers, encyclopedias, comic books,

letters, diaries, journals, and other children's writing. Since reading skills are a major means of gathering data, children must have such skills. If the child is deficient in certain reading skills, he will have successful experiences in social studies only to the extent that the teacher is willing and able to fit the material to the child. It would be folly to expect a child reading on the second grade level to gain much information from materials written for the fifth grade level of reading ability. Although the scope of this book will not allow us to include the teaching of beginning reading skills, you will find helpful information for the teaching of information processing skills in Chapter XII.

Writing.

The purposes for writing in the social studies include such practical experiences as writing to resource people for information, composing thank you letters, recording data obtained from reading or observing, and writing reports.

Writing of a more creative nature can be seen in the following example of cinquain (five line poem) which was the result of experiences in a unit on automation.

Robot
Strong, silent
Working and Whirring
Getting the job done
Mechanical man

The following example of diamante (seven line diamond-shaped poem) was the product of a pollution unit:

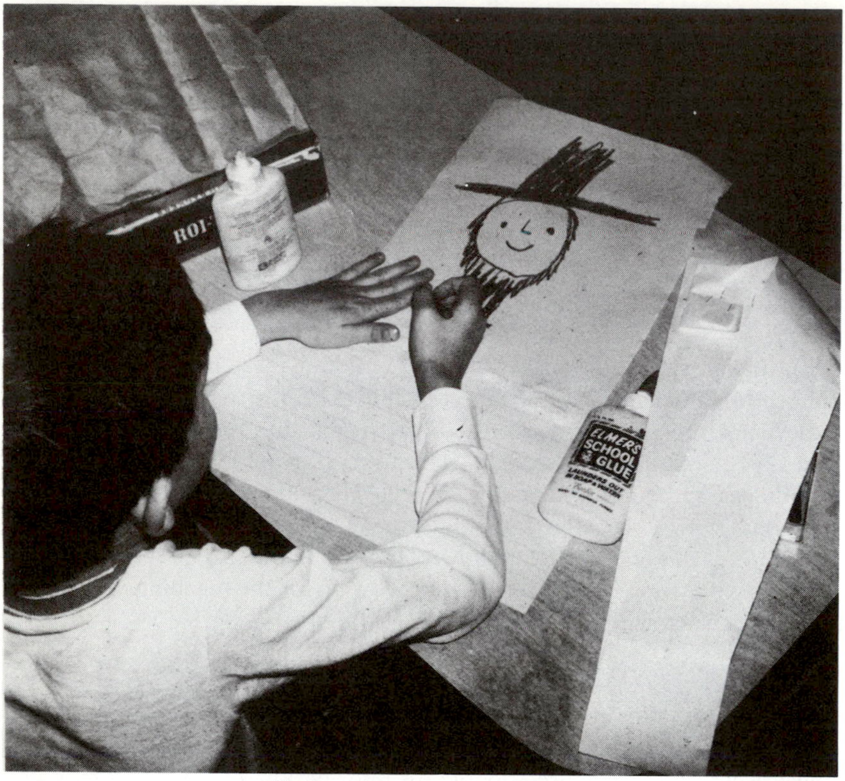

This primary child is drawing a picture and will write a story as part of a unit on Abraham Lincoln.

Pollution
Hazy, smelly,
Billowing, belching, suffocating,
Smoke, steam, clouds, breeze,
Blowing, gusting, refreshing,
Clean, pure
Clear air.

The many forms of poetry which elementary school children can write help them express their ideas and feelings.

Prose need not be neglected. Many intriguing titles can be used to help children pull their thoughts together about a certain social studies topic. The following are some examples:

If Columbus Lived Today
Rounding the Cape

If Machines Could Talk
Diary of a Pioneer Family
How I'd End Pollution
But ________ Did it
The Time Machine

Although these are fictional stories, they require the child to use concepts and generalizations he has accumulated. For example, if the child were preparing a diary of a pioneer family, he would need to know something of frontier life. In order to write about "Rounding the Cape," the child would need some knowledge of sea travel.

Mechanics of language.

Mechanics, the conventions of language, allow us greater efficiency and effectiveness of communication. They are not ends in themselves but rather means to an end—clarity. The social studies provide content through which mechanics can be taught meaningfully.

The importance of correct spelling, handwriting, capitalization, punctuation, and letter form becomes evident to the child writing for information about national parks. The significance of careful word selection required to communicate a precise meaning is obvious to students writing a report to share with another class. These activities provide motivating reinforcement for mechanical skills.

Objectives

The reader will be able to:

Name (1.0) and describe (1.0) at least ten of the communication techniques discussed by the authors.

Suggest (3.0) appropriate communication techniques which could be utilized when given a sample lesson from Chapter III.

Communication Techniques

One problem faced by the elementary school teacher is the selection of interesting ways in which children can share their thoughts, feelings, and beliefs. In the past, teachers relied upon reports prepared by pupils. Such reports were usually read orally to other members of the class. Too often, these "reports" had been copied verbatum from unevaluated sources of information, because the children had not been taught how to prepare reports. Reporting is just one of many techniques that can be utilized to encourage the exchange of information. Although this is a viable technique when it is properly used, anything that is used too much loses its effectiveness.

The following communication devices provide excellent means of exchanging ideas and feelings:

Class discussions.

The class discussion is possibly the most commonly used group technique. Frequently, however, children lack the skills required to carry on a class discussion successfully. There are definite subskills involved that need to be taught. Children must learn how to take turns, listen critically to others, respond at appropriate times, and keep the discussion focused upon the topic. The leader, who may be the teacher or another student, steps in only to refocus or to maintain the theme of the interaction. Purposes for discussions vary widely. Sometimes, a discussion will involve problem solving. At other times, it may include a review of shared experiences, a sharing of different experiences, or group decision making.

Current events in social studies provide excellent opportunities for class discussions. Classes preparing for group work often carry on discussions. This same type of activity is used in group planning of a unit for study.

Panel discussion.

A panel discussion usually consists of a selected group of "experts" chosen because of differing points of view or experience. The moderator, or leader, calls upon panel members in turn. The participants give short presentations on the selected topic. Then, there is an opportunity for the panel members or the leader to ask specific questions of the other members. After the panel members have given their views and discussed differences of opinion, a general interaction with the audience follows.

The panel discussion usually takes less time than a class discussion because it is focused more carefully by the participants. It provides individuals with opportunities for recognition in an area of their interest. The disadvantage is that there is not as much opportunity for general interaction among all members of the class.

One fifth grade class organized a panel on the topic of "Resources of the Oceans." Experts consisted of class members who had done extensive reading on different aspects of the ocean environment including minerals, plant life, animal life, transportation, and pollution. The class was amazed by the findings and resultant discussion.

Buzz Groups.

Buzz groups are formed to encourage greater participation in discussions by all class members. The class may be divided randomly into fairly equal groups. A leader is usually selected and a recorder appointed to write down the contributions of the group. This group organization also allows the discussion of a problem or topic in greater detail in a shorter period of time. The same skills are required as in the class discussion, since this activity is actually a microcosm of the larger discussion.

Buzz groups may be utilized for the same purposes as the class discussion, but they have the advantage of enabling the children to participate in smaller groups. Also, they encourage a divergence not possible in large groups.

On the topic of drug abuse, for example, buzz sessions can help focus upon the common concerns of the student, thereby giving the teacher direction in unit planning. Often, these sessions can be used to search out alternatives in problem situations.

Brainstorming.

This technique allows groups of any size to suggest as many unevaluated alternative actions as possible, within a short span of time. Children are encouraged to use their imaginations. No response is rejected regardless of how "way out" it may seem. The stress is placed on divergent thinking and volume of ideas.

One second grade class won a PTA room attendance award of five dollars and was faced with the dilemma of spending such a great amount of money. Their brainstorming produced these suggestions: let's have a party, buy books, see the Walt Disney show playing at a local theater, buy the teacher a present, get a room aquarium, take an airplane ride, and buy a hamster. After the brainstorming session, the merits of each suggestion were discussed. The final decision was to augment the classroom library through the purchase of two of Dr. Suess' latest productions.

Puppets.

Puppets are among the many dramatic techniques which can be utilized to teach and reinforce concepts in social studies programs. They can be used by both the teacher and students and provide instant motivation. Children typically enjoy making and working with simple hand puppets. These can be constructed out of paper bags, socks, paper cups, styrofoam balls, ice cream sticks, tongue depressors, or scrap materials.

A puppet show, written and directed by the children, can be a fitting culmination for a social studies unit. After studying a unit on "Prehistoric Man," one imaginative class produced a puppet show which involved the visit of a "cave man" to their school.

Younger children enjoy animal puppets. With the help of the teacher, a group of kindergarteners constructed puppet "pets" and put on a show telling what they had learned about caring for household pets.

Puppets also can be used as a projective technique. Children are more likely to release pent-up emotions through the dialogue of a puppet. They are less inhibited when speaking through puppets from behind a table or screen. Puppets are particularly valuable when used to re-create a problem situation which may have arisen in the classroom or out on the playgound. The child who is a bully or the new child in the classroom having a difficult time adjusting to the group offer possible problem situations.

Plays.

Plays are dramatizations having a definite structure. Scripts for plays may be written by the children and/or the teacher. Usually, plays are rehearsed before presentation. Costumes and scenery add interest to this dramatic activity.

Plays are excellent for data sharing. Concepts and generalizations, as well as attitudes and values, may be brought out and reinforced during the course of a play. Sometimes social issues are aired in this way. One of the greatest benefits to be derived from this activity, however, is the "teamwork" required of the groups in planning for and presenting the play. Many diverse activities are involved, such as writing the script, preparing scenery, making costumes and props, directing, as well as participating in the play itself as part of the cast. Thus, every child in the class can have a part in the production and gain a measure of recognition.

Many plays in social studies are concerned with a holiday theme. After studying the origin of St. Valentine's Day, a fourth grade class wrote a short play on this topic and presented it to the rest of the school.

The sixth grade class in another school with a large proportion of military dependent children was interested in Christmas customs around the world. Their families had traveled widely, and the children had collected many articles from foreign lands. The children not only gained much additional information about these countries but, also, had opportunity for recognition. This was particularly important for these children who lacked continuity of school experiences. The play was so successful that the children were asked by the Supervisor of the Intermediate Grades to present their play to students in several schools in the city.

Skits.

Skits are short dramatic presentations which are similar to plays because scripts are used, and they are usually rehearsed before presentation. However, scenery and props are either very simple or absent entirely. Because they are brief, little rehearsing is required. Generally, skits are used for the same purposes as plays.

Pageants.

Pageants in the elementary school are similar to plays, with the exception that they are usually part of a school-wide celebration or holiday observance to promote greater understanding of and appreciation for our American heritage. They may be concerned with such holiday observances as Thanksgiving Day, Veterans Day, Lincoln's Birthday, Washington's Birthday, and Memorial Day, as well as certain state and local observances. Scripts are used, as well as costumes, scenery, and props. Generally, as many children as possible participate in a pageant.

Tableaus.

A tableau is a picture or scene made up of one or more suitably costumed persons and including props and scenery. There is no motion or speech during the tableau itself, which often represents some stirring moment in our history. The landing of the Pilgrims at Plymouth Rock, the raising of our flag on Iwo Jima, the astronauts' first steps on the moon—these are samples of themes suitable for tableaus. The purposes of presenting a tableau are to promote pride in our nation and appreciation of our heritage by recalling great moments in our history. Although the tableau itself lacks oral communication, the poses struck by the participants in the tableau *do* communicate to the audience. The greatest values to be derived from tableaus, however, arise from the group planning and activities which these presentations require.

Dramatic play.

Dramatic play, although completely unstructured, is mentioned here because it forms an important part of kindergarten and early primary programs and enables children to experiment with adult roles. This is important in the social development of the young child. Generally, teachers provide interest centers which are related to the familiar home and family life of the children. Props such as toy stoves, refrigerators, irons, ironing boards, dishes, cooking utentils, and groceries are arranged in the centers. Often "grown-up" articles of clothing, such as hats, ties, aprons, handbags, gloves, and even dresses, jackets, and shoes make the dramatic play more fun and realistic for children. Dolls become the "babies" for the make-believe parents. Often the children are permitted to select the interest center of their choice, as well as the role they wish to assume. They are free to play this role during the allotted time for the dramatic play experience, often 15 to 30 minutes.

Although unstructured by the teacher, dramatic play is important in social studies education. The children gain important understandings and attitudes which will help them in getting along with others. They learn to discriminate the roles of various family members. Also, children learn to share, to exchange conversation and ideas, and to experiment with language and living through dramatic play activities.

Role playing.

Role playing differs from dramatic play in that the roles students will play are selected previously. Also, it usually involves a problem situation which calls for the examining of alternative behaviors. This technique is suitable for individuals of all ages and can be just as successful when used in a college class as with primary children. Only the situations will differ. No costumes or scenery are needed although a few props may be used. Generally, little preparation is required to use this technique.

Effective role playing should evolve out of a definite need in the classroom; some problem or issue which requires examination in detail. It is excellent for promoting understanding among individuals whose attitudes and values differ widely. Role playing does not attempt to provide pat answers for children. Rather, it permits them to scrutinize alternative ways of behaving or responding, as well as to examine the logical consequences which may follow certain choices. The latter is often accomplished in a class discussion which follows the role playing activity. Sometimes the solution to a problem is reached in this way.

The first step in role playing is to help the children focus on their problem or an issue at hand and select the participants, usually from two to six. The participants may desire a short planning session to set the stage. Actual rehearsing is to be avoided, however, as it detracts from the desired spontaneity of the role playing. When the interest of the participants and audience wanes and purposes have been served, the teacher or group leader will call the role playing to an end. Sometimes it is valuable to have participants exchange roles and begin anew. At other times, a new group of children may be selected for the roles to show different ways of responding in the same situation.

Children should be helped to evaluate the role playing in order to make it a more effective technique in the future. The audience should be given the opportunity to discuss the alternatives portrayed and the logical consequences which might ensue; it is important that a free and open climate be maintained. Biased criticism is to be avoided. Although it is difficult to keep from imposing our beliefs on others, we must recognize that this is not our task as teachers and the purpose of role playing. Role playing remains a most valuable technique to help children explore their own feelings, beliefs, attitudes, and values, as well as those of others in a free and accepting atmosphere.

A second grade class was having difficulty accepting the "no fighting on the playground" rule of the school. Many of the children had been taught by their parents to settle their differences in this manner. To do otherwise was considered a mark of cowardice, even for little girls. Here was a clear cut conflict between home and school. The teacher decided to use role playing to help the children look at other ways of settling differences. Several groups of pupils were permitted to participate directly in a role playing situation involving a fictitious playground disagreement. The children concluded that there were many ways to resolve arguments on the playground besides resorting to fighting which was unacceptable at school. However, they also concluded that fighting at home was all right. Although this conclusion conflicted with the teacher's views, she felt that she had accomplished her purpose when she helped the children understand the reasons for the "no fighting" rule and discover other ways of settling playground differences.

The following story was related to one of the writers and is presumed to be true. If it should be fiction, you'll probably agree that it makes a good story anyway!

> Jerry was a continual disturbance in the classroom. From tapping his pencil and shuffling his feet to popping his gum and whistling, his behavior was a source of unending irritation to the teacher, as well as his classmates. Jerry was bright and really not a bad boy—just not easily motivated toward school work. Much of the time he was unaware of what a pest he was. Jerry, you see, was a happy-go-lucky boy who would have preferred fishing in the lake to school on just about any day of the week.
>
> One day, the teacher at last had had it! He decided to try a little role playing as a last resort. He called Jerry to his desk and asked him to play the role of the teacher while he (the teacher) would assume the role of Jerry. Jerry was delighted by the attention he was receiving and blithely continued reading to the group the story which the teacher had selected. "Jerry" (the teacher at this point) began to exhibit the typical annoying behaviors—tapping his pencil, shuffling his feet, and the like. (The teacher was certain from the outset that Jerry would not be embarrassed by this role playing activity.)
>
> About five minutes was all that the real Jerry needed in order to "see the light." Suddenly, Jerry ceased playing the role of the teacher and quipped. "I think I get the point Mr. ________!" Jerry

had been perceptive enough to see through the teacher's purpose for the role playing. He was helped to gain insight into his own behavior. Jerry's annoying mannerisms diminished, and he and the teacher lived happily ever after!

Pantomimes.

A pantomime involves acting out a situation without employing verbal communication. Gestures, facial expressions, and bodily movements are used to communicate non-verbally. "Charades" utilizes pantomine in a game situation. This activity is not commonly used in the social studies but, nevertheless, does have some application. Children may pantomime certain customs of other countries, depict different occupations, or "right" and "wrong" procedures for doing certain things, such as crossing streets or riding a bicycle. A contrast of behaviors is often involved.

Sociodramas.

The sociodrama is very similar to role playing because both are unstructured dramatizations that deal with a problem or issue to be examined. The sociodrama, however, is always concerned with a social problem. Like role playing, the sociodrama is unrehearsed and lacks a structured plot. Participants in both of these dramatic activities make up the plot as they go along. However, the sociodrama may call for a bit more preplanning on the part of participants in setting the stage. Most often it is directed toward solving a pressing social problem facing the group. Opportunity is usually provided for several "casts" to present possible solutions. The audience then arrives at a consensus in order to determine the course of action members will follow. This is an excellent technique which can be employed to help children grow in group decision-making processes.

Structured dramatizations.

The structured dramatization differs from the sociodrama in that a script is written for this dramatic technique, before the presentation. It differs from a play, however, because most often it centers around a problem and the lines may be "read," rather than memorized. The structured dramatization is particularly valuable in the intermediate grades when children can write their own scripts. If the teacher writes the script, ample time should be allowed for discussion at the conclusion of the presentation. Structured dramatizations can be employed to help children develop attitudes, values, and appreciations. Again, the teacher must avoid "preaching" and imposing his beliefs on the class.

Open-ended stories and problem stories.

The open-ended story is another technique utilized to bring a relevant problem or issue before the class. It is suitable for person of all ages. The story may be written by the children and/or the teacher and, then, read to the class. Since the story lacks an ending, the children are free to supply their own. Several different endings may be suggested and the possible implications of each can be discussed by the group. The teacher may wish to prepare questions for the discussion which ensues. The open-ended story can help children form opinions, attitudes, and values, as well as develop empathy for others.

The problem story is very similar to the open-ended story except that at its conclusion it poses this question to the reader, "What would you do?" It has the same general purposes as the open-ended story and is also suitable for all ages. *Today's Education*, the journal of the National Education Association, is a good source of unfinished stories suitable for classroom use.

Problem pictures.

The problem picture is an excellent projective technique which can be used to aid children in understanding human behavior and help them "walk in the other fellow's shoes." The picture may portray a situation commonly faced by children in which they must choose from several possible courses of action.

A picture used successfully by one of the writers showed the anguished face of a boy behind a pane of glass obviously broken by a baseball. The children described what they thought might have occurred before the picture was taken. They were helped to identify with this child through such questions as, "What do you think happened here?" "How does the boy feel?" "Why does he feel that way?" "Have you ever felt like that?" "When?" "What made you feel that way?" "What do you think the boy will do next?" "Why do you think so?" As the children suggested several courses of action the boy might take, the teacher helped them perceive the possible consequences of each. No suggestion was rejected. A teacher avoided "telling" the children what the boy *ought* to do. Rather, they were encouraged to determine, in their opinion, the best course of action for the boy.

Although many problem pictures can be purchased commercially, the picture mentioned above was taken from an advertisement in a popular monthly magazine. Such advertisements are often eye-catching and have general appeal. If the commercial portion can be removed without ruining the picture, many of these advertisements can be used as problem pictures in the elementary classroom.

If the teacher is unable to locate an appropriate picture for a specific problem situation, he may wish to consider making his own on a transparency. Transparencies for use with an overhead projector are simple to prepare, as well as relatively inexpensive.

Films and filmstrips.

These media materials can be used essentially in the same ways and for the same purposes as still pictures for open-ended discussions and problem solving. Again, there are commercial materials available specifically for these uses, but the resourceful teacher will find that many ordinary films and filmstrips can be adapted for the same purposes. Films may be stopped before the conclusion, allowing the children opportunity to discuss possible endings. After viewing the actual conclusion, the children can discuss the ending and determine why they think it ended in this manner.

Running a film with the sound track "off" can be used to analyze human behavior. The children can attempt to determine the dialogue and plot of the story from the pictures and discuss the reasons for their responses.

Storytelling.

Storytelling can be used by the social studies teacher to initiate a unit, to stimulate discussion, to arouse interest in a topic, as well as to convey information to children. It differs from reading to children since the teacher "tells" the story without using a book. If the teacher knows the story well enough, he will be able to tell it with ease. It is not recommended that you memorize the story, as forgetting the lines may cause the storyteller obvious distress and detract from the informality and spontaneity of the storytelling situation.

Flannel boards or lap boards may be used to illustrate portions of the story and capture children's interest. Flannel boards are easy to construct, or they can be purchased commercially. Cutouts for use with the flannel board can be made by backing pictures with flannel or felt. A piece of cardboard or plywood can be used as a lap board. Instead of placing cutouts on a flannel board, the teacher may make toy figures and props for use with a lap board, which, as the name implies, is placed on the lap of the storyteller.

Also, stories can be told through the use of puppets. However, there is a closeness with the audience which develops when the teacher gathers the children around and tells a story without the benefit of props.

An enterprising student teacher introduced a unit on the "Westward Movement" with a storytelling session. After recess one day, she appeared in front of the class dressed in the authentic garb of a pioneer woman complete with bonnet and high-button shoes. She said she had been invited to tell them about the adventures and perils that she and her family had faced in traveling across the country to settle in the untamed West. The children responded enthusiastically to her presentation and flooded her with questions about her "family" and "life on the frontier." This was a most creative way to introduce the unit. She did admit that she had done much reading of background materials in order to prepare for her role.

Children can use storytelling to share information gained through individual and group work. Also, storytelling promotes the creative oral expression of the children. It is excellent when used as a culminating activity for a unit. Storytelling is similar to creative writing except that oral, rather than written communication is involved.

Summary

This chapter has given the reader a general view of communication skills taught in the elementary school. The origin and sequence of language development of the individual were reviewed.

The interrelationships which exist among the language arts were explained and summarized in Figure 10–3. The major difference in the language arts, command of vocabulary, was discussed.

The individual language skills were examined in detail to show applications in the social studies program. Various communication techniques were surveyed and applied to social studies.

References

Green, Harry A. and Petty, Walter. *Developing Language Skills in the Elementary Schools.* Boston: Allyn and Bacon, Inc., 1967.

Michaelis, John U., Grossman, Ruth H., and Scott, Lloyd F. *New Designs for the Elementary School Curriculum.*New York: McGraw-Hill Book Company, 1967.

Smith, James A. *Creative Teaching of the Language Arts in the Elementary School.* Boston: Allyn and Bacon, Inc., 1967.

XI

Exploring Values in Social Studies

Chapter Outline

Exploring Values in Social Studies

Mrs. Martin was busy with a reading group at the front of the classroom. The other children were diligently pursuing different activities at their desks and in the several interest centers in the room. Although attentive to the responses of her readers, Mrs. Martin, nevertheless, kept a careful watch on the other children. Suddenly, she noticed that George was nowhere to be seen. Had he entered the boys' restroom at the back of the room? She quickly rejected that hypothesis as the door to the restroom appeared to be ajar indicating that it was vacant. She continued with the reading lesson for a few moments. Then, she decided to check the coat room which was part of the rear of the classroom and separated from the rest of the room by a partition. She rose from her chair and moved swiftly and quietly to the rear of the room.

"George! What are you doing?" She had discovered George in the coat room, as she had suspected, with a half-eaten sandwich in hand and a most guilty expression on his face.

"George," Mrs. Martin continued, "is that *your* lunch?" No reply was forthcoming. "George! Now tell the truth. I'll find out anyway. Is that *your* lunch?"

"N-n-n-no, ma'am."

"Whose lunch is it?"

No answer.

"George! That is stealing! Don't you know that stealing is wrong? That's a very bad thing to do."

George received a stern lecture on the evils of stealing. Mrs. Martin meted out two swats with the paddle as Mrs. Berger, her colleague from the next classroom, witnessed the act. The rest of the day was a waste for George. He was too upset to think about school. The child whose lunch had been pilfered was delighted to receive a ticket for a hot lunch, courtesy of Mrs. Martin. Then and there, the entire class received a lecture on the evils of stealing!

You may wonder what the foregoing incident has to do with values. Obviously, the teacher was acting on a certain pattern of values which had been inculcated in her. She honestly felt she was doing the right thing. To Mrs. Martin, a wrong was always wrong; no extenuating circumstances were permitted.

Take a minute to reread the incident, and jot down your impressions about the wisdom or folly of Mrs. Martin's actions. Perhaps you raised some questions similar to the following ones:

Did George have breakfast that morning?

Did he know that the lunch he was eating was not his own? (Brown paper sacks are easily confused.)

What did George's lunch contain? Had he already eaten his own lunch? Perhaps he knew he didn't like his lunch. (Bread and bologna does get monotonous as a daily diet.)

Why didn't George tell the teacher he was hungry, if that were really his problem? (Aren't teachers, like policemen, supposed to be our friends?)

Why did the teacher act so hastily in punishing George?

Did she have to make such a scene?

Why did Mrs. Martin interrupt her classroom routine to give the entire class a lecture? (Isn't punishing the group for the actions of one member a way to create hostility?)

In Chapter I, we discussed values in terms of institutional influences on individuals. We indicated that the individual in a pluralistic society is influenced by the dominant institutional values. In this chapter, we shall examine values from a different viewpoint—the cultural, rather than societal perspective. These two views of values will help you understand the nature of the conflict with the values of society that we illustrated in Figure 1–1. In addition to the institutional pressures on individuals in society, individuals, through the cultures in which they participate, exert pressures on institutions. Hence, institutions change to resolve these conflicts.

Currently, values are receiving a great deal of attention on the educational scene. Because social studies are so vitally concerned with attitudes and values, we are devoting this chapter to a better understanding of these facets of the affective domain. First, we shall consider a definition of values. Next, we shall examine the affective hierarchy. Then, we shall take a look at the important factors in helping children acquire values. Lastly, we shall examine conflicts in values which arise when teachers and students behave in accordance with differing value systems.

Objective

The reader will be able to:

Define (1.0) values.

What are Values?

In previous chapters, we have examined and discussed the cognitive domain at length. Attitudes and values lie in the affective or "feeling" domain. Attitudes are defined as predispositions to respond in certain ways. Values are formed from attitudes. Values, too, predispose us to behave in certain ways. They are the criteria against which we judge the worth of things, objects, and actions. Values are stronger than attitudes and are organized into a value system or complex.

Objectives

The reader will be able to:

Describe (1.0) the value hierarchy.

Apply (3.0) the affective hierarchy in illustrating how a value, such as human dignity, develops in the individual.

Explain (1.0) the relationship between values and emotions.

Describe (1.0) the polycultural nature of our society.

Explain (2.0) the relationship between cognition and affection.

The Affective Hierarchy

In Chapter V, we have seen the hierarchy in the affective domain as presented by Krathwohl, et al. The affective hierarchy developed by Rooze and Foerster, which is found in Figure 11–1, may help you to perceive the relationship between attitudes and values.

Let's illustrate the hierarchy using an example. We shall see how an individual might incorporate *cooperation* into his value system. In the beginning, the child would have to experience cooperative behavior and *discriminate* this behavior from behaviors which might be termed non-cooperative. The child might see how a puzzle is solved more efficiently with a partner; a block building is constructed more quickly by a group than alone; fun on a see-saw is only possible if there is teamwork, and

Level 1: Discrimination of behaviors.

Level 2: Labeling of behaviors and formation of attitudes.

Level 3: Trying out behaviors in a number of situations; generalizing, resulting in strengthening or weakening of the attitude.

Level 4: Incorporating or rejecting the behavior. (Incorporation implies the modification of the total value system to accommodate the new value.)

Level 5: Characterization—consistently behaving in accordance with the value system.

Figure 11–1.

so on. The child will need many such experiences if he is to discriminate cooperative from non-cooperative behaviors. Note that much of this covert, internal behavior of the child may occur below the threshold of awareness.

At the next level, the child would *attach a label* to instances of cooperative behavior. It is through labeling that the child is able to manipulate thoughts and feelings internally. He would begin to form attitudes about cooperative behavior. Hopefully, these would be positive and ego reinforcing.

The child would then *try out* cooperative behaviors in a variety of situations. If the feedback to the individual continues to be favorable, he may *generalize* that "Cooperation benefits me. It is something good for me." (If he receives negative feedback, however, he might generalize the opposite or continue to test.)

Now that he has developed positive attitudes toward cooperation, he will *incorporate* this behavior into his developing value system, and he will value cooperation. Incorporation implies that the total value system is modified in some way to accommodate the new value; it's rather like adding another ingredient to the cake batter.

At the highest level, similar to that of the taxonomy, we find *characterization.* This implies that the individual will consistently behave in a cooperative way. We might call him a cooperative person.

The affective hierarchy is a highly theoretical model. It is a simplification of the value development process. Yet, it may serve as a tool to help you understand something of the nature and relationship of attitudes and values. Educational psychologists simply do not know enough about values and valuing. We are just beginning to scratch the surface with research in this area.

We should note, too, that our value systems are open to revision and change, at all times. The greater the backlog of positive reinforcing experiences, the stronger will be that particular element in the value system of the individual. However, should the individual begin to receive negative feedback, the strength of the value will likely diminish.

Returning to our earlier example about cooperation, let's assume that later the child has some unfavorable experiences with cooperative behavior. Perhaps another student with whom he was working "took over" the project leaving this child with nothing to do but watch; or in group work, maybe some of the members stood by idly while the others had to do all the work; perhaps, he had a toy stolen while playing with a group of children. A stockpiling of experiences of this kind can change one's attitude toward cooperation. It may lead that individual to delete *cooperation* from his value complex.

Values and emotions.

Emotions are another dimension of feeling. As such, they are closely related to values. In our example of cooperation above, the emotions which accompanied the behaviors were conducive to developing positive attitudes toward cooperation. Hostile or aggressive emotions in these situations could have resulted in negative feedback. This, in turn, could have produced the opposite reaction in the individual—valuing non-cooperation—if these behaviors had resulted in ego reinforcement. Emotions can cause the individual to perceive differently. At the extreme, they may result in a warping of the personality and may interfere with learning in both the cognitive and affective domains.

Democratic values.

We live in a democracy. We believe in the democratic way of life. Our society is not only pluralistic but, also, polycultural. By society, we mean a network of people. By culture, we mean the ways of people. We belong to a society, and we have a culture. When we say that society is pluralistic, we mean that it consists of many institutions. When we say it is polycultural, we mean that there are many subcultures. Inherent in a democracy is respect for the rights and differences of others. There are, however, certain values which citizens of a democracy must internalize if that democracy is to survive. These are values such as cooperation, respect for human life, belief in the dignity of man, equal rights for all, due process of law, and so on. Schools in a democratic society then, as one socialization agency, have a responsibility to help children acquire the values which are necessary for full participation in that society. We shall call these values "core values" because they are at the very heart of our way of life.

Developing pride in our heritage is this teacher's purpose for using the teaching bulletin board presented.

Cognition and affection.

In order to understand the relationship between cognition (thinking) and affection (feeling), we need to return to an examination of these two hierarchies of the taxonomy. These were displayed on pages 111–125 in Tables 5–1, 5–2, 5–3, and 5–4 of Chapter V. You will recall that the first two levels of the cognitive domain are knowledge and comprehension. These levels form the basis for value development, but they are not sufficient to allow valuing. We once subscribed to the notion that telling children "honesty is the best policy" was sufficient to inculcate these values. Reading textbooks which were used in schools at the turn of the century were full of moral teachings. However, "knowing" does not assure that the individual will accept and incorporate attitudes and values into his personal value complex. For this to happen, the child must have tested the behavior and found it to be satisfying. It would appear that value formation is based upon the lower levels of cognition but requires higher levels of cognition for characterization. Terminally, the individual makes a judgement about the worth of the value to him. This evaluation is the highest level in the cognitive hierarchy.

Within the individual, the cognitive and affective domains are inextricably entwined. We don't know the exact degree or nature of this relationship, but it appears that affection is contingent upon cognition. Conversely, cognition is accompanied by strains of the affective. The higher levels of affection, such as value organization and characterization, call for higher levels of cognition.

Objectives

The reader will be able to:

Provide (3.0) an example from his own experience to illustrate how the traditional approach is ineffective for value development.

Describe (2.0) a classroom setting which would be conducive to value exploration.

Describe (1.0) the role of the teacher in value development.

Suggest (3.0) from his own experience, an instance of inconsistent teacher behavior.

Present (3.0) an illustration of inconsistent verbal-nonverbal behavior from his own experience.

Employ (3.0) the three types of experiences in value exploration.

Can We Teach Values?

No, not directly. Attitudes and values are learned but cannot be taught. We can teach *for* value development. The fact of the matter is that we must teach for development of the "core values" if our society is to be perpetuated. We can help children explore values, but we simply cannot teach values to another person. We merely set the stage and, at times, act as a catalyst for learning, which includes value development. In helping children acquire knowledge and skills, we plan and select experiences carefully. Development of attitudes and values also requires careful planning and sequencing of experiences. Value development is too important to be left to chance. Later in the chapter, we shall examine ways in which we can encourage attitude formation and value development. Now we shall look at some of the more general considerations in this sphere.

The traditional approach to value development.

Raths, et al. (39-40) offer the following seven traditional approaches to helping children develop values:

1. *Setting an example*—either directly or indirectly by pointing to models such as Washington's honesty.
2. *Persuading and convincing*—by presenting arguments and reasons for or against sets of values.
3. *Limiting choices*—giving children choices only within the range of values that we personally accept or slanting the choices so that it is highly probable that children will choose the one we wish.
4. *Inspiring*—by dramatic or emotional pleas.
5. *Rules and regulations*—to condition students and mold them through the use of rewards for conformity and punishments for divergent behavior.
6. *Cultural or religious dogma*—presented as unquestioned wisdom or principle. Appeals to tradition may also fall in this category.
7. *Appeals to conscience*—arousing feelings of guilt.

These authors, Raths, et al., (41) are of the opinion that none of the above lead to value development since values represent the free and thoughtful choice of intelligent humans interacting with complex and changing environments. The only difference we would have with these authors is on the matter of the first item above, setting an example. We believe that the teacher can influence the attitudes and values of his students through his own behavior. We shall discuss this point later.

From your own experiences, no doubt you can refute the worth of most of the above methods for value development. If these traditional methods have largely failed in the past, what recourse do we have if we are to promote the value development of our students?

Classroom climate.

The climate of the classroom is a crucial factor. It is the social-emotional climate to which we refer here. If a child is to develop values, he has to be free to grow and learn in an atmosphere of acceptance. Children learn how to assume responsibility by being allowed to assume responsibility, to cooperate with others by having opportunities to cooperate. The child must be free to try out a variety of behaviors, to explore, to find out for himself. The classroom climate which allows the child to experiment in this fashion is what we shall call a democratic one. Perhaps, it will help to contrast the traditional authoritarian classroom with what we shall describe as a democratic classroom setting.

The traditional authoritarian setting This classroom might be described as follows:

1. The teacher is the central figure in the classroom
2. The teacher and textbook(s) convey knowledge to the student. Teaching is equated with "telling" and then "testing."
3. The student passively meets the demands of the teacher and has no participation in decision making.
4. The teacher's authority goes unquestioned. He assumes responsibility for all actions in the classroom.
5. Great stress is placed on conforming to the dictates of the teacher.
6. There is little opportunity for student interaction. Most interaction is from teacher to student to teacher.
7. Little attention is given to individual differences. All learners are treated alike.
8. There is a rigid classroom arrangement with little grouping.

The democratice classroom setting If we are to encourage development of the "core values" of our democratic society, children need to experience democracy in the present. If the classroom is viewed as a microcosmic democracy, students will have first hand experiences with democratic processes. The following are some characteristics of what we call the democratic classroom:

1. Students are the central focus of the classroom.
2. Teachers don't "teach." They set conditions for students to learn. The classroom is viewed as a learning laboratory. The teacher utilizes many means of mediating instruction, including himself.
3. Students are actively involved in learning utilizing a variety of experiences.

4. Students share in planning and decision making. They share with the teacher the responsibility for what goes on in the classroom.
5. Teachers set purposes for learning *with* students.
6. There is a great deal of interaction among students.
7. Instruction is individualized when needed.
8. There is flexible grouping for a various purposes—skill development, social-emotional needs, interests, and so on.

The climate we have described above will permit children the freedom to test behaviors in a non-threatening atmosphere. This is crucial in attitude and value formation. We can't expect children to value democracy if they have not experienced it. The behavior of the teacher, too, is another factor we shall consider.

The teacher as a model.

Whether he wants this role or not, the teacher through his daily behavior with students is another key in attitude and value formation. Frequently, the teacher is somewhat of a hero to his students in the elementary school. Children look up to him as someone very special, someone to be trusted and loved. There are times when we fall short of deserving this trust and love, however. This is especially true when we tell students one thing and, then, do another ourselves.

Inconsistent behavior Inconsistent behavior on the part of the teacher causes students to doubt him and may promote "unlearning" of the very attitudes and values we strive for children to learn. Let's consider a case in point.

The principal of School X has established a no-talking rule in the cafeteria. Children have been told to raise hands if they need something. Teachers have been instructed by the principal, who thinks of himself as a democratic fellow, to help students understand the "need" for this rule in the cafeteria. He reasons that it is rude to eat and talk, and our job in the cafeteria is to eat; noise upsets our nerves and causes indigestion; it will take too long to eat if we talk, and we need to vacate the cafeteria as soon as we can.

The teachers have duly passed on the rule and the reasons for it to their charges. Teachers, serving as cafeteria wardens for the day, circulate around the room to ferret cut offenders. The faculty lunch table rests in the center of the cafeteria. On any day of the school week, you can enter the cafeteria, and you will be greeted by the din emanating from the teachers' table—talking, giggling, laughing—no superimposed silence here or raising of hands when something is needed! What would be your impression when you walked into School X's cafeteria for the first time? If your were a teacher in School X could you think of any ways to eliminate this display of inconsistent behavior?

Unfortunately, incidents like this are not rare. Have you seen the coach exiting the school with a package of cigarettes tucked in his shirt pocket? Then there is the teacher who expects children to assume their responsibilities but spends his playground duty ignoring the children and conversing with another teacher. Occasionally we find the teacher who "preaches" about the need for a balanced diet but skips lunch in the presence of his students.

The above examples are illustrative of inconsistent behavior on the teacher's part which can interfere with promoting desirable attitudes and values in students. Sometimes, we are unaware of the behavior we are displaying to students. This is often the case in the realm of non-verbal behavior.

Non-verbal communication We communicate thoughts, feelings, and ideas with our bodies, as well as words. Let's look at an example of non-verbal behavior which may have destroyed all the learning in one area which had taken place previously.

In Miss Davis' second grade class the teacher had placed great stress on helping transfer students to adapt to the school setting. Their school had many such students during the year because it had a large proportion of military dependent children in attendance. Miss Davis had employed several techniques to provide her pupils with some insight into ways in which they could help newcomers feel at home in their room. She used role playing, puppets, as well as flannel board stories.

One morning, things didn't go well for Miss Davis from the moment she got out of bed. First, the milk she had poured on her cereal had turned sour so she went without breakfast. Then, her car wouldn't start. Upon her arrival at school, after getting a ride with a neighbor, she remembered that this was the morning for faculty meetings. She was ten minutes late, and, above all, the principal abhorred tardiness at faculty meetings.

She had ushered her children into the room at 9:00 A.M., had run through opening exercises for the day, had assigned seatwork activities, and had just called her first reading group to the table to read when—the door opened. Miss Davis glanced at the clock. It was 9:18. In popped the school secretary with a little lost creature reluctantly following in tow—eyes as big as saucers. The secretary gave the child a gentle nudge forward and stated: "We have a new little girl for your room this morning. Her name is Donna Lake." Miss Davis appeared angry and disturbed. Her brow furled, she drew a deep breath and said in a very icy tone, "How nice. We are glad to see you, Donna." Briskly, she pointed to a desk at the rear of the room and instructed the children to lend the new child a pencil and to give her some paper.

Miss Davis was obviously annoyed. She may not have realized the feelings she communicated with her facial expressions, gestures, posture, and the intonation of her voice. She went through the motions of welcoming the child, but, all the while, she was communicating non-verbally such thoughts as: You are annoying me; I am displeased; you have upset my morning schedule; I can't bother with you now; you are not that important to me.

We can unknowingly communicate hostile, negative feelings non-verbally while we are expressing the opposite feelings with words. Teachers need to analyze their own non-verbal behavior. Also, they need to make children aware of non-verbal communication. It should be noted, too, that if the teacher is sensitive to non-verbal clues, he can discover much about the feelings and attitudes of his students by "reading" these cues.

If consistent behavior patterns on the teacher's part are a factor which we must consider in helping children develop attitudes and values, then, teachers need to examine their own value systems and provide the best model possible for students. Much introspection is required for the essential understanding and acceptance of self. Understanding ourselves permits us to understand and accept others.

Techniques.

We have stated that there are techniques for promoting learning in the affective domain. We need to set purposes and objectives for affective learning as precisely as we do for cognitive learning. Also, we need to plan a variety of such experiences for affective, as well as cognitive learning.

Because most of the communication techniques for promoting value development were discussed thoroughly in Chapter X, we shall take a different approach here. Basically, we can talk in terms of three types of experiences for value development. The first type of experiences includes those in which children are physically involved in exploring their own behavior. The next type of experiences are those in which the teacher uses devices for promoting class discussion. The third type of experiences includes ways of working with individual students in value exploration.

Type I experiences The first type of experiences includes techniques in which students directly participate in "trying out" alternative behaviors. These experiences provide the most effective means for the testing and exploration of alternative ways of behaving. Among these devices are such dramatic activities as role playing, sociodrama, and puppets. Of the three, role playing appears to be the most effective and widely used for this purpose. As we stated in Chapter X, role playing permits the "players" to examine alternative behaviors in an non-threatening situation. Its effective use is contingent upon a classroom in which students are secure enough to bare their innermost thoughts and feelings. It allows them to examine the logical consequences which follow the decisions they make.

Perhaps the best guide for the use of role playing for value exploration has been written by Fannie R. and George Shaftel (see references). This book provides a comprehensive guide to the uses of role playing in social studies. The authors offer a set of problem stories which can be employed in the classroom and provide suggestions for the teacher in the utilization of this technique.

We cannot look upon role playing as a panacea which will cure all ills. The first attempts that children make at role playing may be frought with embarrassment and, perhaps, suspicion. With practice, students learn to role play very skillfully. You will find that as they grow in confidence in using this method, they will become quite open and honest in the roles that they play and provide you, the teacher, with further insight into value differences of children in your classroom.

Occasionally, a teacher will find that he has a child in his group with "sticky fingers." The reasons why children steal are complex, indeed. Sometimes, it is impossible to determine causes for this anti-social behavior. Perhaps the child doesn't understand what it means to "own" anything. Maybe he is accustomed to sharing in the home and perceives taking another's pencil or crayons as "sharing," rather than "stealing." Also there are homes in which children are encouraged to steal. They may learn this behavior at an early age. By the time they enter school, they may have found that stealing is an effective way to obtain what one wants—just don't get caught!

One of the authors had the experience of witnessing this philosophy in action recently.

> While driving through a "depressed" neighborhood, in an effort to find a shortcut to the main highway, I came upon a Coke truck at the end of the block. It was almost blocking the narrow street as the driver was unloading his wares into a small neighborhood store. Having slowed considerably, I noticed a small boy, still in diapers, and his mother, with babe in arms, standing at the open door of the shack which apparently was their home. The mother appeared to say something to the tot and pointed to the truck. As the driver disappeared into the store with his goods, the boy darted in front of me, grabbed two Cokes from the truck, and dashed back

to his mother. Subsequently, they all disappeared inside their dwelling.

When that child enters school, he may have established certain feelings, habits, attitudes, and values which will be contrary to the "core values" of the school and our society. The task of the teacher in dealing with these conflicts will be weighty, indeed.

Role playing, as well as the other devices we have mentioned, will provide experiences in which youngsters, such as the one in the example above, may gain valuable insights into their own behavior, as well as that of others. Telling the child that stealing is evil does not permit the individual to explore and test alternative ways of behaving.

Type II experiences The second type of experiences involves the student in witnessing a presentation of some kind and then talking about it. In other words, the teacher uses one of the many devices for initiating a class discussion in which children will talk about their feelings, beliefs, attitudes, and values. Such devices include plays, puppets (when the children merely watch the teacher use them and are not involved in the performance themselves), open-ended stories and questions, problem stories and pictures, plus other media, such as books, films, filmstrips, audio and video tape recordings.

The benefit from these mediated experiences is derived from the intensive discussion which should follow. In such discussions, the teacher will act as a facilitator, questioner, or prober, attempting to get the children to think and respond. If the teacher injects his biases into the discussion, the children may feel that they must respond in the way he wants them to respond. This destroys the effectiveness of the discussion.

Perhaps, in some discussions the teacher may want to play the role of "devil's advocate." Raths, et al. (127–29) have stated that frequently in value-related discussions only two sides appear, those who care and those who don't. The teacher may want to assume the role of the individual who takes the unpopular side of an issue in an attempt to help the children examine their thinking and clarify their beliefs. The "devil's advocate" role injects another dimension into what might otherwise become a rather lopsided and, perhaps, ineffective discussion. Also, some students may feel the way the "devil" does but fear the teacher's censure if they were to bare the truth about their feelings. This permits these students to "side" with the "devil," at least psychologically, if not actually, in the ensuing discussion.

The "devil's advocate," then, may take a stand against civil rights, for segregation, against honesty, for crime, and the like. It should be noted, however, that when the teacher assumes such a role, he should alert his students to the fact that this is a role he is playing and, thus, not necessarily his true feelings in the matter. Students must be mature enough to recognize that the teacher is actually playing a role. If not, what you say might be misinterpreted and cause parents and administration to demand an explanation from you. This is true whenever the nature of the discussion is particularly controversial.

The class discussion, though perhaps not as intensive an experience for children, remains a useful tool for affective learning. It can provide the teacher with valuable insights into children's thinking. The many devices which we mentioned earlier can be used by the teacher to get the discussion going. How beneficial it is, in terms of value exploration, will lie in the openness of the classroom climate and the skill of the teacher in objectively helping students explore the innermost reaches of their "self."

Type III experiences Both types I and II provide suggestions appropriate for classes and smaller groups of children. The third type of experiences consists of techniques useful in helping individual children who are having social-emotional adjustment problems in school. Two kinds of experiences are worthy of note here. The first consists of the use of books to help children view their problems in a different perspective. This technique is called "bibliotherapy."

Many times, it helps children to read about a child having a problem similar to their own. Books which have therapeutic value are available on various reading levels. For example, a child having difficulty adjusting to a new school situation might be referred to a book, such as Berquist's *Speckles Goes to School.* For a class in which some of the children are from different cultural backgrounds the teacher might encourage the reading of Clark's *Little Navajo Bluebird. Personal Problems of Children,* a booklist compiled by Elvajean Hall on specific problems, is available for 15¢ from Campbell and Hall Inc., P.O. Box 350, Boston, Massachusetts 02117.

The other kind of experience we would like to note briefly, consists of the use of individual conferences. If such conferences are to be beneficial, the teacher must have the trust and confidence of the student in question. When severe adjustment problems are involved, it would be wise for the teacher to seek the advice of personnel who have had special training in this area—school counselors and psychologists. In the conference, as in the other devices we have mentioned, it is important that the teacher remain objective and avoid "preaching" to the student. It isn't likely that much will be accomplished with one or two conferences. Generally, the teacher and student will confer frequently throughout the year if much benefit is to be derived from this technique. The conferences need not be formal. Perhaps just a few minutes from time to time when the other students are not present will be helpful.

In the next section of this chapter, we shall focus upon value conflicts which arise in the school setting. As you read this section, consider ways in which you might apply the above techniques to alleviate such conflicts.

Objectives

The reader will be able to:

Identify (4.0) value conflicts in the college or university environment.

Describe (1.0) the subcultural milieu of our schools.

Explain (2.0) the polycultural nature of our society as illustrated in Figure 11-2.

Identify (4.0) possible points of conflict between his personal values and those of our schools.

Conflict of Values—Teacher vs. Student

Mr. Madison taught sixth grade at any elementary school in a middle-sized town. Desegregation laws had caused the student population of the school to change from almost totally white middle class to a mixture of whites, blacks, and Chicanos (Mexican Americans). Mr. Madison was disturbed at the way the school was "going down hill," as he put it. He was looking forward to retirement in six years. There were days when he felt he might not "make it" another six years. To Mr. Madison, things at school seemed to be going from bad to worse with each passing year.

One day, Mr. Madison was at a local variety store purchasing a few items. He was cruising the automotive section of the store to check spark plug prices when a little farther down the aisle he spotted a couple of students from his school. Apparently, they were unaware of his presence and continued with what they were doing. Suddenly, he noticed one of the boys stuffing some merchandise inside his shirt. Then, the other boy picked up something off the counter and put it in his pocket. Mr. Madison was so amazed that he was speechless. By the time he had recovered from his surprise, they were nowhere in sight.

Upon his return home, Mr. Madison was most disturbed indeed. Some of the comments to his wife were as follows:

"That riff–raff. That's a good example of what we're getting in our school. Those kids are just no good. They'll lie, cheat, and steal, and the worst part of it is that, when you catch them, they act as if they've done nothing wrong. It just makes my blood boil. Kids like that simply won't try to learn anything in school. They're just putting in their time until they can drop out of school legally, and I say good riddance! Meanwhile, they cause as much trouble as they can for us and prevent other students from learning. It's gotten so that I just ignore them in my class and send them to their counselor if they act up."

The following Monday morning, Mr. Madison appeared in the principal's office at 7:55 A.M. He was determined to report those two thieves. The principal listened as he related his tale, but stated flatly that there was nothing he (the school) could do. Even if the culprits had the merchandise on them, it isn't likely that it could be identified as the stolen goods or that the students would admit to the theft. All of the evidence would be too circumstantial. To accuse the students outright could result in some very angry parents and, perhaps, a lawsuit which would be more trouble than the incident was worth. Consequently, the principal strongly advised Mr. Madison to forget the incident.

The behavior of the boys was shocking but not surprising to Mr. Madison. He found it difficult to accept the life styles and backgrounds of children from homes which did not adhere to the values that he had been brought up with. The two boys involved in the variety store theft were from a different subculture. Mr. Madison had established a mental set concerning students from this group. He did not like or understand them. What's more, he had given up on them. It is likely, however, that the two boys in question did not share anything like the same frame of reference that Mr. Madison possessed. If they had been students in his classroom, undoubtedly they would not have understood, liked, or trusted Mr. Madison, either.

Values of the school.

The school, of course, does not "possess" values. When we talk about the values of the school, we are referring to the values of the mainstream of American society which is white, Anglo-Saxon, and Protestant. Values have to be examined within a social or cultural setting. Basically, teachers are drawn from middle class, Anglo society. They help to perpetuate the values of the "system" in which they were raised.

Some have described the school setting as a subculture. Let's examine a description of the subcultural milieu of our schools. The Protestant work-success ethic is stressed—if you work hard today and save for the future, you will become successful and earn the respect of your neighbors. Thus, the emphasis is on hard work in the present and delaying gratification of wants for the future. The school, then, is future-time oriented. Competition plays a vital role in the school. Traditionally, children are expected to be honest, truthful, obedient, cooperative, and conforming. They are supposed to respect the person and property of others; to solve their differences verbally rather than physically; and to understand the language of the school—standard English. The school is routine-oriented. The teacher posts the daily schedule in his room and, within reason, is expected to adhere to it. If we were to sum these characteristics, we might make the following statement in conclusion: Basically, our schools are monocultural in orientation. That orientation is Anglo middle class.

Subcultural values.

Do we prize the right to be different in this country? One might wonder, after examining the orientation of our schools. We have stated that our society is polycultural. The dominant culture, however, is Anglo middle class. To participate in the dominant culture, one must subscribe, at least in part, to Anglo, middle class values. Does this mean that one must give up one's personal values if these should differ from those held by persons in the dominant culture? To a certain extent the answer is yes. However, since we live in a materialistic society in which the dollar speaks quite loudly, it appears that if a person has an abundance of material wealth, he may be as different as he wishes without losing status in the dominant culture. Perhaps you have heard the old saying that if you're rich and "different" you're called "eccentric"; if you're poor and "different," you're just plain crazy. The illustration in Figure 11–2 will help you understand the polycultural nature of our society.

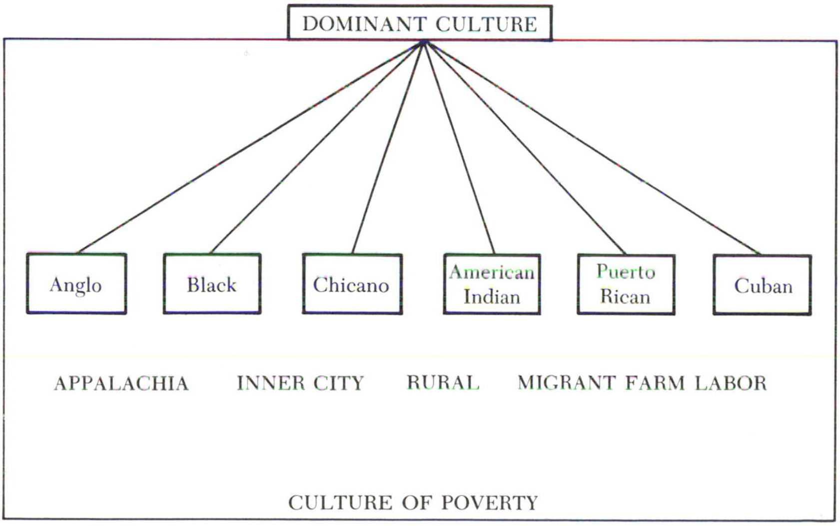

Figure 11–2. *Polycultural society*

Examining the illustration, we see that there are at least six subcultures which can be identified readily. Each of these subcultures could be divided further on the basis of degree of acculturation which might be viewed as a continuum. The individual's or group's point on the acculturation continuum is based to a great extent on economic factors. The greater the economic participation of the individual in the mainstream of American society, the more likely it is that the person or group will adopt the values of the dominant culture.

CHICANO___$___$___$___$___$___$___$___ MIDDLE CLASS ANGLO

Based on education and/or skills ______$______ Result(s) in social status and open(s) the doors to participation in the dominant culture

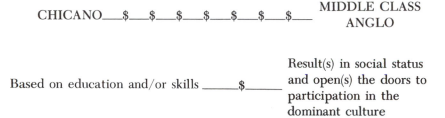

Because of the strong economic factors operating in our society, some have identified a general "culture of poverty," which characterizes most persons who are economically deprived, regardless of race or ethnic origin. For a discussion of the "culture of poverty," its effects on people, as well as an examination of subcultural groups within the culture of poverty, the reader is referred to Chapter XIII. The various subcultural groups differ in their life styles and value systems. Thus, their children may be very confused when a differing value system is imposed upon them in school. When the value system of the home clashes with that of the school, undesirable results are assured.

Examining value conflicts.

How, then, do we, as teachers, deal with value conflict situations? "Very carefully," at first might appear to be a rather ridiculous answer. Yet, it is probably the soundest advice we can give. Consider this example and the way in which the teacher extricated herself from a rather tight spot.

A *case study* Mrs. Jacobs taught first grade in a predominantly lower socioeconomic school. She had a room full of twenty-nine average-to-bright youngsters. Except for Debbie Janicky, she was experiencing a delightful year. Debbie had a weight problem. She was a tall six-year old and was almost as broad as she was tall. The children teased her and called her "fatty" when they were out of hearing range of the teacher. Her father had taught her to fight back—literally—whenever the children taunted her or things didn't go her way. Consequently, early in the school year it was evident to Mrs. Jacobs that Debbie was always in trouble for fighting on the playground.

Because Mrs. Jacobs was concerned about Debbie's obesity, she made out a referral slip for the nurse. After chatting with Mrs. Jacobs about Debbie, the nurse made a home visit. Mrs. Janicky welcomed the nurse into her modest, but spotless home, and was most cooperative in answering questions about her daughter's diet. Only recently Mrs. Janicky had had another baby, so Debbie had been used to getting her way for a number of years. The nurse found out that Mr. Janicky preferred pies and other sweets for breakfast. So this is usually what Debbie had, too. Mr. Janicky worked hard at the foundry and required a lot of food. Mrs. Janicky tried to keep the food budget down by using a lot of "fillers," such as potatoes and beans, and relying on the cheaper cuts of meat which were generally quite fatty. Snacks of potato chips and soda pop were frequent. As the nurse was about to leave the home, Mr. Janicky, who happened to be working a later shift that week, came out of the bedroom. He was a huge man who was almost as wide as he was tall. It was obvious at the outset that the nurse's visit did not please him. He used the opportunity to vent his rage on the nurse for all the problems Debbie was having in adjusting to school.

"Them teachers at that school let them kids call Debbie fat and don't do nuthin' about it," he ranted. I tol' her to stick up fer her rights. Sock 'em one. They ain't got no right to pick on that kid of mine like that."

It was obvious to the nurse that little would be accomplished by remaining and attempting to reason with Mr. Janicky. So, she decided to make a hasty retreat. She thanked Mrs. Janicky, a slender, nervous woman, for the coffee and returned to school.

The nurse had a conference with Mrs. Jacobs, filling her in on all the details of the visit. She said that Mrs. Janicky seemed willing to take Debbie to the doctor to see what could be done about her weight problem. However, the mother appeared reluctant to approach her husband on the matter. Apparently, overweight was a sore subject in the Janicky household.

So meanwhile, all of the teachers got to know Debbie quite well. Rarely did a day pass without Debbie's having been reported for fighting out on the playground. The teachers didn't hear the children tease Debbie. The children usually retreated to the far reaches of the playground, well out of hearing range. Although the teachers tried to prevent such occurrences, they knew that the children were unkind to Debbie and didn't like her. When the children teased, Debbie used her fists to retaliate. And she could really hit! In fact, she was so successful at fisticuffs that she was fast becoming a bully. Whenever the slightest thing went wrong, she would fly into action with her fists in order to get her own way.

Naturally, the children avoided her, at all cost. She didn't fit in with the girls. She was even too rough and tough for the first grade boys. She was a virtual outcast, and Mrs. Jacobs knew she would need to have a conference with the parents, soon.

Mrs. Jacobs contacted Mrs. Janicky, and they set a time for a conference at the school. Mr. Janicky was to be present, too, but he failed to appear at the appointed time. Mrs. Jacobs found Mrs. Janicky understanding and apologetic for Debbie's behavior.

"My husband wanted a boy. He's raised Debbie just like a boy. He says he was taught to fight for his rights and that's why we have as much as we have today. He's taught Debbie to do the same. I know there's rules against fightin' here at school. Debbie says the other kids don't like her. They call her names and won't play with her. That's why she fights. I'll talk to her. Maybe that'll help."

Apparently Mrs. Janicky did have a talk with Debbie. For awhile she stayed out of trouble on the playground. Mrs. Jacobs tried various techniques to integrate Debbie into the group. The children continued to shun her, but, at least she wasn't pestering them and getting into fights. Then——it happened!

Mrs. Jacobs was working with one of the reading groups. The silence of the room was broken only by the activity of the readers. Suddenly, there was loud thud followed by a piercing scream. Mrs. Jacobs looked up to determine what had happened. Debbie had thumped her neighbor, a delicate little girl, on the back with the full force of her fist. The child was sobbing loudly by this time, and Mrs. Jacobs jumped up from her chair to comfort her. "What happened, Debbie?" queried Mrs. Jacobs. "She got her elbow on my desk and was botherin' me." (The children's desks were pushed together in rows to facilitate communication.)

Mrs. Jacobs calmed the victim who actually was more stunned than hurt. She reprimanded Debbie sternly for her actions and turned her attention to returning the class to the morning's activities.

Mrs. Jacobs neglected to contact Debbie's parents after school that day. She assumed she would see them at Open House, the following week, and would relate the incident to them at that time. Mrs. Jacobs went home, took off her shoes, picked up the newspaper, and proceeded to dismiss the memory of the hectic day at school from her weary mind.

By the next morning, she had all but forgotten the incident, as she prepared her classroom for the morning's work. At 8:55 A.M. the bell rang and Mrs. Jacobs walked to her classroom door to greet her students as they entered. At the end of the line was Debbie and Mr. Janicky! There was fire in his eye, and all 250+ pounds appeared ready for a battle. As he approached the classroom door, his face reddened and his fists clenched.

"What's this I hear you done to my kid yesterday?" raved Mr. Janicky, as he placed a mighty hand on the open classroom door.

"Uh, yes, Mr. Janicky. We did have an incident in the classroom involving Debbie," replied Mrs. Jacobs attempting to "keep her cool."

"My kid says you chewed her out in front of the class when all she done was protect her rights. Now I ain't gonna have that. I. . . ."

Mrs. Jacobs interrupted him, wrenched the door from his hand and said, "It's time for class to begin, and I cannot discuss the matter with you now. I shall be happy to discuss the incident with you in the presence of Debbie and the principal after school today." (She knew intuitively that talking would accomplish little this morning.) With that she briskly closed the door, quickly regained her composure, and began the day with her students, whose eyes, at this point, were as big as saucers!

Mr. Janicky did not appear after school. When he and Mrs. Janicky arrived at the Open House the following week, he meekly apologized to Mrs. Jacobs for being so "hot under the collar" as he put it. Mrs. Jacobs talked with the Janickys for quite awhile that evening. Without telling Mr. Janicky that he was wrong to have made a bully out of Debbie, she pointed out the many reasons why fighting was unacceptable behavior *at school.* She advised the parents to take Debbie to the family physician in an attempt to correct her obesity problem. The parents appeared receptive to this idea.

Meanwhile, at school, Debbie continued to have a rather miserable year. She was achieving satisfactorily, academically, but despite Mrs. Jacob's efforts, the children continued to reject her.

Can you perceive the value conflicts in the foregoing situation? From a tiny tot, Debbie had been taught to play rough and fight for her rights. Mr. Janicky had come from a lower socioeconomic home. His parents had been immigrants and were barely able to eke out an existence. He lived in a tough neighborhood in which physical violence was part of the life style. He equated "fighting back" with courage and manhood. To attempt to settle disagreements with words was unheard of; not even the girls in the neighborhood did that. Although, through vocational training and exceptional skills, Mr. Janicky had risen in economic status to the middle class, he clung to many of the values of his childhood. Some of these values ran contrary to those of the school. They had caused problems for Mr. Janicky when he was in school. Now they were causing problems for Debbie.

The following are some questions which might be raised about the "Debbie incident:"

a. What are the value conflicts involved?

b. Should Mrs. Jacobs have counseled with the parents earlier?

c. Should she have "paddled" Debbie for her fighting?

d. Should Mrs. Jacobs have taken time out when Mr. Janicky appeared at school that morning to confer with him?

e. Is Debbie's behavior the result of hostility or merely training?

f. How can Mrs. Jacobs help Debbie become a more cooperative child?

g. How could Mrs. Jacobs have helped the class in accepting Debbie?

h. What are the teacher's feelings toward Debbie?

A reexamination Let's return to the two incidents presented earlier in this chapter. "Ethnocentrism" is a term which anthropologists use in referring to the bias we tend to possess in thinking that our own culture is superior to all others and that any variance from it has to be due to ignorance, stupidity, or baseness. We seem to view facets of the culture in the same way. We lean toward the belief that the values we hold, personally or as a group, are superior to the values of others. We grow in acceptance of others as we study about them and learn to view cultural differences in a more objective way. There are no "good" or "bad" cultures. The labels "goodness" or "badness" become attached to the behaviors of participants in the culture, on the basis of their conforming to cultural norms—what is expected of them.

Perhaps our brief discussion of values as related to the cultural or subcultural milieu will help you view value conflicts more objectively. We shall attempt to refocus your attention on two incidents related in this chapter, in order to provide you with the opportunity to exercise your objectivity.

(1) You will recall that the incident at the beginning of the chapter found George pilfering someone else's lunch. Here are some questions which you may wish to ponder and discuss.

a. Should Mrs. Martin have ignored George's behavior and permitted him to finish the lunch?

b. Does George understand the meaning of "stealing?"

c. Since George is a member of a minority group in the culture of poverty, can we assume that he has been taught honesty in the home?

d. Should Mrs. Martin have determined if George were hungry? If so, why didn't he eat his own lunch? How might this information have affected Mrs. Martin's actions?

e. What effect do you suppose Mrs. Martin's paddling had on George's behavior?

f. What effect do you imagine her lecture had on the class?

g. Is honesty a trait we wish children to have? If so, how can we help them acquire this characteristic?

(2) Another incident we discussed concerned the out-of-school behavior of two sixth grade boys who had pilfered merchandise from a variety store. Obviously, the teacher Mr. Madison had a fixed set of values and used these values as a criterion to judge the behavior of others. You can use the following questions to guide your rethinking of this incident:

a. If the boys had recognized Mr. Madison as a teacher in their school, do you think they might have altered their behavior in any way?

b. Why is Mr. Madison so hostile toward the culturally different children attending his school?

c. If you were the principal of the school in which Mr. Madison taught, how might you help your teachers acquire more positive attitudes toward culturally different children?

d. If you had been in Mr. Madison's shoes in the variety store, how might you have reacted when you noticed the boys stealing?

e. If you were the principal, would you have recommended any punitive measures?

f. Is there ever a time when stealing might be justified?

The teacher and his values.

Examining one's own value system is a tricky task, somewhat similar to chasing a bar of soap around the floor of the shower. Few of us have such static sets of values that we know them well and can verbalize about them readily. One wonders about those who are so sure of themselves that they can make dogmatic pronouncements on a variety of topics, at the drop of a hat. Adults, like children, constantly test behaviors in a variety of settings. We adjust and readjust our attitudes and values on the basis of the feedback we receive from our environment. Then, too, we sometimes try to fool ourselves, and say we believe in a certain way, yet behave in a manner which contradicts our beliefs. At times, we fall short of the ideals we set for ourselves resulting, perhaps, in disgust and shame. But the wonderful part of life is that with a new dawn we can wipe the slate clean and resolve to do better next time.

Teachers are human. We all have self-doubts and anxieties. Perhaps we are bothered by the things we see around us—injustice; man's inhumanity and indifference to man; the poverty, disease, and hunger which continue to run rampant in parts of our country; unsettled world conditions; lack of concern for ecological problems; the power that the almighty dollar wields over the lives of people. If we are bothered, this is a good sign. It means that we care. It means that we want to leave a better world for future generations.

It is the teacher who lacks strong feelings and a set of values to live by, who, perhaps, doesn't belong in the classroom. Maybe he is the type of person who feels that teaching is just a way of earning money and that his personal life is his own business. It just doesn't work that way. As a teacher, you cannot help but inject something of yourself into your relationships with students. The affective dimension is ever present in our dealings with others. The old cliche remains true—we teach *children,* after all, not subject matter.

We are not suggesting that each teacher subscribe to an identical set of values. We have pointed out that valuing, like other learning, is personal. There are expected differences, even among persons in the same culture. Yet, unless one has a set of values, even though fluid, that guide his actions, he hardly can be expected to help students develop attitudes and values.

Let us emphasize that we believe that teachers need to incorporate into their personal value systems the "core values" of a democratic society. We do not condone stealing, cheating, lying, breaking the law, and so forth. If our nation is to survive, we need youth who are honest, truthful, loyal, law-abiding citizens. This may seem an impossible task when we see hypocrisy about us in our institutions, as well as in our personal relations with others. Yet, teachers need to "tell it like it is" and work toward change and improvement.

The teacher remains the key to the value development of children in school. Much of the task of value learning lies in helping students explore alternatives. As with cognitive learning, the teacher needs to determine where his students are before he can begin. If students are participants in a subculture which has a vastly different value structure from his own, the teacher must be aware of these differences and avoid "preaching" to children. This only serves to create a wider chasm between teacher and student, school and the home. There is no substitute for knowing the life style of your students well. This involves visiting with parents in their homes and developing a "feel" for their way of life. You cannot map a plan of action if you don't know what you are to begin with.

If we are to provide students with a well-rounded program in social studies, one in which both cognitive and affective learning will take place, we shall be unable to ignore attitude and value development. Yet, we lack sufficient research to guide us in planning for this most important segment of education. Hopefully, this chapter has provided you with some information, as well as techniques, which you will be able to apply in your own teaching.

Summary

In this chapter, we have offered an overview of value development in social studies. We defined values and provided a model of the affective hierarchy which may prove helpful in understanding how an individual develops his value complex. We discussed the set of "core values" which persons in a democracy must hold if that society is to survive. It is the development of the "core values," particularly, with which social studies is concerned.

We pointed out that values cannot be taught directly. This is why we have referred to this segment of learning as value development or acquisition. We stressed that it is our task to provide children with opportunities for value exploration.

Three factors in value development were stressed. They were the classroom climate, the teacher as a model, and specific techniques for value exploration.

Certain value conflict situations were presented, and the reader was challenged to consider the underlying conflicts in these examples. The values of the school were described. Lastly, we took a look at the teacher and his values. We stressed that the teacher, after all, is the key to value development in the school setting.

References

Raths, Louis E., Harmin, Merrill, and Simon, Sidney B. *Values and Teaching: Working with Values in the Classroom.* Merrill's International Education Series. Edited by Kimball Wiles. Columbus, Ohio: Charles E. Merrill Publishing Company, 1966.

Shaftel, Fannie R., and Shaftel, George. *Role Playing for Social Values: Decision-Making in the Social Studies.* Englewood Cliffs, New Jersey: Prentice-Hall, Inc., 1967.

XII

Information Processing Skills in Social Studies

Chapter Outline

Information Processing Skills in Social Studies

In Chapter I, we pointed out that one of the basic purposes of social studies is to teach the child to think. It was further stated that in order to do this we had to teach the individual sources of information and methods of organizing data to draw conclusions. These are the skills required to promote thinking and to which we shall refer as information processing skills. In this chapter, we shall examine these skills in greater detail. First, we shall discuss a few generalizations which have been advanced concerning the teaching of these skills. Second, we shall list the skills, and, third, we shall present selected procedures teachers have designed to enable students to acquire these skills. The lessons presented are not offered as exemplary. They are simply *a* teacher's way of attacking the problem of aiding children in the development of information processing skills. Since the gathering of data from written materials, listening skills, field trips, and the communication of ideas has been discussed in other sections, it will not be discussed in this chapter.

Objective

The reader will be able to:

Identify (5.0) the three generalizations the authors present on teaching information processing skills.

What We Know about Teaching Information Processing Skills

It is not unusual for a beginning teacher to be assigned a classroom full of bouncy youngsters, given a set of texts which range in age from a few months to several years, and provided with a brief outline of what he is "supposed" to teach. Then, the door is closed for the first day of class. The neophyte frequently may fail this "baptism of fire" because he assumes that children have the skills necessary to begin at the point the teacher selects. Some teachers admit that they have expected children to possess many of the same skills that they themselves possess—a rather ridiculous assumption.

Acquaintance with related research as well as many bitter personal experiences have convinced teachers that they can assume little about children and nothing about the skills they possess. As we have indicated in previous chapters, you must analyze the task you expect children to perform. After you have identified the skills which will be needed, you must assess the level of skill attainment to determine whether children have the required skills. If they don't possess these skills, then, the teacher must help children acquire the skills before they are asked to perform the task. The question, then, is "How does the teacher go about this? Can he teach the skills incidentally?" The answer Schiller (201–03) would give is a resounding, "No." For example, incidental teaching of skills did not aid the achievement in geography of a group of seventh graders. The children who were taught skills systematically showed a significant gain on a measure of geography achievement over students receiving incidental instruction. What does this mean? Simply, that you must design your units so that they teach children specific skills in a planned sequence. You may recall that such a planned sequence in reporting has been presented in Chapter V. "Does this mean that I must teach skills in isolation?" you may ask.

Again, the answer is, "No!" Skills must be taught in a realistic and functional setting, or learning will not transfer to the areas you intend. Perhaps the reason for this lack of transfer is that the purpose for learning is not readily apparent to the learner unless he is faced with a meaningful situation which forces him to use the skill. Many times, in each of our academic backgrounds, we have advanced rapidly after recognizing the need for a specific skill. As we have indicated previously, developing the need for learning is a motivational step.

Objectives

The reader will be able to:

In cooperation with a group of peers

1. **develop (5.0) a question which can be answered using the interview technique.**
2. **develop (5.0) an interview instrument.**
3. **collect (2.0) the required data.**
4. **analyze (4.0) the data by one means suggested by the authors.**
5. **prepare (5.0) a graphic summary of the data, and**
6. **draw conclusions (6.0) from the data gathered.**

Listing the Information Processing Skills

Skills result in the ability to do something with some degree of expertness in repeated performances. In the social studies, the performances we are attempting to elicit from the child are locating information, organizing data, drawing conclusions, and communicating these ideas and conclusions to others. Essentially, these are information processing skills.

Few people in our history have been forced to make so many choices. Take career choices, as an example. How much choice of careers did your grandmother have? Your mother? What about your choices? As citizens, we must make choices, too. The important aspect we must consider is the quality of these choices.

The following table is an attempt to identify a systematic listing of skills which can be used to improve the quality of our choices as citizens. Table 12–1 is a listing which was patterned after one created by Eunice Johns and Dorothy McClure Fraser for the National Council for Social Studies in 1963. (311–327) Since the presentation of that listing, many ideas about children's abilities have changed. In the summer of 1971, a group of eighteen graduate students, experienced elementary teachers, looked at the former list and decided that it needed revision. Using the list compiled earlier as a organizer, the students developed the revised Table 12–1. No attempt has been made to validate this listing, to this date. The authors would encourage you to test and revise this inventory from time to time as you teach.

The authors have arranged the listing in the form in which it would be used, from the collection of data to means of communicating findings to others. Unfortunately, it is not a complete inventory. In some cases, the delineations included here will also be found as listings in reading texts. Remember, however, that social studies and science are considered the content sources of the elementary curriculum. It is natural that the areas which produce the tools needed for this content—language arts and mathematics—should be integrated with content areas. None of the skills listed should be conceived of as the sole province of the social studies. Remember, these skills are needed to make decisions. They can be used in all curriculum areas.

Another important point must be discussed. You will note that check marks placed in the columns denote early primary (EP), primary (P), early intermediate (EI), and intermediate (I). These assignments mean that the skill is introduced at that level. Mastery will be achieved at any of the following levels. The grade level of mastery is dependent upon individual differences. If one looks at skills in this way, it will be evident that all teachers are responsible for testing for the level of their students, individually, and progressing from that point. Last year's teacher is not *really*

Table 12–1

A Listing Of Social Studies Skills

	EP	P	EI	I
I. Locating Information Through:				
A. Past Experience				
1. Recalls what is known	√			
2. Evaluates information		√		
3. Decides what additional information is needed		√		
4. Lists questions which can be used to guide inquiry		√		
5. Attempts to gather data to answer these questions		√		
B. Observation				
1. Describes things he observes	√			
2. Determines reliability				√
3. Determines validity				√
C. Interviews				
1. Identifies purposes	√			
2. Identifies important questions			√	
3. Selects a procedure for obtaining answers			√	
4. Summarizes the results			√	
D. Books				
1. Uses titles as guides	√			
2. Uses tables of contents	√			
3. Uses alphabetization	√			
4. Uses indices			√	
5. Uses title pages	√			
6. Uses topic headings			√	
7. Uses glossaries, appendices, lists of illustrations			√	
8. Uses fictional and factual materials			√	
9. Chooses appropriate books	√			
10. Scans for required information		√		
11. Skims to identify general ideas				√
E. Efficient Use of the Dictionary				
1. Alphabetizes to third letter		√		
2. Uses guide words		√		
3. Uses pronunciation keys			√	
4. Syllabicates correctly		√		
5. Selects appropriate meanings		√		
6. Uses entry words			√	
F. Newspapers and Magazines (at age and interest level)				

	EP	P	EI	I
1. Recognizes as sources of information	✓			
2. Recognizes purposes and coverage of various materials			✓	
3. Selects appropriate materials			✓	
4. Uses lists of previous published articles as reference tools				✓
5. Identifies biases of publishers or writers				✓
6. Identifies mass persuasion techniques				✓
G. Materials in the Library				
1. Uses the card catalog				
a. Title		✓		
b. Author		✓		
c. Subject		✓		
d. Publisher			✓	
e. Date of publication			✓	
2. Uses various categories of books				
a. Historical fiction			✓	
b. Realistic fiction			✓	
c. Biography		✓		
d. Folk stories and myths			✓	
e. Music and art		✓		
f. Religion			✓	
g. Factual		✓		
H. Gathering Data from Written Material				
1. Identifies topic sentences		✓		
2. Identifies main ideas		✓		
3. Summarizes needed ideas			✓	
4. Organizes material from several sources			✓	
5. Prepares reports				✓
I. Using Field Trips				
1. Identifies purposes	✓			
2. Identifies important questions	✓			
3. Identifies procedures for obtaining answers		✓		
4. Summarizes results of interviews or field trips	✓			
J. Listening				
1. Attentive listening				
a. Grasps speaker's purposes		✓		
b. Detects main idea	✓			
c. Relates supporting details			✓	
d. Notes evidence to support statements			✓	
e. Draws conclusions		✓		
f. Follows directions and instructions	✓			

	EP	P	EI	I
2. Analytical listening				
a. Finds main events in sequence	√			
b. Finds supporting ideas		√		
c. Finds emotional persuasion			√	
d. Detects opinion statements or bias				√
e. Distinguishes fact from opinion			√	
f. Makes comparisons	√			
g. Finds relationships	√			
h. Make judgements	√			
i. Makes inferences	√			
II. Organizing Information Through:				
A. Evaluating Data				
1. Lists data	√			
2. Establishes criteria for accepting or rejecting information		√		
3. Compares information drawn from two or more sources	√			
B. Arranging Data in Some Useful Way				
1. Constructs diagrams and flow charts		√		
2. Makes outlines			√	
3. Designs tables or information accumulation charts	√			
4. Prepares graphs	√			
III. Drawing Conclusions By				
A. Making Tentative Generalizations	√			
B. Evaluating the Generalizations	√			
C. Verifying the Generalization by Looking at a Similar Situation		√		
D. Verifying the Generalization in a Situation Changed in One Respect		√		
IV. Communicating Ideas Through Graphic Materials				
A. Prepares Charts			√	
B. Prepares Graphs		√		
C. Reports Information to Groups		√		
D. Prepares Summaries of Information Through Group Discussions			√	
E. Prepares Written Reports Containing Several Graphic Methods				√

the one to blame. You have the responsibility of helping the child gain the skills he needs to perform a given task.

Locating information.

There was a sign in many computer centers a few years ago which displayed these letters: G I G O. It stood for "garbage in; garbage out." In other words, if one fed the computer poor programs and data, it gave poor answers. We differ from computers in that we can locate and evaluate the information we use. Our task with children is to help them make use of "good" information. The best way to accomplish this is to teach them, first, to use many sources of information, and then to evaluate the data they obtain from these sources. A fountain of information we have neglected in the past is the child's own experiences. Perhaps one of the most effective ways to teach children to use their own experiences is through the techniques developed in Hilda Taba's research. These procedures aid children in understanding that their own minds are a source of data. The task, then, becomes one of helping them evaluate their experiences.

Past experiences The things we know are the keystones of our beliefs. We establish our ideas through the experiences we have. We can make some generalizations about these ideas we have accepted.

1. Preference for one idea indicates some evidence in favor of an idea.
2. What we believe changes from time to time according to the data we have.
3. Ideas we hold should be consistent. Inconsistency indicates a need for more data.
4. Decisions must be made on available data. We hope to find the best evidence upon which we can make decisions. We seldom have all the data we need.
5. Ideas must be tested through exposures to the beliefs of others.
6. There are things we can't prove. These ideas are open to refutation.

Many times, after we have evaluated the data available to us, we must seek additional data. In order to accomplish this, we ask ourselves questions. So, children must be taught to ask productive questions, too. Lippitt, Fox and Schaible (17–18), in their guide for teachers, list criteria for questions which can be summarized as follows:

1. Questions must be answerable by data which can be collected. If data can not be gathered, it is a poor question.
2. Questions should not be asked which depend upon unestablished conclusions.
3. Questions should be asked which allow us as broad an application as possible.
4. Questions should not ask for value judgements.

These authors have identified and presented a list of types of questions. This list can be useful to the teacher in helping children arrive at questions which aid in the accumulation of data.

1. *Descriptive:* What happened? What are they doing? What is going on? How many different kinds are there?
2. *Comparative:* How are they different from each other? How are they similar? How would the scientists do it?
3. *Historical:* When did it get started? How did it get started? Has it changed from the way it used to be? What have they found to be true in the past?
4. *Causal:* What caused him to behave that way? Why did it turn out that way?
5. *Prediction:* How will it end? What's going to happen next?
6. *Experimental hypotheses:* If I do this, will he do that? If the bright ones help the slower ones, will the total amount of motivation increase? What would happen if I . . . ?
7. *Methodological:* How can we find out? Where can we locate resources? Are these observations reliable? How valid are our data?
8. *Value inquiry:* Which way is best? Is it always bad to get angry? Is that a good way for things to end?
9. *Relevance of application:* How does this apply to me? How does this idea or generalization apply to other situations? at home? after school? (Lippett, Fox, and Schaible:19)

Another source of information when helping children locate data is observation.

Observation Children are natural observers. Many parents know this is true. In fact, there is a saying that states, "Do something you don't want a child to do, and watch him repeat it." There are some guidelines for observation which we must follow.

Two basic requirements of systematic observation are validity and reliability. Reliability refers to the ability of two or more persons observing the same act to report similar results. Reliability in observation is notoriously poor. We know from watching court trials on T.V. that the descriptions of witnesses are very unreliable. Descriptions of observations tend to be poor unless observers are trained. Children can learn to be more reliable observers through the use of observation games in the classroom. They can be taught that in order to obtain a reliable observation, it is better to have several observers and compare observations.

The lack of validity is the second error which often creeps into observation. The validity of observation means, "Did we really see what we thought we saw." We often see what we want to see and not what is there. The best example of this is an audience watching a magician. How many times have you seen a levitation act? What really happened?

Children can be made aware of validity, too. A feeling box can be constructed in such a way that children can feel objects in a box but can not see them. The task for the children is to describe the object and, then, make guesses about the identity of the object. It is difficult for the early primary child to refrain from making careless guesses before he has accumulated data. The task is describing what we actually see or feel and not what we *think* we see and feel.

In the same way, children can differentiate between fact and opinion. What is the difference? A fact is a statement about what we see, taste, smell, touch, and hear, which can be verified through others' observations. Opinions are interpretations of facts built upon assumptions of our feelings about what happened. We label something as bad or good, better or worse on the basis of our opinions. These opinions come from our interpretations. An example may help. If we see one child strike another and say, "Johnny hit Ricardo," we are making a statement of fact. If we say, "Johnny hit Ricardo because he was angry with him," we are making an interpretation. Merely observing the two children is not enough to make the latter statement. More information is needed.

As long as we know when we are making interpretations and upon what assumptions we are basing them, there is nothing wrong with interpretations. The problem, of course, arises when we make evaluative interpretations and accept them as facts, objective data.

Interviews Many times we must obtain data through conversations with other people. Opinions of others are useful data. Their experiences allow us to take shortcuts to new knowledge. Social scientists often make use of interviews or surveys to obtain data. Interviewing is a skill useful to children and they can be taught to employ this technique reliably. Lippitt, Fox, and Schiable suggest the following rules for observers:

> 1. The purpose of the interview, or some orientation to the interview, should be given at the start.
> 2. The interviewer should be friendly. He should seek to elicit and maintain the cooperation of the respondent.
> 3. The questions should be asked *exactly as stated,* and usually into the order given.
> 4. The responses should be reported as given. The interviewer should not show that he either agrees or disagrees with the answers. (It might be a good idea to have interview teams of two for each interview—one person to ask the questions and probe for the answers, the other to record what is being said.)
> 5. The interviewer should prompt or probe for some answers. This should be done especially when the answer is not clear, when it is very brief, or when the respondent is reluctant to answer. This is especially important. (77)

The technique for teaching these skills is used in most graduate schools today. Many undergraduate students have been taught them. The teacher sets the stage so that the student derives the purpose for learning to use the device, demonstrates a good interview, and, then, guides children in role playing and analyzing interview sessions. Children can also obtain interview data through development of useful survey questions. Social scientists have identified the forced choice, rank, scale, and opened-ended question as useful tools.

The forced choice question requires the respondent to provide either a *yes* or *no* answer. Ranking questions require that the interviewee place things in the order he thinks best. Scale questions present several possible choices along a continuum, such as illustrated below.

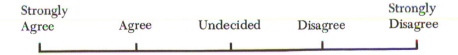

Strongly Agree	Agree	Undecided	Disagree	Strongly Disagree

The open-ended question is utilized when you want to place little restraint on the interviewee. Often, this technique is used to gain a great number of alternatives such as, "What should the school do with the money it received from the paper drive this year?"

As a society, we have tended to leave research techniques to upper graduate levels, advertising, industry, and business. However, in a study of high achieving sixth grade youngsters, Torrence and Meyers (1–6) indicated that elementary school students were able to perform historical, descriptive, and experimental research. These students were able to use the simple statistical concepts of mean, median, mode, variance, levels of confidence, and the t-test. Since their research study, several statistical concepts have been introduced into children's social study. We will spend a few minutes discussing the simpler of these procedures and indicate possible uses for them in the classroom. Since most math series introduce several statistical concepts in the intermediate grades, we shall assume that teachers could use social studies statistical data to aid in the teaching of these concepts. Levels of confidence and t-tests will not be discussed here. Teachers wishing to use these techniques should refer to Henry E. Garrett's, *Elementary Statistics*. This book presents these concepts simply.

Table 12–2 summarizes the various procedures indicated above. As presented, the percentage is a useful statistic. If one were attempting to survey the class or several classes about how they would vote in an election, the simple percentage statistic would be useful. If one were attempting to determine a point which would indicate the average amount of time students spend watching T.V., the mean could be helpful. Since the median and mode are types of averages, too; they could be employed to indicate, for example, the point at which 50% of the group watched T.V. and those points at which members seem to group, in terms of the hours spent watching T.V. Also, the range might be interesting because this could tell us the difference in hours between the student who watches T.V. most and the student who watches it the least.

In analyzing the results, the several graphing devices mentioned in Chapter VIII should be utilized. The circle graph could be used in the intermediate grades to show percentages. The amount of time spent by individuals watching T.V. could be plotted on a line graph. Either a line or bar graph could be constructed to show the mean, median, and modes of the T.V. habits of the various groups.

Books Books have been the most popular data sources in the elementary school. Yet the skills required to use books effectively have often been neglected. Many of these skills can be developed in the early primary grades as indicated in the chart listed in Table 12–1. One tradition of American education must be changed before we can begin using this data source correctly. That tradition has been ingrained into everyone of us—books must be read from cover to cover.

This belief is sheer idiocy. An analogy on approximately the same level would be the developing of a computer program to do a specific job and, then, expecting the computer to regurgitate all of the other data

Table 12–2

Statistical Procedures For Social Study

Method	Use	Computation
Percentage	To determine portion of group responding in a given way	Take the number responding in a given way (n) and divide it by the total number (N) responding
Mean	To find the point on a scale around which the greatest numbers of the distribution fall	Take all the scores, (X) add them (Σ) and divide by the number of scores (N) $M = \frac{\Sigma x}{N}$
Median	The point at which 50% of a group fall above and below	Count halfway through the group $Mdn = \frac{N}{2}$
Mode	The most frequent or popular score or scores	Find points at which the greatest number or numbers of scores fall
Range	The spread of scores from the highest to lowest score	Subtract the lowest score from the highest

in its memory bank to be sure we haven't missed something. Textbooks and other informational books are merely data banks. Man has invented many procedures for entering these data banks so that he can solve specific problems. In the first place, titles were developed. These act as guides to types of data we can find within a particular book. They are guides which even young children can use. The table of contents is more specific than the title. The most exacting means of entering this storage of information is the index.

Since some books require special terminology and vocabulary, they contain a glossary which enables the reader to understand peculiarities of the vocabulary found in the book or data bank. The following are other ways of finding specific types of data within the text, which may be of interest to the reader: bold-face headings, picture captions, pictures, maps, and graphs. It is unfortunate that children are sent to other sources of information when the data they need is in some portion of the books they are reading, and they don't know it. It's exasperating to a parent to find that children taught from textbooks don't know the format of this data source sufficiently well to use it to advantage.

One fourth grade teacher wanted to aid her students in learning about sources of data available in informational books.[1] She integrated the following unit on the glossary into the study of farming and ranching.

Entry behavior: The student will have had sufficient experience with a dictionary to be familiar with phonetic spellings, diacritical markings, and multiple meanings of words.

Behavioral objective A: The student will be able to analyze (4.0) the glossaries in reading, science, health, social studies texts, and other informational books.

Teacher action: The teacher will ask the children to open selected books and discuss what they find in the glossary of each. The teacher will use the similarities and differences procedure according to Taba and attempt to develop generalizations that: glossaries contain specialized definitions, and that glossaries have distinct elements which are identifiable.

Media: Required books and chalkboard.

Students' actions: Examine glossaries and enumerate similarities and differences. Draw generalization indicated.

Behavioral objective B: Using the information he gains in the above objective, the student will develop and illustrate (5.0) his own glossary on farming or ranching.

[1] Mrs. Kay Knight of Lubbock, Texas, furnished the ideas for this unit.

Teacher action: The teacher will call the children's attention to the vocabulary lists they have developed during the study on farming or ranching and review the elements they discovered about glossaries. She will ask the children to develop a glossary using a listing of words and their discovered meanings.

Media: The data organizing charts on vocabulary and glossaries. Various materials children request.

Students' actions: Collect a list of words, arrange them with their meanings in an illustrated glossary using the elements they have discovered about glossaries.

You will note that in the beginning the teacher did not focus entirely on social studies texts. This would be a disadvantage because glossaries are common to many books. Children should be aware of the types of books in which glossaries are found. This is another example of a resourceful teacher's efficient planning. He teaches the skill once, for all subjects. It is easier for children to transfer skills if they are shown several possible applications from the beginning.

Efficient use of the dictionary. Although the use of the dictionary is considered a language arts skill, both social studies and science are the content areas within which it must be used. We have stated previously that skills are taught most effectively in situations where they are needed. The intermediate grades are important in the development of these skills. Although such skills are introduced during the primary grades, alphabetization to the second and third letter is usually not mastered until the fifth or sixth grade. The selection of appropriate meanings remains a problem in junior high school. Appreciation for this skill can be developed in the area of social studies by requesting that children attempt to find the word that "really expresses" what they want to say. After all, the dictionary is the standard of convention in our language usage. It can be employed to facilitate communication. Children can be taught to use it as an expressive, as well as interpretative device, in social studies.

The use of guide words is important, too. Surprisingly, many adults fail to use them correctly. How many of us continue to scan the dictionary page, rather than use the guide words at the top?

Newspapers and magazines. The most misused media in the classroom today are the newspaper and the magazine. Although the authors have seen many accounts referring to the successful use of newsstand papers and magazines, their experiences indicate that these media forms are basically useless in grades K-6. Perhaps this statement should be tempered by noting that there are some articles of a historical or current events nature that have sufficient appeal to children to be understood by them. There is that variable of motivation which can not be denied—if a child wants to, he'll read it.

The problem appears to be more one of journalistic style, rather than difficulty of reading level. Journalistic style includes idiomatic language, as well as unelaborated language structure that throws the young reader. Until the child has had sufficient experience with this writing style, adult news magazines are relatively unusable. Magazines and newspapers written for children are very useful, and, as we have indicated previously, they can provide the background for the child's later use of adult material.

As neophytes begin to search for information, they have no sense of what they need or of the types of material they can uncover to fulfill fuzzily defined needs. This is as we would expect. Since most children entering school have not experienced the process of formal problem-solving, we can not expect them to possess these skills.

It is only through contact with informational media that children begin to develop a feel for sources of information. After a semester of experience with a magazine such as *Nature and Science* or a Scholastic publication, for example, children begin to recall the kind of information published in them and, thereby, are able to identify the usefulness of such magazines.

Earlier, in the primary grades, you may find children turning to a fictional story for information. At times, even intermediate children can be found doing the same thing. So it is not only a problem of possible sources but, also, of identifying the type of material for which one must look. Again, the stumbling block is the lack of experience. For the child to grow in these abilities, he must have experiences with many kinds of materials.

The teacher can begin attacking the above problem in the primary grades by calling the children's attention to a story and asking such questions as, "Is this a true story?" "Do you think that this could really happen?" "Was ________ a real boy?" You are helping children to differentiate between what is factual and what is fanciful. In the early intermediate grades, most children make this distinction easily. A fourth grader is rarely fooled by fairy tales. A third grader, early in the year, may not be sure that a specific story *is* a fairy tale. Third graders can distinguish books which are likely to be fictional stories, but there are often shades of gray which are difficult for them to categorize.

Experienced fifth graders can tell you in a minute where you are likely to find such and so. Their memories may produce the page number, the name of the paper, and the picture under which the information can be found. Notice that the modifier we used in the previous sentence was

COMB, WASHTUB REMAIN

Half-Dugout In Brownfield Seems Untouched By Time

(Special To The Avalanche-Journal)

BROWNFIELD — Starting your automobile at the courthouse here and within five minutes you will arrive at a structure of yesteryear.

It is within the city limits of Brownfield.

Driving northwest and across the railroad tracks, then making two turns to the west, you hit N. Bridges Street. This is the Wheatley Addition.

* * *

Half-Dugout Remains

ACROSS FROM the abandoned school building, in plain sight, is a hal'-dugout. It was owned by the late L. D. Ray.

The dugout is on a four-acre plot and the area is kept clean by the city and residents of the addition.

Entering the dugout, one knows a man lived here. There are such items as comb, shaving cream and washtub there still. Over the door is a heavy iron cotton hook, of the type used to handle bales of cotton. Two automobile license plates are tacked beside the entrance. The door was not locked.

Dirt steps lead in. Two "shelves" hewn in earth apparently were bed bunks. The living quarters are one "room" of about 10 by 16 feet. A small window is at the south end. It was covered with heavy wire.

A single electric light cord, drops from the roof. It is frayed and worn.

THE WALLS are earthen up to about four feet. The rest is made from scraps of lumber. The roof is covered by tin.

I. H. "Grandpa" Harris, age 94, longtime Wheatley resident, said the dugout was there in 1934. He added the original location was on a 260-acre plot that belonged to W. R. Bridges.

The old dugout has remained unmolested all these years. The residents around it appear more interested in street lights and paved streets they want than in the historical significance of the dugout.

★ ★ ★

This motivating newspaper article and museum picture illustrate the type of materials that enhance natural interest in the child's own environment.

"experienced." Children's attention must be called to magazines, as a source of information. One teacher accomplished this task with his classes by having students identify main ideas or write summaries from time to time throughout the year. Near the end of the year, he would have the students return to articles they had summarized previously about such topics as transportation, automation, population growth, ecology, or welfare. He had the children formulate conclusions or recommendations from what they had read. This focused their attention on the current events materials as sources of information. Also, he collected five or six magazines from each issue over the year and bound them. Similarly, children could also use articles from past years as sources of information.

This leads to another important skill which is a prerequiste to one in the junior high school—the use of the *Reader's Guide.* Since intermediate children have difficulty digesting adult magazines, it is senseless to teach them to use this reference. You can help them, however, by collecting back issues of children's magazines and binding these along with the yearly index of published issues printed by most children's newspaper and magazine publishers. Often, these indexes are cross-referenced like the *Reader's Guide.* Here, the child begins to use a retrieval system that will provide him with a useful skill in later life.

Bias is another problem faced by all information consumers. We should constantly ask these key questions: "What are the author's or speaker's assumptions?" "Are his conclusions valid?" But, alas, we don't always do so.

In our attempts to develop citizens who will evaluate assumptions, one of the skills on which we must focus is identifying bias. To fulfill this purpose, an innovative junior high teacher furnished the ideas for the following unit which appears to have merit for the sixth grade. Notice that this lesson plan makes use of both magazines and newspapers. You will note, however, that these materials are of a type to provide high motivation.

Skill: The Identification of Bias in Magazines

Purpose: To enable children to understand and identify bias found in magazine articles.

Entry: The student will be able to differentiate between a factual account and a statement of opinion.

Pretest: The teacher will reproduce an obviously biased report of an incident and ask the children to record their reactions to the article.

Behavioral Objective A: The student will be able to define (1.0) orally what is meant by biased reporting.

LESSON 1:

Teacher actions: The teacher will assign two class members who like opposing professional football teams to describe the last quarter of a current game. The following Monday, the students will be asked to describe their accounts. The teacher will video tape this portion of the game without the students' knowledge and play it back to the class after the students have given their accounts.

Media: Accounts of the football game. Video tapes of the game.

Student actions: Selected students will observe and write accounts of the assigned game. The remaining students will listen to the above accounts and describe likenesses and differences of the accounts. They will identify biases in these accounts.

LESSON 2:

Teacher actions: The teacher will provide students with a copy of an objective news story and an editorial on the same event. He will conduct a class discussion finding likenesses and differences in the accounts and gather inferences which explain them.

Media: A news account and an editorial on the same event.

Student actions: The student will list the likenesses and differences they observe and make inferences to explain them.

Evaluation: Students will generalize that bias is interpretive reporting, rather than an objective view of an incident.

Behavioral Objective B: The student will be able to detect bias through an analysis (4.0) of oral presentations.

Teacher actions: The teacher will record an interesting session of "Meet the Press" on video tape.

Media: Video tape recording of stated program.

Student actions: Students will watch tape and attempt to identify bias in the presentation and possible reasons for the speaker's bias.

Evaluation: Observations of students' abilities to identify bias.

Behavioral Objective C: The student will be able to identify bias in magazine articles and discuss the possible reasons for this bias.

Teacher actions: The teacher will assist in the selection of articles in such magazines as *Flying, Hotrod, American Girl, Seventeen,* or *Boy's Life.*

Media: Magazines which the children enjoy. Xerox one copy and develop Thermo-fax masters for copies of selected articles children agree upon.

Student actions: Select and identify bias in articles discussed in class. Identify the assumptions the authors are making.

Evaluation: The teacher will supply an editorial which will appeal to students. The students will identify the position of the writer and state his assumptions in a one page paper.[2]

Another skill which we must help our youthful associates acquire is that of debunking information, in other words, identifying mass persuasion techniques that impinge upon us from every direction for both "good" and "bad" purposes. A popular article by Crowder, a professor of social studies education, underlines several techniques familiar to many adults around election time or during the snack times on T.V. (normally referred to as commercials): name calling, glittering generality, transfer, testimonial, card stacking, plain folks, and bandwagon procedures. Crowder points out that we must teach children to recognize when these devices are being used, to understand the intention of the communication, and to identify the power of emotional appeals. A sixth grade teacher developed the material in Table 12–3 to aid in developing activities which would enable children to become critical readers. This teacher reminds us that skill development requires step by step instruction over a period of time.

Materials in the library There are more central libraries in elementary schools as a result of funds which were made available through the federal government in the late fifties. Unfortunately, it is common practice to schedule classes in the library once or twice a week. This makes libraries less usable than they should be. Some schools have defied tradition and follow the philosophy that this facility should be open to every child throughout the day. However, availability does not automatically assure us that children know how to use the library. Library skills must be taught.

The systematic teaching of library skills begins in the early primary grades. One teacher developed the individualized sequence on page 335 for her third grade class.[3] You will note that this sequence is similar to the Identifying Topic Sentence sequence the authors presented in Chapter VI.

Her abbreviated sequence lists each behavioral objective last. These objectives are numbered so that you can read the two sequences listed.

---

[2] The ideation for the above unit was furnished by Mr. Phil Lago of Midland, Texas.

[3] The unit (Figure 12-1) is abstracted from materials prepared by Mrs. Mattie Lou Ellis of Plainview, Texas.

Table 12–3

Directing Critical Reading[4]

Purpose	Activity
Distinguishing Fact from Opinion	Select from textbooks short passages which contain statements that are basically opinion. Have students read statements and select words or phrases which led them to conclude that they were statements of opinion
	Have students rewrite selected sentences from their textbooks, leaving out or rewording the parts which are basically opinion.
	Have students bring interesting editorials from the local newspaper and examine the style that differentiates them from news stories on the same subjects.
	Have students read and compare a biography of a famous person with a fictionalized story about that person.
Recognition of Assumptions	From material in other content area textbooks, select statements for the students to examine for assumptions and vague expressions.
	Help students identify statements containing assumptions in class newspapers and magazines.
	Devise statements containing assumptions and ask students to react to them on paper before they are discussed and the correct answers are revealed.
Recogizing Propaganda Techniques	Discuss the various categories of propaganda ("common folks," "band-wagon," "repetition," "testimonials," "snob appeal," etc.) to help students become more conscious of the techniques of mass persuasion

[4] This table was developed by Mrs. Hazel King of Lubbock, Texas.

Purpose	Activity
	Have student bring to class and examine political brochures and advertisements to illustrate the use of propaganda techniques and irrelevant material by office seekers.
Judging Competence of the Writer	Assist students in the use of biographical dictionaries, card catalogues, and other sources to determine the background and knowledge of a writer on a given topic.
	Emphasize the importance of finding out two things about a writer: (1) if there is any reason to believe that he does or does not have accurate information, and (2) whether the writer is known for complete reports which give a clear picture.

The specifics of a prepared unit are omitted so that this sequence could be included in any unit plan the teacher designed. The teacher could employ this same series of lessons as many times as the children needed it. Mastery was not the goal of this sequence, although some children could attain mastery after two or three specific units which contained this sequence. In other words, the following chart is a skeletal series of lessons. A teacher using this chart would place the titles, authors, and subjects he would need in order to implement this plan into a teaching unit. Notice also that this teacher uses the deductive method of development. She first makes the generalization and then presents examples. The experiences are contrived experiences developed for the children. This teacher physically arranged the children in alphabetical order in an attempt to make the experience less abstract.

The Dewey Decimal or the Library of Congress system used to categorize and locate books in the library should not be memorized. This is a senseless waste of time. These systems are extremely useful, but even college students don't know the numbers unless they have worked in libraries where the need for knowledge of the complete system was required for them to shelve books. Charts showing the numbering system used and the location of various collections should be made by the librarian or a sympathetic teacher and displayed in convenient places in the library.

Many of us recognize only factual books as sources of information about man and his enviroment. This is an unfortunate mistake. We can learn

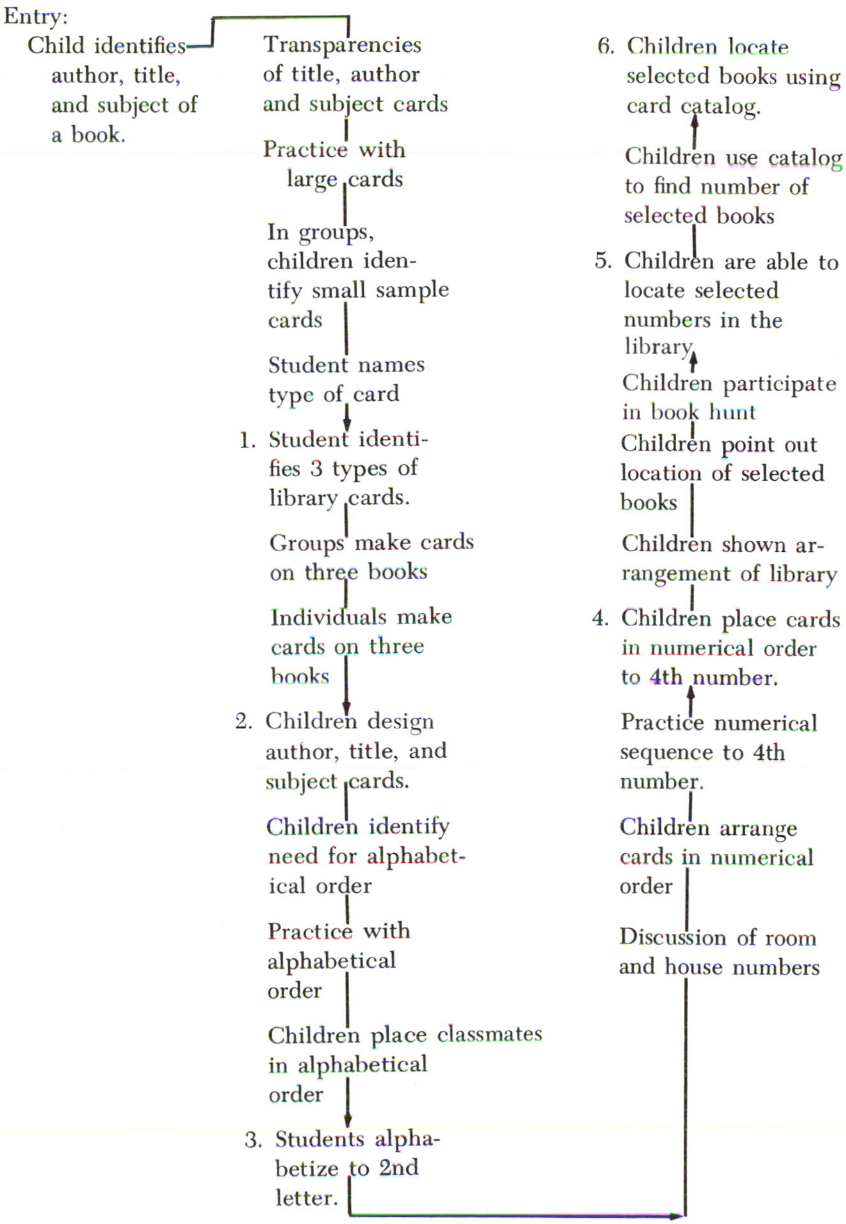
Entry:
Child identifies author, title, and subject of a book.
Transparencies of title, author and subject cards
Practice with large cards
In groups, children identify small sample cards
Student names type of card
1. Student identifies 3 types of library cards.
Groups make cards on three books
Individuals make cards on three books
2. Children design author, title, and subject cards.
Children identify need for alphabetical order
Practice with alphabetical order
Children place classmates in alphabetical order
3. Students alphabetize to 2nd letter.
Discussion of room and house numbers
Children arrange cards in numerical order
Practice numerical sequence to 4th number.
4. Children place cards in numerical order to 4th number.
Children shown arrangement of library
Children point out location of selected books
Children participate in book hunt
5. Children are able to locate selected numbers in the library.
Children use catalog to find number of selected books
6. Children locate selected books using card catalog.

Figure 12–1.

much about people from the many kinds of literature. One of the most life-like places to learn about history and the lives of people who lived in our past is historical fiction. Books such as those listed below are useful in understanding our history.

Alice Dalgliesh, *The Thanksgiving Story.*

Laura Ingalls Wilder, *Little House in the Big Woods.*

Marguerite de Angeli, *The Door in the Wall.*

Elizabeth Coatsworth, *The Sod House.*

Katherine B. Shippen, *Leif Erikson.*

Carol Ryrie Brink, *Caddie Woodlawn.*

Walter Edmonds, *The Matchlock Gun.*

Harold Keith, *Rifles for Wattie.*

These books are standards which bring American history to life and teach many of the concepts and generalizations present in the new social studies.

Realistic fiction also allows children to understand their own lives or the lives of other people. Many of Ann Nolan Clark's books about people in North and South America accomplish the task of illustrating cultural differences very well without making the people "seem odd." Also this category of children's books can be used to study the family and family differences, the peer group, racial differences and conflict, regional differences, the impact of governments, and poverty.

The following book are useful for such purposes:

Eleanor Estes, *Rufus.*

Gladys Yessayan Cretan, *All Except Sammy.*

Annabel and Edgar Johnson, *The Grizzly.*

Mary Urmstron, *The New Boy.*

Helen Griffiths, *The Greyhound.*

Mary Hays Weik, *The Jazz Man.*

Kate Seredy, *A Tree for Peter.*

Folk stories and myths are useful in explaining the beliefs of ancient and primitive peoples. One caution should be observed, however. Children must realize that people who inhabit the regions from which these stories came don't necessarily retain the same beliefs today. This probably means that these sources of understandings should be reserved for study at the intermediate level. Children in primary grades can enjoy the stories, but again, the real and fantasy worlds seem to merge at the lower grade levels. *Man: A Course of Study,* developed under the direction of Jerome Bruner, is one of the new social studies curricula that uses myths of a primitive people to show their system of beliefs. Children gain great understanding about their own beliefs through this study.

Fantasy can have its place in social studies, too. *Ben and Me* and *Mr. Revere and I*, by Robert Lawson, are excellent examples of "dessert" and can aid in creating motivation. Of course, the fairy tale, *Animal Farm*, contains many political science concepts. This section can be summarized by stating that literature is about life; therefore, it contains many of the concepts and generalizations which we help children acquire.

Organizing Information.

After children have located the information they need to solve a problem or answer a question, some systematic method of evaluating this data must be applied. Most individuals find that the best way to deal with information is to place it where it can be seen. In actual practice, data is evaluated as it is arranged into some useful form. Since we can't handle both acts at the same time,however, it this presentation we will separate the two.

Evaluating data To solve problems and make decisions, we must collect and use reliable data. Scientists or investigators in any field develop a feel for evidence that our beginning detectives will not possess. This intuition can be developed through some device that will provide an artificial feel. The first of these artificial devices is to help the child determine whether the data he has collected is the best obtainable within the limits in which he must operate. The second device is to request him to support the validity of the data he has gathered. It is conceivable that some investigations can come up with surprising results. Usually, our data may point to conclusions early in the problem-solving episode that make us realize that we must accumulate careful documentation. An example may clarify what we mean.

Two fifth grade groups in one school were burdened continually with relieving a chainlink fence of its decoration of paper after windstorms which were quite common in this Midwestern community. Needless to say, the class soon tired of this chore and decided to find the cause for the accumulation of litter. They hypothesized that since most of the litter was notebook paper, candy wrappers, and the like, it must be the result of carelessness on someone's part, rather than the effect of faulty garbage removal. The class set out to find the culprits.

Observers were selected and given the task of watching children walk to and from school, to determine who was throwing the trash on the park-like field behind the school, the area from which the wind blew. It took very few sessions of data collection before it was obvious that a trend was developing. The data pointed in the direction of junior high students who passed the site on their way to the new junior high school. It is obvious that such a finding required careful documentation. This finding countered the popular belief that careless children from the school the fifth graders attended were guilty of the littering.

A third device is to help the child determine relevance of the data. It must clearly relate to the problem being solved. It is obvious that the data being collected above is relevant. The field, wind direction, and the adorned fence clearly indicated what relevant data was necessary. Of course, the competence of the data-gatherers was important, too. In the above situation, the direction of movement of the individuals was carefully recorded. Observers were trained and randomly assigned. Their observations were validated by the observations of a group of fourth graders who were not "in" on the purpose of the project.

A fourth device is to help the child determine whether the evidence drawn is fact or opinion. Of course, opinions ran wild in the above episode. The policing task had originated from a community opinion about the elementary children. The fifth grade class set out to change the opinion with carefully gathered facts.

Fifth, children must be helped to understand that the data gathered must be primary source material. That is, the material gathered as evidence must be first hand data, not hearsay. The teacher who was the "sob sister" for the group could not accept the "we didn't do it" offered her by the class. A survey of the elementary school involved would not have sufficed. The class needed first hand data. That is what they obtained.

The final device is aiding the child to draw logical conclusions. Again, in the above case, the data allowed the students to establish their case. Since students seen walking to and from the junior high had been observed littering during certain hours of the day, the fifth grade class could establish that the seventh graders were the litter bugs. The data further indicated that there was a five to one ratio between subjects identified as junior high and those identified as elementary school children.

The cross checking of data is an important activity for children, especilly if we are to teach critical thinking. Reliability and validity are measures of cross checking which we have discussed previously. Many times, however, children find conflicting data in sources they use. They don't have sufficient experiences to judge the validity of a source. Usually, we can only alert them to possible errors, such as dates of publications, and attempt to aid them in placing some evaluative judgement on the data sources. Perhaps checking with a third source is the best solution, but at times, this presents a third and different answer.

Arranging data in useful ways Although we have discussed the use of data organizing devices previously, we must remind you that data must be organized. Children can not see the relationships among isolated facts. Adults can't either. Data must be manipulated before relationships begin to appear. If, as a teacher, you recognize that a possible sequence seems to be emerging, question the children until they see this relationship. Clearly, the best organizing device to show sequence would be the diagram, flowchart, or outline. A table or information accumulation chart is useful for showing likenesses and differences. Graphs are invaluable in underlining trends and quantitative data which we would list under other relationships. Note that these tools aid in the organization, as well as the reporting of data.

Drawing Conclusions.

The results of our investigations are always tentative. This is true because we look at a given situation, make some assumptions which we formulate into questions, gather information to answer these questions, and draw conclusions from this data. Our answers must be tentative because of our assumptions, methods of gathering information, and processes of analysis. We can check resulting generalizations by testing them against similar situations as we did in Chapter IV. However, in cases, the same situation can not be tested. For example, if we were to make generalizations about change, it would be useless to test this generalization in the same setting. Our generalization would be more valuable if we could test it in many types of settings. You will find examples of these means of testing generalizations in Chapters III and V.

Summary

We began this chapter by stating that one of the major purposes of the social studies was to teach the child to think. We have delineated four basic information processing skills which will aid the child in achieving the ability to think. These skills involve the locating of information, the organization of this information, drawing conclusions, and communicating this information. The latter of the skill areas was examined in a previous chapter. They dynamics of group communication will be discussed in Chapter XIV.

Perhaps the most important idea we have discussed concerning skills in general is that they must be taught in a realistic setting, rather than in isolation. Such skills can not be left to incidental teaching. If children are to acquire the skills we have listed, a systematic program must be established and used in your classroom.

References

Crowder, William W. "Helping Elementary School Children Understand Mass Persuasion Techniques." *Social Education* 31 (February 1967): 119-21

Garrett, Henry E. *Elementary Statistics.* New York: Longmans, Green and Company, 1956.

Johns, Eunice, and Fraser, Dorothy McClure. *Skill Development in Social Studies. Thirty-third Yearbook of the National Council for the Social Studies.* Washington, D.C.: The National Council for the Social Studies, NEA, 1963.

Lippitt, Ronald, Fox, Robert, and Schaible, Lucille. *The Teacher's Role in Social Science Investigation.* Chicago: Science Research Associates, Inc., 1969.

Schiller, Philomene, S.L. "The Effects of the Functional Use of Certain Skills in Seventh-Grade Social Studies." *Journal of Educational Research* 57 (December 1963): 201-03.

Torrence, E. Paul, and Meyers, R.E. "Teaching Gifted Pupils Research Concepts and Skills." *The Gifted Child Quarterly* 6 (Spring 1962): 1-6.

XIII

Social Studies for the Exceptional Student

Chapter Outline

Social Studies for the Exceptional Student

Sally is a lovely child. Her parents dress her well and she comes to school looking like a precious, little, china doll. The teacher is delighted to have Sally in her first grade. Sally sits quietly and smiles sweetly when the teacher talks to the class. Lately, however, the teacher is becoming concerned about her school performance. She appears unable to follow directions, even the most simple ones. Her manual coordination is poor. Sally is easily frustrated when she cannot complete a task and cries frequently. Is Sally an exceptional child?

Gilberto comes from a home in which almost no English is spoken. His parents are American citizens who grew up in the Rio Grande Valley of Texas and dropped out of school at an early age to help their parents as agricultural workers. Gilberto has been retained once in first grade. Now, in the fourth grade, Gilberto reads first grade material very poorly. Is Gilberto an exceptional student?

Margie is in the third grade. She is small for her age and doen't care for silly games like "jacks" or "hide-and-go-seek." Indeed, Margie would rather spend her recess talking with the teacher or reading library books. She is an avid reader and has no problem reading her sister's fifth grade textbooks. What about Margie? Is she an exceptional child?

Objective

The reader will be able to:

Demonstrate (3.0) how the Model of Instructional Design (MID) could be employed to modify the program for the exceptional child.

Suggest (1.0) general ways in which students differ from each other.

Introduction

With the limited knowledge of each student presented above, it is very difficult to determine if Sally, Gilberto, and Margie are exceptional children. Undoubtedly, you recognized that these children were different from what you would expect of normal children at each of the grade levels cited. Yet, they were different in divergent ways. Shall we label all three children exceptional? Labels are only useful, however, if they are employed to aid the labeled. How can we help exceptional children accomplish what there is to be learned in social studies? What changes do we need to make in our social studies program to accommodate exceptional students? These are some of the questions which we shall endeavor to resolve in this chapter.

Who is the exceptional student?

Before we begin a discussion of the exceptional student, you will need to know what we intend when we utilize this label. For the purposes of this chapter we shall define the "exceptional" student as any student whose performance in school varies sufficiently from the average for that level to warrant a major modification in our program for that child. Thus, we shall eliminate at the outset the bulk of children whose school performance would fall within the rang of normality. We individualize instruction for these students by minor modifications in the school program, such as additional practice on basic skills, grouping for common interests and needs, extra tutoring, and the like.

We also intend to eliminate from our discussion reference to the child who is so exceptional that he is unable to attend public schools. This would include children with severe learning disabilities or physical handicaps, such as deafness, blindness, paralysis, and the like. These children require the services of special schools staffed by teachers trained specifically to work with children having these handicaps. Neither are we talking about the child with severe social—emotional problems. His very presence in a regular school classroom could jeopardize the safety of the teacher and other students because of his extreme antisocial behavior. We are not discussing the hyperkinetic child who cannot tolerate the routine of the classroom—the distruber whose presence would prevent any learning from taking place. Nor are we referring to the child with an emotional problem who cannot cope with living. All of these children need the attention of specialists. They do not belong in a public school classroom.

When we discuss the exceptional student, we are talking about the child who appears normal in many ways but simply doesn't "fit into" the existing program. Obviously, there are many kinds and degrees of exceptional children. In the limited space of this chapter, it would be impossible to deal with all of them.

Therefore, we shall limit our offering here to three kinds of exceptionality: the child who is exceptional because he simply takes longer to learn things than his classmates; the child who is exceptional because his environment or subculture has not prepared him for success in our middle class schools; the child who is exceptional because he learns very quickly and outshines his classmates.

Fitting the program to the student.

In the past, students were expected to "fit into" the curriculum. Diagnostic-prescriptive teaching would instead fit the curriculum to the child. Utilizing a stategy such as the Model of Instructional Design (MID), the teacher individualizes instruction for the class taking into account the widely varying needs and abilities of his students. We hear much about meeting the needs of students. This is a well-worn cliche, often ignored in practice, commonly used in educational literature and in conversations among educators. However, it is our philosophy that merely meeting the needs of students is insufficient in itself. Our task, after all, is one of increasing the range of individual student differences so that when we move children on to the next grade or level, we pass on a group of students who vary more than they did when we received them. As children proceed through the grades, then, the range of differences among them will become increasingly greater. The teacher who is either unable or unwilling to individualize instruction, to fit the program to the student, does not belong in our public schools. Teaching to the average is no longer considered good pedagogical practice.

Children differ in many respects. Basically, they differ in factors related to heredity, environment, and the interaction of the two. Children vary in innate capacity for learning, learning rate, growth patterns, emotional traits, personality characteristics, motor development, social maturity, family background—including socio-economic status, linguistic abilities, experiences, interests—as well as a myriad of other characteristics.

The exceptional child we have described is not much different from other children in the class. You will find that some of our suggestions for working with exceptional children will be suitable for other members of the class as well. However, for the child who is a slow learner, culturally different, or gifted, the modifications that we make in the program are particularly crucial if the child is to have successful experiences in school. Fitting the program to exceptional children, then, merely carries the individualization of instruction which we provide for all students a step or two further.

Objective

The reader will be able to:

Describe (1.0) the characteristics of the slow learner.

Suggest (1.0) some possible causes for slow learning.

Identify (1.0)the special needs of the slow learner.

Suggest (1.0) modifications in the social studies program for the slow learner.

Plan (3.0) suitable experiences in social studies for the slow learner when given a topic or theme.

Offer (3.0) ways in which paraprofessionals and parent volunteers might be utilized when given a topic or theme.

Working with the Slow Learner

Sally, whom we briefly mentioned at the outset of this chapter, is an exceptional child. There is label for Sally. She is what we call a slow learner. Sally will have a most difficult time in school unless she has teachers throughout her school experience who recognize that she has special problems and who are willing to work with her on her level and at her pace.

Most of us can only speculate about the frustration that a child must endure when he is required to sit in school day after day and is asked to do things that are beyond his capabilities. However, perhaps you have had an experience similar to the following: Have your ever enrolled in a college course thinking that the course title sounded most interesting but neglecting to notice the prerequisites in the catalog? Eagerly you bound into the classroom on the first day and sit in the front row so that you may catch every pearl of wisdom as it drips from the professor's lips. The lecture begins. Immediately, you are transfixed with horror. Why, you don't understand what he's saying! Perhaps you squirm during the entire period, but being naturally polite you appear to take notes and provide the professor some positive reinforcement in the way of a smile from time to time. However, the minute the bell rings, you spring out of the room and to the Dean's office to pick up a slip of paper which will entitle you to drop the course and rid you of your misery and frustration. You know that the experiences in the course are failure oriented for you from the outset and you are wise to get out while you can.

Now let's return to the child in the elementary classroom. If he is a slow learner and simply can't keep up with the rest of the group, he has no recourse but to remain in the classroom. He can't go to the principal's office and drop third grade or first grade or any grade! If Sally's teachers are prudent in their planning of learning experiences for her, there will be no problem. Sally can find success and happiness in school just as her faster counterparts.

Identifying the slow learner.

The slow learner is a child whose measured intelligence falls in the subnormal range (70–90). A score of 70 on an IQ test is frequently considered the cut-off point for placing children in special education classes. However, it would be most risky to judge a child purely on the basis of one intelligence test. Therefore, the diagnosis should be based on more than one type of test and substantiated by teacher judgement.

The child who is a slow learner has a more difficult time learning language. Therefore, his communication skills are generally weak. For this reason, he is usually far behind the group in reading skills. Listening skills are underdeveloped and attention span is short. Math skills are usually weak, too. Because communication and math skills are basic to success in school, the slow learner is characterized by low achievement. This low achievement and repeated failures will be damaging to the child's self concept. The slow child appears to be less flexible in his thinking—less imaginative, less resourceful, less creative. More than likely, he is a follower, rather than a leader. Often, he is easily influenced by his peers.

Obviously, with as broad a description as this for the slow learner, many children will fall into this category. Yet, experienced teachers frequently admit that they know little about working with the slow learning child.

What causes slow learning?

Frankly, we do not know. Obviously, there may be certain genetic limitations which affect learning rate. Brain damage is another possible cause. The diet of the very young child may be a factor. If it is deficient in protein and the child is severely malnourished over a period of time, it is likely that development will be retarded. There are environmental factors, for example, lack of stimulating experiences in early childhood. Emotions are a consideration. Various factors may combine to cause the child to learn more slowly. The picture is complex, indeed.

Just as the medical doctor cannot spend the bulk of his time trying to determine *why* his patient has appendicitis, you cannot dwell at length on why the child is a slow learner. The important thing is to deal with the situation now before it gets worse! Of course, it is important to know students well, but it is urgent that we identify the slow learner early so that we can adjust our program to fit his special needs before he has been subjected to a myriad of failures.

Special needs of the slow learner.

The child who is a slow learner needs reading materials that are on his level. Further, he will need additional help with interpreting what he reads. Often, he is unable to use context clues to aid reading comprehension and finds it even more difficult to "read between the lines."

The slow learner must be helped to increase his attention span. You can accomplish this by employing a variety of motivating devices and by gradually increasing the demands placed on the child's listening. As with reading comprehension, the slow learner has problems with comprehending what he listens to. He must be taught how to use context clues, as well as how to "read" the speaker's intonation patterns, gestures, and facial expressions. The slow learner, then, needs much help in developing his listening capabilities. He needs to be taught *how* to listen, as well as *what* to listen to.

Because the slow learner has communication problems, his study skills are generally poor. He finds report writing extremely difficult. He will need more practice in using reference materials, writing topic sentences, paragraphs, and the like, than other children. Creative writing will be an unsuccessful experience unless he is helped with spelling, phrasing, selection of vocabulary, and sequencing of events.

Since the slow learner may quickly build a back-log of failure experiences in school, it is imperative that the teacher break down learning experiences into segments which can be attained realistically. For this reason, programmed learning generally works well for the slow learner. Goals are short term, and the learner has immediate feedback from his responses. When programmed materials are available and suitable for the needs of the child and purposes of instruction, they can be utilized successfully to help these children acquire the needed knowledge or skills at their own pace without slowing down the rest of the class.

The slow learner needs more opportunities for development of positive concepts of self than the average child. Educators will continue to debate the issue of intrinsic or extrinsic rewards. It is not for us to resolve this controversy here. Indeed, there may be no solution. Success in a task is intrinsically rewarding or reinforcing. However, as the slow learner has not had as great a share of success in school as other children, he may need extrinsic rewards until the cycle of failure has been broken. Extrinsic rewards range from lollipops to remarks from the teacher like "that's fine," or perhaps just an approving nod or smile. The teacher, then, will need to increase the extrinsic rewards for the slow learning child to the point that negative self concepts are replaced by more positive ones, and the child develops a willingness to try new things without fear of failure. These are some of the special needs of the slow learner which should influence our choice of materials and teaching methods for social studies, as well as the other content areas.

Strategies for teaching social studies.

The new multi-media approaches to teaching social studies, as well as other subjects, are a boon for the slow learning child. Included in many of these programs are pictures, slides, transparencies, films, records, tapes, as well as a variety of reading materials which students can use for reference. By employing various mediating devices, you can provide the slow learner with the additional reinforcement he needs without boring him.

Along with the multimedia approach, utilizing the unit method of organizing instruction will permit greater individualization. This is essential if the slow learner is to participate in the on-going activities of the class and become a contributing member of the group. Because unit instruction allows for a variety of activities, you can select for the slow learner those activities most suitable for his needs, taking into his account his limitations. Since he will be able to make his contribution to the class, there is less likelihood that he will feel left out and develop negative self concepts.

Since the slow learner is weak in reading skills, you can capitalize on social studies content to develop these skills. Reading is not taught in a vacuum. Children need to read *about* something, talk *about* something. Thus, content in social studies provides a most useful vehicle for helping the slow learner acquire the needed communication skills prerequisite for success in school, as well as full participation in society later.

There are several problems, however, which you take into account when utilizing materials in social studies to develop reading skills. First of all, you must recognize that social studies materials employ a specialized vocabulary. For example, the following terms might be found in a unit involving the use of a globe:

longitude	temperate	time zone	axis
latitude	tropical	equator	hemisphere
meridian	frigid	polar	continent

It is important that the teacher employ many different methods to help slow learners develop the concepts and vocabulary which are prerequisite for comprehending text materials.

Frequently, social studies material is accompanied by pictures, graphs, tables, and illustrations of different kinds which help convey meaning to the reader. The slow learner must be taught how to "read" pictures and interpret graphs, tables, and other matter which will greatly aid in understanding the topic at hand. As with all learning, you have to meet the student on his level. Thus, you may need to devise simple practice materials within the range of the child's abilities before he will be ready to tackle the more complex illustrative materials found in social studies matter. Avoid making assumptions about the child's ability to use graphic materials as aids in understanding of content.

For the slow learner who is severely retarded in reading, you may find it necessary to write suitable social studies materials. The last decade has witnessed an explosion in the number of books written for children. Particularly important has been the increase in the amount of high interest, low vocabulary books on the market. Easy-to-read books on many topics are freely available. Nevertheless, at times you may find it difficult to find suitable reading materials on particular topics in social studies which will meet the needs of the child, as well as those of the program.

Writing materials for students is not a difficult task. You can begin by preparing an outline of the content you wish to convey to the student. Utilizing the outline, continue by filling in the important details which are essential for comprehension of the topic. Now the task becomes one of translating this outline into vocabulary and sentence patterns which are on the child's level. Frequently, subheadings in the outline can be expanded into topic sentences for the paragraphs that you write. If new vocabulary must be employed, you may want to prepare a short glossary of terms.

The older "fact-stuffing" approach to the teaching of social studies works less well for the slow learner than for the average or gifted child. This approach relied heavily upon expository teaching in which the teacher spends much of his time lecturing to students. Because the slow learner is characterized by a short attention span and poorly developed listening skills, it is understandable that he was at a disadvantage when the greatest part of the instructional period was spent in listening to the teacher or reading material he didn't understand. The type of testing which went along with this instruction and the heavy reliance on learning isolated facts further handicapped the slow learning child.

First of all, he has difficulty retaining what he has learned in a short span of time. He needs many experiences in order to "fix" the learning. Next, unless the slow learner is helped to fit the learning into his existing cognitive structure, it isn't likely that the learning will make sense to him. This, too, will block retention. Whereas the gifted child can make giant cognitive leaps and the average child, perhaps, needs a minimum amount of help in perceiving relationships, the slow learner needs much guidance in this very crucial area. Thirdly, the slow learner has difficulty in following written instructions. Also, if the test is the same one provided for the rest of the class, it is unlikely that he will have sufficient reading skills to complete it successfully. Lastly, the slow learner does poorly under pressure. He is at a distinct disadvantage in a timed test situation. He may become frustrated and give up completely, or he may want to please you and go through the motions of completing the test with little regard for his responses. Thus, a heavy reliance on memory work and the concomitant type of testing which requires giving back the facts is definitely not suitable for the slow learning child.

In contrast to the approach described above, there are strategies which entail a high degree of active student involvement. The slow learner needs this kind of involvement if learning is to be meaningful and, hence, retained. You need to plan a variety of firsthand perceptual experiences so that the slow learning child will have opportunities to utilize as many sensory avenues as possible. Field trips can be valuable experiences for the slow learner, particularly if he is encouraged to ask questions during the experience and to verbalize about it afterward. Demonstrations in which he can play a role are profitable, too. The many kinds of what may be called enrichment activities are particularly valuable experiences for this child. There are art and music activities, dance and other movement experiences, as well as the many types of dramatic techniques which can be employed. Thus you can provide the slow learner with the additional experiences he needs, as well as opportunities to practice basic skills.

Because the slow learner needs to be reached through more than one sensory channel, it is important to use pictures and other illustrative materials, especially when new concepts and vocabulary are involved. At times, it may be necessary to "boil down" facts to the essentials and present them to the child in a simple table, if it is necessary to know the facts in order to make inferences and applications. The slow learner would have a difficult time gathering and retaining such data on his own. Charts and tables may help him synthesize data so that he can deal with it in an organized manner.

Working models are important, too. For example, the child may not be able to conceptualize a spinning wheel by reading about one in a book. Viewing pictures of spinning wheels may not help. Even a film showing the spinning wheel in actual use may "lose" the slow learner who finds abstract thinking more difficult than the average child. By providing a working model of a spinning wheel and allowing him to use it to spin some thread, we may help him grasp concepts which otherwise would have been too difficult. We need to provide concrete and semiconcrete experiences for the slow learner which will help him build a stock of concepts and vocabulary.

Concepts of time and chronology are quite abstract and, thus, difficult for the slow learner to perceive. A sense of chronology (sequence of events) is developed in children by helping them understand the order of events in their own lives. The daily routine of classroom activities can also be employed. Arranging pictures in the order of their occurrence is another useful activity. Young children, particularly, need many such experiences before they are ready to treat the sequencing of events which occur over a long span of time and which have little relationship to their daily lives. In dealing with events in history, it is crucial to work with time rolls, time lines, and other devices which are semiconcrete in nature. These are valuable experiences for all children but mandatory for the slow learner. A time line is constructed by marking key dates and events on a long sheet of paper employing a set measurement, such as an inch to serve as a one, five, or ten year span of time. The time line is usually constructed by students and can be displayed in the room as long as it is appropriate to the on-going activities of the classroom. This helps the student see, at a glance, the relationship of events in time.

Economically disadvantaged children appear to have more difficulty with time concepts than other children. Thus, time lines and time rolls are discussed in greater detail in the section of this chapter concerning the culturally different learner.

We have discussed previously the nature and use of deductive and inductive teaching strategies. Because of the additional reinforcement that the slow learner requires, it may be profitable to vary your strategy in succeeding lessons. For example, if you introduce material to the slow learner utilizing an inductive strategy, it may be profitable to employ a deductive strategy the next time you work with the same concepts. Conversely, if you begin with a deductive strategy, you may follow up with an inductive one. Approaching the learning task from a different vantage point is helpful to the child who is attempting to assimilate new material and strengthen understandings. It is wise to include a lot of class discussion with any strategy that you select. Your slow learner may need much encouragement to ask questions, as he may have been embarrassed previously by asking questions which other students felt were "dumb." Also, the slow learner may need to be taught how to ask appropriate questions. His discussion skills may be weak. This will be an area in which you will need to work with the slow learning student. Provide opportunities for small group discussion before involving him in a class discussion. You may wish to supply cues to the slow learner when you are employing a questioning strategy. Cueing simply means that you supply him with bits of information that the rest of the class doesn't have. This allows the child to respond correctly and, thus, facilitates the development of confidence in the discussion activity.

The employment of team teaching strategies, the use of paraprofessionals and parent-volunteers, as well as multi-age grouping of students are other means which can result in more effective instruction. They permit greater individualization. Team teaching capitalizes on the strengths of each teacher and permits him to develop his teaching potential to the fullest. The use of auxiliary personnel in the classroom is desirable because the teacher is freed from many routine classroom matters and can spend more time in actual instruction. Multi-age grouping is "team-learning" in the sense that older children who are having difficulties in a particular subject or skill area are teamed with younger children having similar problems. Research appears to indicate that both benefit from this scheme in which the older child tutors the younger in the problem area.

Our discussion of the slow learner is far from exhaustive. Hopefully, however, it will encourage you to seek new and better ways of working with students who fall below the average and simply do not learn at as fast a pace as other students.

Objectives

The reader will be able to:

Identify (1.0) the culturally different.

Describe (1.0) the characteristics of the culture of poverty.

Explain (2.0) why the poverty child is disadvantaged in the school setting.

Design (3.0) a course of action you will follow in preparing yourself to teach in a poverty area school.

Select (2.0) the outstanding characteristics of each of the subcultural groups discussed in this section.

Explain (2.0) the relationship of linguistic differences and school failure.

Offer (3.0) suggestions for avoiding stereotypes in social studies teaching.

Explain (2.0) why social studies is frequently disliked by the culturally different student.

Suggest (3.0) teacher actions which can indicate his acceptance to his students.

Explain (2.0) why the culturally different child frequently is characterized by a negative self concept.

Describe (1.0) ways of building cross-cultural understandings.

Identify (1.0) the guidelines for selection of content.

Indicate (1.0) ways of providing successful experiences in social studies for culturally different children.

Suggest (1.0) ways of teaching concepts of time and chronology to culturally different children.

Helping the Culturally Different

We referred to Gilberto at the beginning of this chapter. Gilberto, whose parents speak little English and are migrant farm laborers, is an exceptional student. There is label for Gilberto, too. He is what we call "culturally different." Actually, many labels have been employed to categorize children like Gilberto. You may hear the term "cultually disadvantaged." It is misleading to label someone culturally disadvantaged. Therefore, we shall use the term culturally different. Gilberto, and the thousands of other children in our country like him, are not disadvantaged, as far as participation in their subculture. They are only disadvantaged when they enter our schools which are geared to middle class Anglo America. They are culturally different, however, in the sense that their culture is unlike that of the mainstream of our society. Thus, we prefer to employ the term culturally different. When we us the term "disadvantaged" in this section, we are referring to the economic disadvantage which stems from lack of sufficient resources for full participation in society.

Who are the culturally different?

We shouldn't be misled to think that racial or ethnic differences alone place children in the category of the culturally different. These factors play an important role. Yet, the most outstanding characteristic and the most binding one as well is that of poverty. If you will turn back to Figure 11–2 on page 307, you will recall that we identified six groups within what we called the culture of poverty. Harrington and others have identified the characteristics of this culture. Each of the subcultural groups has its own life style and value patterns. Yet, all encompassing is the restriction that poverty places upon these people. We have economic stratification in our society. People who lack the education and/or training to obtain the better paying jobs or who are unable to work for one reason or another, compose the lower strata and are able to participate in our society only in a very limited way. Economic resources, then, determine to a large extent the family's ability to enjoy the "good life" which society has to offer.

Characteristics of the culture of poverty Harrington (21) has stated that the poor live in a culture of poverty which differs considerably from middle class America. The economically disadvantaged have many characteristics in common, because they comprise the unskilled labor force. They hold jobs which tend to be seasonal or part time in nature. Frequently, they are the last hired and the first fired.

An important facet of poverty is the psychological effects it has upon the individual. The person who looks all about him and views our land of plenty, unable to obtain his share of the wealth, cannot help but feel left out, rejected, and bitter. There is a helplessness and a fatalistic attitude which develops as one experiences misfortunes and feels unable to extricate himself. As a result, levels of aspiration are low and the poor are, in a sense, crippled psychologically.

Generally, their housing is substandard. Yet, many families may be paying rather high rents for poor housing which is crowded and lacks proper heating and sanitary facilities. Often, they are characterized by a high degree of mobility. Living in furnished flats, the poor may pick up the few belongings they have and move on when it's time to pay the rent once more.

Nutrition of the families tends to be substandard. Often the cheapest cuts of meat are purchased. Thus, protein intake is low and fat and carbohydrate intake very high. Fresh fruits and vegetables may be a rarity on the table except among the rural poor. Snacks, sweets, and soda pop may provide fillers to quell healthy appetites, but they offer little in the way of nutritional value or a balanced diet.

Since housing and diets are generally inadequate, those living in the culture of poverty may be ill much more frequently than their middle class counterparts. Yet, they visit doctors and dentists less often. These are "luxuries" that the family may feel it cannot afford.

The family structure of the poor differs from that of the dominant culture. Family ties are not as strong or as stable. There are many fatherless homes; there is less marriage; there are larger families and more unwanted children. Poverty families with close ethnic ties may have strong religious bonds, but, by and large, people in the culture of poverty do not attend church frequently.

There is more crime within the culture of poverty. This is partially due to the crowded living conditions, particularly in inner cities, and increased use of alcohol and narcotics. Prostitution, gambling, and practically any other vice you can think of may run rampant in ghetto areas.

Except for the black subculture, particularly in inner cities, the family is dominated by the male, whose authority in the home is supreme. Masculinity is highly prized. As boys reach puberty, there are strong social pressures to prove themselves as "men." Frequently, this is accomplished by the number of romantic conquests the boy can make or the amount of liquor he can consume.

Children living within this culture lead a much different kind of life than others living on "the other side of the tracks." They are exposed to the vicissitudes of life at a much earlier age. Violence is a part of daily living.

We hear a lot about the lack of experiential background of the culturally different. This is true in the sense that their background of experiences has not prepared them for success in school. They have not had the many toys, books, and other objects in the home which build this readiness. Often, the language of the home is what sociolinguists have termed a "restricted code." It is characterized by short, unelaborated messages and an absence of detailed explanations. There may be little verbal exchange between adults and children. The linguistic code is generally a nonstandard dialect of English which communicates well within the home and neighborhood but is very limited. Further, it varies considerably from "school language" which is a more elaborated code. Thus, these children may be called linguistically different. Children are not encouraged to ask questions at home. When they come to school they may appear more passive and silent than other pupils for these reasons.

The child from the culture of poverty may have a shorter attention span and may be distracted rather easily. Because of the noisy environment in which he lives, he may have learned to tune out noise very skillfully. He needs help in learning *how* to listen, as well as in *what* to listen to.

Yet, children who function in the culture of poverty may have had many experiences of a different nature than other children. These experiences include the assumption of a great deal of responsibility in the way of caring for younger brothers and sisters and earning money for the family. Actually, they are more wordly-wise. They are more concerned with the here and now and are not motivated easily by long term goals. Their subculture has taught them that you can't count on the future for the future may never come.

Cooperation and sharing in the home are more a part of their way of life. There is little private ownership of goods. Many children will have had no experiences with owning anything. It is little wonder, then, that when they enter school they may consider objects in the room as things that are to be shared. Taking someone else's pencil, for example, may be an extension of the sharing behavior learned in the home. Yet, to the teacher, perhaps this is stealing. The teacher's understanding of the child's home environment may prevent situations in which the child is punished for acts at school which are acceptable in the environment of the home and neighborhood.

The value systems of people in the culture of poverty generally differ from those of the mainstream of American society. They may have little regard for property, both public and private, since they have had little opportunity for ownership of goods. They view the police with suspicion and fear. Respect for law and order may be nonexistant. They tend to be pragmatic, viewing anything that "works" or benefits them in some way as "good." Refer to Chapter XI for a discussion of values.

Conflicts of values are a plaguing source of frustration and, at times, even hostility for middle class teachers, as well as their lower class students. The fact that beginning teachers frequently are assigned to lower class schools does nothing to alleviate these problems. Working with the poverty child is more challenging and rewarding for the teacher, than working with middle and upper class students. Yet, there is no substitute for teaching experience in order to make decisions in the classroom that will be fruitful and prudent.

If you are assigned to a "poverty" school, one of your first actions should be to become familiar with the neighborhoods in which the children dwell. Determine the kinds of homes in which they live. Talk with residents, if you can. Begin to immerse yourself in their subculture. Speak with teachers in your school in order to find out more about the life style of the families whose children attend your school. Read to gain more information. Find out if courses are available in a college or university near you which will help fill your own learning gaps about people from different subcultures. These may be courses in sociology, anthropology, or education. By broadening your own background of experiences you will find that you are less apt to be ethnocentric in your outlook and better prepared to accept the child whose home environment is vastly different from your own.

Who resides within the culture of poverty? Functioning within the culture of poverty, we find Black citizens in inner city ghettoes, as well as rural Blacks who depend upon agriculture for a livelihood. We have many persons who have emigrated from Puerto Rico in an attempt to find better economic opportunities and a chance to live the "good life." There are Cuban refugees who have left their homes because of political oppression. We have a large proportion of Mexican Americans, particularly in the Southwest. Many of these are involved in agricultural occupations. We find many of our American Indians who function on incomes which are below subsistence level. Also, to be considered are poor Whites residing in rural and urban sections of Appalachia. These six groups then, by and large, make up the residents of the culture of poverty which we have described. We shall take a brief look at five of these groups, in an effort to provide you with some insight into the different life styles of each.

1. Blacks in the culture of poverty. Black people are the largest minority group in our country, numbering about 22 million. (Burma, 13) Not all Black persons live in poverty. We have an increasing number of Blacks who are educated, who hold well paying jobs, and generally participate in the mainstream of American middle class society. On the other hand, we find that many exist on the fringes of society, lacking the economic resources that are prerequisite for full participation and still fight discrimination in jobs, housing, and the like.

Many Blacks continue to live in the South. However, we have a great proportion who have migrated to large urban centers of the North in search of better jobs and less discrimination.

The Black subculture differs from that of the Mexican American or Puerto Rican, although the culture of poverty tends to bind people by common needs. One of the striking characteristics of this subculture is the different linguistic code. Blacks, in the culture of poverty, generally speak a nonstandard dialect of English. Further, this dialect varies more from standard English than most other nonstandard dialects. Some linguists have traced the history of Black dialects and feel that they have a common base and rich history of their own. (Stewart, 351-79) The Black child who speaks nonstandard English may face a greater disadvantage in school than the child who comes from a Spanish-speaking home. Frequently, the teacher makes linguistic assumptions about the Black child that he wouldn't make about the child who is learning English as a second language. Also, because nonstandard English dialects are closer to standard English than is a foreign language, there may be greater interference in learning the new code.

Another characteristic of the Black subculture of poverty is that many families are fatherless (Crow, et al, 18) and thus female-dominated.

Black people are no longer content with second-rate educations, second-rate jobs, second-rate housing, and the like. They are vocal in their demands for equal opportunities. In the past, our schools have failed to meet the needs of Black children from the culture of poverty. The situation is improving, but we still have a long way to go.

2. Puerto Ricans in the culture of poverty. Although a precise figure is not available, it is estimated that there are approximately one million mainland Puerto Ricans (Burma, 13). Many of these people living in the culture of poverty can be found in New York City, as well as other large urban areas of the North. They are not faced with the problem of citizenship as are Mexicans who emigrate to this country, they are already citizens. If Puerto Rico gains its independence, as some groups wish, then this situation would change. Because Puerto Ricans speak Spanish, they face a linguistic barrier similar to the Mexican American. Further, they are separated from the mainstream of American society by differing customs and life styles.

Traditionally, the Puerto Rican family is male-dominated. However, this situation may be altered on the mainland because the women are more likely to find employment. Thus, conflicts may arise in the home over the roles that the mother and father play in the family. Many of the men fail to find employment because they are hampered by lack of facility in English and because they lack the education and skills required for employment in industry. Therefore, many are slum-dwellers, who reside in substandard housing with little hope for betterment of their lot. *West Side Story* attempted to portray something of their subculture, but, realistically, there is little to sing and dance about in their daily lives, when each day begins anew another struggle for their very survival.

As in the case of most Spanish-speaking peoples, they are devout Catholics with strong religious and familial ties. Perhaps because of these ties, many Puerto Ricans overcome what might seem like insurmountable barriers and "make it" in the Anglo world.

The children of Puerto Ricans who have recently come to the mainland often find our schools unfriendly places where a different language is spoken. Because of language, as well as experiential differences, their first school experiences may result in utter failure. Succeeding years in school, frequently continue to be failure-oriented for them with the result that they drop out of school as early as possible. Education, the very element which could help them break the poverty cycle, is rejected by them. You can easily understand why. No one likes to discover that he is lower class, unworthy, unacceptable, and that he will never enjoy full participation in American society. Yet, such feelings may be reinforced continually by schools which force children into preconceived molds for which they are neither ready nor able.

In defense of educators, we must state that the special problems of Puerto Rican children have been of great concern and have received much attention in areas where they attend schools in large numbers. We are learning more about working successfully with these children, but innovation in education proceeds at a snail's pace and there are no pat answers.

It is an undeniable fact of our pedagogical lives that we must change our schools to fit children, rather than change children to fit existing schools.

3. Mexican Americans in the culture of poverty. Mexican Americans comprise the second largest disadvantaged minority group in our country. There are approximately five million people of Spanish-Mexican descent residing within our borders (Burma, 13). They are found in large numbers in five states: Texas, New Mexico, Arizona, Colorado, and California. Not to be discounted, however, is the fact that the number of Mexican Americans found in large urban areas of the North, such as Chicago, appears to be on the increase. Demographic data on Mexican Americans is difficult to obtain because such counts are based upon Spanish surnames which are frequently misleading.

By and large, Mexican Americans, living in the culture of poverty, are employed in agriculture or related occupations. Many are migrant farm laborers who follow the crops. Thus, their employment tends to be seasonal. Many are paid below-minimum wages and are at the mercy of their employers.

One must be cautious not to over generalize about Mexican Americans because many have been able to break the poverty cycle and appear to function quite well in both worlds, the Anglo, as well as the Chicano. The characteristics we shall present in brief discussion here, then, are drawn from the more traditional Mexican Americans who live in the culture of poverty and are the least acculturated of all.

Perhaps another distinction is in order here. The term "Mexican American" or "Chicano" refers to persons who are citizens of this country but whose heritage is Mexican, not Spanish. Many Chicanos stress their Mexican heritage and are much opposed to being referred to as "Spanish." On the other hand, there are pockets of Spanish Americans who reside in northern New Mexico and southern Colorado who would be angered if they were referred to as "Mexican." These people are proud of their Spanish ancestry. Many can trace their family trees back to the Conquistadors who came to this country from Spain more than 400 years ago. Their heritage is Spanish, not Mexican.

Mexican Americans are deeply religious. Many are Catholics, although the number of Protestants among them seems to be increasing.

The traditional Mexican American family unit is a strong one. Next to allegiance to God, Chicanos prize the allegiance to family. The Mexican American does not view himself as an individual first. He is a member of the family, and family obligations are filled before personal wants and needs. This is in contrast to our highly individualistic society. "Family" to the Mexican American means more than parents and children. It is the extended family pattern which is characteristic of this subculture. The family will include grandparents, aunts, uncles, and cousins. School absences of Mexican American children may be the result of parents' placing family obligations ahead of school attendance for their children.

Also to be noted is the position of authority held by the father or oldest male in the household. What he says or does is never questioned. He is the disciplinarian in the family. The mother is respected and revered but plays a subservient role. Male and female roles are clearly defined. No self-respecting Mexican American male would be found doing the dishes or pushing a vacuum cleaner. *Machismo,* or the cult of manliness, is so strong in this subculture that it has some important implications for working with Mexican American children. Female teachers may find it difficult to discipline Mexican American boys. They simply are not used to this kind of role for a woman. Communication with parents may be difficult because the mother may be reluctant to leave her home. Teachers may need to plan home visits at a time when the father can be present. If you are a male teacher, it may be very unwise to visit in the home at any time when the father is not present. Mexican American males feel a strong sense of protection for their women.

Mexican Americans tend to be fatalistic in their outlook. They are more accepting of misfortunes and disasters which strike, than are Anglos. A typical reaction is, "It is God's will" or "Que sera, sera" (What will be, will be). This is due to their strong faith in Divine wisdom which is never questioned by man.

The subculture of the Mexican American stresses cooperation, humility, sharing and obedience. Shame, pride, and modesty regulate the behavior of its members. Competition is not valued. Thus, Mexican American children may appear overly passive and conforming to the teacher who is unacquainted with these characteristics of the subculture. Further, their culture does not encourage climbing the ladder of success. Mexican Americans do not generally share our middle class Puritan work-success ethnic. Work is not viewed as a virtue in itself. In fact, the person who rises above the lot of his father, who moves into a "better" neighborhood and begins to prize material wealth, may be rejected by family and friends. Mexican Americans who succeed in the Anglo world frequently do so at the expense of losing respect among those they love. Success, to a traditional Mexican American, is based upon the role one plays in the family and neighborhood, not upon his status in the larger society.

Generally, Mexican Americans are a courteous and friendly people whose love of life and living could well be emulated by Anglos. They seem to have an absence of concern over the future, trusting that things will take care of themselves. They do not run their lives by the clock as Anglos do. They take the time to enjoy family and friends. Frequently, they are artistic and creative. There are many such positive traits in the Mexican American subculture.

More than language barriers have prevented the success of Mexican American children in our schools. The many cultural conflicts, as well as the need for additional income for the family have resulted in a high dropout rate among Mexican American youth. Unless they are encouraged by the family to remain in school, they may find life in the outside world much preferable to fighting an uphill battle to succeed in school.

Like our Black minority, our Chicano citizens are becoming more vocal in their demands for better education, housing, and jobs. They are determined to keep their language and cultural heritage as they seek access to the Anglo world. The Spanish-speaking people of the Southwest are a sizeable minority who will continue to affect school programs as educators strive to make school experiences for their children successful and relevant to their life style.

4. American Indians in the culture of poverty. Our "vanishing Americans" are not really vanishing after all. The Indian population in the United States now numbers approximately one million (Van Til, 280), and it appears to be on the increase. It is difficult to generalize about Indians because they are members of diverse tribes, numbering approximately 315, some of whom continue to live on reservations amounting to 52 billion acres distributed across 26 states. (Deloria, 47) Others, around 500,000, live in urban areas. Controversy continues over whether reservations should be continued or abandoned. Further, the type of education which is "best" for the American Indian child is open to great debate. Consequently, there are many patterns of schooling. For a long time, Indians had little control over the public education of their children. It is only recently that they are beginning to shape educational policies through the creation of Indian school boards for reservation schools run by the Bureau of Indian Affairs (BIA).

Indian poverty on reservations is well documented. (Osborn, 229-30) Unemployment is extremely high, with family incomes well below the national average. The overwhelming majority of Indian families live in housing that is far below what we refer to as substandard. Drive through a reservation area and you will find that "home" for many Indian families is little more than a pile of sticks, a lean-to shack, or a mud hut. The death rate is far above that of middle class America.

The level of educational attainment among Indians is quite low. Undoubtedly, linguistic differences constitute an important factor in the high dropout rate. There is no such thing as a single "Indian language." There are over a hundred native Indian languages, not including dialects, spoken by Indians in the United States and Canada.

We need to recognize that the American Indian is not an immigrant who chose to come to this country in search of better opportunities. He was here first. The struggle of the American Indian to retain his cultural identity in the face of great pressure from "palefaces" to adopt "white man's ways" has been long and arduous. The American Indian has become somewhat acculturated, however. For example, a status symbol on the reservation may be a shiny new pick-up truck, rather than the number of cattle or sheep one owns. More Indians are going to college these days and "making it" in the white man's world. Many of the young reserve the "dress" of their tribe for tribal functions and, otherwise, follow the latest fashion fads of white youth. Many continue to resist any and all attempts at acculturation and cling to the traditional ways of their tribe.

In order to gain a measure of understanding of the problems which Indian children face in public schools, we shall examine, briefly, some highlights of the traditional Navajo culture. It should be understood that Indian cultures vary considerably and that our discussion of the Navajo should not be generalized to all other Indian tribes.

The Navajos are over 100,000 in number and live on reservations totaling over 15 million acres located primarily in Arizona and New Mexico. (Bahti, 31-32) Because the reservations have limited resources, however, numbers of Navajos must leave to seek employment. Many work in agricultural occupations. Some personal income is provided by the beautiful craft work for which the Navajo is famous. Tribal income is derived from timber, as well as oil and gas leases. (Bahti, 34)

Navajos appear to be adjusting to modern living in various ways. Many follow the traditional pattern of sheepherding and gardening. Others, however, find employment with the Bureau of Indian Affairs both on and off the reservation. Some few are urban dwellers in such cities as Phoenix, Denver, and Los Angeles. (Zentz, 181)

The family organization of the Navajo appears to be in a state of flux. Traditionally, the father was considered the head of the family. However, as theirs is a matrilineal society, the woman generally shared the management and decision making of the family. (Zentz, 176-77) The family was regarded as part of the mother's extended family group, and she owned much of the family's worldly goods. As the men seek jobs off the reservations and they earn money to support the family, the women's position is weakened as they must rely upon their husbands for support. Also, the husband frequently demands a greater role in the ownership of goods. Thus, the matrilineal extended family is weakened and may be replaced by a nuclear family pattern. Sometimes the women work, too.

Navajos stress such things as looking after one's own property; getting along well with others; doing as told; sharing wealth with relatives; righting wrongs; avoiding the unfamiliar and staying away from strangers; seeking escape in the presence of danger or frustration. (Zintz, 179-81)

The Navajo child attending non-Indian schools faces many handicaps and frustrations. We have mentioned linguistic differences. Some Navajo children have almost no knowledge of English. Few white teachers have sufficient command of Navajo, an extremely difficult language to learn, to initiate instruction in the children's native language. When Navajo children come to school with a fair degree of facility in English, generally this is a nonstandard dialect. They continue to have difficulty with vocabulary and pronunciation. Textbooks are being rewritten in Navajo. Generally, this is a local project, as the market is not sufficiently large to tempt publishing companies to produce editions in various Indian tongues.

Frequently, white teachers complain of the passivity, apathy, shyness, lack of interest, incentive, motivation, and competitiveness in their Indian students. Perhaps, there are two basic causes for their observations. First, these characteristics may be the product of the lack of fit of public schools for Indian children. Also, there are differences between the life styles and value systems of Indians and whites.

Zintz (183) has offered an interesting contrast between what the American public school teaches and the traditional Navajo culture stresses. For example, the Navajo culture teaches harmony with nature, whereas our schools point with pride to the harnessing of nature's forces to work for man. Within the Navajo culture is belief in the supernatural, mythology, witches, and sorcery. Our schools teach that there is a scientific explanation for all natural phenomena. The Navajo is similar to the Mexican American in that he tends to be present-time oriented. Sun time is used instead of clocks. Our schools schedule everything by the clock. Teachers attempt to motivate children with long-term goals. In the Navajo culture, people who amass wealth are looked upon as selfish and stingy. In our schools, we preach the importance of saving for the future. How many white teachers have used "Horatio Alger" type stories to spur on their students to greater heights? Success to the Navajo means being a good person. Our schools, as agents of society, tend to equate success with material wealth. The Navajo society is matrilineal and based upon extended family organization. Our schools tend to portray the family as consisting mainly of parents and siblings with father as the head of the household. Since traditional Navajos do not believe in the germ theory, children may not understand when the teacher talks in terms of germs, sickness, cleanliness, and good health habits.

These are just a few of the differences which we could mention. You can see readily how such additional differences as are found in religion, clothing, shelter, and diet would contribute further to the lack of relevance of public schools for Indian children. All encompassing are the vast differences in thinking and behavioral patterns which must be taken into account when planning programs and teaching strategies for these culturally different children.

5. Poverty in Appalachia. There are pockets of poverty all over our country. However, the poverty of the Appalachian Mountain whites is

outstanding and worthy of special note. These people inhabit the mountainous regions found in West Virginia and parts of Pennsylvania, Ohio, Maryland, Virginia, Kentucky, Tennessee, North Carolina, Georgia, and Alabama (Crow, et al., 20). As a group, they are characterized by low level of income and educational attainment, high unemployment, much illiteracy, as well as a certain detachment from the rest of society. Some work land which is insufficient to support the needs of even one family. Others rely on employment in the coal mining and lumber industries which have incorporated much automation and, hence, do not require as large a labor force. Many of the older unemployed miners and lumberjacks refuse to retrain and relocate in another region. There is little industry, other than the mines or timber, to support a large semiskilled labor force. Because of the poverty, industries are reluctant to come in. Most of the youth leave Appalachia and seek their fortunes elsewhere, but many of the mountain people continue to live out their adult lives in the place of their birth in dire economic circumstances. Welfare has become a way of life for many of these people who have been known in the past for their pride and independence. It has been estimated that it would take more than a million new jobs to revive the economy of Appalachia and get this region back on its feet. (Van Til, 297) It is unlikely that this many new jobs will be created in the near future. Meanwhile, many families are kept from absolute starvation by government food stamps and surplus commodities.

The characteristic family patterns of the depressed Appalachian mountain people have been described as revolving around specific duties allotted to various family members. (Crow, et al., 21) Children are assigned chores or help care for the younger ones. The father tends to be the authority figure. The family, by and large, remains aloof from involvement in social, community, or governmental activities. However, many attend church regularly and practice their religion with great zeal. Generally, they are not interested in schools or schooling. However, this attitude may be changing. Frequently they resist offers of help and tend to retain some of their independent spirit in the face of having to accept help from the government to keep the wolf from their door.

The children speak a nonstandard dialect of English which is different from the other groups we have discussed previously. Because of their isolation, their speech is full of colorful expressions and idioms. These dialect differences, however, obstruct school learning and result in low achievement. Until parents are convinced of the need for school for their children and are willing to learn along with them, it is unlikely that education will make much of an impact on the Appalachian mountain people.

Strategies for teaching social studies.

Nowhere in the total elementary school curriculum is the lack of relevance of school experiences for the culturally different children more pointed and obvious, than in social studies programs. In the past, these programs have been almost totally ethnocentric, in the sense that they portrayed the white middle class way of life in our country as the *only* worthwhile way to live and generally ignored any aberrations as unworthy or unimportant. Damage was often done in the form of stereotyping groups of people. The Mexican was pictured wearing a serape, napping against a saguaro catus, sheltered from the afternoon sun by a huge sombrero. The Black was shown as that "funny song and dance man" or polite servant in a white household. The "quaint" mountain people played their fiddles, danced around, and produced moonshine in great quantity. The Indian was a bloodthirsty savage who scalped people for the fun of it. Not only are such stereotypes unfortunate, but they provide stumbling blocks to the understanding of and appreciation for all peoples.

Frequently, social studies is the most unpopular school subject for the economically disadvantaged child (Dimitroff, 183-97) because reading has been the key to success. Many of these students are reading two or three years below grade level, and, therefore, social studies is a symbol of failure. Concepts and generalizations cannot be formulated without a factual foundation. Children with a different language background have difficulty in forming generalizations because these statements involve complex sentence structures. The size and format of textbooks and other materials used in social studies programs may offer further discouragement to the child who lacks highly developed communication skills. Another stumbling block has been that the content may be too far removed from the lives of children who face daily the cruel vagaries of life.

Learning the skills associated with the social studies may be somewhat bewildering to disadvantaged students. Critical thinking is not, generally, a part of their background. Lack of skills, poor attitudes toward school and learning, and an inclination against organization and postponing conclusions until all data have been evaluated, make the teaching of critical thinking quite difficult.

Two skills which require both imagination and organizational ability are perceiving cause-and-effect relationships and understanding graphic representations. (Dimitroff, 186) Children often cannot fathom how events occurred and fail to comprehend the connection between events in the past and those of the present. Due to the lack of appropriate background materials and experiences, the culturally different have problems with these learnings to a much greater degree.

The child from an economically depressed environment needs to learn how to form generalizations which he can apply in variety of situations. (Loretan and Umans, 89-90) Basic concepts in the social sciences should be established as reference points. Generalizations should be derived from seeing the relationship between understandings and facts. A sequential spiral approach over a thirteen or fourteen year period (pre-kindergarten through twelfth grade) is more useful for learning generalizations in social studies than the cyclical approach, often used in the past, in which the same content is repeated throughout the grades. In the spiral or sequential approach, basic concepts expressed in the language of the children are taught in the earliest years and are increased in depth in later years using new content, increasingly higher levels of abstraction, and more difficult problems. There are real gains to be reaped from this approach. It helps them develop the ability to make applications of basic principles to new situations and strengthens associational thinking.

In this section, we shall look at the economically disadvantaged child and show you how social studies can become a meaningful and profitable element in this child's education. We shall consider these factors: teacher attitude; self concept; building cross-cultural understandings; content selection; and providing successful experiences.

Teacher attitude Teacher attitude is a key factor in the degree of success of any program. However, here we refer particularly to the teacher's attitude toward children from a different subculture.

The teacher's feelings toward these children must reflect total acceptance, not necessarily of his subculture and value system, but of the child himself. Children are extremely perceptive of feelings. If you as a teacher reject them covertly, no amount of overt expression of acceptance on your part will be sufficiently genuine to indicate complete acceptance.

Please note that we prefer to say "acceptance," rather than "tolerance." Tolerance has the connotation that "I'm just putting up with you." "Acceptance" connotes that "I appreciate you and value you for what you are."

A prerequisite for acceptance is understanding. Understanding is based upon knowledge—the facts. This is why we have provided a brief acquaintance with the major subcultures in our country, as well as the all-inclusive culture of poverty which is so debilitating and crippling to all, regardless of race or ethnic origin. Your first steps, then, in learning to accept the culturally different are to find out as much as you can about them and, then, build your personal understanding of their life styles, beliefs, customs, attitudes, values, and needs.

Your acceptance of culturally different pupils in the classroom will be reflected in your faith in them, the respect that you show them, the openness with which you approach them and a myriad of other little ways ranging from a smile to a pat on the back.

Self concept The culturally different child frequently has a poor or unrealistic concept of self. This is understandable. Self concept is learned from the reactions of others to us. The dominant culture may have reinforced such feelings as "I am no good," "I am not wanted," "People don't like me," "It's bad to be ________ (Black, Chicano, etc)." By the time the child enters school, he may have had sufficient negative reinforcement that he's convinced he's not an acceptable person.

One of the tasks of the teacher of the culturally different, then, is to build in each child a positive concept of self. Your acceptance of the child certainly will help, but the child will also need many successful school experiences if negative concepts are to be unlearned.

In the past, social studies classes have failed the culturally different miserably, in this respect. Often, the pupil was doomed to failure from the outset. When a textbook, "fact-stuffing" approach is employed, this is inevitable. As we have indicated, the culturally different child typically has communication problems. He has poor command of standard English. The higher he proceeds in the grades, the greater is the gap between grade level expectations and his reading achievement level. A single textbook approach to social studies does not provide this student with the successful school experiences he needs in order to build healthy concepts of self.

We can change the materials we use for teaching social studies and modify our methods to build a backlog of successful experiences for the culturally different child. Perhaps, however, the most critical contribution which social studies can make is in the area of developing pride in one's cultural heritage and strong feelings of identity. This may be accomplished by creating in each child a cultural and personal awareness.

Building cross-cultural understandings One of the positive features of the integrated school is that within its walls can be found a microcosm of the real world in which people of varied backgrounds work together for the common good. Thus, in most classrooms we find children from different social strata and subcultural backgrounds. Certainly, in developing cross-cultural understandings, the teacher would begin with the subcultures of the children in the classroom. If you have Black children in your room, you will want to include some "Black Studies" in your social studies program. This is true in every grade level. For example, "Black Studies" should not consist of one unit at the fifth or sixth grade level but, rather, should be a part of the total elementary program at increasingly higher levels of complexity as children proceed through the grades. If you have some Mexican American children, you will do the same with "Chicano Studies." For the American Indian or Puerto Rican, you would follow a like procedure—begin building an understanding of the children's own heritage first. Even the Appalachian mountain people have customs, traditions, and heroes which can be studied along with the history of the region from its early settlement to the present.

Some cultural awareness and appreciation may be accomplished by giving attention to the art and music of the different groups of people. Such dramatic activities as role playing, plays, pageants, tableaus, and the like are also profitable experiences.

Involving the parents of your children in school activities is another way to build understandings and appreciations. Perhaps, you can invite Maria's mother to help the class make *tacos*. Maybe Bobby's mother could involve the children in preparing "soul food." If you have Indian children, it may be that you can coax a parent to demonstrate the making of "squaw bread." If some of the parents have special talents or are engaged in occupations which they might talk about or demonstrate in your classroom, you may build such experiences into your social studies program. By involving parents in these ways, you have the additional benefit of helping them learn more about what goes on at school and, perhaps, selling them on the importance of education for their children. They may become the best goodwill ambassadors that any school ever had! A few such persons within the neighborhood community may help to modify the attitudes of many people within that community towards school and the importance of school attendance for their children.

Certainly, if the children are to have the opportunity to achieve full participation in the dominant society, they need to know and understand the characteristics of the dominant culture. This should not be achieved by contrasting this culture with subcultures as this tends to make it appear as if the subcultures are inferior to the dominant culture. The approach used should be a positive one, examining alternative ways of behaving without making value judgements.

If we help children examine our society realistically, they will discover that it is dynamic—constantly changing. They will also discover that since it is a product of man's efforts to live in harmony with fellow man, it is imperfect and needs improvement. These are not "secrets" that the child should have to discover on his own as he interacts in his world. We can and should begin building an awareness of the nature of society together with its conflicts and problems, early in the grades.

We must not stop here, however. We need to guide children toward ways of finding solutions to critical societal problems and help them discover acceptable means of initiating social changes. We live in a democracy. If our democracy is to survive, then, by "acceptable" we imply that these means would consist of actions compatible with democratic principles and practices.

Content selection We have mentioned including ethnic studies and the history of the local environment. If our goal is to be relevance, we will need to exercise a few additional guidelines in content selection. The culturally different child may comprehend events far removed in time more effectively than those which are closer to the present. In the early primary grades we begin our teaching with an emphasis on the present and leap back in time to events which occurred a very long time ago. Young children find dinosaurs and cave men fascinating study!

Another guideline we might stress is that of providing models of alternative family patterns. Many children are members of families in which there is no adult male present. Other families include more than parents and siblings—grandparents, uncles, aunts, cousins, and the like. These alternative family patterns should be explored so that the child is not led to believe that the "typical family" follows a nuclear family pattern with father as the main breadwinner.

In selecting content about community helpers, we need to portray these people *as people* and make a careful distinction between the person's role as a community worker and his other roles such as citizen, family member, etc. In the past, people like policemen and teachers, for example, were portrayed as near-perfect individuals who always made the "right" decisions in everything they did. Teachers, policemen, and others are people who make mistakes both on and off the job. By portraying persons realistically, we are less likely to turn off our culturally different students. We must keep in mind, too, that, frequently, these children have much different attitudes toward community workers than we have. In fact, the policeman may be a person that they fear greatly or even hate.

Often, disadvantaged children are most concerned with problems within the neighborhood or larger community. Certainly, we would recommend including local problems in your social studies program. Such problems are meaningful and relevant for the children who face them outside of school each day. These problems provide excellent opportunities for exploring possible solutions and discovering community resources which are available. Frequently, these children know too little about local resources and agencies.

Content can be meaningful and relevant for culturally different students if we exercise care in selection and apply these guidelines. If we know our students well and are familiar with their backgrounds and life styles, we are less likely to plan experiences for which they are not ready or in which they have little interest.

Providing successful experiences If we are to provide successful experiences for our culturally different students, there are several considerations which are important. First, we shall give attention to the development and assessment of children's skills which are related to what we are attempting to teach. We have mentioned pretesting previously, but it is worthy of particular note here, when we discuss the culturally different child. The materials and resources we select and the activities we plan for students are additional elements which we shall discuss. Finally, because social studies deals with concepts of time and chronology which are particularly difficult for many economically disadvantaged children, we shall give special attention to this facet of the social studies program.

1. Skill development and assessment. Social studies can provide a vehicle for the teaching of communication skills in a meaningful context. We have stated that, generally, the culturally different child is weak in all areas of language skills. If he is weak in listening skills, then we may teach him to be an attentive and critical listener employing social studies materials. The same is true for reading skills. In both listening and reading activities, the teacher must check for comprehension continually. Avoid making assumptions about the child's ability to use context clues to determine meanings of new words which he hears or reads. It is important to give special attention to new vocabulary and the terminology used in many social studies units.

Because research skills involve a more complex application of communication skills, the teacher of the culturally different may need to spend additional time to improve these skills. An inquiry or problem-solving approach to the social studies will offer many opportunities for teaching these skills at the time when they are needed. This should result in more proposeful learning for the student.

Assessment of skill attainment is important in any instructional sequence, but it is crucial in the case of the disadvantaged learner. We cannot assign tasks to students for which they do not have the prerequisite skills and expect them to accomplish these tasks successfully. Pretests come in many forms, ranging from simple observation to complex batteries of testing instruments. Select the method of pretesting which best suits your purposes and the skills which you are attempting to assess. Then, build your instructional plan around this information. If the child does not have the skills which are prerequisite to success, then, either teach him the skills before you begin the instructional sequence or build your program of skill development into your instructional plan. Either way, at least you will be assured that the child will have success-oriented experiences.

2. Materials and resources. The need for many firsthand perceptual experiences is generally based upon the age of the child, as well as his background of experiences. The child living in the culture of poverty rarely comes to school with a sufficient backlog of experiences which have prepared him for school. Thus, we would recommend that the teacher fill in learning gaps by providing a variety of such experiences. Dale's Cone, which we displayed on page 139, can be of help to us in selecting materials. Certainly, we would recommend selecting experiences toward the base of the cone before planning those more abstract in nature. As the child discovers many new things, it is advantageous to work on language

development. Capitalize on opportunities to label things, to find likenesses and differences, cause and effect, to discuss, write stories, and the like. Rather than simply bombarding children with experiences of many kinds, take the time to get the most out of each you select. Quality, not quantity of experiences, is important.

When choosing written materials for the culturally different, it is vital that you select materials within children's abilities to read and understand. This is not always possible to accomplish. Perhaps such materials simply are not available at the child's reading level, or maybe you do not have access to these materials. In either case, you may need to write your own. This can be achieved by taking the more advanced materials and translating them into words and sentences which the children will be able to read with understanding. You may wish to put the materials you have written in book or pamphlet form or record information on large chart tablets. Perhaps, you will wish to use transparencies and an overhead projector. An alternate way of accomplishing the same goal is to record the material you have written and let the children listen to the tapes you have made. By writing your own materials you may avoid one of the problems that has plagued social studies teachers for many a year—that of finding materials simple enough to be read and understood by children who are reading far below grade level.

Relevance should be another consideration in selecting materials and resources. Teachers need to select topics which will have meaning for the culturally different—which are within the realm of their experiences, at least in part. Frequently, textbooks fail here. Newspapers and magazines may provide relevant information. Also, there are paperback books, pamphlets, radio and television programs, films, and many other sources of information. Comic strips and cartoons should not be overlooked.

Inviting resource people from the community may help to bridge the gap between the real world and school experiences. If your resource persons are members of minority groups, they may be able to communicate with students more effectively than you could yourself.

3. Activities. The activities that you select for your culturally different students should be placed within the context of their life style, when this is appropriate. For example, if you are teaching about economics, you may approach this in the context with which your students might be familiar—selling newspapers on a corner, or soft drinks at a sporting event.

This child learns more effectively when he is actively involved. Thus, we would recommend increasing the number of activities in which the learner is an active participant. Simulation games are excellent devices if the teacher selects games which are meaningful for the children in terms of their different backgrounds of experience. Also to be noted is that several subcultures we described earlier value sharing and cooperation above competition and amassing of material wealth. You can readily see how a game like Monopoly might lack educational relevance for economically disadvantaged children. The buying and selling of properties may be too remote from their lives. Also, it could be that their sharing tendencies might result in the giving away of properties and breaking the bank by passing "GO" whenever a player needs money!

The culturally different child should be given objects to manipulate and models to work in order to enhance learning. He needs many concrete experiences. Art and music activities, too, can provide profitable reinforcement or enrichment. The more sensory avenues which the child uses, the more effective will be the learning. The teacher should select activities for children accordingly. We must remind you that if the learning task is extremely difficult, only one sensory path should be used at a time.

4. Concepts of time and chronology. Concepts of time and chronology (sequence of events) are in the realm of the abstract. Therefore, the disadvantaged child appears to have a greater difficulty in learning these concepts than other children. This statement is substantiated by research. A recent study was conducted by one of the writers (Foerster). Approximately 400 sixth grade students were examined using an oral test of concepts of time and chronology constructed by the researcher. Significant differences were found between the achievement of disadvantaged children in poverty schools and other children. Implications drawn from this research study were that teachers need to give special attention to the teaching of concepts of time and chronology when they are working with children from the culture of poverty. First, we shall explain why there is a need for special attention to these concepts. Then, we shall provide some specific suggestions for their teaching.

Frequently, the life style of the poor includes a different time orientation. (Crow, et al., 129) Also, the various subcultures we have discussed previously were characterized as having a different time perspective. The small child learns the rudiments of time and sequence through the household routines which he observes. However, in many families within the culture of poverty there is an absence of regular routines. Each day seems to evolve out of the previous one, and parents take one day at a time. There is little planning for the future, as present problems must be surmounted first. Thus, the child has little exposure to a regular sequence of happenings in the home and vocabularly dealing with the future. Many of the homes lack clocks and calendars. If there is a clock or calendar present, it may not have much importance, as far as the family is concerned.

In the average middle class home, the father and, perhaps, the mother leave for work at the same time each day, and the small child is exposed to a routine which he follows at home, at the babysitter's, or at nursery school. His life is organized for him at an early age. Meals come at the same intervals each day. So do his nap and play periods. The adults around him frequently talk about the clock and calendar, and he learns that these things have an important effect on his life. Thus, he gains some understanding that clocks measure time and that things happen in a sequence. Also he is exposed to a time vocabulary.

Some specific suggestions for the teaching of concepts of time and chronology to young culturally different children would include capitalizing upon the daily classroom schedule to show how the clock helps us measure time and how events happen in regular order each day. The importance of maintaining a regular daily sequence for these children cannot be overstressed. By calling attention to the time and order in which activities occur, you will begin building some understanding of what time means in the lives of people and how we measure it.

The school week and school events can be used to teach some understanding of the calendar. The holidays and special days also provide excellent opportunities to discuss the calendar and mark off days in anticipation.

It is important to build children's time vocabulary, including both indefinite and definite expressions of time. Social studies materials are full of such references. It should not be assumed that every child will understand these expressions the first time he meets them. In the lower grades, such words and expressions as "clock," "hour," "minute," "second," "noon," "midnight," "calendar," "day," "week," "month," "year," "yesterday," "tomorrow," as well as "soon," "always," "never," "before," "after," "now," "later," "in a little while," and the like will need to be taught. Older children need to gain an understanding of "decade," "century," "era," "age," "epoch," "in the near future," "a long time ago," "in colonial times," "in the days of the cave man," as well as a myriad of other terms frequently found in social studies materials. Children should be taught how context clues can aid in the understanding of indefinite time expressions.

In teaching a sense of chronology, it is most effective if the teacher will work within the child's own life space. The ordering of events in the child's life is important to him. For example, the teacher might begin by having children discuss the events which occur between getting up each morning and leaving for school. Later, such activities can be extended to include longer periods of time in the child's life.

When young children are arranging events or the parts of a process they understand in the order of their occurence and are relating dates to personal experience, they are beginning to develop a sense of chronology. (Spieseke, 185) By the time the child is ten or eleven, he should be encouraged to think of happenings in relation to the continuous passage of time and to learn the importance of dates as the accepted way of marking events.

Time lines are useful for teaching many aspects of time understandings by encouraging students to think of time graphically. (Fraser and West, 183) They are especially important for working with the culturally different so that the child is provided with a visual referent. Time lines help in establishing a sequence of events, comparing the length of historical periods, developing a time vocabulary, and a worldwide framework of time relationships. The first time lines that the child works with should be simple, covering a short time span. Later, more complex time lines and multiple time lines can be constructed by the children.

If time lines are to be useful as teaching devices, we must ascertain that pupils are able to work with them and interpret them correctly. They should be used frequently for clearly defined purposes related to the unit of work. Some time lines may be saved and used to compare with those developed in later units.

Time lines can be helpful in reviewing and deepening an understanding of the system of chronology in which centuries are numbered backwards and forwards from the birth of Christ. Also, they are useful for showing and relating pivotal dates and clusters of dates. In the upper grades, parallel time lines may be helpful in aiding the development of a comprehensive mental time framework needed to study relationships among contemporaneous events around the world.

Children should be encouraged to construct their own lines. However, the teacher should supervise this construction so that the time lines will be easy to interpret and mathematically correct. Some of the cautions which need to be exercised are that the time line should be continuous, enabling the eye to travel in one unbroken sweep. (Preston, 218) Also, it should be scaled accurately and consistently. Generally, the time line should have a single theme.

A pocket chart may be combined with a simple classmade time line in the intermediate grades, making the time line a visual referent for any specific event discussed much in the same way that a map is used for reference. (Merritt, 263) As a child reads or hears about important events, these may be noted on cards and placed in the appropriate pockets. As the pockets accumulate dates concerning events noted, the contents may be used as the setting for a story. The dates themselves are of little importance except as they help children with the relationship of time and events.

Time lines can fulfill an important function in the social studies program, especially for the child whose experiential background has not encouraged the learning of these concepts. If attention is given to selecting appropriate time lines, in terms of children's readiness to use these devices, and supervision is provided during their construction and use, they can be most helpful.

Not only are time lines beneficial, but family trees and time rolls can be utilized as well. (Johnson, 205–07) The children themselves may make and keep time rolls consisting of strips of paper fastened together to make a strip five or ten feet long, or even longer. One end of the strip may be fastened to a round stick. The children enter dates as they appear in lessons, being careful to keep spacing between the dates mathematically accurate. To be of use in the classroom, all of the time rolls should be of the same length and should be spaced in the same way.

In our discussion of the culturally different, we have attempted to point out subcultural differences and to give you some help in planning your social studies program. If you have economically disadvantaged children in your classroom, you will want to individualize your teaching to the extent that you will be able to incorporate many of these suggestions. The net result will be success for the learner and satisfaction for the teacher.

Objectives

The reader will be able to:

Explain (2.0) how the term "gifted" is used in this section.

Suggest (2.0) ways of identifying the gifted.

Explain (2.0) the relationship between intelligence and creativity.

Discuss (2.0) the special problems of the gifted.

Suggest (3.0) appropriate activities for the gifted child when given a topic or theme in social studies.

Challenging the Gifted

Perhaps you recall Margie whom we mentioned at the outset of this chapter. Margie's parents are both high school graduates. Her mother is a secretary and her father is an automobile salesman. Margie has two sisters, age two, and the other age ten. Margie's parents have tried to provide the girls with all the "advantages." Although the family is not wealthy, the parents have been able to supply the children with most of the things which children need and want. In short, they are enjoying the "good life." Margie had learned to read before she entered the first grade. Her speech is characterized by complex sentences and an extensive vocabulary. Margie is an exceptional child, but she is not the type of exceptional child which we have discussed previously in this chapter. She is what we shall call gifted.

What is giftedness?

There are many kinds of giftedness. Some persons are said to be gifted because they display extraordinary talents in music or art. Others are said to have the "gift of gab." The kind of giftedness to which we refer here is that associated with school learning. We are talking about the academically talented child who is above average in intelligence and ability, causing him to excel in the school environment. This child learns very quickly and retains much of what he learns. He is precocious in language development and appears to have an insatiable curiosity and thirst for knowledge. It is not likely that you will have many children like Margie in your classes during your teaching career unless you work in some sort of special school. Those that you *do* have, you will never forget!

Perhaps the greatest need of many gifted children is to be challenged. In the past when few programs were individualized to accommodate the differences in children, the gifted child frequently found school a dull, boring place. Many learned to escape the humdrum routine by resorting to daydreaming and thinking of ways to keep the teacher on his toes. There are gifted children, however, who seem to have the knack of challenging themselves. Their greatest need may be to be "turned loose" by the teacher to pursue their interests independently.

We passed through a period in the history of education when it was customary to "double-promote" or even "triple-promote" academically talented children. The line of reasoning here was that the child should be moved up to the grade in which advanced work was provided in order to present the learner with a real challenge. As a result, there were students who had completed high school before age sixteen and college before they were twenty or less. However, it was found that the social adjustment of these children was frequently poor. They simply did not have the same interests and were not as physically and emotionally mature as their older classmates. Thus, the practice of advancing the gifted in the grades was largely abandoned.

Current educational thought places stress on providing enrichment materials and activities for the gifted child, while keeping him with his age-mates. This does not mean that the teacher loads on more of the same kind of work in which most of the class is engaged. The gifted child is not interested in doing more of the same thing. He should be encouraged to pursue many topics in greater depth and to broaden the spectrum of his interests and abilities.

Intelligence and creativity.

Intelligence and creativity are related, but this relationship is not a reciprocal one. All highly creative people are extremely intelligent, but not all highly intelligent people are very creative. It seems that intelligence provides the resources with which an individual can engage in creative behavior. However, it appears that in some highly intelligent persons creative behavior has been discouraged at an early age.

Creativity cannot be taught. All persons are born with some measure of creative ability. The environment serves either to nourish or nip-in-the-bud the individual's latent creative potential. As teachers, we design the classroom environment. This environment can either nurture or squelch the creative efforts of students. The kind of classroom environment to which we have alluded throughout the book is conducive to bringing out children's creative efforts. Social studies provides many opportunities for divergent thinking and problem solving. Naturally, you can expect the gifted child to excel in creativity if you provide him with the encouragement and opportunities that are needed.

Special problems of the gifted.

Because the gifted child may be recognized easily as "different" in the classroom, he will have some problems with social adjustment. He is not well accepted by his peers. If he has spent a lot of time with books, models, and the like, he may lag behind his age-mates in physical development and skills. This may be an area of great weakness for him. Part of the teacher's task may lie in helping the child develop a better-balanced way of life.

The gifted child may act very grown-up most of the time, but behind this exterior, we must remember, exists a child. He is no different from any other child when it comes to basic needs such as security, love, a feeling of belonging, positive concept of self, and the like.

Another problem the gifted child may face is that of not being accepted by his teacher. Many gifted children are very conforming and make teachers happy by doing what they say and accomplishing tasks very successfully. Some are less willing to conform and may be rejected by teachers as troublemakers. If the teacher feels challenged or threatened by a student, he may react by punishing the child or by exerting great pressure for conformity. Most teachers, however, are willing and able to individualize the instructional program so that the gifted will be challenged, while other members of the class engage in success-oriented experiences, too.

One way in which you can utilize the talents of your gifted children is by permitting them to tutor other students in the school. The self concept of the gifted child may be greatly enhanced in this way as he gains the respect and admiration of other children. Some schools may encourage older students who have completed their assignments for the day to work with children in the lower grades. The gifted child may wish to utilize his special talents in this way. Other possibilities for service include working as an aide to the librarian or school nurse, helping out in the school's office, or helping teachers prepare materials. It is not a matter of finding busywork for the gifted child. The intent is to provide opportunities for service as well as for broadening the child's experiences.

The teacher of the gifted child who is patient and understanding, sensitive to his special needs and problems, and who encourages him to put forth his best efforts in everything he does will make a substantial contribution to the life of this child.

Strategies for teaching social studies.

The social studies program for the gifted will need to be modified just as for the culturally different or the slow learner. The changes that we make, however, will not be the same because the needs and abilities of the gifted are different.

To begin with, the gifted child is capable of much more independent work and much greater self-direction than other children. Frequently, all he may need is a suggestion from you and, perhaps, a little encouragement. Generally, his powers of concentration are greater and thus he is able to remain at one task for a longer period of time. He is capable of sustained research which is complex. However, he has a low tolerance for frustration. He may be able to follow a problem-solving model quite readily and require little direct guidance from the teacher except when he hits snags in his efforts.

The gifted child has well-developed communication skills. Thus, he is able to utilize a greater variety of learning resources, as well as more complex ones. Generally, he will be reading substantially above grade level. Thus, the older gifted child may be capable of utilizing adult sources of information with ease. He does not need many concrete perceptual experiences because of his advanced verbal and conceptual development. He can perceive relationships readily and work with abstract concepts.

It is important, however, that the gifted child retain his place in the group and that he not become an outsider. There will be many opportunities in which he can work with other members of the class and feel that he belongs. Also, it may be well to encourage his leadership abilities. In this way, he can retain his place in the group as he works on projects which interest and challenge him.

Remember that the gifted child has a greater potential for creative behavior. He should be encouraged in his efforts at divergent thinking. Provide him with many opportunities to use his imagination and his problem solving abilities. Guide his unending curiosity and insatiable thirst for knowledge.

Summary

This chapter was initiated with a description of three exceptional children. Each child was exceptional in a different way. We discussed some overall considerations for working with exceptional children before proceeding into sections concerning three types of exceptionality. The slow learner was examined first. Some causes for slow learning and the special needs of the slow learner were taken up next. Then, suggestions were given for teaching social studies.

The section following dealt with the culturally different child. The culturally different were described as children living in the culture of poverty. This subcultural mileau was described in detail. Then, we examined five other subcultures: Black, Puerto Rican, Mexican American, American Indian, and Appalachian white. Suggestions were given for helping the culturally different in the social studies program. Particular stress was placed on providing success-oriented experiences.

The last section concerned the gifted children in our schools. Giftedness was explained along with the relationship of intelligence and creativity. The special problems of the gifted were considered and suggestions were offered for working with these children in social studies.

References

Bahti, Tom. *Southwestern Indian Tribes.* Las Vegas, Nevada: KC Publications, 1968.

Burma, John H., ed. *Mexican-Americans in the United States.* Cambridge, Mass.: Schenkman Publishing Co., Inc., 1970.

Crow, Lester D., Murray, Walter I., and Smythe, Hugh H. *Educating the Culturally Disadvantaged Child.* New York: David McKay Company, Inc., 1966.

Deloria, Vine, Jr. "The War Between the Redskins and the Feds." *The New York Times Magazine* (December 7, 1969): page 47.

Dimitroff, Lillian. "Teaching Social Studies to Culturally Disadvantaged Pupil." *Teaching the Culturally Disadvantaged Pupil.* Edited by John M. Beck and Richard W. Saxe. Springfield, Illinois: Charles C. Thomas, 1965.

Foerster, Leona M. "The Development of Time Sense and Chronology of Culturally Disadvantaged Children." Unpublished dissertation. University of Arizona, 1968.

Fraser, Dorothy, and West, Edith. *Social Studies in Secondary Schools.* New York: Ronald Press, 1961.

Harrington, Michael. *The Other America: Poverty in the United States.* Baltimore, Maryland: Penguin Books, Inc., Penguin edition, 1963.

Johnson, Henry. *Teaching History.* New York: The Macmillan Company, 1940.

Loretan, Joseph O., and Umans, Shelly. *Teaching the Disadvantages.* New York: Teachers College Press, Teachers College, Columbia University, 1966.

Merritt, Edith P. *Working with Children in Social Studies.* San Francisco: Wadsworth Publishing Company, Inc., 1961.

Osborn, Lynn R. "Language, Poverty, and the North American Indian." *Language and Poverty: Perspectives on a Theme,* Edited by Frederick Williams. Chicago: Markham Publishing Company, 1970.

Preston, Ralph C. *Teaching Social Studies in the Elementary School.* New York: Rinehart and Company, Inc., 1950.

Spieseke, Alice W. "Developing a Sense of Time and Chronology." *Skill Development in the Social Studies.* Edited by Helen McCracken Carpenter. *Thirty-third Yearbook of the National Council for the Social Studies.* Washington, D.C.: National Education Association, 1963.

Stewart, William A. "Toward a History of American Negro Dialect." *Language and Poverty: Perspectives on a Theme.* Edited by Frederick Williams. Chicago: Markham Publishing Company, 1970.

Van Til, William. *Education: A Beginning.* Boston: Houghton Mifflin Company, 1971.

Zintz, Miles V. *Education Across Cultures.* Dunbuque, Iowa: Kendall ˜Hunt Publishing Company, 1963.

XIV

Group Dynamics

Chapter Outline

Group Dynamics

In our pluralistic society where we come into contact with a great number of individuals whose values differ and are often in conflict with our own, interpersonal relations are critical. No longer can we maintain the detached philosophy of our isolated, agragrian ancestors. In Chapter I, we indicated that the values of the individual must be consistent with those of society if the individual is to achieve his wants and needs through the institutions of that society. From an analysis of the pluralistic society, we abstracted a set of values appropriate in a democracy and to which the school should expose children.

We shall review that listing, briefly, to determine why social studies educators are placing so much emphasis upon group involvement in the new social studies. After completing this study, we shall turn to a discussion of how you, as a teacher, can help children explore these values in group situations. Finally, we shall describe a developmental sequence which allows you to assess progress of your group toward productive involvement.

Objectives

The reader will be able to:

Identify (1.0) the values with which the authors associate group work.

Explain (2.0) the authors' rationale for using group work in the social studies.

Values and Group Activities

The first value we abstracted from our analysis of a pluralistic society was that all men have inherent worth. In order for children to develop this frame of reference, they must acquire positive perceptions of others. Children must experience involvement in situations where the ideas and abilities of others are valued. They must also experience situations where their own ideas and abilities are appreciated, so that they can develop trust in self and others.

A second value we identified was that all men have the right to think, feel, act, and speak according to their own beliefs. Implementation of this ideal requires that the individual develop sufficient independence to think, act, feel, and speak for himself. If we don't value our beliefs, we will not support the beliefs of others.

The third value can be described as the ability to establish and follow norms. As individuals who are members of groups, we follow rules of behavior established by groups in our society. These rules of behavior must be revisable in a changing society. As an interacting member of various groups, through communication with our fellows, we have the right and responsibility to establish and revise rules. We also must perceive the relevance of such rules to our success and failure as productive individuals.

Elements of communication come into play in our assessment of success or failure. Success and failure are often the result of our use or misuse of information. It is through communication with our fellows that we structure our behavior. Since our vocations and avocations are group oriented, they are dependent upon communicative exchange of cognitive and affective content.

The resolution of conflict is dependent upon at least three traits democratic individuals possess: a positive self concept, positive concepts of others, and an ability to communicate with others. Unless we have a strong self concept, we are likely to perceive ourselves as always wrong. This is disasterous in group problem solving. It is equally disasterous to assume that others are always wrong. In group interaction, it is not necessarily the cognitive content of communications that upsets our associates. It may be the way they perceive we are behaving toward them—the affective content. "Its not what you say; it's the way you say it."

What does all this mean in terms of what we expect from children? If we return to Edgar Dale's Cone of Experience, it means that we must provide children with real and contrived experiences in the area of group interaction. It requires, also, that we must view the school environment as one which facilitates such interaction. It must be one in which there is a chance for the child to play roles he will be expected to play as an active member of society. If we are to produce citizens who can make decisions themselves, work with others to make decisions, and implement the decisions they make or help to make, they must experience this environment in the school. The passive school environment of the past will not allow us to attain these purposes.

Objectives

The reader will be able to:

Identify (4.0) the behaviors which the teacher must develop in order to facilitate group involvement.

Teacher Actions Which Facilitate Group Involvement

In the teaching situation, the only behavior you can control is your own. It is through *your* behavior as a teacher that you develop the environment of the classroom. Several authors, such as Gorman (40–41), have listed goals toward which teachers must move in attempting to develop group skills in children. In the first place, the teacher must become a participating member of the group. He must move from the role of director toward group centered leadership. The group must feel that the teacher can lead, if necessary, but that their own opinions count in decision making.

Second, the role of decision making and opinion giving must pass from individual to individual. Even after the teacher has assured the group that all opinions count, every member must feel that his individual opinion will be recognized. All of us have participated in groups when we knew our ideas would be thrown out. Such a group is disappointing to some of its members. Sooner or later it will disintegrate. Every member must have his say.

Third, teachers must realize that there is more than the cognitive element in group products. There is an affective element that must be considered, too. Every member must have his say, if he wants one. In addition, there is a morale factor to consider if the group is to maintain itself. There must be encouragement, praise, a sharing of feeling, dependence, and support among members of the group.

One incident will help to illustrate what we mean. Alfonso was a slow, determined, but shy child. He seldom participated. One day as he sat, seemingly withdrawn from the group, a problem developed in pulling together the information the group had been working with. Suddenly, a light appeared in the round face. "Those are the resources of iron making," he blurted.

Carol turned, half facing Alfonso and commented praisingly, "That wraps it up fine!" Alfonso picked up his chair and physically moved closer to the group. His nonverbal behavior indicated that he felt more a part of the group with which he was working.

Fourth, the teacher must help the group focus on growth and progress, rather than on grades and passing tests. The teacher of the group discussed above might have allowed Alfonso to see his own progress in becoming a group member even though Carol had helped this. Carol might have been made aware of her own behavior, too. She had provided Alfonso with needed positive reinforcement. As a teacher, this is one behavior pattern which you will want to encourage. Children should become aware of the feelings of others and their own role in influencing such feelings. Reinforcement obtained from peers, frequently, is more important to the child than that from the teacher. The distribution of the power of reinforcement is the fourth principle of good group management.

Evaluation of group participation is another need. This is the fifth principle we shall consider. Such evaluation should not be negative, tension producing, or in the form of ridicule or sarcasm. Further, it should not be directed toward particular individuals. Negative criticism creates hostility, emotional upset, fear, and fault finding within the group. It is divisive and, therefore, destructive of group unity. Positive evaluation is necessary to aid groups in their progress toward achieving established goals. You will recall that we have discussed the development of procedural charts for use in group problem solving. Children set their own objectives and work toward becoming more productive as a group and more successful as participants.

Communication is the sixth important element of group interaction. How many classes have you attended in which the instructor did more than half of the talking? Did you feel you had much in common with others in the group? Were you able to express your feelings? What about your ideas?

There are many times that the teacher should remain quiet. He can move from group to group, assuring children that he is there if they need him. Often, in class discussions, the verbal interaction should move from child to child, eliminating teacher talk—the teacher's verbal interaction. The teacher's task is one of maintaining interaction, encouraging wide participation, ensuring that the group stays on focus, and raising conversations to higher levels of thinking. During the more advanced stages of group development, even these activities become the responsibility of the group.

As teachers, we must become aware of nonverbal, as well as verbal behavior, in each situation. Alfonso's physical behavior in the above incident revealed much about his feelings. An alert teacher observing the above group at work would have been concerned about this child's seating position in relation to the group. The teacher would have been rather uncomfortable until he saw Carol's act. He probably would have been mulling over ways to accomplish the child's inclusion in the task group. As any good teacher, he would have refrained from taking direct action as long as he could. The above incident seems to indicate either that the timing of Carol and Alfonso's teacher was excellent or that the incident itself was most timely.

Blank stares, inattentive postures, disdainful frowns, and teasing actions are all nonverbal behaviors to which teachers must attend. If you observe such behaviors, wait to determine whether members of the group include the member about whom you are concerned. If they don't, then you must attempt to help in an unobtrusive way.

Communication, verbal and nonverbal, transmits our true feelings to children. If you are an open teacher, the feelings you express will be truthful. If you are a closed and insincere teacher, this will be communicated, too. Children distrust insincerety. They should. If you are open about your feelings, children will be open about theirs. The communication of feelings is as important as the communications of ideas in the achievement of any task. This is particularly true of any group-oriented endeavor.

To summarize, in order to create and maintain cooperation within a group, the teacher must distribute authority, encourage participation, accept and give feelings, focus on the growth of the group toward the achievement of common goals, distribute the power and the presentation of rewards, and maintain channels of communication among members.

Objectives

The reader will be able to:

Identify (1.0) the four stages of group development described by the authors.

Contrast (5.0) the stages of development, using the likeness and difference method described in Chapter V.

Sequential Development of Group Interaction

Sociologists have indicated that there are identifiable stages of growth through which groups pass (Schmuck and Schmuck, 114–22). As in human growth and development, the growth rate varies among individual groups, and there is a tendency to regress to lower stages of development when the group meets a new or unfamiliar situation. Progression proceeds toward more advanced stages, as long as the group is maintained.

The generalizations we shall develop in this section will apply to the classroom as a whole, as well as to task groups—groups organized to complete a short-term, assigned task. Each time a new task group is formed, if the membership is changed, it will pass through the same phases. There is some carry-over of skills from the larger to the smaller task group in that relationships established in the larger group may be maintained.

The stages Schmuch and Schmuck list include the following behaviors. In the first phase, students obtain acceptance by being included in the group and begin developing a mutual trust among members. In the second phase, influence patterns emerge, assignments are made, and the group develops its lines of communication for exchange of task information and the expression of feelings. The third stage sees the group attaining its goals both in terms of the task and the feelings of its members. As the group enters the final stage, it recognizes each of its members as individuals. It allows for differences among the abilities and interests of these individuals. When problems arise, they are solved within the group.

You have encountered each of these phases in one group or another in which you have been involved. In addition to discussing these phases, we shall suggest ways for you, as a teacher, to help groups move through each phase. Progress and group maintenance require careful planning and thoughtfulness on the part of the teacher.

Creating group trust.

As indicated above, the first task of the teacher is to aid the group in acceptance. Acceptance requires that the group include all of the children in its membership. It must also create the trust these individuals will need to become actively participating members. Although teachers are infrequently assigned classes in the elementary school in which members are totally unknown to each other, most beginning teachers are completely unfamiliar with the situation and, consequently, must begin at this point. Generally, there is a period of approximately two weeks during which everyone is trying to determine the limits of behavior, threats to status, and to establish status with the group. It is evident from children's behavior that this is the critical time in the establishment of group cohesiveness. The teacher must avoid negative criticisms, threats to individuals, and prevent himself from becoming the group authoritarian.

The teacher should establish himself as an individual who can be a trusted leader, but one who allows others to lead. He must open channels for the flow of information and feelings among members of the group—child to child, as well as teacher to child. It is important for each member to gain a feeling of worth, although not every member will be accepted equally. The group must also be a source of pleasure.

What are the types of activities that will create such an environment? Simulation games like the one mentioned in Chapter I could get a group off to a good start. In these games, the task is group and goal centered. Also, they are interest-creating and offer a possible source of enjoyment. In the intermediate grades, panel discussions can be developed so that children can become "experts" and report on different segments of a subject for which only they are given responsibility. The latter activity allows the student some recognition, if only for a few minutes.

These first weeks are more or less a pretesting period for the teacher. He should attempt to establish some idea of existing relationships within the group, in terms of leadership, membership, and general status. This is an excellent time to establish the teacher role of facilitator. During panel discussions, when questions arise, you can learn to count to five or ten before you answer the question. This creates what radio people call "dead air." It is rather perplexing when it occurs during a radio program, but, in the classroom, it makes students sufficiently uncomfortable that they may begin thinking of possible answers to questions. When they learn that you are going to allow *them* to answer questions, group members become more spontaneous.

During such discussions, especially early in the year, discourage negative comments. This does not mean that ideas and suggestions should not be evaluated. Granted, there is often a fine line between constructive critical analysis and negative criticism. What you must attempt to prevent is the critic who continually degrades the thoughts of others. The following are some comments which you can use to encourage participation:

"We'd like the thoughts of everyone."

"Let's listen to ________'s idea."

"Can you tell us more about that?"

"Let's be sure we get all of the suggestions we may need.

Often, the teacher can turn negative comments in useful directions. Children soon learn that responses from *all* members are truly sought. Children who normally don't respond should be encouraged to participate, too. The classroom segment below illustrates how this might be accomplished.

> "We're discussing the ways the Indians we have read about used the things around them in their lives. Are there other things we can add to our list?" Miss Kelly turned toward her third grade class to gather more items. "Kim?"
>
> "They used flint they got from rock."
>
> "How shall I record your suggestion?" Miss Kelly queried.
>
> "Flint."
>
> "Fine. Anything else?" The teacher continued as she recorded the item. There was not an immediate response. Noticing that a chubby little blonde had not responded, she asked, "Sandi, do you have something you'd like to add?" Noticing that the child seemed to feel pressured, the teacher added, "If you have something you'd like to add, just hold up your hand and I'll come back to you."

Miss Kelly may not get a response from Sandi during this lesson. Often, children like Sandi *will* respond to such a technique. At least, it allows *them* to know that *you* know they are there. This simple act of inclusion will aid reluctant children in their entrance into the group.

The Taba Strategies, the procedures developed by the staff working under Hilda Taba, are excellent for creating group unity. Everything the group says is accepted as information or data. Every child's response is sought. The group is able to work toward a common product.

Encouragement and positive reinforcement are important. Search for good things to say about your group. Although you may doubt that this is possible for every group, when you begin looking at groups with positive criteria, soon you may be surprised by the results. Remember, you must be sincere. Insincerity may allow you to get through the first couple of weeks, but children are going to find you out sooner or later.

Don't be afraid to recognize feelings. If the group expresses anger, accept anger. "I know you are angry about________. Do you have any ideas on how we could do this in a better way?" It's often surprising how many problems can be solved constructively in terms of feelings and group unity when children are allowed to express their feelings without reservation. One caution is in order, however. If you are given a group decision, you should move in the way the group decides. Variance from this decision creates distrust. If we are not going to follow recommendations, we shouldn't ask for them.

Anxiety must also be dealt with. Often, groups express their anxiety by hesitancy. A degree of anxiety is one step in the learning process. However, anxiety may cause us either to push ahead with increased fervor or to quit. The task of the teacher is to help the learner push on toward the established goal. Accept the group's feelings of anxiety. "I know that this seems like a difficult task, but I can help you get it done. What is the first step?" And on you go . . .

Groups must occasionally face failure. Placing the blame on________ is not necessary. Try: "This didn't seem to work. Does anyone have an idea about what we should try next?" People, especially children, shouldn't be placed on hooks. When we find that they are, however, our task becomes one of finding ways for them to get off those hooks!

Here are some other group activities which will aid you in developing group trust and membership, and promoting acceptance.

buzz groups	brainstorming
group sings	puppetry
creative dramatics	role playing
murals	storytelling

We would like to refer you to Chapter X where many of these techniques are discussed in greater detail.

At times, you will encounter groups which are, or later become, organized negatively. In order to change these groups, you must identify the group leaders. Find ways to structure subgroups of the larger group so that the negative tendencies are not as severe. The development of a sociogram helps. Figure 14–1 will also be beneficial since it facilitates the identification of lines of communication as well. Other tools which will aid in such an analysis are provided in the following book:

Fox, R.; Luszki, M., and Schmuck, R. *Diagnosing Classroom Learning Environments.* Chicago: Science Research Associates, 1966.

Developing influence patterns.

The next stage of group development is the structuring of lines of communication for the completion of tasks and the expression of feelings. By now, the students have developed a relatively high degree of trust. This is voiced frequently in terms of whom they can depend upon. The observational guide developed below will indicate these patterns and should be employed at this stage of development. It should be used in observations of the total group and task groups as well. Such knowledge will aid the teacher in facilitating group growth.

For the sake of group unity, task groups should be assigned in such ways as to separate cliques which develop in some groups. Although friendship patterns are natural and normal, closed groups are destructive to total classroom unity, as well as task group production.

It must also be pointed out that group structures are relatively resistant to change. Rearranging the communication patterns of the group for a short time will not restructure the relationships in a group. It takes a great deal of time to get groups working in certain ways. In an experience of one of the authors, it took a period of six months to restructure the communication patterns of a group of intermediate children which was tightly controlled by three girls in as many separate cliques. With the assistance of these young ladies, the group finally became highly productive.

Observing task groups working on assigned problems at this level, you may note that there is a great deal of testing of ideas and procedures. The group may seem to be moving in a particular direction as you listen to their conversations. Feeling they are on the right track, you move to another group. When you return to the first group, you may be surprised to find they have changed directions completely. This is characteristic of this phase of development. The lines of communication have not been completed, so the group vacillates in one way and then another.

Very often, groups have false starts at this stage. At the end of the work period, you may find a group which seems to be off and running.

Act	Student
Who gives ideas and suggestions in group discussions?	
Who voices opinions that differ from those of the teacher and other members?	
Who takes initiative and performs work independently?	
Who tries to put ideas over and get them implemented?	
Who suggests things to study or tasks to perform?	
Who suggests ways of presenting products completed by the group?	
Who offers help to others?	
Who tells others of good movies, records, activities?	
Who organizes play activities?	
Who helps children with out of school problems?	

Prepared from suggestions given by Schmuck and Schmuck pages 34–35.

Figure 14–1. *Analysis of Intergroups Relations*

When the next work period begins, you find they are dissatisfied with their direction. They may begin their exploration anew. Usually, the problem seems to center around personal interrelationships, rather than the value of ideas themselves. An incident in an undergraduate class meeting will illustrate this point.

The group consisted of five students whom we shall call Bill, Christi, Anne, Yvonne, and Pam. The task assigned was the preparation of a lesson which would teach seasonal changes. As the instructor listened, he found that the group had decided that they would use charts. Although they had discussed the use of a projector and the globe earlier, this idea seemingly had been discarded. The class period ended, and the group rose quite happy that their task was near completion.

During the first half on the next class meeting, the instructor noted that there seemed to be a rather heated debate among the members of the group. He strolled in their direction.

"Yes, but the drawing of charts takes too long!" Pam was saying. "It would be better if we borrow a projector from the media lab and use that globe over there."

"Sure, but how are you going to get the right angle?" Christi inquired.

"The dole moves. Dr. Williams has that one set in the upright position," Yvonne reminded Christi.

"I think this is a cruddy assignment!" Bill complained to Christi as the instructor approached. Both students laughed nervously as the instructor pulled up a chair.

"What's the objective you are attempting to fulfill?" The instructor began. Seemingly, he had not noticed the last comment.

The group had vacillated in its approach to the assignment because communication lines within the group had not been established. The task procedure was not finalized until this bit of dynamics was settled. The question you may be asking is "Will the best idea become the one which the group decides to accept; or will it be any idea the most influential member of the group decides is best?" There is not really an answer to that question. In fact, it depends upon the personalities of the various members of the group and the type of behavior that the teacher encourages.

Let's notice the orientation the instructor had taken in his questioning of the group. He asked, "What is your objective?" This question focused the students away from personalities toward the problem they were attempting to solve. He was implying, "Look Bill, Christi, Anne, Yvonne, and Pam, obviously you are in conflict because you are dealing in personalities; let's focus on the problem. Where are you trying to go? What's the best way of getting there?" There was little doubt that one, or possibly more, of the group would become leaders. Christi was becoming a type of leader. She was the person, in this instance, through which feelings were being channeled.

Turning to feelings, the instructor ignored an expression of negative feelings, which is as it should be. Possibly, it was a sincere evaluation, or the student may have been testing his opinion against others in the group. Actually, we cannot make this judgement on the basis of a brief episode.

Important elements are illustrated in this example. In the first place, this is the stage of decision making, in terms of the procedures which will be used to solve the problem at hand. It is also a time for channeling feelings, the second characteristic of this stage. Teachers who observe groups at this point often see some horseplay. This expression of feelings is important. The third point is that groups can be guided toward task solution, but only after *they* have settled upon a procedure.

Teachers can facilitate growth through this stage by asking questions which encourage all students in the group to talk and to participate. Should the teacher repeat questions which individuals ask? This may seem a bit ridiculous, but consider for a minute the effect such an act may have on a group of children. Repetition by the teacher or group leader usually lends support to the question. Also, it causes the original questioner to think through his words. Both acts are of value. Summarizing what the group or an individual has said has the same effect. These are our ideas, or my ideas, he is repeating. They are all ways of reinforcing behavior.

Accepting and sharing feelings are also important means of aiding the group in weathering this phase of group growth.

There will be times when children will fail in working toward their goals. They may become sidetracked because they do not understand the task. Here, the teacher must help, encourage, accept, suggest, and provide alternative solutions to tasks the group has chosen. Group problem solving takes time. Individuals usually can accomplish a single task faster, but, frequently, depth of thought is lacking. The same objectives are not achieved. Patience is the watchword. Help; don't force. Assist; but don't do.

We may be confusing you by jumping from large groups to small task groups and back again. The same stages are encountered in both large and small groups. Some of the stages will be reencountered in new situations. In order to clarify one possible source of confusion, it must be realized that each year groups may require one to three months at each of these stages.

Growth within groups will vary, also. You will have some task groups that are more mature in their development than others. This shouldn't surprise you. Remember, we are talking about group interrelations. Groups will naturally vary in their growth because of the individuals of which they are composed. Moving successful group participants into less successful groups may facilitate the slower group's growth, but it does not guarantee it.

There are some activities which seem to help groups acquire influence patterns.

- group problem solving
- group reports
- developing plays
- puppet plays
- task centered evaluation
- murals
- exhibits of children's work

Productivity.

Before this stage, there actually is no group work in a technical sense. While children work in groups, their products are mainly a pooling of individual efforts. After the distribution of influence has been accomplished, the group has developed trust and has established clear communication lines, the actual goal of group involvement begins. Previously, goals and procedures have been established primarily through the direction of the teacher. At this point, however, groups begin to establish their own goals and procedures. The teacher aids the large group or the task groups to evaluate their goals and procedures and to develop some means of evaluating the quality of their products.

It must be emphasized that growth within the group is uneven in terms of individuals. There is always the individual who fails to accomplish his task. Sometimes, this is because he fears the group and personnally has not developed as rapidly. At times, the student simply has not acquired the data processing skills needed for the task. Obviously, it is the role of the teacher to diagnose the problem. The strength of the group is in evidence when members of the task group express this feeling to the teacher, "Miss ________, Debbie can't find the information she needs, can you help us?"

Such a reaction from a group means that you have achieved your goal. The members of this group at least, and, probably, the large group as well, have realized that the teacher is someone who can and will help them. Equally important, the lines of communication have been left open so that the children can express their concern. On the other hand, the expression, "Mr. ________, dumb ol' Debbie's not doing her part," is divisive, illustrative of fear within the group, and indicative of the lack of open lines of communication.

The use of large and small group planning sessions, inventories of group progress, and charts providing suggestions of evaluation of group work procedures are excellent developmental activities. The Developing of Generalizations procedure patterned after the work of Taba is excellent during this stage. Since children will enjoy group work, it is unrealistic to expect a quiet classroom during work sessions with groups in this stage of development. Enjoyment creates exuberance.

The most effective teacher may talk very little during this stage. The major task is one of facilitating: asking probing questions, suggesting resources, solving individual problems, and aiding individuals in the development of necessary skills. In terms of time, this is the longest stage of development. Activities which aid children to pass through this stage are listed below.

- developing generalizations
- testing generalizations
- intergroup competition
- student developed plays
- community projects
- group problem solving
- committee work
- art shows
- interclass sharing of products

Group maturity.

When a group can accept each member's individual learning style and personality, it has arrived at the ultimate in development. Such groups are able to establish their own goals, design their own procedures, and assess their achievement of these goals.

Perhaps, to the uninitiated in the area of group involvement, arrival at this point by a disparate group of children, or even adults, seems "ivory towerish." It isn't! It happens more often than you might imagine. "In the traditional school setting?" No? It can't happen in that setting, but the schools in which you will be teaching are not as traditional as you might imagine.

Let's step back five years and look at a school with a student enrollment of around six hundred in an average community setting. The principal of this school was a head teacher, a master teacher qualified to step into any classroom at any time and pinch hit or demonstrate a new method to a reluctant teacher. The only relatively new concept besides the usual curriculum revision was a team teaching arrangement in the intermediate grades. The staff ranged in age from 22 to 57 years. The median age was 40. Every staff member was equally responsible for every child in the building. Corporal punishment was not allowed.

One day, a relatively young teacher was called out of school near the noon hour with a routine family crisis. Since the teacher needed to be away from the building for a short period of two hours, he arranged with the principal that the latter would take over the classroom while he was out. The class was divided into several small groups, each assigned a portion of a larger project. As usual, the work schedule, previously decided upon in a group planning session, was written on the board before the teacher left. The principal's role was to be that of the facilitator.

Two hours after the noon bell rang, the teacher returned and walked into a busily humming classroom. Noticing that the principal was not in sight, the teacher assumed that a problem had arisen to call him away for a minute. His suspicion was aroused, however, when Sue came to him and said, "We can't find a way to put these things together."

"What did Mr. Ellis suggest?" the teacher asked, so that he would not be covering ground the principal had already plowed.

"He wasn't helping us!" This seemed strange. The teacher knew that this was a rather basic problem which would have needlessly delayed a group working with an astute leader like Mr. Ellis. The teacher was puzzled; he began questioning the group to help them find a common element or two in what seemed to the task group to be a collection of unconnected facts. After the day was over, the teacher, passing by the principal's office on the way to a routine task, stuck his head into the half-open doorway, "Thanks, Jack. I appreciated your filling in for me."

"Filling in for you—Good heavens, I forgot!"

No, this is not a "traditional school" in the sense most of us would think, but it is only unusual because of its democratic atmosphere. There was respect for all individuals in this school. There were lines of responsibility, but there were also open channels of communication.

There was something else that was rather unusual. A group took responsibility "beyond their years." Five years ago, this was unusual, but today there are schools where small groups of children are responsible for their own actions for nearly the entire day. The point is simply, given proper training and motivation and a democratic climate, children can carry the responsibility of citizens. Group behavior of the type illustrated above doesn't "just happen." Children are taught to be independent of adult supervision. Although the teacher of the group above was unaware of the power of the experiences he was providing, it obviously was successful.

Did everything run happily ever after? No. All groups have conflicts within them. That is why we call the subject we are discussing, group dynamics. Groups are always changing. Changes may bring about unfriendly behavior, occasional expressions of rejection, withdrawal, and the many other behaviors characteristic of lower levels of development. In mature groups, however, these conflicts are resolved within the group in a mutual desire to preserve the group for its own sake.

Objectives

The reader will be able to:

Explain (2.0) the concepts of formal and informal channels of communication.

Present (2.0) examples from his experience when he has used the three means of communicating wants and needs, and explain (4.0) the consequences of each.

Intergroup Communication: Implementing Decisions and Recommendations

One problem we have, as citizens, is getting people to act on our conclusions and recommendations. Many times, the things we accomplish with children in the classroom require little action outside the group. Classrooms, however, are also influenced by external pressures in the same way the average citizen is affected by external forces. How do we as citizens react to such pressures? How do we make our wants and needs known? This is a basic question.

There are channels of communication through which we can react. Children must learn to seek out these channels if they are going to influence their world. Since the classroom can be viewed as a microcosm of our democratic society, then, we must teach children to use correct channels of communication.

To illustrate what we mean, let's return to Chapter XII and the example in which the fifth grade group developed an observational procedure to determine who was littering their play area. You'll recall they concluded that the culprits were junior high school students. The problem facing them was getting action on recommendations they had developed from their study of the problem. You can imagine what their recommendation was. "Since the junior high students were making the mess, the junior high students should remove the litter from the chain-link fence."

The teacher's problem was obvious. How was he going to help the class get this recommendation implemented? Actually, what he had to consider was the kind of lines of communication which were open to the group. It is what military personnel call the "chain of command." The diagram below illustrates a formalized channel of communication.

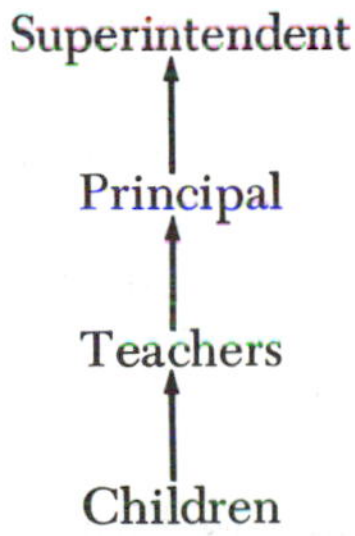

This is the way the educational institution intends for communication to flow. According to this illustration, the children express their wants and needs to the teacher. The teacher screens these recommendations and presents them to the principal. The process continues until someone either stops the communication or acts to fill the want or need.

The children's problem could not be solved in this chain because there was no way for them to interact with the junior high school in our schematic. Let's look at another diagram.

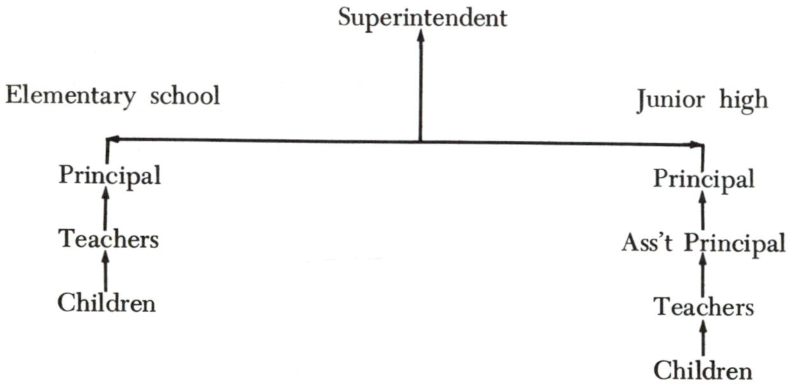

This diagram illustrates a possible channel for the message the children were attempting to communicate. The teacher decided to talk to the principal. The principal asked representatives of the group of children to bring the recommendation to him, and he'd try to get some action. To make a long story short, the junior high principal relieved the fifth graders of the task.

The important point here is that this group of children learned to use the formal, established structure to channel their findings and recommendations. Children must learn the chain of command in any situation if they are going to be able to communicate. As we have pointed out previously, communication is an important element in democratic living. Children are much happier and schools run much more smoothly when the lines of communication are open and children are able to express their wants and needs.

Also, there are informal structures within groups. Returning to our diagrams, you will note that there are no direct lines of communication established between the elementary and junior high school, except through the formal structure at the principal's level. What if the formal channel of communication had failed? How would the group have communicated their findings?

Perhaps the teacher could have used what is called the informal channel. Possibly she could have communicated with teachers in the other school.

The principal or assistant principal might have cooperated. Children, like adults, must learn that there is some risk in using informal channels of communication, but these are acceptable means of communicating cognitive and affective information.

Children rarely need much guidance, especially in this day and age, in identifying another channel of communication, the most risky of all. They are likely to label it "demonstration," but the formal name for it is "conflict." The class simply could have refused to pick up the litter the next time there was an unfavorable wind. There is no need to hide the facts from children. They use informal channels, but few adults realize that we apply such strategies in our daily lives. We are so familiar with these techniques that we fail to recognize them. We would be remiss, however, if we let children think that there would not be a reaction to such an action. The question the teacher must always ask is, "And then what will happen?" Such a question allows children to see the possible consequences of their actions.

Summary

The dynamics of groups are present whether we take note of them or not. Since our purposes in social studies include the development of citizens for a democratic society, we must attempt to focus children on group interpersonal relationships so that children can learn to function in a democracy. To accomplish this purpose, a democratic environment must be established in our schools, and children must receive guidance toward successful functioning within it.

The objective of this chapter has been to focus you on your role in such an environment. Your task is to guide groups of children through the various developmental levels we have described. The greatest task of all is maintaining the lines of communication so that your children can function as citizens of a democracy.

References

Gorman, Alfred A. *Teachers and Learners: The Interactive Process of Education.* Boston: Allyn and Bacon, Inc., 1969.

Schmuck, Richard A., and Schmuck, Patricia A. *Group Processes in the Classroom.* Issues and Innovations in Education Series. Dubuque, Iowa: Wm. C. Brown Company Publishers, 1971.

Index